Literary Critique, Modernism and the Transformation of Theory

For my father

I have come into my garden, . . .
Song of Songs

Nothing more wretched than the word, yet it is by the word that one mounts to sensations of felicity, to an ultimate dilation where one is completely alone, without the slightest feeling of oppression.
Emil Cioran

Literary Critique, Modernism and the Transformation of Theory

Mena Mitrano

Edinburgh University Press is one of the leading university presses in the UK. We publish academic books and journals in our selected subject areas across the humanities and social sciences, combining cutting-edge scholarship with high editorial and production values to produce academic works of lasting importance. For more information visit our website: edinburghuniversitypress.com

© Mena Mitrano 2022, 2024

Edinburgh University Press Ltd
The Tun—Holyrood Road
12(2f) Jackson's Entry
Edinburgh EH8 8PJ

First published in hardback by Edinburgh University Press 2024

Typeset in 11/13pt Adobe Sabon by
Cheshire Typesetting Ltd, Cuddington, Cheshire

A CIP record for this book is available from the British Library

ISBN 978 1 3995 1322 7 (hardback)
ISBN 978 1 3995 1323 4 (paperback)
ISBN 978 1 3995 1324 1 (webready PDF)
ISBN 978 1 3995 1325 8 (epub)

The right of Mena Mitrano to be identified as the author of this work has been asserted in accordance with the Copyright, Designs and Patents Act 1988, and the Copyright and Related Rights Regulations 2003 (SI No. 2498).

Contents

List of Figures — vi
Acknowledgments — ix

Introduction — 1

1. What is Critique?: Three Types of Indocility — 46
2. Theory: Thinking with Literature — 68
3. What is a Critic?: Weak Thought, Weak Theory, Italian Theory — 90
4. Language: The Return to Saussure — 123
5. Tradition: Eliot and Work — 148
6. Text and Method: Cixous–Joyce–Lispector — 189
7. Poststructuralism: Faith and Lacan — 215

Conclusion: Depending on Your Neighbor — 239

Bibliography — 247
Index — 270

Figures

1. Airan Kang, Installation view of *New Romance—Art and the Posthuman*, Museum of Contemporary Art, Sydney, Australia, 2016. Courtesy Airan Kang.   2
2. Airan Kang, Installation view of *New Romance—Art and the Posthuman*, Museum of Contemporary Art, Sydney, Australia, 2016. Courtesy Airan Kang.   3
3. Airan Kang, *Textual Landscapes*, Bryce Wolkowitz Gallery, New York, USA, 2009. Courtesy Airan Kang.   4
4. Airan Kang, *The Luminous Poem*, media installation, Gallery Simon, Seoul, Korea, 2011. Courtesy Airan Kang.   10
5. Airan Kang, *Light of the World, Light of the Intelligence*, Art Front Gallery, Tokyo, Japan, 2006. Courtesy Airan Kang.   11
6. T. S. Eliot, postcard to Virginia Woolf, 1926. T. S. Eliot Collection of Papers, The Henry W. and Albert A. Berg Collection of English and American Literature, The New York Public Library. Courtesy Eliot Estate.   162
7. George Platt Lynes, T. S. Eliot, twelve photographic portraits undated. T. S. Eliot Collection of Papers, The Henry W. and Albert A. Berg Collection of English and American Literature, The New York Public Library. Photographic Portrait N. 11. Courtesy Joshua R. Lynes.   164
8. George Platt Lynes, T. S. Eliot, twelve photographic portraits undated. T. S. Eliot Collection of Papers, The Henry W. and Albert A. Berg Collection of English and American Literature, The New York Public Library. Photographic Portrait N. 1. Courtesy Joshua R. Lynes.   168
9. George Platt Lynes, T. S. Eliot, twelve photographic portraits undated. T. S. Eliot Collection of Papers, The Henry W. and Albert A. Berg Collection of English and

American Literature, The New York Public Library.
Photographic Portrait N. 2. Courtesy Joshua R. Lynes. 169
10. George Platt Lynes, T. S. Eliot, twelve photographic portraits undated. T. S. Eliot Collection of Papers, The Henry W. and Albert A. Berg Collection of English and American Literature, The New York Public Library. Photographic Portrait N. 3. Courtesy Joshua R. Lynes. 170
11. George Platt Lynes, T. S. Eliot, twelve photographic portraits undated. T. S. Eliot Collection of Papers, The Henry W. and Albert A. Berg Collection of English and American Literature, The New York Public Library. Photographic Portrait N. 4. Courtesy Joshua R. Lynes. 171
12. George Platt Lynes, T. S. Eliot, twelve photographic portraits undated. T. S. Eliot Collection of Papers, The Henry W. and Albert A. Berg Collection of English and American Literature, The New York Public Library. Photographic Portrait N. 5. Courtesy Joshua R. Lynes. 172
13. George Platt Lynes, T. S. Eliot, twelve photographic portraits undated. T. S. Eliot Collection of Papers, The Henry W. and Albert A. Berg Collection of English and American Literature, The New York Public Library. Photographic Portrait N. 6. Courtesy Joshua R. Lynes. 173
14. George Platt Lynes, T. S. Eliot, twelve photographic portraits undated. T. S. Eliot Collection of Papers, The Henry W. and Albert A. Berg Collection of English and American Literature, The New York Public Library. Photographic Portrait N. 7. Courtesy Joshua R. Lynes. 174
15. George Platt Lynes, T. S. Eliot, twelve photographic portraits undated. T. S. Eliot Collection of Papers, The Henry W. and Albert A. Berg Collection of English and American Literature, The New York Public Library. Photographic Portrait N. 8. Courtesy Joshua R. Lynes. 175
16. George Platt Lynes, T. S. Eliot, twelve photographic portraits undated. T. S. Eliot Collection of Papers, The Henry W. and Albert A. Berg Collection of English and American Literature, The New York Public Library. Photographic Portrait N. 9. Courtesy Joshua R. Lynes. 176
17. George Platt Lynes, T. S. Eliot, twelve photographic portraits undated. T. S. Eliot Collection of Papers, The Henry W. and Albert A. Berg Collection of English and American Literature, The New York Public Library. Photographic Portrait N. 10. Courtesy Joshua R. Lynes. 177

18. George Platt Lynes, T. S. Eliot, twelve photographic portraits undated. T. S. Eliot Collection of Papers, The Henry W. and Albert A. Berg Collection of English and American Literature, The New York Public Library. Photographic Portrait N. 12. Courtesy Joshua R. Lynes.   178

Acknowledgments

This book is beholden to many people. First and foremost, I would like to manifest my admiration for artist Airan Kang. My book is indebted to her generosity in granting permission to reproduce images of her installations, including the image on the cover. I am honored for the opportunity to thank her publicly. I also thank the following people and institutions: Josh Lynes for granting permission to reproduce the twelve photographic portraits of T. S. Eliot by George Platt Lynes housed in the Berg Collection of the New York Public Library; Carolyn Vega, the curator of the Henry W. and Albert A. Berg Collection of English and American Literature at the New York Public Library, and her staff for their work and their kind assistance during my research in the summers of 2018 and 2019, and for responding to my queries after that time; the Eliot Estate for granting permission to quote from T. S. Eliot's letter to Lincoln Kirstein and from a postcard to Virginia Woolf, and include the image of the postcard in Chapter 5 of this book; the librarians and staff of the Jerome Robbins Dance Division, The New York Public Library for the Performing Arts for assistance during my research there; the Bryce Walkowitz Gallery in New York for letting me visit the gallery to see samples of Airan Kang's digital books in the summer of 2019; the Special Collections Division of Biblioteca Nazionale Centrale of Rome for assistance during my research on Adriano Tilgher; the Elmer Holmes Bobst Library of New York University and Michael Stoller, former Associate Dean of Collections and Research, for ensuring my access to the library resources; Loyola University Chicago, John Felice Rome Center, particularly Anne Wittrick, for the research resources made available to me before my move to Ca' Foscari University.

My research could not have translated into a book without two fundamental actors: my editor, Jackie Jones, and my institution, the Department of Linguistics and Comparative Cultural Studies at Ca' Foscari University of Venice. From the beginning, I wanted to publish with Edinburgh University Press for the kind of conversation that Jackie Jones carries on with her authors. I thank Jackie for the exchange of missives that tracked the discoveries and progress over time and across space, and Susannah Butler together with the rest of the team at EUP for seeing the book through production. My institution, the Department of Linguistics and Comparative Cultural Studies at Ca' Foscari University of Venice, provided important financial support toward the publication of this book. I am very pleased to thank my Director, Antonio Trampus, for being at the helm and offering various kinds of support. My debt extends to Virginia Turchetto, Francesca Bernardi, and Caterina Fusaro for their work, and especially to Alberto Parolo, who embodies that rare combination of talent and kindness. He made a difference.

During the time in which the project was in the making, I benefited from the feedback of two anonymous readers whose generosity in offering criticism, comments, and suggestions for revisions has given me real sustenance. They have detected my attempt at uniting worlds, and have encouraged me to follow through. Their commitment to the conversation has been vital to the transformation of the initial project into this book and to the book's overall architecture. While I take responsibility for all the flaws, I am very pleased to thank my anonymous readers for the role they have in my account of the life of critique.

The writing that went into the book builds on conversations and presentations at various events and conferences. I thank all the colleagues of the Italian Thought Network. The list of names would be too long, but, in representation of them all, let me thank Enrica Lisciani-Petrini and Roberto Esposito for introducing me to the network and welcoming my work. The debates at the International Conference on *Italian Thought*, Unversità degli Studi di Salerno, Fisciano, in October 2015 and at the subsequent founding meeting of the Italian Thought Network in March 2016, at Università degli Studi di Bari Aldo Moro, Dipartimento di Studi Umanistici, can be said to have marked the beginnings of the book. I thank the Modernist Studies Association for the travel grant that enabled me to present my early research on Modernism and Italian Theory at the "Culture Industries" conference in Pasadena, in November 2016, and the British Modernist Studies Association for welcoming the panel on "Modernism/Italian Theory," at the annual conference in June 2019, where I especially treasured the exchange with Vittoria Borsò. The questions from colleagues at the "Histories of Psychotherapies and Literature" conference, at the Faculty of Medicine and Psychology of Sapienza University of Rome in June 2019, and our interaction during the pre-conference seminar helped with the last chapter.

Mario Martino invited me to present my research at the interdisciplinary seminar he directs at Sapienza University of Rome in May 2017 and in May 2018, and asked me to teach the newly instituted course "Critical Methodologies." I thank Mario and all the students who, in the academic years of 2018–19 and 2019–20, took the first and second editions of "Critical Methodologies," especially: Zahra Abushova, Hanieh Aghaie, Alina Akmatbekova, Rauana Alakbarova, Turan Aliyva, Joseph Arnold, Sahar Asharioon, Ayda Atrzadeh, Toloue Sara Bidokhti, Eleonora Boncompagni, Aglieszka Calka, Francesco Camiciola, Roberta D'Alessandro, Gulinur Davutva, Giulia De Niedellis, Alessandra Diori, Francesca Eboli, Elmira Afshar Farokhi, Miriam Ferraglioni, Melissa Fisher, Giacomo Frate, Sara Galliani, Silvia Gatti, Sara Ghazaleh, Anna Gornik, Hasti Gorrjipour, Anish Gulfam, Aytakin Guzbanzade, Maedeh Hosseinpoor, Sadat Shakiba Housseini, Chiara Iannini, Sara Israfilbayova, Faraj Saeed Jalal, Vafa Karimli, Tahmina Khudayarova, Krystsina Kniukh, Erica Laricca, Amir Latifi, Zeynep Lebe, Ruzigar Luftalayeva, Andrea Lupi, Zhala Mammadaliyeva, Jennifer Marano, Marco Marchesini, Humay Mejidova, Arzu Mikaylova, Mona Mohammadinasab, Lida Mohammadrezah, Caterina Napolitano, Irene Raponi, Andrea Raso, Asal Rustamil, Bezhad Saedpanah, Narmin Safarova, Alena Salenik, Martina Scibilia, Valentina Seminara, Sisi Shen, Lucia Alessia Solla, Raja Suryaraj, Ehsan Tabarizadeh, Aygun Tahmazova, Francesca Titolo, Davide Zakarian, Mozhgan Zare.

I thank: Jewel Spears Brooker who, since our first meeting in Florence in 2015, has been my real introduction to T. S. Eliot; Grace Schulman for an unforgettable afternoon of stories about Edmund McKnight Kauffer and T. S. Eliot at 1 University Place in the summer of 2019; Rajni Singh and Catharine R. Stimpson, as ever; my Venice colleagues for welcoming me in the Department; Pia Masiero for our ongoing conversation; all my Venice graduate students for the interdisciplinary adventures that kept me company as I was finishing the book; Tina Cawthra for her collaboration.

Projects cannot be completed without a magic circle of friends. My affection to: Bridget Gellert Lyons and Bob Lyons for their friendship and our ritual gatherings at *La Boite en Bois* over the years in which this book was in the making, and for Bob's predictions; Patrizia Sorge for the well-being and inspiration that I draw from her loyal friendship; her daughters, Chiara, Isabella, Sofia; Leon, for being our Angel.

I reserve my deepest gratitude for my family. I thank my family for their love, especially in times of loss. Will words help? Gino gave me the gift of life and taught me about history; now, he is teaching me to speak *that* silence—gently. This is one of the things for him, with love.

Introduction

Hollow forms

South Korean artist Airan Kang uses books to transform space and incorporate them in ordinary life. This is especially the case with *Digital Book Project* (2000–present), which has been shown at several galleries around the world (Figures 1–3). I first saw it in 2016 as part of the exhibit *New Romance—Art and the Posthuman*, at the Museum of Contemporary Art in Sydney, Australia. Kang's project consists of installations made of sculptures in the form of books created with resin and LED devices that emit colorful lights programmed to change in luminosity, chromatic nuances, and intensity. Kang's books are not books in the traditional sense. We cannot open them. They are virtual books, that is to say, hollow book forms. Hong-Hee Kim defines a virtual book as "an electronically luminescent book; EL (Electro Luminescence is an optical phenomenon in which a material emits light in response to an electric current passing through it) light is embedded in a hollow book form cast from transparent synthetic resin" (9). But Kang's hollow forms are not a statement against real books. Her virtual books do not oppose real books; rather, the two join forces to extend the role of books as supplements of human existence. The artist creates synesthetic environments in which the book is present and engages the visitor at a multisensory level. Within these environments, her books invite and support reflection on reading as a human activity.

Describing *Digital Book Project*, Anna Davies, the curator of the 2016 Sydney exhibit, proposes that Kang explores "the book as a symbol of human knowledge," and that, in doing so, she raises

Figure 1. Airan Kang, Installation view of *New Romance—Art and the Posthuman*, Museum of Contemporary Art, Sydney, Australia, 2016. Courtesy Airan Kang.

Figure 2. Airan Kang, Installation view of *New Romance—Art and the Posthuman*, Museum of Contemporary Art, Sydney, Australia, 2016. Courtesy Airan Kang.

Figure 3. Airan Kang, *Textual Landscapes*, Bryce Wolkowitz Gallery, New York, USA, 2009. Courtesy Airan Kang.

questions about our capacity to protect and preserve what we know: "'How will we store information in the future?', 'What bits of it will we value?' and 'Will we still absorb it in the same ways?'" (n.p.). Davies captures an aspect of Kang's work that resonates in particularly striking ways with literary studies today: the idea of texts as "wounded and vulnerable artifacts" (Felski, "Introduction" 217). For if the questions posed by Kang's art concern our capacity to preserve and to understand what we value, those questions bear on the core activity of literary studies, that is, criticism. For the purposes of this Introduction, until fuller discussion takes off in Chapter 1, by the term "criticism" we can provisionally understand the practice of reading with the purposeful aim of interpreting a literary or aesthetic artifact, explaining and making sense of it. Lately, doubts have been cast on the fitness of the literary critic to the task of protecting, preserving, and caring for those vulnerable artifacts. The debate on something called "postcritique" has gained momentum because it is representative of an impasse in the figure of the critic. Critics of course have been shamed before, but this time the impression is that the critic in this debate comes off as a fascinating figure, a practitioner who, having taken upon him- or herself the task of interpreting literary texts in order to unlearn mastery (critique), now finds that he or she has unlearned it incompletely and is at a standstill, like the woman in Dürer's *Melencolia I* who is stopped in her tracks, her tools and instruments lying on the ground.

Questions about what we will preserve and what we will value flow directly from the practice of reading but they also tie reading in with related questions about the ways in which we know and create knowledge. Kang's hollow forms call attention to this tie.

Kang's digital books develop from her beginnings, with her concern with the act of "packing" knowledge. She started with books arranged in a bundle wrapped with *bojagi*, a type of stitched textile traditionally used as a wrapping cloth that is a key element of Korean culture, especially in the ordinary life of women. She moved from "*bojagi* books" made of aluminum casting before 1997 to books bundled in silk in later years. Her gendered perspective has been noticed, and commentators have remarked that her bound books "bear social and cultural implications," as if "to alleviate" the negative side of patriarchal culture and history (Kim 12). From this perspective, her extensive array of books not only symbolizes "the cognition of the world" (Okabe 55) but raises questions of documentation, of what we can know because we can document, what it means to document, and the ways in which reading is crucially interwoven with the problem of documentation (a fact to which the act of binding draws attention).

Kang's art assumes the poststructuralist lesson about the link between knowledge and power.[1] As commentators say, her early work suggests "the act of hiding or concealing something precious in secrecy or packing to leave and be liberated from an oppressive environment" (Kim 11–12). In other words, Kang's work suggests a shared condition that consists in the double bind of being both subjected to regimes of truth that shape us right through our bodies and engaged in resisting them with our lives. How is this double bind documented in books? The gesture of binding seems a purposeful interrogation of what we can collect and how we think by making a whole from pieces and fragments, all questions that bear directly on the problem of what is (or is not) documented in books. Talking about her project *Otheca Luminosa—Cella Penthesilea*, the artist manifests her intention of collecting photographs, videos, and testimonies regarding feminist movements:

> I intend to contemplate on the legacy of their cultural history and establish an enlightening vision for the future. While looking into the life of female workers in contemporary society and the violent working environment for them, I want to draw up a blueprint for the future of women with great anticipation for feminist resistance and creative changes. (Kang 121)

The bundles therefore suggest a frayed whole that needs documenting and enlightening. Hollowed out of content, the digital book presses the issue of reading as a type of luminosity that is achieved through making, by stitching together what is and what is not yet there.

In 2009 Kang built both on Michel Foucault's concept of heterotopia and on the notion of virtual reality inherited from media art to convey a "liminal space" that cannot actually be experienced physically, a space "that has the quality of non-being though undoubtedly existing" (Jeong 117, 119).[2] The space resulting from Kang's reading of Foucault is actually highly evocative of what Hannah Arendt called "space of appearance," meaning a potential public realm "brought forth through action and speech in public" (*Human Condition* 204). For Arendt, the space of appearance is a relational space of mutual recognition because there one can gauge the reality of the world by "its being common to us all" (208). In Arendt's rendering, the public realm which we all need "in order to appear at all" is immaterial; yet without it, neither "the reality of one's self . . . nor the reality of the surrounding world can be established beyond doubt" (208). Turning to Foucault, in her reflection on how virtual reality might actually produce heterotopic in-between zones within reality, Kang, therefore, looks back to Arendt's own "in-between," as the German-American philosopher also called the space of appearance (Arendt, *Human Condition* 182). This means that, assuming power-knowledge as a given, Kang's digital book project recuperates the question of the role of language in humanizing practices. If I dwell at some length on Kang's recuperation in this first section of the Introduction, it is because it encapsulates my own reintroduction of critique in this book.

Kang's *fil rouge* is something like Arendt's in-between. Since the earlier stages of her work, she has juxtaposed real books and transparent virtual books. By installing them next to each other, she could ask about what is and what is not documented.[3] The question is inseparable from an attempt to bridge the distance between the spaces of the book and "those of everyday life" (Jeong 120). Often her virtual books are superimposed by images of libraries, an attempt at bridging the separation between more conventional spaces of knowledge like libraries, "heavily laden with [...] independent and absolute time," and "the daily lives of ordinary human beings" (Jeong 120), as indicated by the LED lights, commonly used to illuminate urban spaces. Kang's wish to create synesthetic environments where the visitor can experience her book sculptures at a multisensorial level and her affirmation that her works "exist not as a sign of but as part of life" (Jeong 121) suggest an in-between in the sense of Arendt: an environment where language and thought, as her luminous books indicate, play an important role not just by virtue of some transcendental function but because they support the kind of active imagining associated with retrieval, reinvention, rewriting. Precisely because we cannot open her virtual books, thus we cannot read in ways that we are used to, Kang's art initiates a reflection on reading that is inseparable from the question of how we produce what we know, and the latter question ties in with the other question of knowing through modes of recognition and recovery.

Her "dematerialized" shells (Kim 11), while presupposing a loss of content, are lit from within; encountering her books implies the question of the recovery of their contents. The titles on display span indiscriminately—art, philosophy, popular culture, poetry, literary criticism, and so on—and often the books are clustered randomly and they are staple items in what we can easily imagine as a general world library, symbols of a shared intellectual legacy—Maya Angelou, Edgar Allan Poe, Vermeer, Klimt, Picasso—and of global turns of the imagination (one of the titles is *Postmodernism*). The sculptures seem to pay homage to certain books encountered and loved by the artist while traveling around the world, visiting and photographing libraries and bookstores in order to recreate each environment as a digital version of the original. Many of them are Western books, especially in *Digital Book Project*, although, as mentioned earlier, Kang works with non-Western women too. The range of titles invites questions of order and selection.[4] Certainly Kang's sculptures are autonomous technological objects, but in memorializing books, and thrusting into relief the question of our relation to them, and by the fact that in the installations the books illuminate dark spaces, the artist seems to use books less as an ornamental appendix of consumerism-driven lives and more to query the notion of encountering them, clothing them in charm. The luminous shells raise more questions about the encounter than we can answer; they tell of something passing between the subject and the object, between one agent and another, "like a smile or a look" whose influence cannot be accounted for completely: "What causes it? What does it consist of? Does it consist of anything to begin with?" (Jankélévitch, *Music* 104). Vladimir Jankélévitch (1903–85) writes: "A charm—like a smile or a look—is *cosa mentale*" (104), and Kang's luminous books seem to literalize this idea. If, as Aomi Okabe proposes, they "satisfy [our] intellectual curiosity" (48), this is not because we can absorb their contents but because the empty shells represent intellectual curiosity as something like an "astrological influence," as Jankélévitch would put it, passing from one to the other (104). The fact that the books often are part of a collective world library and their synesthetic perception in the installations combine to balance the influence so that the initiating agent (the artist), the one who wants, may not want too much, and keep the agent who is being acted upon (the visitor/reader) giving rather than withholding his or her consent.[5]

Kang's sculptures suggest an act of reading that takes place at the level of memory and dream. In some installations, selected quotes in LED run across the open book while in other installations the hyperbook remains open, as if to mark a particular page of the text, alluding to the kind of daydreaming encouraged by absorption in a particular detail or moment of the text.[6] The fact that the content is not accessible directly holds the promise of an augmented semiosis in which a thought (held in the book) addresses future thoughts (in the reader) that may then be drawn into the light.[7] Selected texts, discourses, quotations, and language fragments call attention to reading as a practice of interiorization and memorization, but the selective access that we are given by the artist to the book's contents underlines not so much those contents or the single quote as the possibility of reconstituting and recreating loved ideas. For this reason, Kang's books are much more than a visual gloss to our reading habits; putting into play local and less local meanings of reading, they do not seem foreign to a reflection on literary interpretation, since they cast the gap between reader and text in affirmative ways. These books do not enable romancing the (tactile) texture of the text; yet, the fact that they are "empty" points neither to a fateful gap between things and language nor to a competitive model (reader vs.

text); they are not about autonomous objects that finally overturn the sovereignty of the human, nor do they lash out against our being of language. These digital books are lit, and they withdraw. They seem to have the stabilizing function of Arendt's things. For Arendt, things, exactly like persons, are caught in the outward movement of appearing; they "supplement each other," forming the extensive relationality without which "things would be a heap of unrelated articles, a non-world" (*Human Condition* 9), and there would not be a self to talk about: I can retrieve myself, my sameness, "by being related to the same chair and the same table" (137).[8] The synesthetic environment that Kang seeks to create in her installations (Figure 4) replicates Arendt's web of relations. The charm emanates from the sincerity with which these world books, much like the chair and the table in Arendt's account of the human condition, are shown in a web of relations, making it possible to speak of a "world." In the beautiful media installation *Light of the World, Light of the Intelligence*, a solitary Merleau-Ponty illuminates a spacious darkness, with Nietzsche not too far in the distance (Figure 5).[9]

There is no doubt that Kang's digital books are attractive. What makes them attractive? In the attempt to answer this question, I initially turned to Graham Harman's concept of allure. Harman grants that allure "is expressed in many ways" but goes on to propose a common theoretical principle according to which each of the forms that allure can take "involves the separation of a thing from its innermost precious features: its notes" (*Guerrilla Metaphysics* 211). By "notes" Harman means "features that seem to be permanently welded to a person or thing" (213). Allure in this sense seems akin to defamiliarization; when we speak of the allure of a person or a thing, we are acted upon by the effect of estrangement or defamiliarization. From this point of view, allure "initiates a rift in the thing that was lacking before" (213). The allure of Kang's digital books might result from their being severed from a whole—they seem randomly selected, from a number of disciplines, and their installation in clusters poses questions about how we collect, select, and classify knowledge—in the same way that the allure of the ascetic is "that of the human severed from all the striving and social climbing too often encrusted onto the human essence" (213). But even though they are severed from a readable content (whole), I am not sure that Kang's books can be a case of allure. Jankélévitch's charm, as proposed earlier, seems a more appropriate comparison. The book covers are not an exact reproduction; they modify the original covers, testifying to the reader's appropriation of the loved book. It is this gesture that

Figure 4. Airan Kang, *The Luminous Poem*, media installation, Gallery Simon, Seoul, Korea, 2011. Courtesy Airan Kang.

Figure 5. Airan Kang, *Light of the World, Light of the Intelligence*, Art Front Gallery, Tokyo, Japan, 2006. Courtesy Airan Kang.

influences us, and it bespeaks freedom: what appears as an unruly array of books modeled for lighting books has been encountered by the artist in her travels and, at the same time, is a recognizable, collectively shared canon. Their luminosity comments not only on the artist's loving appropriation but also on the sheer fact that the books are available, in the first place, because they circulate, thus emphasizing a movement in space beyond local boundaries and cultures.[10] The question of the encounter is foregrounded within the context of a cultural circulation that should not be taken for granted. The latter aspect, I think, contributes to the charm of *Digital Book Project*, which encourages questions on the experimental, imaginative side of reading that are particularly attuned to the current search for "fresh ways" of interpreting texts in literary studies (Anker and Felski).

Postcritique

> He told us, *with the years you will come*
> *To love the world.*
> And we sat there with our souls in our laps
> And comforted them.
>
> Dorothea Tanning, "Graduation"

> I have been feeling a mounting perplexity about the role of the critic.
>
> Carla Lonzi, Autoritratto[11]

Discussion about new ways of reading has been going on for a while, inaugurated by privative descriptors such as "surface reading" (surface, not depth) or "just reading" (reading, not something else, and not some other aim) which announce the wish to be liberated from the burden of a style of reading insistently called symptomatic (Marcus and Best).[12] This style of reading is generally associated with poststructuralism, and has come under attack for construing "presence as absence and affirmation as negation" (Marcus, *Between Women* qtd. in Marcus and Best 12), with the consequence that the critic is placed in competition with the text, endowed with a greater freedom over it (Marcus and Best 18). Like all labels, poststructuralism of course is the inadequate name for a multiplicity of developments; nevertheless, it may be taken to refer to the displacement and relocation of French philosophy and criticism (from Roland Barthes's semiology to French feminisms to deconstruction) to the U.S.; it consists less in a movement and more in a series of authors who "were read and classified or compartmentalized" (Dillet 517) and, together, have facilitated the dialogue between different branches of knowledge, including psychoanalysis and Marxism. Its principal effect on literary studies has been an increased autonomy of the critic, an autonomy that has come to be perceived as the emblem of the political excesses of the turn of literary criticism called Theory, seen to have encouraged "opportunist uses of texts from the past, primarily fueled by ideological or deconstructive purposes" (Collini n.p.). The excesses imputed to poststructuralism play a role in the rise of postcritique but it was the success of Rita Felski's articulation of the problem in her book *The Limits of Critique* (2015) that accelerated the debate.

Felski defended the confluence of aesthetics and politics as the defining trait of critique, explaining that the latter is a "matter of connecting, composing, creating, coproducing, inventing, imagining, making possible" (*Limits* 18), but her point was that when this kind of critical reading settles in standardized critical gestures underpinned by negative affects, such as suspicion, opposition, and hostility, what we miss is the life of the text, a life that is always in excess of the context of production, of the relations, and of the movement in which texts are inevitably entangled. The epigraph from Dorothea Tanning (1910–2012), an artist who had two lives, first as a modernist painter, later as a poet, speaks of a remarkable transformation. Coming "to love the world" suggests a process that begins in its elided opposite: to hate the world.[13] Put briefly, this is the graduation sought by Felski: "Perhaps it is time to start asking different questions: 'But what about love?' Or: 'Where is your theory of attachment?'" (*Limits* 17–18). In other words, casting her gaze at what is neglected and damaged, must the critic necessarily expose the offenses of the world? Must critical reading be necessarily associated with the force of those offenses and with the depth of negativity? Talking about the limits of critique means asking some valid questions, questions that had been waiting to be asked. In asking them, Felski, with other scholars like Toril Moi, was also trying to put wonder back into critical practice (Moi 233), reclaiming for the literary critic what philosophers are currently claiming for the sciences: "the adventure of interpretation" and a new type of thinker who gives things the power to challenge "his well-defined categories" (Stengers 372–3).

The attempt to put wonder back into critical practice implies giving an account of the past, and, even though this may not have been the intention of Felski or of the scholars championing postcritique, the search for fresh ways of interpreting texts has been received not just as a rejection of but also as "a backlash against critique" (Bérubé 971), variously called theory, poststructuralism, deconstruction, symptomatic reading, or the hermeneutics of suspicion. At this point, it might be good to understand what exactly we are rejecting.

Felski's work has elicited some interesting responses from early career scholars who do not feel addressed by the future-oriented thrust of postcritique, not only because they live precarious academic lives but also because, and this is the point, more than for new ways of reading they feel the need for "different modes of scholarly articulation": "I didn't want to talk differently about texts; I wanted to talk differently about how others were talking about texts," writes Pardis Dabashi in her introduction to a *PMLA* cluster called "Cultures of Argument" (947), which grew in response to Felski's *The Limits of Critique* in a paper first presented at the 2019 MLA in Chicago, when she was still a graduate student. Dabashi calls for different styles of being in the common space of academic appearance, and the "epistemic modesty" that she proposes (947), far from endorsing a more or less tacit rejection of critique, helps recover what I believe is the defining question of critique. As I shall propose in this book, the stake of critique for the literary practitioner is the sense of a proximity to thought or, as I call it in Chapter 2, thinking with literature.

Dabashi's intervention has been taken to mark a generational rift, coming from an early career scholar who like multitudes of early career scholars leads a precarious life. Yet, it might be helpful to remember that the decades of Theory, with its on-and-off backlash and supposed death, in fact correspond to a serious cross-generational academic precarity also in countries other than the U.S. From this perspective, the remarkable trait of Dabashi's intervention is her reminder that the stake is the link between literary studies and thought: "the sense that we might do a better job of thinking with patience and being patient with thought" (947). Responses like Dabashi's and the others in the "Cultures of Argument" cluster, in manifesting the need for modesty and generosity in intellectual endeavors, suggest that the question of what goes by the name of postcritique includes the search for grace in the academic sphere. From the vantage point of those who want different ways of arguing, postcritique does not signal yet another version of the avant-garde procession of destruction and novelty, hence it does not come *after* critique but is part of the question of critique. From this vantage point, Wai Chee Dimock's essay on "Weak Theory" (2013) is an example of postcritique. As we shall see in Chapter 3, Dimock's theme is a literary critic who seeks a different scholarly posture, who wants to be somewhere else, where ideas happen and "other meanings" are ("Weak Theory" 744). Here we have a literary practitioner with a highly unstable identity, who, whatever her mode of analysis—hermeneutic depth, surface reading, description, and so on—wants more than to interpret literature; she wants to think *with* it.

The examples of postcritique offered by Dabashi—especially the references to Sophie Seita, author of *Provisional Avant-Gardes* (2019), whose affinity with the many poets she writes about results in her reluctance to make a "final argument" about them (Dabashi 950), or "the fragmentary form" favored by Alix Beeston to reflect the "chanciness and fitfulness of everyday research practices" (Beeston qtd. in Dabashi 950)—counter the assumption of argumentative mastery. They provide examples of the restitution of the practice of critique. To clarify what I mean by restitution of critique, I will refer to the example of Carla Lonzi. Lonzi's revolutionary *Autoritratto* (Self-Portrait), first published in 1969 and reissued in 2010, is a montage of the conversations of an art critic with some of the major artists of the 1960s, from Pietro Consagra to Lucio Fontana, from Mimmo Rotella to Giulio Turcato, from Jannis Kounellis to Cy Twombly. In assembling the text, Lonzi, the critic, erases her questions and blends her voice with the voices of the artists. Lonzi feels that the task of interpretation exceeds disciplinary confines and requires a style of scholarly articulation for which her profession has not trained her. In the preface to *Autoritratto*, Lonzi writes:

> This book is a collection and a montage of conversations that I had with some artists. But the conversations were not intended to be the materials for a book: they respond less to the need to understand and more to the need to be with someone in a manner that is pre-eminently communicative and humanly rewarding. The work of art has been felt by me, at a certain point, as the possibility of an encounter, as an invitation to partake issued directly by the artist to each of us. It has seemed to me a gesture for which I had not been professionally trained. (4)

Lonzi's idea of encounter does not only trouble the critic–art object hierarchy but suggests that interpretation crosses over to "a thought that sees in art practice the place of true critical practice" (Iamurri, "Prefazione" viii; my translation). By pointing to the disposition of criticism to appear in other practices, Lonzi in her time raised the question of critique in similar terms to those in which Dabashi and others raise the question of postcritique today.

Lonzi negates the role of the critic as subject of mastery and opts instead for the kind of language and analysis developed through feminist practice (see Iamurri, *Un margine*). Her journey away from mastery and toward feminist thought was guided by a hermeneutic question: How do we reconstruct what Lonzi termed "the individual itinerary"? In other words, how does the critic reconstruct the making of the individual artist? How does the critic account for the work of art and, by extension, for the literary text? She laments constraining theoretical models because, as she puts it, there is always "a margin that eludes," a remainder that it is nevertheless possible to perceive in practices other than criticism, for example the interview form, memoirs, conversations. These can help capture, even if only remotely, the complexity of an artistic vocation. Lonzi was concerned with theoretical models that cannot do justice to what in the groundbreaking essay "La solitudine del critico" (The solitude of the critic), she called "the affective and verifiable tangibility of the work" (355).[14] She went on to ask for a critical method attuned to the "operation of truth," which she associated with the modernist avant-garde, whereby each viewer/reader (seen as a member of society) is invited to accept as truth "what flows from a spontaneous constitution of consciousness" (356). This operation of truth results in knowledge that cannot be certified by an authority, let alone a patriarchal authority (*patres*), and exceeds disciplinary classification (philosophy, criticism, social sciences, etc.). The task of criticism is that of identifying the kind of artistic production that appears as

> the creation of techniques of life through which we react in a non-neurotic way to the fall of social myths, to the clash of cultures and traditions, to dissolving boundaries and to what, in general, it seems apt to call a new planetary condition (*una nuova condizione cosmica*). (Lonzi, "Solitudine" 356)

Lonzi was taken with the idea of criticism as somehow parallel to "the act of seizing freedom," the same that determines contemporary works of art, in the conviction that this would be the only tool in the hands of the critic who hopes to establish a contact with the work of art ("Solitudine" 356). I have dwelled at some length on Lonzi's pursuit of a criticism outside criticism because it suggests that to take up the question of critique means to return—tirelessly, that is, lovingly—to the conundrum of the conjoining of method and form of life. I began with the example of Airan Kang because it helps me put the stakes of reading critically as a transformative form of life on the table.

Overview and roadmap

The main obstacle in the way of this book was names. There is something unsatisfying in names, especially when, after extended use, they turn into labels, or, as is implicit in the etymology of the word "labels," they become badges, assisting us in ordering and classifying without necessarily soliciting any labor of understanding in the sense of explanation. This is the case with critique, poststructuralism, deconstruction, theory, postcritique, all names that need to be invoked here without ever hoping to explain them adequately. Yet, the attempt to understand what is meant by critique implies the intersection and the overlap of all those names.

This book started a few years ago, but the necessity of the act was brought home when I tried to introduce a group of graduate students to the notion of critical practice at one of the largest public universities in Europe. My course was entitled "Critical Methodologies" and many of the attending students were international students coming from non-Western countries such as Turkey and Iran. My syllabus began with T. S. Eliot and Susan Sontag and ended with Italian Theory, with deconstruction, feminist genealogies, gender theory, queer studies, and postcolonial theory in-between. It was in this rather animated course that I learned the truth of what Toril Moi says in her wonderful *Revolution of the Ordinary* (2017). Moi proposes that, unless we want to encourage our students "to take a given theory and apply it to a text" (179), which would mean encouraging them to the standardized reproduction of particular reading styles, we need to confront the core problem of literary criticism as a field, which is reading. Reading, Moi reminds us, is a practice, not a method. As I will mention later on in this Introduction, the attempt to overcome critique, especially when it is reduced to the political and theoretical excesses of the past, has revived a search for method as a cure for those excesses. I believe that this view of method can put at risk the great opportunity that we are given by the debate on postcritique to think through the constitutive instability of the literary field and of the practitioner at its center—the literary critic—whose unique strength is also his or her weakness: a dependence on the neighbor (of which I will say more in the next section).

In this book, I turn back reconstructively to the notion of critique and, taking in hand certain aspects of the "postcritique" orientation, I offer a more inclusive, ampler view that recovers aspects of critique that might be further developed in literary studies. These aspects might be summed up under the question of the ethical underpinnings of critique. Before being a specific method or disciplinary practice, critique is an attitude and stance toward others, including both affective and gestural-embodied relations to the object of study. Italian Theory becomes a vector traversing the book because it allows me to specify these ethical underpinnings through two subthemes: (1) language; (2) the link with modernism.

Italian Theory causes us to revise the temporality of theory. I understand it primarily, though not exclusively, through Roberto Esposito's notion of "living thought," which refers to the recovery of a latent thought, not opposed to poststructuralism but *eccentric* to it, both ahead of the linguistic turn and preceding it because it "perceives the inadequacy of the linguistic horizon with regard to something that is irreducibly corporeal that juts out of its boundaries" (*Pensiero vivente* 10).[15] Esposito's Italian Theory is a thought that issues from the "perception or the production of a new 'turn,' after the linguistic turn and, in some ways, comprehensive of the linguistic turn, which, overall, might be summed up in the paradigm of life" (10). As shown by Federico Luisetti, the turn toward life is deeply attuned to the Anthropocenic and posthumanist reconfiguration of the "natural contract" between human life and the world of the living, "whether things, technological objects, biological species, geological or atmospheric formations," and it participates in the reinvention of the "semantics of ... modernity" made necessary by the troubling of the nature/culture boundary and the manifest insufficiency of the old political and historical categories (152; my translation). In this book, Italian Theory is particularly helpful because, unlike the major currents that today wield influence on literary studies, like the "speculative turn" and realism (which I discuss in the next section), it does not wish to return to reality as if language did not exist, thus going in the opposite direction of poststructuralism, which decreed the sovereignty of language.[16] Italian Theory "does not wish to disown the relevance of language but to recover the relation that ties it on the one hand, to the biological fold of life and, on the other, to the dynamic order of history" (Esposito, *Pensiero vivente* 10). Italian Theory enables me to probe the potentiality of language less as an autonomous object and more as a space of attachment where, in Felice Cimatti's words, "the body itself needs symbolic recognition in order to live, not just to think" ("Introduzione" 16; my translation), something that allows me to query language at once for its beneficial resources and its openness to human externality.

Now, for the second subtheme: the link with modernism. The intimate tie between modernism and Theory implies the development of Theory as a complement and moment of modernism in its relation to language and textuality. Hence, the apparent burnout of theoretically driven literary criticism would seem, as well, to compromise the legacy of literary modernism. Felski, for example, rejects modernism's "adversarial schemes that counterpose" dominant interests to "the ruptures and innovations of a marginal avant-garde" ("Introduction" 217). This book presents the transformation of critique as a further step in the transnational migration of modernism into new contexts (see Chapter 6). But the main point is that Italian Theory and its turn to the horizon of life recirculates occluded modernist motifs which show their lingering force, first and foremost the Life vs. Form conflict. This recirculation allows for the reading of modernist texts with attention to the motif of the repression of life and the contrast to this repression, while, at the same time, pointing to the enfolded temporalities of modernism and critique, defamiliarizing the anglophone concept of modernism.

I order materials around a cluster of basic terms in literary studies: critique, theory, critic, language, tradition, text and method, poststructuralism, with each chapter discussing a keyword. The book, however, is not organized as a lexicon, and the structure makes room for presenting the primary dispositions of critique such as indocility, receptiveness, openness to transformation, awareness of relationality, attention to language, distance and displacement, attunement to the body, externality, and wonder, and there is a narrative to it.

The narrative begins with the slippage between criticism and critique (Chapter 1). Having retraced the difference in meaning, discussion focuses on the metamorphosis of the literary critic after the rise of Theory in the U.S. (Chapter 2). From the distance of time, when looked at from the vantage point of the recent phenomenon of Italian Theory, Theory appears as a transatlantic phenomenon of Euro-American modernization whose dissolution reveals an ampler movement of intellectual and geographical displacements. Critique advances as a dynamic, self-transforming, ampler arch of reflection whose defining trait is the movement toward an outside "that is wider than a local or national one" (Esposito, *Pensiero vivente* 3). With the help of Italian Theory, in Chapter 3 I discuss the symbol of this movement: the plane of coevalness, where the cultural logic of circulation borders on *méconnaissance* and repetition. The plane of coevalness specifically thematizes the problem of temporalities, suggesting occluded, eccentric lines of thought hosted in the folds of an ongoing critique, which can only fully emerge in the present. A split temporality appears that parallels Anglophone Theory, with concerns that seem like lingering motifs from the past, residual, occluded, latent but also vital (Esposito renames Theory "living thought) because they hail from the intractable notion of "another" modernity, modernity understood as a mechanism for the repression of life. I glean some of the motifs, more specifically: the (im)possibility of community, the search for the locus of a true plurality beyond cruel dynamics of humanization (the gaze and desire), and, above all, the notion of life as always in relation and in tension with history and politics. Together, these motifs seem to defamiliarize Anglophone Theory from its intimate link with the concept of modernism and create a parallel theoretical temporality, whereby certain recognizably modernist atmospheres—the sense of a vaster world, a paralyzing sense of human multiplicity (the many), how to be safe in the world—are altered in their contours as if through a technique of erasure (of the kind used by American painter Robert Rauschenberg when he erased a work by his colleague Willem de Kooning), and linger on like incomplete strands of thought.[17]

The lingering and the incompleteness and the uneven temporalities are a product of Italian Theory's deep reliance on the resources of feminism and psychoanalysis, with the former emphasizing *bíos*, the body in relation/tension with history and politics, and the second stressing the wedge between words and things, the experience of speech. The affinity causes a rift in the stale image of critique as the iterative debunking or desire-squelching postponement of truth that seems assumed by the debate on postcritique, producing the effect of incomplete motifs that come and go in a movement of returns. I deal with those returns in chapters on Saussure, Eliot, and Joyce–Lispector (Chapters 4, 5, and 6). Italian Theory winds around feminist and psychoanalytic notes, allowing me to focus on language not as an object but as an attachment. The return to Saussure, which foregrounds the preindividual and suprapersonal dimension of the institution of language, helps me identify, in the folds of Ferdinand de Saussure's (1857–1913) theory, the fascinating figure of the speaker (the delectable speaker) who is an agent positioned as receiver. Consequently the notion begins to appear of a beneficial resource stored in language which makes it possible to think of the speaker as a member of a social mass (language as a social relation), hence as a subject defined by its relation to others, but also always in potential proximity to a beneficial attachment. My chapters on Eliot and Joyce pursue this beneficial resource, with Eliot refusing the artist as a technology of the self and figuring himself as the affected receiver, while the transnationalization of Brazilian writer Clarice Lispector allows feminist theorist Hélène Cixous to reorient Joyce's modernism beyond the Oedipal structure of combat and aggression and toward the reparative scenario of a paternal adoption in language. Discussion of this emergent motif culminates in the last chapter, Chapter 7, where a focus on the experience of speaking from the double perspective of psychoanalysis and religion brings out the reparative scenario in the folds of poststructuralism, which, through its attention to a radical otherness, opens to an exploration of faith approached as the reorientation of an *affectus* for language.

The obsession of Hannah Arendt's heroine Rahel Varnhagen to exit "the mute spell of mere happening" (her phrase for naked life) and exist among others remains an overriding concern here (*Rahel* 248). As we seek outside the human for less cruel dynamics of humanization, scholarship is supported by an array of brilliant work that, within the broad range of the posthuman, explores "transspecies identification, and cross-species solidarities and the queer collectivities" (Singh 126). Thinking her way through these possibilities Julietta Singh, for example, in her recent book *Unthinking Mastery: Dehumanism and Decolonial Entanglements*, proposes what she calls dehumanism as "a practice of recuperation, of stripping away the violent foundations (always structural and ideological) of colonial and neocolonial mastery that continue to render some beings more human than others" (4). Her dehumanist dispossessions are the product of an affirmative labor of the negative and, from this perspective, resonate with the critic's search, as presented in this book, for a different epistemic position that could be called unmasterly. I am sympathetic to that side of the conversation, and my book is invested in the less cruel dynamic of humanization, beyond, for example, the gaze of the human other. We do not exist in the gaze and desire of another, but we do subsist—not just in the mind but also in the body—in a space of symbolic recognition. While of course the notion of recognition extends to a horizon beyond the human other, and, as I shall mention later on in this Introduction, I turn to Esposito's Italian Theory because it thinks "after man," my focus is more on the externalities to mastery that language makes possible. I am fascinated by the possibilities of the linguistic relation. What needs to be emphasized is that for Arendt it is not possible to speak of language without also speaking about the world. The "world" means less a product of human thought and more the problem of our proximity to things; it is the name for our inclusion in a web of relations outside of which it would be difficult, if not impossible, to feel that we are. This web has expanded. Yet, as mentioned in the opening of this Introduction, when discussing artist Airan Kang, the multiple things that make the "world" stabilize our lives to the extent that we can retrieve a sense of our self (our sameness) by being related to them. As we become aware of—and take our distance from—ways in which we have enthroned the fantasy of human uniqueness and disavowed our materialities, the human is redrawn but it does not mean that it disappears ecstatically in those unmasterly re-encountered materialities. The things that stabilize our life connect us to others that we scramble to imagine (i.e. understand) as best as we can, more often than not feeling the pang of failure.

At the opening of the Introduction, we saw that Kang's luminous books conjure reading as the problem of recovering, reconstituting, recognizing, and recreating knowledge, the implication being that it often corrects the omissions of the book. Kang's luminosity, like the luminosity sought by Arendt's Rahel, indicates that the activity of reading is reminiscent of and moves in parallel motion to the activity of imagining others. In the remaining sections I will try to explain further; in order to do so, it will be helpful to dwell in detail on the book's premises, beginning with the themes of postcritique that I take in hand.

Reality

> But all the same this too you will learn, how it was inevitable for things seeming to be
> to be assuredly, ranging throughout all things completely.
> <div align="right">Parmenides, <i>On Nature</i>[18]</div>

When considering the phenomenon of postcritique, what stands out is the theme of the critic: the critic and her metamorphosis, through the pursuit of symptomatic reading and, more broadly, Theory, into a misguided reader whose dulled senses make her see what is absent and hear what is not uttered. It is significant, however, that even those who seek to take a distance from Theory are not ready to give up Marxism and psychoanalysis, which are thought to remain central to the activity of interpretation (Marcus and Best 19). The need to preserve Marxism and psychoanalysis indicates that the problems imputed to a critique understood as the habit of debunking and deconstructing reach further back into the past and amount to the larger question of reality.

After Marx, it is strange to think of reality in empirical terms. Change comes to inhere within the concept of reality, and the task of thinking is "restituting living substance to the real" (Esposito, *Pensiero istituente* 94).[19] Psychoanalysis joins Marxism and plays an important role in the restitution, since its central interest lies in "the coming to being of the new that was not there and that becomes real" (Lacan, "Discorso" 136).[20] How can reality contain the exigency of its own transformation? Those who perceive the exigency do not necessarily want a revolt against reality. Once reality is understood in non-positivist and non-empirical terms as praxis, the thought related to it is "objectively inclined to change it" (Esposito, *Pensiero istituente* 194). The metamorphosis of the critic lamented by postcritique may be understood as a legacy of this question of reality.[21] Once Marxism and psychoanalysis, together, show that change is not an addition to knowledge but that knowledge is synonymous with change, language takes on a preeminent role in the task of understanding reality.

The entire arch of contemporary modernity is dominated by the idea that experience is mediated by language. What is referred to with the label "poststructuralism" may be grasped as a name for this continued climate.[22] The idea that "experience has a transcendentally linguistic character" (Esposito, *Da Fuori* 161) is central to the twentieth-century philosophical reflection (one thinks of Martin Heidegger and the idea that language is the dwelling of man), and the belief that no truth exists that is not mediated by human conceptual systems extended to literary studies (Fleissner 103). The theme of language bridges the distance between philosophy and literature (broadly understood), bringing into the foreground a zone of contact between two neighboring fields, especially with the rise of the new discourse of Theory.[23] Today, the primacy of language is being challenged by postcritique's contiguity to relational ontologies that assert the limits of the category of the human—as a construction of modern capitalism and colonialism—and emphasize the shared life of human and non-human agents or objects. This has led to a rapprochement with reality and a reopening of the question of reality. Philosophers Levi Bryant, Nick Srnicek, and Graham Harman pair "realism" with the term "materialism" to indicate that they want to talk about the reality of the physical world. They are examples of thinkers who want to encounter the world in all its dazzling physicality and concreteness.

On opening Parmenides' poem *On Nature*, the decisive lines of the prelude first present us with the bifurcation of a persuasive or "round truth of things" (*alēthēs*) and the opinion of mortals (*doxa*), but then go on to point to a learning that concerns a sense of things that are presumed to be and are that ranges through everything "completely." This learning concerns, then, things that are in every sense, at the confluence of incommensurable meanings. In comprehensive accounts of Western thought, the forgetfulness of this complete sense of things makes for a remarkable motif, countered in the twentieth century by Heidegger, who takes his cue from the forgetfulness of being to redraw the idea of the world as a place populated by the concreteness of things (Sloterdijk 79).[24] The concreteness, however, becomes enmeshed with the immaterial shell that covers them: language. Language becomes itself world, shelter, and dwelling of the human. Today, the new relational ontologies drive a wedge between the world and language.

In their introduction to the volume *The Speculative Turn* (2011) Bryant et al. associate this new interest in reality with the birth of "a new breed of thinker" who, regardless of the discipline he or she comes from, asks anew "questions about the nature of reality independently from human thought and from humanity more generally" (3). Two of the thinkers included in the volume, philosophers of science Bruno Latour and Isabelle Stengers, have recently wielded significant influence on anglophone literary studies because they do not reduce reality to the empiricism of facts but reclaim, as Stengers puts it, "the adventure of interpretation" (372). Stengers understands interpretation as observation guided by the capacity for accepting what we see beyond the dogmas of reason. This view of course resonates with those literary scholars who, in the past decades, have hoped for the potential of interpretation to see beyond dominant dogmas and established schools of thought (372).[25] Like Stengers, Latour argues for the exigency of our time "to raise the question of what the real world is really like" (*Reassembling* 117). In his case, the stress on the physical world modifies received accounts of modernity in ways that have been helpful in literary studies. In his alternative account, modernity departs from its identification with rationalism and industrialism that had been traditionally assumed in the study of literary modernism, for example. He looks back to the old debate about the "two cultures" and, by updating it, he proposes a new ontology of relations. Following up on predecessors like C. P. Snow, who pleaded the cause of an aesthetic and critical investigation of the "intellectual depth" of the physical world, and Aldous Huxley, who lamented the "crudeness of thought" when it came to "matter, which is dynamic beyond any imaginable limit," Latour overcomes the divide between the two cultures by integrating human and non-human actors (artifacts, objects, organizations, etc.) in the same conceptual framework, where all actors are indistinctly given the same potential for agency (Actor-Network Theory).[26] Stengers's and Latour's conceptual framework has exerted an influence on literary studies because it seems to restitute to the literary practitioner what Andrea Tagliapietra calls "the gift of thought" (61): the sense of proximity to thought felt as the capacity to see more the things before us and around us. The gift in question is the gift of surprise and unpredictability, of the "wonder that precedes the instalment of the cognitive and (foundational) subject/object divide" (61).[27] Stengers wants to mobilize "the power of wonder" to liberate scientists "from the role of guardians of rationality that has captivated them and put them at the service of power, both state and capitalist power" (375).[28] As for the literary critic, the gift of wonder promises to rescue him or her from what is perceived as the poststructuralist imperative of "a panoramic vision of the social order" (Felski, *Limits* 157).[29] The gift of wonder is palpable in certain metaphors put into play by Felski, who opposes the "impassive, scrupulously judgmental" poststructuralist observer (pointing to Michel Foucault) to quite another observer, ready "to trudge along . . ., marvelling at the intricate ecologies and diverse microorganism that lie hidden among the thick blades of grass" (*Limits* 74, 158).

But the new thinker of the realists no longer relies on concepts like text and discourse (Bryant et al. 3), and this poses problems for the literary critic. Postcritique might wish a welcome transition toward more reparative ways of reading, and Felski indicates as much when she speaks of "guarding, protecting, conserving, caretaking and looking after the wounded and vulnerable artifacts of history" ("Introduction" 217), but how might a practitioner pursue such a reparative task without the notion of the text, if only to think of the text in different ways or, to put it in Dabashi's terms, to "talk differently about how others [are] talking about texts" (947)? Moreover, if we consider texts as "artifacts of history," then what might their "wounded" status and their vulnerability consist in?

Such questions are related to the central issue in criticism, which is the field's reliance on other disciplines, and hopefully they will not be eliminated by the new craving for objectivity that has resulted from the shift toward reality. Though by no means the sole strain of postcritique, a craving for objectivity is one of the forces of this complex phenomenon. Among a number of departures from critique, Jennifer Fleissner highlights the present tendency to start from the assumption that there is a cluster of objective facts that the critic should discern. The task of the critic is seen as that of grasping these objective facts in as accurate a manner as possible. When taken into consideration, the critic's subjectivity is advantageously enlisted in the process of discerning objective facts (Fleissner 102). Thus, scholars, turning to the cognitive sciences in an attempt to correct the excesses of the past decades and to contrast "an insistence on criticism as a forthrightly political act" (102), advocate a search for method.[30] Mary Thomas Crane, for example, asks for a "methodological tool kit" that might supplant the consolidated but problematic "practice of reading for symptoms of hidden contradictions within cultural systems" (77). There is truth, however, in what Moi pointed out: that the search for method may distract us from the more radical problem of our field, which is the fact that reading is a practice. Following up on Moi, we can say that the central activity of our field determines the precariousness of the field, advising among its resources a certain openness to transformation. This is not to say that there are no tools available for those who wish to pursue literary interpretation, to reflect on its aims, how to best conduct it, and how to best use texts when interpreting them. There is no shortage of theorizing around the activity of reading in literary studies, including a long tradition of literary hermeneutics which expounds on the rules of interpretation and the sense of the critical act, which cannot be properly investigated in the space of this book.[31] From this point of view the field is stable and there is an abundance of "schools" from which to choose to launch the investigation. However, the fact that our central activity is reading, and that reading is a practice (not a method), by definition privileges the unforeseen; it implies an openness to transformation that has fostered the critic's reliance on other disciplines—linguistics, psychology, philosophy, and so on—for theoretical grounding. Such a reliance has been condemned in the past;[32] it is now lamented by scholars who are advocating a turn to objectivity after the waning influence of symptomatic reading (Crane 78). Why should the critic's dependence on the neighbor be a source of anxiety? If, as Moi contends, literary criticism means the practice of reading, and if the field therefore cannot be said to "have anything that we can call competing methods" (178),[33] then close proximity with other disciplines may itself be constitutive of the field. Perhaps, it is precisely in that proximity that criticism is enabled to perceive itself, in Fredric Jameson's phrase, as "genuine thinking": not a philosophy or a systematic set of rules, but reflection—thought in the making (*Marxism and Form*).[34]

For the practitioner of literary studies, the urgency of this proximity has been brought home by modernism. Aesthetic modernism has caused criticism to open up to the transcoding of ideas from other disciplines, especially philosophy in the form of critical theory and psychoanalysis. The literary concept of modernism has required and encouraged forms of theoretical criticism adequate to its experimental vocation. An undeniable intimate link exists between modernism and Theory, which, over time, have mutually forged each other, to the extent that the demise of Theory for the reasons articulated by Felski has led to predict the dissolving of the field of modernism (Saint-Amour). One of the arguments that Felski has with critique is precisely about its intimate link with modernism. In literary studies, modernism is synonymous with rupture and, undoubtedly, that is part of the attractiveness of the term, which has traditionally suggested an aesthetic reaction to industrialized modernity (Rainey and von Hallberg; Friedman, "Musing" 498), and fostered what Felski now calls "adversarial schemes that counterpose" dominant interests to "the ruptures and innovations of a marginal avant-garde" ("Introduction" 217). Critique and modernism have mutually sustained each other through their entanglement in this model of rupture which, as Felski argues, "has lost its last shreds of analytical purchase" (217).[35] Felski aligns herself with thinkers who reject any human-centered notion of rupture, but the relational ontologies favored by postcritique do not reject modernism, quite the opposite: the philosophers that attempt to emancipate the world from human perception (loosely called realists here), in fact, recirculate modernism's neglected strains.

Latour and Harman return to modernist thinkers like William James and Alfred North Whitehead (1861–1947), who have receded into the background during poststructuralism. Far from assuming that reality appears "only as the correlate of human thought" (Bryant et al. 3), these thinkers think of it exclusively in terms of relations and becoming (Shaviro 286). As a result, while literary scholars may appear to seek an alternative to modernism's supposedly worn discourse on the new (tradition vs. the avant-garde), the philosophers seem to return to the question of the new. Steven Shaviro's essay "The Actual Volcano: Whitehead, Harman, and the Problem of Relations" will be discussed here in some detail as an example of the recirculation of modernism. I do so with the hope of clarifying further that the stakes of my account of critique are in the ethical underpinnings of critique.

Persons and volcanos

Shaviro focuses on the modernist thinkers William James and Alfred North Whitehead, presenting them as philosophers not of being but of becoming. For James and Whitehead, being thrown in the world means being immersed in a bustling democracy of neighboring creatures (Shaviro 287). In Shaviro's discussion the two modernists embody an alternative line of reflection that values the "hidden life of things" and stresses the importance of "conjunctive relations" among entities (287). With regard to Whitehead, author, among other things, of *Process and Reality* (1929), Shaviro explains that the British philosopher spoke of "really real" things that simultaneously constitute the universe and are entities and opportunities (284). Because Whitehead thinks of entities in terms of a "constructive functioning" (convergences, alliances) associated with "an infinite wealth" of possibilities that we can choose from, Shaviro can thrust into relief the aesthetic component of the modernist predecessor's thought (286). As an example of this aesthetic component, he singles out Whitehead's notion of "patterned contrasts," a phrase that indicates differences that are reconciled and adapt to each other. Shaviro argues that Whitehead's aesthetic component proves his affinity for the twenty-first century—our present.[36] According to Shaviro, the modernist philosopher helps to detect the pervasive relationality of our time, which manifests first and foremost in a predominant aesthetic practice involving "sampling, synthesizing, remixing, and cutting-and-pasting" (290). Thus, relying on Whitehead, Shaviro can go on to raise the following questions: "How can recycling issue in creativity, and familiarity be transformed into novelty? Through what process of selection and decision is it possible to make something new out of the massive accumulation of already-existing materials?" (290). These are familiar questions; it is possible to hear in them the problem of the new in the same terms in which Walter Benjamin posed it, that is to say, in terms of the copy: can the copy produce diasporically (departing from the original) the new and the unexpected? (Groys 104).

Shaviro then translates, through Whitehead, the problem of the new into the question of relationality in the contemporary world, where "all manners of cultural expression are digitally transcoded and electronically disseminated, where genetic material is freely recombined and where matter is becoming open to direct manipulation on the atomic and subatomic scales" (289). This translation recuperates the world grasped as surface: there are no "hidden depths"; "nothing is hidden" (289). If we consider Shaviro in conjunction with the postcritical rejection of depth (symptomatic reading) in literary studies, then both philosophers and literary critics would seem to converge on the celebration of surfaces. In fact, Whitehead's "patterned contrasts" enable Shaviro to shift a little closer to an aesthetic view of reality that is rather familiar to the literary critic. But from the latter's point of view, this literary-philosophical celebration of surfaces might occlude what once prompted Carla Lonzi to be concerned with a margin that eludes and today prompts Moi to insist that reading is a practice.

When Shaviro discusses Whitehead's concept of real entities *as* real forces to be reckoned with, he offers the precursor's example of the volcano: Whitehead talks of the real entity "volcano," not different perceptions of the thing; he affirms "the actuality of the volcano" not by "isolating *it* from the world" or by "reducing its dynamism to a sort of sterile display" but by showing its "direct effects upon other entities" (Shaviro 288). Shaviro's point is to specify that things are not "just available to us," but they are "unavoidable": we "cannot expect to escape [the volcano's] eruption" (290). The volcano, however, is a strange example. If it illustrates the pervasive relationality of the "'universe of things'" (290), it also conjures the great moving shadow that Arendt, in her account of the human condition, called *animal laborans*, comprising the slaves of ancient Greece and the precarious lives of all sorts of workers in advanced capitalism and beyond, a condition of subjection to the all-consuming nature–human cycle. In other words, the example has a way of reminding us of our human insignificance; this is why it works well as a warning against the tedious "human-centered mandate of contemporary thought" (Harman, *Guerrilla Metaphysics* 104).

What if we try to replace the volcano with another of the things present in the universe of things, for example a croissant with jam? It might have happened to you. It is early morning; the place is drenched in the glorious light of spring, and you are sitting at a table outside a coffee place, when a woman (you hear the rustle of a long skirt) stops, wishes you a sunny "Good morning!," and asks for money. You respond, proposing that she get something at the coffee place. She goes in, comes out, waves a small paper bag. She has chosen a croissant, "a croissant with jam," she specifies, and in reply you catch yourself saying, "So, next time I will know," meaning it. Does the relationality illustrated by this anecdote confirm that nothing is hidden? Does it comfortably illustrate that everything is transcoded, translatable, without hidden depths? Perhaps the example is farfetched; after all, the volcano and the croissant have nothing in common, but the volcano and the woman do: they are equally unavoidable. While the example of the volcano showcases the impact of an agent on another agent, reducing language and human thought to insignificance, this is harder to do in the example of the woman. What happens there is not all that clear. The scene is not a humanitarian scene. The mediating role taken on by the croissant only serves to withstand somehow the unavoidability of the woman. Questions arise: What makes you pay for the croissant? A debt toward the woman, a complete stranger? If so, could the debt ever be extinguished? If you are someone who, for some reason, cannot have croissants with jam and experience an emotion if the complete stranger has them for you, what kind of thing is this? The croissant points to a relationality of entities connected but also withdrawn in themselves. This of course is nothing unique; we are talking about the experience shared by most people that Toril Moi refers to as "human separation": most of us have found ourselves in "situations in which we feel powerless to know the thoughts and feelings of another human being" (206). The croissant anecdote is one of the many examples of human separation; and yet, the unavoidability of the woman does not prove that human separation is a tragic condition. It remarks on a distance that, proper to the realm of ordinary life, never disappears once we engage in the activity of reading as critics, that is to say, with the purposeful objective of interpretation. As mentioned earlier, the scene of the woman and the croissant is not a humanitarian scene. This is crucial. The croissant clearly offers no relief to speak of. Yet, it "says" that sustenance is a question here; the sustenance of bodies—the two speaking bodies—in the vital space of symbolic recognition. The "croissant with jam" is the faintest trace of a dialogism of bodies that is not immediately reducible to verbal language, does not necessarily result in linguistic behavior, and is likely to raise the problem of forms of experience that go beyond understanding and explanation. The example tells us that language is not an autonomous, transcendental object.

As long as we read, we are called (we decide to accept the call?) to bridge the hermeneutic distance between reader and text through thought and language, but such a labor does not remain confined to the hermeneutic enterprise. Elaine Scarry had the problem of hermeneutic distance in mind when she called for the labor of imagining others (45). Even the realists and the new materialists acknowledge that Scarry's labor is a "pressing concern," as when Ilya Prigogine and Isabelle Stengers, speaking for the physicist, consider the notion of sensibility:

> What is a being sensitive to? What can a being be modified by? What do its reactions to the world make a being capable of? Similar questions already make sense for simple "beings" like physical-chemical systems. But how could they not be an even more pressing concern for anyone who studies living beings endowed with memory and capable of understanding and interpreting? (64; my translation)

Today, far from having disappeared, Scarry's imaginative labor has been extended. As Latour writes: "Hermeneutics is not a privilege of humans but, so to speak, a property of the world itself" (*Reassembling* 245), suggesting that the problem is not to get rid of language and thought, though they may no longer have, in Harman's words, a "human-centered mandate."

Human separation haunts hermeneutics. Looking at harrowing images, in *Regarding the Pain of Others* (2003), her second study of photography after her groundbreaking essays of the 1970s, Susan Sontag grasped the tragic ossification of the distance between subject and object in the deadlock of the executioner–victim pair. This is why she ventured the controversial assertion that photographs do not make us understand; "they haunt us" (*Regarding* 89). What haunts the observer in this case is the closure of the space of symbolic recognition, with the impression that understanding happens only when the two trade places (in harrowing photographs trading places with the victim means death).[37]

In Biblical hermeneutics the distance between the text and the reader must be preserved: because of the authority of the Scriptures the aim is not to reach a plenitude between the Scriptures and the reader's interpretation, but one can return endless times to the question of the meaning of the Scriptures. By contrast, in literary hermeneutics, distance is not necessarily a founding principle. Literary criticism, as the explication of texts, assumes the search for meaning, and the task of arriving at meaning. But it is possible to observe that at important turns in its recent history, criticism has renewed itself through moments of impasse, when that distance between reader and text persists as a problem and is spectacularized. For New Criticism the moments of impasse in the text (ambiguity and paradox, for example) are also the ones that keep the reader searching for its meaning; deconstruction is irritated by the notion of hermeneutic distance and voluptuously gets rid of it, intensifying the play of the signifier; more recently, speculative realism affirms that meaning depends on the impossibility of any integration of a structure and its components. Tom Eyers writes:

> Literature stages better than most phenomena the manner in which, far from shutting down the possibility of meaning, the impossibility of any final, formal integration of a structure and its component parts is the very condition of possibility of that structure. (8)

The assumption of a necessary loss, which was a precondition of Biblical hermeneutics, seems to have transferred to literary interpretation, to the extent that "it is [the] very resistance to semantic recuperation that, paradoxically enough, lies at the root of literature's capacity to refer, even to transfigure, annul, boost or remain strikingly indifferent to, its historical and political conditions" (Eyers 9–10). It is in this very resistance to being repaired, somehow, that literature can have any dealings with its outside. In dealing with literature, one begins under the sign of damage, incompleteness. This damaged condition causes untiring, endless, loving returns to meaning even when meaning has been reached. This is why Felski speaks of texts as "vulnerable artifacts," urging a practice of care that is more generous than critique as she depicts it. It is this depiction that has elicited the most controversial responses. Her account of critique has seemed inaccurate, spurring work that rather than promoting fresh interpretations takes flight from the core business of literary studies (see Liming).

The abridgment of critique to a set of oppositional gestures that ought now to be replaced with reparative gestures of preserving and protecting is part of a larger epistemological shift, but there are other factors in the demise of the *againstness* commonly associated with critique that I will expand on in the next section.

Againstness (and Euro-American relations)

The limits of critique are entangled with political factors that seem hard to ignore because of the influence they exert on scholarly research and on the production of knowledge in academia. First among these factors is the value of literary studies in the University, which has become increasingly dependent on the quantification of research and on the kind of money it brings in. Second, and related to the first, in the face of the quantification of research that also drives universities' rankings and reputation, a great number of academics—regardless of the stage of career they are at—live precarious lives, a fact that can indenture their intellectual output to fear and shame, while it also pressures them to disavow these negative affective underpinnings. This is also called the phenomenon of adjunctification of academic labor; but it is important to bear in mind that the phenomenon encompasses tensions that are not just generational tensions and forces that, far from being limited to the post-2008 financial crash, concern the constraint of knowledge production in the University, with the ossified disciplinary sectors that keep research, thinking, and teaching within confines that often do not reflect the critical practice of many interdisciplinary scholars. Combined with these problems is the fall of the critic from his or her role as public intellectual; and, should he or she opt for what formerly had been the virtue of critique, that is, "the suspension of ordinary beliefs and commitments" (Felski, *Limits* 25), the risk of being perceived as a destructive agent unable to defend the value of literature and art outside academic circles. It is in this climate that critique might be perceived as an obstacle in the adventure of interpretation.

In a way, the simplification of critique as againstness, an adversarial attitude usually associated with leftist scholars, has resulted from the transformation of fields of study that are immediately related to it. We remarked earlier on the intimate bond between modernism and Theory, conjoined in their reliance on rupture with the dominant culture. But as modernism becomes more geographically decentered, more lateral and paratactic (Friedman, *Planetary Modernisms*), the conceptual objects of attachment that it had produced for the uses of criticism fade into the distance, among them: the opposition between center and margins, an anti-institutional stance against power, iconoclastic negativity, and so on. In 2013, Wai Chee Dimock registered the effect of the disappearance in the phrase "weak theory": it may be taken to refer to the weakening of the critic's conceptual object of attachment, first and foremost, the center–margin opposition, and the ensuing feeling of being stranded in a zone of "noncommunicability" ("Weak Theory" 751). Dimock's zone recalls a lot the subject/object deadlock that haunted Sontag. What wanes with the modernist critical objects is also the idea of the new as the child of discontinuity and rupture, with the logic of the avant-garde borrowed as a template for the classification and ordering of critical schools,[38] which appear only to be destroyed and superseded by the next: German Critical Theory, French Theory, Weak Theory, Italian Theory, in a continuum called "critique" that entangles "aesthetic and social worth" but makes both intelligible only "in terms of a rhetoric of *againstness*" (Felski, *Limits* 17).

From this vantage point, what is meant by critique too often represents a localized phase of modernization and an instance of acculturation that the term "postcritique" makes visible at its crepuscular moment. As an example, I will draw on Eric Hayot's account, in *Critique and Postcritique* (2017), which is worth quoting at length:

> It is in the nature of idealisms to disappoint. You start out planning to change the world; you end up teaching in a university, changing one small thing or another in yourself, your students, or the curriculum, while the world goes on without you. Or you end up changing quite a lot—perhaps as one small soldier in the giant army of what used to be called lesbian and gay studies, and is now queer studies, an army that helped make possible the stunning national and international transformations in the political status of homosexual, transexual, and transgendered men and women, and in the civic recognition and legitimation of their sex and love. Or perhaps as a teacher of teachers who have rewritten high school and university curricula in the United States to include engagement with the bleak, inspiring history of ethnic struggle, or with the fight for women's rights, and with the art and the literature of those battles, a change that seems radical and huge to someone who in his American high school English classes never read a single book written by a woman, or a person of color. (282)

Only by recounting the fall of critique can one fully realize its local achievements. In the narrative above, the waning of critique, abridged to the necessity of debunking, produces the appropriate distance from the past; it, in fact, creates the narrative of a critical past. The relocation in the U.S. of foreign thinkers in a succession of critical schools—"the way that Foucault succeeded Derrida, Bourdieu Foucault, Badiou Bourdieu, Rancière Badiou, and so on"—effects "the Theoretical revolution in the American academy" (Hayot 287). At the same time, such a narrative makes clear that critique is an episode in Euro-American relations, an important phenomenon of transatlantic communication and modernization. While it may be boring to dwell on the prefix "post," we might just say that one of the reasons for the fortune of the term "postcritique" lies in its promise of a departure from that process of modernization (and from that procession of great men).³⁹ The new beginning that it announces affords a sense of relief. Perhaps, however, it would be helpful to recall that critique, in its transatlantic crossing, has tended to feel like an unstoppable search for relief. The reconstruction of critique that is offered by Eve Kosofsky Sedgwick in *A Dialogue on Love* (1999), which might be read as a classic of postcritique, is clear about *that* mood.

Sedgwick's *A Dialogue on Love* is at once a self-portrait and a collective intellectual biography, which centers on the abandonment of poetry for the ethical responsibility of theory. The theme is the vulnerability of the critic: as her body is undermined by cancer and beset by mortality, she tries to account for her critical formation and presents critique as the process of what in our postcritical times Singh would call "unthinking mastery."⁴⁰ In Sedgwick's self-portrait, criticism can only be defined in its difference from poetry; it is the "song" that poetry could not sing for those post-Vietnam War generations that felt the increasingly invasive power of institutions and sought a discourse fit to oppose it.⁴¹ Sedgwick herself casts her acclaimed criticism as a secondary writing, a translation of her first love, poetry, a translation made necessary by both personal and national circumstances (*Dialogue* 65). Being abandoned by the muse of poetry is not an incident in the *Bildung* of the introspective academic but an event of national dimensions shaping postwar American history marked by anti-Vietnam protests and the experience of anti-communist fury. In such a climate the muse must oppose her "No." Theory is a kind of "poetry" fit for a time when it becomes especially clear that institutions shape individual acts. The extraordinary trait of Sedgwick's narrative is the presentation of theory as a necessary form of intellectual self-fashioning that is at once a reparative labor. Her second muse, in fact, enables her to distance herself from the anxiety emanating from haunting personal origins, particularly her grandmother Nanny's ugly "fishwife voice" against which Eve's mother opposed her own teacherly voice, the first object of child Eve's hatred. The mother's teacherly voice is not simply an object forged by power but testifies to Eve's mother's consent to the work of power in the attempt to distance herself from the anxiety of permanent intellectual robbery radiating from Nanny's roughness. It is to these workings of power, amplified in the larger public and national arena, that Eve opposes her supple intellect and her allegiance to critique. She would invent Queer Theory. In Sedgwick's account critique amounts to the laborious, patient making of a fragile artifact. The psychoanalytic setting of the narrative, which unfolds around the sessions with her Ferenczian analyst, Shannon, is there to remind us that language and speech are irrenounceable in the task. Shannon's psychoanalytic affiliation to Ferenczian tenderness (Sándor Ferenczi was a dissident disciple of Freud accused of practicing the "kissing technique"), in concomitance with the critic's acceptance of her dying body, helps to envision a shift from the colonizing dynamics of power to the possible overlap of cure and love in critical practice. As in Lonzi's transition from art criticism to feminist critique understood as a "technique of life," in Sedgwick's shift from power to love the fall of certified forms of mastery entails the appearance of a discourse without a specific genre, with permeable boundaries, which, in fact, gathers its strength in the weakness of its unclassifiable genre.

This turn in criticism is not stressed in Hayot's account, which assimilates critique to a temporal stretch, to a sense of a time that is lost and cannot be retrieved—"What we know is that something has been lost, that literary criticism, today, floats adrift on an open, darkling sea, while the sailors search desperately for new compasses. Something has changed" (279)—to an intercultural, transatlantic reciprocity that evaporates once the realization sets in of a vaster world of "global patterns" of development whose "sheer scale" neutralizes "the possibilities of individual and social resistance to capitalism and violence" (283). From this perspective, the prefix "post" in the word "postcritique" signals the end of a phase of Euro-American reciprocal modernization and the exposure of the U.S. to what Jean-Luc Nancy would call "the game of the world" (Nancy qtd. in Esposito, *Da Fuori* 218). While Hayot's account highlights the procession of great men, Sedgwick outlines a genealogy of againstness that is at the same time deeply personal and public and is based on a transformative vital labor.

Like Hayot, Felski attributes the demystifying posture of critique to its transatlantic formation: it is "transmitted across the Atlantic" (*Limits* 76). The phenomenon of Italian Theory addresses itself precisely to such accounts. As a name given from within the anglophone context, Italian Theory addresses this context meaningfully but also defamiliarizes the postcritical narrative of critique.

This work of defamiliarization is accomplished above all by Roberto Esposito. On more than one occasion, Roberto Esposito has reflected on critique understood as something transmitted across the Atlantic. In *Pensiero vivente* (Living Thought) (2010) he traces the beginning of "Italian Theory" to the success of living

Italian thinkers among American scholars in American universities (3). The phenomenon closely recalls the rise of French Theory and, before French Theory, the German Critical Theory of Adorno, Horkheimer, and Marcuse (Esposito, *Living Thought*). In "German Philosophy, French Theory, Italian Thought" (2015), Esposito modifies the name circulated in English, "Theory," into "Thought" to call attention to the ordering of the waves of Theory and to question that sequence. For Esposito the sequence points to the movement of deterritorialization which, since its decline in the 1930s and 1940s, has propelled European philosophy outside its boundaries, in the attempt "to reinvent itself along other trajectories" ("German Philosophy" 105). Focusing on the displacement of the Frankfurt School and later of French Theory, without neglecting the difference (the first ensues from traumatic historical events, the second is devoid of any tragic resonance), Esposito argues that they provide examples of the inventiveness and the productiveness linked to geographical displacement, which "resulted in a contamination and in a circulation of ideas that took on the traits of a veritable hegemony in a number of disciplines, from literary criticism to gender studies and postcolonial studies" (106).[42]

In the series of geographical-intellectual displacements, within the context of the Euro-American exchange, the given name of "Italian Theory" suggests a third wave of theory, continuing the movement and modifying the emphasis of the previous two: if German Critical Theory emphasized the social dimension and French Theory the textual dimension, Italian Theory emphasizes the "constitutively conflicting space of political practice" (Esposito, "German Philosophy" 107). Although *Pensiero vivente* does attempt to reconstruct a genealogy of Italian philosophy,[43] what Esposito ends up calling "living thought" refers to a line of reflection that is far from national, comprising Dante and Machiavelli but also Spinoza, Nietzsche, and Foucault. It refers to a thought that unfolds as if in a countermovement vis-à-vis the transcendental orientation of modern philosophy, and, rather than being based on the constitution of subjectivity or on theories of knowledge, leans outside, toward the world, unfolding along the three main axes of life, history, and politics (Esposito, *Pensiero vivente* 12). For this reason, "living thought" names a philosophical thought that is defined as "latent" and appears to be a non-philosophy, raising the problem of genre that concerned Sedgwick.[44] In Esposito, the adjective of nationality performatively calls attention to the Anglo-American incorporation of European philosophies in linear chunks of national traditions:

post-World War II German Critical Theory first, poststructuralist French Theory later, and now Italian Theory, with one school, as noted by Hayot, superseding and replacing another. In renaming Italian Theory, Esposito invites us to see it as a line of reflection that moves along at an eccentric pace, at once preceding and exceeding "analytic, hermeneutic and deconstructive philosophies" (Esposito, *Da Fuori* 161). As such, "living thought" reorients critique as a larger, dynamic movement, with the result that Theory, rather than coming with the melancholia for a lost transatlantic past, signals the emergence of a latent body of thought that is particularly attuned to the "dynamics of globalization and immaterial production of the postmodern" (Esposito, *Pensiero vivente* 5). Revising the standard account and associating critique with a series of geographical-intellectual displacements that admit of a different "affirmative tonality," Esposito sees critique not as inadequate to the current global patterns and their overwhelming scales but as coterminous with these changes ("German Philosophy" 110).[45]

Esposito shares Felski's disaffection for rupture and, like the realists, he proposes a thinker turned outward—toward the world. But he neither champions a pervasive relationality, that would risk being an aestheticized version of reality, nor abandons human thought; rather, he participates in the larger conversation on the defamiliarization of the human by probing the most basic categories like person and community. This labor of estrangement began with *Bíos* (2005) and, more strikingly, with *Terza persona* (2007), where the towering notion of a biological fold of transindividual flesh rises to trouble previous notions of thought and critique, and continues in the attempt to think "after man" as the subject of humanistic discourse (*Bíos* 105).[46]

As already mentioned, Italian Theory defines itself as eccentric to poststructuralism, somehow comprising its linguistic turn. It does not assume the sovereignty of language and focuses the problem of things stripped of their reality by language, but the latter remains a central question not only because it is a space of what Felice Cimatti calls "symbolic recognition" ("Introduzione" 16; my translation), but also as a space of simultaneous (and violent) inclusion and exclusion (through language and thought we build limits and margins and decide who/what is included and who/what is not, who is more human than others and who is not).[47] Language therefore remains an important space where the labor of imagining others that I conveyed in my croissant anecdote is important to the inquiry into less cruel dynamics of humanization (*Terza persona* 135).

The plane of coevalness

Thus, sharing the urgency of an exit in a larger world with other disciplinary discourses, Italian Theory does not take as its main target the rejection of poststructuralism or againstness. Againstness is understood as part and parcel of the production of the new within European thought, a production which Esposito sees as inseparable from the production of an "anthropic margin" to defend ourselves from. In his analysis, the production of the new is made possible by "the construction of a threshold—whether anthropological, epistemological, or institutional—which shelters from something primordial and constitutive, that cannot be governed by reason but instead threatens reason" (Esposito, *Pensiero vivente* 24). This "anthropic margin" has variously been occupied by magic and myth, and is still "too contiguous with the animal dimension" (24). In this pattern, "something primordial and constitutive" is deferred but always returns aggressively, a "pre-reflexive magmatic substance" (*sostanza magmatica pre-riflessiva*), that makes its spectral return—whether as the Other, animality, or inhumanity—as something fundamentally unknowable. The new appears when we defend ourselves from the returns of the magmatic pre-reflexive substance and seek a new beginning. This standard pattern evaporates in the notion of a plane of coevalness where "the origin is made available as a resource rather than something to be subjected to as if to a spectral return" (25).

In positing the plane of coevalness, Esposito, unlike Felski, does not feel compelled to reject modernism, but neither does he tap modernism, like the speculative philosophers, to celebrate a pervasive relationality bent on disposing of the idea of depth. Assuming, via Foucault, that power-knowledge implies forms of life that resist it, Esposito reactivates the modernist motif of the conflict of Life vs. Form (as we shall see in Chapter 3). The "living thought" that he outlines, eccentric to poststructuralism, actually activates occluded modernist motifs which are thereby shown to be incomplete, first and foremost what he calls *bíos*, life or the living, referring to the weave of life, history, and politics. The plane of coevalness differs from the surfaces and the radical relationality of new materialism and new realism as well as from Latour's bustling network of actors. Like them, it is interested in disposing of a model of rupture in our intellectual endeavors; unlike them, it mobilizes a line of reflection that refocuses and recovers, by folding back on feminism and psychoanalysis especially, the notion of life as always in tension with its context and with history.

If a linear modernity which presupposes an unevenness of cultures has overshadowed the multiple locations of ideas and the effects of their circulation, the plane of coevalness is the plane of circulation where the new appears through a circuit of recognition and misrecognition or *méconnaissance*. Which leads us to the question of reading and back to where we started with Airan Kang's luminous books. The plane of coevalness is a plane of defamiliarization (in tune with critique's traditional labor of the de-). Kang's lit books suggest a plane of circulation that is a plane of beneficial defamiliarization; by being lit and withdrawn, the books invite us to entertain the notion of imaginative reconstruction.

Like "living thought" her work, as we saw at the start of this Introduction, may be said to have a poststructuralist (as well as a feminist) matrix, stemming from a consciousness of the link between knowledge and power and an interest in the politics of knowledge. This transpires in the questions Kang poses: What knowledge will we store? What will we value? But also: How do we recognize knowledge? Such questions concern literary criticism, a practice which relies on a strange relation between the text and the critic. Traditionally literary criticism has acknowledged the difficulty in reconciling the literary object and its explanation because explanation has been suspected to diminish the capacity for wonder. As Wolfgang Iser once wrote:

> The effectiveness of the work depends on the participation of the reader, but explanations arise from (and also lead to) detachment; they will therefore dull the effect, for they relate the given text to a given frame of references, thus flattening out the new reality brought into being by the fictional text. (10)

As a professional reader, the critic can only secure an unstable identity, often taking flight in the freedom of the common or lay reader. The bifurcation between professional and lay reader returns in Felski's most recent work, *Hooked: Art and Attachment* (2020). As Kang's luminous books remind us, when reading we are addressed by something that withdraws. Her use of LED, marking the crossing of public space and the one-on-one dialogue with the book as well as her attempt to include it in ordinary people's lives, struck me as a good beginning for this book which, in dealing with critique, deals with the problem that has allowed critique to take up lodgings within literary studies, and that is the figure of the critic, his or her task, and the constitutive instability of the reader/critic who not only wishes to think with literature and through language but also seeks to envision forms of human agency that contribute to a just society.

Notes

1. Her early work is thought to suggest "the act of hiding or concealing something precious in secrecy or packing to leave and be liberated from an oppressive environment" (Kim 11–12).
2. Airan Kang, *The Sublime. The Space of Heterotopia*, Solo Exhibition, Gallery Simon Seoul, Korea, 2009, in Kim et al. 100–9; Motoe.
3. See, for example, the series "Reality and Virtual Image," in Kim et al. 11.
4. Okabe explains that art books are frequently used for a rather practical reason: "thick art books have the advantage of having LED and digital equipment built-in easily, which are necessary for the specification of lighting books, and additionally, more autonomous standing and stable display is possible" (48).
5. Jankélévitch writes: "Charm functions only by means of entirely spontaneous and nascent suggestion on the part of the agent. Because if the agent wants too much, then the one acted upon will no longer desire; if the agent begins to work too hard, then the one acted upon withholds his or her consent: and the Charm is broken" (*Music* 88).
6. For example, *Lord Byron (Hyper Open Book)*, 2010, LED lights, resin shell, electrical circuits, 24 1/2 × 16 1/2 × 4 in.
7. Charles S. Peirce said of thought: "a thought is what it is, only by virtue of its addressing a future thought which is in its value as thought identical with it, though more developed" (84).
8. For Arendt, as for Augustine, the self is a void; it can be remembered; it is a weave of memory.
9. *Light of the World, Light of the Intelligence*, Solo Exhibition, Art Front Gallery, Tokyo, Japan, 2006; Kim et al. 186–7.
10. Okabe presents Kang's career in terms of a shift from "her sentiment about her self-history" to an interest in "books symbolizing the cognition of the world" which parallels the circulation of her own work outside Korea and Japan (55).
11. All translations from Lonzi, *Autoritratto* are mine.
12. "Just reading" is used by Marcus in *Between Women*.
13. "Graduation" was first published as "Evening" in *The Antioch Review*, vol. 62, no. 1 (2004): 102 and is included in Tanning's book *A Table of Content* (20).
14. All translations from Lonzi, "La solitudine del critico" are mine.
15. I am working with the Italian edition, *Pensiero vivente*, and all translations from it are mine; for the English edition, see Esposito, *Living Thought*.

16. On this topic, see Cimatti, "Vita" 88.
17. Robert Rauschenberg, *Erased de Kooning Drawing*, 1953, San Francisco Museum of Modern Art.
18. I am quoting Parmenides as translated by Vishwa Adluri, *Parmenides, Plato, and Mortal Philosophy Return from Transcendence* (Bloomsbury Academic, 2011) 139.
19. For Esposito this interrogation of reality reaches back to include Machiavelli (*Pensiero istituente* 193–207). All translations from Esposito, *Pensiero istituente* are mine.
20. I am drawing on the Italian text of Lacan's "Discorso di Roma," the stenographic transcript of the speech pronounced by Lacan in Rome, 26 September 1953, that introduced "The Function and Field of Speech and Language in Psychoanalysis." My translation.
21. I return to the critic in Chapter 3.
22. In literary studies, it translates into a marked attention to resistance, struggle, difference, to the limits of knowledge, and to the undoing of oppositions and binaries, as criticism tries to renegotiate the proper distance between critic and text (Williams; Bertens).
23. Discussed in Chapter 2. Here I use the capital initial to indicate not only a new genre of literary criticism but also a historical moment localized in the U.S. and the connected anglophone world.
24. Accounting for the fall from things in the long time of thought, Sloterdijk points to the sphere as the seductive image of totality, representing the point of view of the observer positioned outside the world: "The sphaira as the highest form of imagining thought, lured mortals into the game of an initially jovial, then lordly observation of the outside that would one day lead to polytechnical dreams of control and the tyranny of knowledge over concretely interpreted life as a whole" (79).
25. To illustrate the subversive potential of observation, in "Wondering About Materialism," Stengers quotes the example of Diderot, who once said to D'Alembert: "Do you see this egg? With it you can overthrow every school" (373).
26. Snow, *Two Cultures*, originally delivered as a lecture, "The Two Cultures and the Scientific Revolution" in Senate House, Cambridge, in 1959; Huxley, *Literature* 1, 118; Latour, *Reassembling*. In the late 1950s and the early 1960s, the "two cultures" debate was led by figures like C. P. Snow and Aldous Huxley. Snow argued that the physical world, as an edifice erected by science, has an "intellectual depth" and a complex articulation that deserves aesthetic and critical investigation. Huxley urged "a not too hostile symbiosis" between the scientific and literary communities, wondering whether language could do justice to the physical world. Both Snow and Huxley pointed to the problem of the literary critic who defined him- or herself against the horror of industrial modernity and the paralyzing power of science and technology. Following up on his predecessors, in *We Have Never*

Been Modern, Latour criticizes those scholars in the Humanities who perceive themselves as guardians of a variety of immaterial objects, including "souls, minds, interpersonal relations, the symbolic dimension, human warmth, local specificities, hermeneutics" (123).

27. My translation. Tagliapietra defines wonder as a peculiar way of seeing, in which things irrupt in the field of vision as if appearing for the first time (69).
28. Reclaiming the "adventure of interpretation" results, as Stengers observes, in certain fundamental questions cutting across different disciplines. For example, the question "What is matter?" does not find a reply in one particular science, but it crosses disciplines and generates new areas of investigation (372). The question has given impetus, in literary studies, building on the work of Donna Haraway and others, to material feminisms and the troubling of what Nancy Tuana calls "substance ontology" as well as to the ecological criticism of Serenella Iovino. See Tuana and Scott; Iovino. See also Alaimo and Hekman and, in the same collection, Karen Barad's probing of the pun on matter as noun and verb.
29. In Wai-Chee Dimock's words, "Latour urges us to think instead about tangential processes, wayward lines of association, oblique to an existing system, pulling away from it and stretching it in unexpected ways. There is no reason why we should not work with these centrifugal forces, these 'long networks' that head out—'mediators' that reopen closed cases and undo any naturalized hierarchies" ("Weak Theory" 736).
30. Along these lines, see Heather Love's project of "meticulous flat description" ("Close but Not Deep" and "Close Reading"), or Franco Moretti's "distant reading," which relies on data mining and cognitive science to confer scientific legitimacy and universal value to the interpretation of texts. Further core readings on description include Marcus et al.
31. On this topic, see Szondi.
32. In her 2006 presidential address, MLA President Marjorie Perloff concludes that "instead of lusting after those other disciplines that seem so exotic primarily because we don't really practice them, what we need is more theoretical, historical, and critical training in our own discipline" (Perloff qtd. in Lesjak 18).
33. Moi writes: "Thus, when we talk of poststructuralism, feminist theory, or simply theory, these are not methods unless, of course, we encourage our students to apply a certain theory to a text, but in so doing we would encourage them to repeat and produce in a mechanical and standardized manner" (179).
34. Jameson will be discussed in Chapter 2.
35. In the same introduction to the special Latour issue of *New Literary History*, Felski worries that the scholar should be able to speak to wider

audiences and to "multiple constituencies" ("Introduction" 219). This preoccupation perhaps says more about the critic brooding on his or her own performance than about critique. At some level, it does feel like a return to the kind of impasse that led intellectuals like Sontag in the 1970s to reject the then dominant narrative linking modernism to the question of the public intellectual, that is to say, to the necessity of an élite that explicates a difficult sensibility to the masses. From this perspective, the rejection of critique, because of the kind of impasse to which it leads, can already be heard in Sontag's work: "I am an adversary writer, / a polemical writer. I / write to support what is / attacked, to attack what is / acclaimed. But thereby I / put myself in an emotionally / uncomfortable position. / I don't, secretly, hope to / convince, and can't help / being dismayed when my / minority taste (ideas) / becomes majority taste (ideas): / then I want to attack / again. I can't help but / be in an adversary relation/ to my own work" (*Consciousness* 397).
36. Shaviro argues that the modernist Whitehead is closer to the twenty-first century than his own contemporary colleagues like Graham Harman who, following up on Whitehead, develops the concept of "allure," a generative principle of new relations among objects that exists *in nuce* in reality, including the inanimate sphere (Harman, *Guerrilla Metaphysics* 244).
37. Indeed, the closure of symbolic space haunts us, and that is why the diffuse experience of human separation visits the critic on the scene of interpretation and can make him tremble in his professional chair.
38. That there are other ways of understanding the term "avant-garde" is compellingly conveyed by Renato Poggioli in his pioneering study, where the avant-garde is a way of reading (and being attached to certain texts) that is also a form of life (91).
39. In my book on Sontag my aim was to study the ways in which she negotiated her place in that procession by turning to Benjamin (Mitrano, *In the Archive of Longing*).
40. I offer a fuller discussion of Sedgwick's text in Mitrano, "Che cos'è la teoria."
41. Sedgwick, "Who Fed This Muse?"; Mitrano, "Che cos'è la teoria" 65.
42. Esposito reminds us of a fact that has been noticed a number of times before: in what Felski and Hayot would call its "Atlantic transmission," the thought of Derrida, Deleuze, or Foucault, "became quite other as decontextualized fragments of their thought amalgamated in a new discourse called 'theory'" ("German Philosophy" 106).
43. On this point, see Claverini.
44. On this point, see Luglio.
45. We should not forget of course that Esposito conducts a philosophical critique of political theology, and that, in transferring his terms from philosophy to the literary realm the risk is that of conceptual deracination and estrangement. At the same time, his description of theory

reminds us that the contact between philosophy and literature (understood as both literary texts and the critical discourse they generate) is fundamental to critique, especially when seen from the experience of U.S. theory. As mentioned above, he speaks of the decontextualization of foreign thinkers whose work is assimilated in multiple disciplines, including literary studies ("German Philosophy" 110).
46. In thinking "after man" Esposito's Italian Theory shares the broader conversation across a number of disciplinary discourses. Queer Theory, Postcolonial Theory, and Race Theory find affinities and intersections around the task. Here I can only indicate some helpful introductory examples: Muñoz et al.; the issue that contains this article features on the cover the extraordinary photograph by Laura Aguilar, *Grounded #114* (2006), which positions the viewer at the crossroads of a withdrawal from the human (including the possibilities of symbolic recognition) and our affinities with nature; Cheng; Singh.
47. On the violence of language, see Esposito, *Persons*; Agamben, *What is Philosophy?*

Chapter 1

What is Critique?: Three Types of Indocility

Overview

The keyword of this chapter is "critique." The inquiry takes as its reference point Judith Butler's 2000 Raymond Williams lecture, "What is Critique? An Essay on Foucault's Virtue," and the fact of Butler's return to and repetition of Michel Foucault's question in his own 1978 lecture "What is Critique?" to suggest that the importance of returning to the question, that is to say, to the institution of that question, is in itself part of critique. The repetition of the question leads us on the trail of a muse: the imago of a movement—slight, divergent—gentle turning or gentle indocility, linked across time, to humanity's emancipation from immaturity, exemplifying, more than a method or a field, an attitude: the critical attitude. The three types of indocility of the title refer to Foucault, Theodor W. Adorno, and Walter Benjamin. They are discussed here to show that the critical attitude is associated with the capacity to connect the particular—single text or event—to a larger pattern. This capacity to connect determines the transition from criticism, understood in its basic meaning as fault-finding, to critique, a transition which, as discussed in this chapter, requires, among other things, a defamiliarization or distancing from the present perceived as weakness especially in the ways in which it suppresses life. By chapter's end, we shall see that today proponents of non-anthropocentric ontologies like Bruno Latour, who has wielded significant influence in literary studies and in propelling the debate on postcritique, are on the trail of the muse followed in this chapter, wondering where the critical attitude is and asking about ways of recovering it.

Reflective indocility

When did literary criticism become critique? In a lecture entitled "What is Critique?," originally delivered in May 1978, Michel Foucault dwells on the desire and the impossibility that simultaneously surround the question.[1] The author of *The Archeology of Knowledge* (*L'archéologie du savoir*, 1969) uses the term "critique" to recall a noble philosophical tradition that bears the indelible stamp of his great precursor, Immanuel Kant, and the loftiness of his enterprise. At the start of the lecture Foucault explains that his admiration for the master prevents him from repeating the title of Kant's essay, "What is Enlightenment?" (*Was ist Aufklärung?*), which is the title that he had wanted to use. In that essay, the precursor depicts a humanity kept in a state of immaturity, by the law, by knowledge, by religion. Foucault begins by making public his own desire with regard to the precursor, speaking of the modesty that he must exert. In this beginning, it is as if the tension between repetition and novelty were itself part of the question of critique: "I had hardly been able to find a title; or rather there was one that kept haunting me but that I didn't want to choose. You are going to see why: it would have been indecent" (Foucault, "What is Critique?" 41). Only after this prelude does Foucault utter the question he wants to speak about: "What is critique?" (41). The indecency of repetition lies perhaps in wanting to utter the question as if for the first time.

Foucault goes on to distinguish between the nobler meaning of critique, when it refers to the conditions of knowledge, to the fact that knowledge operates within limits, and the less noble meaning of the word, when it refers to "polemical-professional activities" ("What is Critique?" 42). The critique he wants to investigate (i.e. give shape to) is located somewhere in-between the properly philosophical modality and the polemical modality. It is born at the margins of philosophy, in the neighborhood of the non-philosophical (42); it is a "project" that does not "cease to take shape, to persist, to be reborn on the frontiers of philosophy—quite close to it, quite against it, at its expense, in the direction of a philosophy yet to come, in the place perhaps of every possible philosophy" (42). The essay opening has an affective tone (the awe inspired by the concept and by those who came before), which is far from peripheral to the theme at hand. The care one should take when attempting to speak about critique, the desire to speak about it, and the difficulty of doing so, all become as central to the text as its actual content. The mixture of desire (for the master and for emulation, but also desire to name something new, which fact, however, would have been "indecent") and hesitation is decisive in the perception of critique as a kind of knowledge. This is why Foucault speaks of critique as a "virtue" (43). If it does not belong to philosophy, neither does it belong to other disciplines; it is a "function" subordinated to the disciplines (including literature), but it is not about correcting the errors of a discipline (42): "There is something in critique that is akin to virtue. And in a certain way, what I wanted to speak to you about was the critical attitude as virtue in general" (43).

Reaching back to the intellectual history of the West, Foucault identifies a "curious activity" ("What is Critique?" 42) and dates its birth between the fifteenth and the sixteenth centuries, when it manifests itself as "a certain manner of thinking, of speaking, likewise of acting, and a certain relation to what exists, to what one knows, to what one does, as well as a relation to society, to culture, to others" (42). Such is the "critical attitude." Etymologically the word "attitude" is akin to disposition (an aptness and a promptitude), but it also means posture or position, as in the posture of a figure in a statue or in a painting. Perhaps, however, the most striking semantic trait of the word "attitude" is that it means a position of the body that is supposed to indicate some mental state. To speak of critique as an attitude means to evoke an alignment of mind, language, and action; it means to suggest a felicitous correspondence of thought, speech, and doing, which are all rendered simultaneous, as if each were the perfect translation of the other. The description captures the agility—even the athleticism—of a human figure stilled in the achievement of lightness, as body, words, and doing become harmonized in one single intent. The presiding image of critique here is a supple human figure; she looms behind Foucault's critical attitude, poised in readiness before "a domain" that her gaze "is unable to regulate" (42). The figure's gaze is detached. She is less an image and more the prototype through which the thinker apprehends his relation to knowledge, the imago of a stilled kinesis, of a certain way of moving distinguished by a unity of intent of mind and body.[2] The virtue of critique flows from this imago of a unison turn of body and thought in another direction with regard to something that has weight in human history. The weighty matter for Foucault is the idea of being governed, and the term "virtue" suggests a graceful handling of that weight, through a suppleness of the body that reflects an equal disposition of the mind not to be weighed down, "not to be governed quite so much" (45).

By his own admission, Foucault's critique is a shadow; it comes on the trail of something "very general and very vague and fluid" borne by the tide of historical time down to us, the prototype of a gentle gesture—"not . . . quite so much"—that nevertheless can settle in a method, providing "the historical anchoring points" ("What is Critique?" 45). History begins to line up from the single perspective of the dominant art of being governed in a sequence of tableaux that reveal just as much the individual letting himself be in a "total, meticulous, detailed relationship of obedience" to someone else (26), as the fascination with the individual's capacity to abandon the relation through the act of turning and diverging, but in a gentle, measured way. As Foucault charges on, the governmentalization of the individual exudes the conviction of the shaping force of a humanity kept in a state of immaturity and of a Europe united in the art of "subjugating individuals in the very reality of a social practice by mechanisms of power that appeal to a truth" (47). The monochromatic sadness of the tableaux—"how to govern children, how to govern the poor and beggars, how to govern a family, a house, how to govern armies, different groups, cities, States and also how to govern one's own body and mind" (27)—only thrusts into starker relief the prototypical gentle movement catching up on us across Europe's historical time. Critique is "the movement through which the subject gives itself the right to question truth concerning its power effects and to question power about its discourses of truth" (47). The figure "seek[s] to escape"; it is the figure of an escape. But it is the "not . . . quite so much" that counts, more than the attempt at distancing ("the subject gives itself the right . . .") and the movement itself (45). Most readings of Foucault make much of insubordination, and in the current debate on postcritique his name is associated with the paradigmatic gesture of cool adversarial exposure:

> To flip though the annals of recent theory is to encounter an unmistakable rhetoric: the vigilant weeding out of any traces of emotion or expressive voice, a syntax that piles one rhetorical question on top of another in an interrogative spiral while steering clear of definite propositions or affirmative statements, a deadpan citation of commonplace phrases in such a way as to expose their hollowness and hypocrisy . . . In the act of distancing herself from received wisdom, the critic models an exemplary self-consciousness and a heightened aesthetic sensibility. Foucault's style, especially, has triggered numerous imitations: famously impassive, scrupulously nonjudgmental, even when portraying sensational facts and shocking acts, it serves as a model and template for much contemporary prose. (Felski, *Limits* 74)

But Foucault's discussion of critique here consigns us to a "general cultural form" ("What is Critique?" 45) preserved as if through the hypnotic charm of a pose that is the enigma of grace in the midst of ugliness. Even his conclusion that critique "will be the art of voluntary insubordination, of reflective intractability" (47) emphasizes less an attitude of againstness and more the memory of a harmony, mind and body in unison in the necessity of a non-servitude, of a reflective indocility.

What Foucault calls "critique" resumes the process of emancipation that his predecessor had meant by *Aufklärung*, but now, once the word "critique" is used to say, modestly, the other name that it would have been immodest to say, the effect is that the uttered word is "reborn on the outer limits of philosophy" ("What is Critique?" 42), in the guise of the critical attitude, "an attitude at once individual and collective of emerging, as Kant said, from one's immaturity" (47) and, one can assume, into a healthier life. Why would *this* critique interest literary studies?

We will try to reply by reflecting on Judith Butler's own repetition of Foucault's question: "What is Critique?" Foucault had turned to a predecessor in awe but had disengaged the philosophical use of critique in favor of his own archeological perspective. Butler, in the text that returns to (and repeats) Foucault's question, does the same. She turns with the same modesty to a predecessor in order to repeat his stance and, in repeating it, she disengages the stance from its original intellectual environment. It is crucial here to bear in mind that Butler's lecture "What is Critique? An Essay on Foucault's Virtue" was first delivered as the Raymond Williams Lecture at Cambridge University in May 2000. Though of course the mention of Williams is an important aspect of the text, the predecessor that Butler turns to is Adorno. Williams, the Marxist literary critic, acclaimed author of *Keywords* (1976), is presented as following in the footsteps of the predecessor, a fact that comments on how much raising what Paul de Man called "the perennial question of the distinction between philosophy and literature" (119) is part of what we call "critique". Like Adorno, Williams was concerned with mechanization, industrialization, and mass society. Like Adorno, he saw that modernity translates into mechanisms of coercion and annihilation. Adorno was concerned most of all with the annihilation of the individual in industrial society. In using Adorno as a figure of reference in order to pay homage to Williams, Butler therefore chooses to call attention to ways of assessing economic and social phenomena based on what they do to life. Adorno is a figure of reference because of his concern for the effects of modernity on life, effects that transfer to modes of thought: as Butler points out, Adorno warned against the "danger . . . of judging intellectual phenomena in a subsumptive, uninformed and administrative manner and assimilating them into the prevailing constellations of power which the intellect ought to expose" (Adorno qtd. in Butler, "What is Critique?" 304–5). Williams comes after Adorno because he reoriented literary criticism and its practitioners away from an evaluative mission that often translated into a sterile administration of ideas and into the government of texts. He moved away from the headstrong and self-willed critic to quite another kind of responsive practitioner. As Butler puts it, in part quoting Williams, he strove to find "a vocabulary for the kind of responses we have to cultural works, 'which [do] not assume the habit (or right or duty) of judgment'" (304). Williams sought to overcome the limits of criticism when it is too often "unduly" associated with "fault-finding"; instead he emphasized the "specificity of the response" and "the practice" of linking specific responses to a larger structure (314). Beginning her essay with a stretch of recent intellectual history noteworthy for the inaugural shift from an evaluative literary criticism based on judgment to an ampler cultural criticism, Butler transfers to Williams the intellectual gesture of Adorno, the gesture that would become paradigmatic of what is variously called suspicious, symptomatic, or (after Eve Kosofsky Sedgwick) paranoid reading: the gesture of exposing. For Adorno "the intellect ought to expose" the larger structure to which our responses relate (Adorno qtd. in Butler, "What is Critique?" 315). In "Paranoid Reading and Reparative Reading; or, You're So Paranoid, You Probably Think This Introduction is About You" (1997), Sedgwick points to the repeated occurrence of the verb "exposes" in Butler's own *Gender Trouble* (1990) as an example of the "paranoid impulse" or "the programmatic argument in favor of demystification" (15–16). In the case of the essay under discussion, Butler's repetition of Foucault's question—"What is Critique?"—harnesses Williams's expansion of the aims of literary criticism to return to the question of the predecessor which the name "critique" modestly signposts: the question of what the intellect ought to do. The next section will expand on Adorno's gesture; by the time we resume Butler's reading of Foucault, critique will be the about the promise of a productive familiarity held in its question.

Incredulity and debt

The *locus classicus* of exposure is the essay that Adorno co-authored with Horkheimer, "The Culture Industry: Enlightenment as Mass Deception." Traditionally the stress has fallen on Adorno's pessimism, which can certainly be heard in the argument about the disappearance of the individual and the transformation of individuals into reified consumers.[3] However, the most interesting aspect of the culture industry essay is not its implied pessimism about social change but the incredulity and the bafflement of the beholder at the reciprocity between the reified consumers and the thinker. In fact, this reciprocity makes for an important strain of the culture industry essay and forms the basis for Adorno's notion of negative dialectics. Standardized production "hems [the consumers] in so tightly, in body and soul" (Adorno and Horkheimer, "Culture Industry" 106) and the thinker, reflecting the same condition, is chained body and soul.[4] Adorno's thinker therefore must proceed as if to the outermost limit of thought, along a trajectory of "perpetual criticism" (as art historian Bernard Smith has renamed negative dialectics [*Modernism's* 288]), in a region that places center stage what to Adorno's philosophical predecessors had appeared ephemeral and uninteresting ("lazy Existenz"). In *Negative Dialectics*, Adorno writes that the

> matters of true philosophical interest at this point in history are those in which Hegel, agreeing with tradition, expressed his disinterest. They are nonconceptuality, individuality, and particularity-things which ever since Plato used to be dismissed as transitory and insignificant, and which Hegel labeled "lazy Existenz." (8)

Ostensibly, the culture industry essay conveys a heroic vision of the thinker whose implicit task would seem to withstand the aggression of production and standardization, processes that rob the consumer of his or her imagination. But the comments on the film spectator raise the question of an entire world of perception that eludes the thinker: once he or she is outside the movie theater and in the streets, the film spectator has the impression that the cinematic spectacle continues because representation wants to reproduce, in the most rigorous ways, the perceptive world of ordinary life:

> The whole world is passed through the filter of the culture industry. The familiar experience of the moviegoer, who perceives the street

outside as a continuation of the film he has just left, because the film seeks strictly to reproduce the world of everyday perception, has become the guideline of production. (Adorno and Horkheimer, "Culture Industry" 99)

How can such an elusive border region between representation and ordinary life be properly described? The protagonist of the culture industry essay is a beholder standing before the seamless continuum of external world and represented world, which in turn matches the equally seamless continuum of interiority (individual consciousness) and cultural production (reified consumers), of particular and universal. Emptying themselves one into the other, they blend and become one a substitute for the other. It is as if an important imaginative and intellectual terrain were closed. At the center of the culture industry essay tower two poles without distance, reduced to a "murky identity" whereby the universal can substitute for the particular and vice versa (Adorno and Horkheimer, "Culture Industry" 102). The closed space of sameness and replacements amounts to the rise of subjectivity as a substitutive model. In the face of this major event, thought becomes indebted to "obscure experience," to "dissipated" and "unheard" life (103).

The culture industry represses and suffocates: it provokes preliminary unsublimated pleasure only to encourage a constant habit of deprivation that causes pleasure to dry up into purely masochistic pleasure (Adorno and Horkheimer, "Culture Industry" 111). But the consumer and the spectator's habit of deprivation mirrors a similar habit of the thinker who must constantly face the repression of life, existence that goes unheard. The indictment of the culture industry resonates with the moments of *Negative Dialectics* where thinking "unconsciously obeys the idea of making amends to the pieces for what it has done" (Adorno, *Negative Dialectics* 19). Adorno cannot imagine the possibility of thought outside the scene of guilt and debt: "Dialectics is the consistent sense of nonidentity. It does not begin by taking a standpoint. My thought is driven to it by its own inevitable insufficiency, by my guilt of what I am thinking" (5).

For Adorno, thought depends on an inner theater of repression and it unfolds along guilt and reparation:

> Thought forms tend beyond that which merely exists, is merely "given". The point which thinking aims at its material is not solely a spiritualized control of nature. While doing violence to the object of its syntheses, our thinking heeds a potential that waits in the object,

and it unconsciously obeys the idea of making amends to the pieces for what it has done. (*Negative Dialectics* 19)

In the chapter of *Negative Dialectics* entitled "Constellation" thought makes amends but only through a circuitous form of reparation that is felt to be insufficient; the new potential "stored" in the object, escaping the continuum of sameness and domination, may be approached in a circuitous way, through neighboring objects which are always in excess and always "more" than the object of cognition, but which constitute an attempt to unseal it, as a key opens a lock (163). The question is much more than denouncing the reification of the individual, or of ideology, domination, and totality; it is about the exodus of the introspective thinker toward an outside that is unforeseen and unforeseeable. The culture industry is a counterpoint to philosophical reflection, an end-station for the introspective thinker who is pushed to the outer border of "the phantasms of profundity" (17). Staring at the bottom of profundity, the thinker can only see total domination, but Adorno cautions against such phantoms and advocates an exodus that leaves philosophy to its incompleteness and its dependence on the outside. Critical theory, a reflection that comes belatedly after the missed moment of philosophy's realization, is a kind of reflection that "makes sure of the nonconceptual in the concept" (12). Thought is driven by its own "inevitable insufficiency" and this binds the thinker even more to guilt for what he is thinking (5). For Adorno thought is a patched-up affair, inevitably remedial, made of limp, abstracting gestures: "no philosophy can paste the particulars into the text" (11).

Yet, while discrepancy, interference, obstacles, and failure are defended as modes of resistance, they are also the ultimate bridge to thought's inner theater of servitude. Nevertheless, they suggest a heroic dimension of the thinker, and this dimension, in turn, is an indication of Adorno's reluctance to let go of the notion of the subject. His purpose, instead, is precisely to show the rise of modern subjectivity as a formal model that is infinitely and indifferently occupied by any concrete individual. As the particular empties out into the universal in the regime of production and consumption, the process of substitution is finalized as everyone replaces everyone else:

> The identity of the species prohibits that of the individual cases. The culture industry has sardonically realized man's species being. Everyone amounts only to those qualities by which he or she can

replace everyone else: all are fungible, mere specimens. As individuals they are absolutely replaceable, pure nothingness, and are made aware of this as soon as time deprives them of their sameness. (Adorno and Horkheimer, "Culture Industry" 116–17)

Subjectivity reaches the highest level of abstraction, and each individual becomes the visible vector of equality in a generalized substitution. This process of formalization bans critical judgment and supports a heroic strain linked to the disappearance of the "thinking subject": "The fight is waged against an enemy who has already been defeated, the thinking subject"—Adorno talks of "the subject who is able to think" as a defeated enemy (Adorno and Horkheimer, "Culture Industry" 120).

The fortune of the phrase "culture industry" is linked to the theorist's biting criticism of American life and culture.[5] It is, however, possible to observe that geographical displacement to the U.S. corresponds to a "philosophical torsion" (Stimilli 180; my translation) that extends the reach of the psychic economy of guilt and debt. On the one hand, Adorno further enhances the privileged link between intellectual judgment and negation, already asserted by Freud in his 1925 essay on "Negation," extending negation as the act of taking cognizance of what is repressed to a general function of thought:

> Thought as such, before all particular contents, is an act of negation, of resistance to that which is forced upon it . . . The effort implied in the concept of thought itself, as the counterpart of passive contemplation, is negative already—a revolt against being importuned to bow to every immediate thing. (*Negative Dialectics* 19)

On the other hand, the local, historical conjuncture of domination exemplified by the culture industry allows for the recuperation of a more fundamental, prior negativity which makes thought appear less as a reaction to an economic regime and more as itself a psychic economy of guilt and debt.[6] I borrow the phrase "philosophical torsion" from Elettra Stimilli, who uses it to describe a longer arch of twentieth-century reflection engaged by "an originary negation," what might be called a native negation at the origin of thought, in the sense of a disinvestment or self-distancing at the beginning:

> as if a potentiality that is ontologically open at the origin of human life, in order to exert the power that it nevertheless has, finds ways of blaming itself for guilt, for a lack, for a debt that as a result becomes what it can invest in to give value to what seems to have no value. (181; my translation)

Like the culture industry consumer, Adorno's thinker is chained body and soul to a scene of debt and guilt at the ontological opening of life, a fact that links thought, as suggested though not overtly stated by Stimilli, to shame. The passivity of the culture industry consumer is more than a local, historical instance but it recuperates for the thinker, who mirrors the same passivity, a larger "self-disengagement" or self-distancing at the origin that can be imagined as a shame at the origin. Interestingly, Adorno argues that this shaming relation to oneself at the origin is a shaping force in history when he harnesses the elusive notion of timeless negation to the more concrete mode of relation that has historically reproduced class difference: a relation based not on a brute exertion of power but on an excess of moral credit given to the materially able other: "However, just as the ruled have always taken the morality dispensed to them by the rulers more seriously than the rulers themselves . . ." (Adorno and Horkheimer, "Culture Industry" 106). The servitude of multitudes of consumers vanquishes the idea of history as a progressive linearity to entangle it with an excess of credit that the mind cannot repair and is repeated like the ritual of Tantalus (111).

If critical theory begins where philosophy fails the particulars—"no philosophy can paste the particulars into the text" (Adorno, *Negative Dialectics* 11)—it also reveals the connection of thought and shame through thought's own insufficiency. The connection has become not only increasingly visible after Sedgwick's landmark essay on the popularity of suspicious or paranoid reading which inaugurated the debate on postcritique, but also problematic, leading to the necessity to overcome critique understood as againstness and opposition, as the overt work of the negative as illustrated by Adorno. When in one of her notebooks Susan Sontag lists among the virtues of the great critical theorists who had inspired her the constant conflict of "melancholy and history," she is thinking of Adorno (*As Consciousness* 401). His local analysis of the culture industry, reaching further back to a temporality preceding the modernity of capitalist production, retraces, as Stimilli puts it, the torsion of a potentiality that is "ontologically open at the origin of human life" in the direction of guilt and debt. This torsion essentially means the recuperation of a native negation: "The effort implied in the concept of thought itself, as the counterpart of passive contemplation, is negative already—a revolt against being importuned to bow to every immediate thing" (Adorno, *Negative Dialectics* 19). But it simultaneously recuperates an antecedent melancholia that keeps thought tied to the same scenario of guilt and debt.

The loss of such a tie would appear unimaginable in Adorno since it allows for the possibility of new ideas in a regime of sameness, posing a writing in reserve which he renders as a "potential that waits in the object" (*Negative Dialectics* 19). Adorno's defense, in *Negative Dialectics*, of discrepancy, interference, obstacles, and failure as modes of resistance implies precisely the profundity of expansive unbroken servitude that is echoed in Foucault's European tableaux in "What is Critique?" only to show how more supple Foucault's turn is than his predecessor's torsion. Discouraged by the accusation of privileging theory over practice, Adorno expresses concern about "the prohibition of thinking" ("Resignation" 199); this prospect is vanquished by Foucault, who reclaims concepts as "a way of living": "Giving form to concepts is not a way of killing life but a way of living; it is a way of living in relative mobility and not an attempt at immobilizing life" (Foucault qtd. in Esposito, *Da Fuori* 151).

In the wake of Adorno's concern for lives lost in obscurity, the inner theater of servitude and repression becomes a much more diffuse cultural climate from the Enlightenment to our days, which is effectively countered by the dust of the archive and by the forms of life that it restitutes.

The criterion of life

As we have seen, Butler's repetition of Foucault's question—"What is Critique?"—rings like a reminder about the limits of criticism in its common meaning as fault-finding, as an activity finalized at administering cultural works. These are limits that the literary critic Raymond Williams (whom the lecture homages) was able to overcome. What appears to have made this possible is a capacity to take a distance from the present, and experience a debilitating sentiment for the present as processes that had been unmistakably associated with modernity are "revealed as an expression of exhaustion and weakness" (During, "Eighteenth-Century Origins" 74).

Building on Foucault's view of critique as a historical formation, Simon During finds that critique "requires division": "The critic and her object are divided from one another on terms that require the critic to align with certain values or allegiances or purposes, if sometimes unknowingly" ("Eighteenth-Century Origins" 74). A critic "is required to choose, or, at least, to assume, standards by which to assess a particular object or field" (74). In general, a critic chooses the strongest criteria, which extend the furthest. To illustrate, During offers the example of Nietzsche, who preferred life to art as a test of knowledge. Nietzsche's object is the present. By turning to the Greeks, he institutes a division from the present which enables him to grasp "the modern requirement . . . to console oneself imaginatively by avoiding the actual conditions of life" (74). Nietzsche sees, above all, that "the modern requirement to be democratic, reasonable, emancipatory, utilitarian, optimistic—to be 'moral'—are signs of exhaustion" (74). From the perspective of his interest in life, modern morality, with its will to critical judgment, becomes "a secret instinct for annihilation . . . the beginning of the end" (Nietzsche qtd. in During, "Eighteenth-Century Origins" 74). In During's analysis, critique consists in "a scalar leap" or "scalar structure": "a discrete and small thing (a text, an image, an event) is examined as an example of or portal into a larger structure (ideological formation, a mode of production)" (75).[7] The capacity for distancing becomes itself an available method—"once progressivism is revealed as an expression of exhaustion and weakness"—though one borne on the trail of affect: "the affect that best bears critique" oscillates between pessimism and laughter (74).[8]

When Butler reads Foucault, she returns to her predecessor Adorno who, like Nietzsche, distances himself from the present by looking at it through the criterion of life. He sees that the view of modernity that is steeped in emancipation requires an "instinct for annihilation." In Butler, Adorno and Williams exemplify Foucault's critical attitude in that they seem to perform the same scalar leap that During observes in Nietzsche, whereby a "specific" cultural work and a "specific kind of response" function as a "portal" into to a larger structure ("What is Critique?" 304). Butler defines this capacity of what During calls a "scalar leap" as "a specific stylization of morality" to convey the urgency and motivation of the critical attitude, demarcating it from the notion of a willful againstness (318).

Achieving a distance from the present can settle into method though it remains on the trail of an affective component, as During has pointed out in his study of Nietzsche. But when Butler returns to Foucault to repeat the question of critique, this affective component is neither specifically pessimism nor laughter. Butler observes in Foucault the pursuit of the scalar structure of critique in During's terms: "It will not comply with a given category, but rather constitute an interrogatory relation to the field of categorization itself, referring at least implicitly to the limits of the epistemological horizon within which practices are formed" (Butler, "What is Critique?" 310). Yet, the distance that During calls "division" is inflected as difference in the sense of a divergence: a "difference from an uncritical obedience to authority" (Butler, "What is Critique?" 321). The affective component has nothing to do with the specific mood(s) of the thinker; rather, it comes with the question of a fit between thinker and task. Butler returns a Foucault to us who is even more intent on the gesture and the pose of turning that, in his account, is sedimented under the question of critique.

Butler brings this to the fore as she explicates his work, coming after Adorno, through a process of "desubjugation," in the attempt, that is, of disentangling himself from something called "the politics of truth" (Butler, "What is Critique?" 315). When Butler calls "virtue" this movement of "voluntary insubordination" (Foucault, "What is Critique?" 47), she suggests that it is not a single moment of resistance; in fact, it may be misleading to call it resistance. It is rather the practice of a unity of intent of body and mind as an imperative or a shaping moral force.

Butler's Foucault performs the scalar leap of critique, and the larger structure he connects to (the nexus of power and knowledge) "gives rise to the field of intelligible things" (Butler, "What is Critique?" 316). When Butler includes Williams in her canon of indocility, we begin to see how critique impacts the literary critic. The critic appears as a position, the position of the thinker before the field of intelligible things, a field practitioner (literature) who both belongs and does not belong to his field, looking at it as if from the outside: his task is to "track the breaking points within the field, the moments of discontinuities, that is to say, the sites where the field fails to constitute the intelligibility for which it stands" (316).

Scholars who have considered the effects of Foucault on literature tend to emphasize the productiveness of a formation of the subject in subjection, with individuals shaped at and by the nexus of power and knowledge. Foucault, however, is more interested in the emergence of the field of the intelligible than in the practice of reading.[9] From the perspective of subjection, literary criticism would be concerned with how literature participates in "subtle institutionally organized processes of normalization and discipline" of the self (Freundlieb 338).[10] Literary criticism would be seen as part of an apparatus "including self-surveillance and self-fashioning, similar to that which operates in religious practices" (Freundlieb 330). One can easily imagine how the rote imitation of this suspicious distance from the text could lead to the dead end of sterile exercise (Felski, *Limits* 74).[11] However, the imago of the human figure turning, implicit in the critical attitude discussed by Foucault, combined with the tug of desire and modesty and the tension of repetition and novelty, also implicit in his discussion, all suggest that, when it is brought to bear on literary studies, critique might mean more than an adversarial attitude, more than just a "no" to power.[12]

Julia Kristeva once wrote that "[t]rue dissidence is thought" (299), and her formulation suggests the close link between indocility and thought, which in the end is what Foucault is suggesting in "What is Critique?" But his type of indocility recalls less a frontal opposition, and more a slight movement of mind ("not . . . quite so much") that is reflected and perfectly translated by a pose of the figure's body. His pose is one with the idea of what it means to think, without Foucault speaking, like Kristeva, of the dissident intellectual. The imago of the movement, of the slight divergence revived in the uttering of the question of critique comes as if from a daydreaming state which, combined with the awe for the precursor, impresses on us the question of critique as the pose of a subject whose grace ("not . . . quite so much") lies in the fact that it is someone who gives him- or herself the right of imagining him- or herself thinking. The need to rise from humanity's immaturity is renewed both modestly and immodestly. The secret (or virtue) of critique does not lie solely in the capacity to purview the past from the distance of the present (we have seen that as the human figure turns, the gaze is detached from it, incapable of laying down the law in the domain that it purviews), but in coming into this pose and position.

Criticism and critique

When Kristeva equates thought with "dissidence," she conjures the familiar image of the public intellectual in the adversarial sense of Edward Said, as someone who speaks up to power (Said, *Representations*). Dissidence is etymologically connected to the verb meaning "to sit apart" (*dis* + *sedeo*). It is different from Foucault's reflective indocility; someone who sits apart is someone who sits on the other side of a cohesive group, at the margins of the noise of public speech. It suggests the act of taking up a position on the side or at the margins of a general assembly. Walter Benjamin would be one of the dissidents in Kristeva's canon. He is an example of those cases in which Foucault's indocility translates into the necessity of anonymity. More than "the art of voluntary insubordination,"

Benjamin champions the art of "(voluntary) confinement."[13] Unlike Foucault's figure, he is above all an observer absorbed, as Graeme Gilloch says, in "a process of destruction and (re)construction" (86). It is from this position of marked separation that Benjamin cares to distinguish between criticism and critique. In "Goethe's Elective Affinities" (published 1924–5), he writes: "Critique seeks the truth content of a work of art; commentary its material content," only to argue for an intersection of the two, whose relation, he proposes, is determined by "that basic law of literature according to which the more significant the work, the more inconspicuously and intimately its truth content is bound up with its material content" (296). He rejects the dominant view that mistakes criticism for the judgment of a work because the critic often limits himself to praising only what he can recognize. Benjamin sees traditional criticism as a process of divination and rather aligns real critical activity with the notion of ideas that arise in an unintentional mode, as if at the neutral point of thought. This relaxation point of thought never stops fascinating him, as is clear in "Letter to Florens Christian Rang," where he champions a "method of [the work's] consummation" (153), another way of saying what Raymond Williams would call "practice."[14]

The slippage between criticism and critique sets in when Benjamin considers that the tie between truth and the material content of a literary text is both inconspicuous and intimate, that is to say, barely legible. The slippage has consequences for the figure of the critic who is relocated not so much before a text that waits to be decoded, but before a field of texts not yet made intelligible. Benjamin uses the metaphor of the paleographer to convey the critical attitude described by Foucault as a certain manner of thinking and of speaking and a certain relation to others, culture, and society. Here is Benjamin in the essay on Goethe:

> More and more, therefore, the interpretation of what is striking and curious—that is, the material content—becomes a prerequisite for any later critic. One may compare him to a paleographer in front of a parchment whose faded text is covered by the lineaments of a more powerful script which refers to that text. As the paleographer would have to begin by reading the latter script, the critic would have to begin with commentary. And with one stroke, an invaluable criterion of judgment springs out for him; only now can he raise the basic critical question of whether the semblance/luster [*Schein*] of the truth content is due to the material content, or the life of the material content to the truth content. For as they set themselves apart from

each other in the work, they decide on its immortality. ("Goethe's Elective Affinities" 298)

Benjamin imports the question of truth in literary criticism but ties it to the expressiveness of texts. For him, as for During's Nietzsche, the test of knowledge is life: "what is alive." Life remains the criterion for that particular scalar leap of modern critique which is necessary to make a field emerge.[15]

Benjamin's critic finds himself before a field of discrete works, with each becoming an "enigma": regardless of our consciousness, it lives; it burns.[16] Critique reassembles such living works on a plane. Benjamin embraces Novalis's expressive view of the text to affirm the autonomous existence of aesthetic objects apart from human consciousness: every work of art has "an implicit necessity to exist" (Benjamin, "Concept of Criticism" 79), thus it exists on the plane of legibility whether we understand it or not. But to what extent might the implicit necessity of the work to exist be dictated by the less visible forces agitating within the folds of a society (Foucault's nexus of power and knowledge)?[17] The interest in this question prompts the differentiation of criticism and critique.

Novalis's notion of a "more resolute, more active, more productive use of our organs" helps Benjamin formulate something similar to Foucault's critical attitude, meaning (by that) the alignment of mind and body that we have discussed above (Benjamin, "Concept of Criticism" 150). He does not champion the adaptation of the intellect to empirical reality but builds on the Romantics' belief that art is a site of thinking to bridge the distance between criticism and reflection. In "The Concept of Criticism," Benjamin relocates the critic near "the point at which reflection arises from nothing," in the zone of the "neutral origin of reflection," thus portraying critique as a thought that touches itself (150). What he calls "method of consummation" foregrounds the fragile boundaries between texts and suggests their neighborliness. Echoing Novalis's "positive criticism," Benjamin outlines the continuous transposition of a text into other languages, in a process that reveals the text not as an inert container but as an act—as an expressive act, something "alive" (54).

In the four years between "The Concept of Criticism" (written in 1919) and his letter to Florens Christian Rang (1923), Benjamin envisions a plane of neighborliness where works are like monads in relation to each other. In his letter to Rang, a field of objects appears: they are "taciturn," enigmatic and self-enclosed, but nevertheless impact on each other: "The essential links between works of art remain intensive" ("Letter" 388). The plane is the figure of "a timeless, intensive process of interpretation" (388). This does not mean that there is no literary history or no canon. As Benjamin explains through a comparison with philosophy, philosophy can be such a plane when it is conceived neither as a history of dogmas nor one of philosophers, but as a history of problems.[18] Similarly, what one wants to avoid in literary criticism is "the history of contents and forms, for which works of art seem to provide merely examples or models" (388). The problem is not whether to see the text inside or outside the box of history and society, but how not to reduce the text to an illustration of content and form, how not to make single works subservient to thematic illustration.

When, exactly like philosophy, criticism is understood not as a history of authors and authoritative ideas but as a history of problems, individual works "pass over" into "a timeless, intensive process of interpretation" (Benjamin, "Letter" 389, 388). A plane of neighborliness appears where "[s]uccession is supplanted by *intensification*" (Schwebel 602; original emphasis). If the transition from criticism to critique requires a scalar leap, Benjamin associates critique with the dynamic sympathy, the affirmative, engendering expressionism that flows from the structure of monads separated by a vacuum but nevertheless in relation (Fenves).

In this chapter we have seen that criticism becomes critique through a style of indocility, which, however, does not amount to destruction. The proponents of new ontologies of relationality that reject the centrality of human consciousness and depart from the long arch of twentieth-century philosophical thought aimed at the destitution of the metaphysical premises of the subject are still concerned with what Foucault called the critical spirit. When Bruno Latour asks, "What has become of the critical spirit?," he repeats Foucault's question—"What is critique?" (Latour, "Why" 225). Latour claims that the hermeneutics of the subject has attended only to a limited version of reality. He responds to the weight of a humanity kept in immaturity with "a stubbornly realist attitude": if the "critical mind is to renew itself and be relevant again, it is to be found in the cultivation of a stubbornly realist attitude . . . but a realism dealing with what I call matters of concern, not matters of fact" (231). By "matters of fact," Latour means "objective statements" behind whose "appearance" we have learned to detect "the real prejudices" (227). He does not want to reduce things to objects and does not want to divide the world into two camps, with inert objects on one side and people debating on the other side. He is concerned with repressive concepts and forms, the same concern of Benjamin when he talked of forms as "a profound externality full of yearning" ("Middle Ages" 239). For Latour the problem is to associate critique with "a whole set of new positive metaphors, gestures, attitudes, knee-jerk reactions, habits of thought" ("Why" 247).

Differently from Foucault's thinker, he turns "stubbornly" toward the world, the gaze outward on the world's minutest details. But the realist attitude is determined by an old problem, the problem of the new: Latour wonders about "generating more ideas than we have received, inheriting from a prestigious critical tradition but not letting it die away" nor "drop into quiescence, like a piano string struck by a hammer" ("Why" 248). The loss of the critical spirit, which he laments, only proves how strong the bond between critique and the new is. Foucault had framed his essay with the same problem, but had spoken about it in a veiled manner (the modesty in repeating the predecessor). Latour uses the metaphor of a piano "in quiescence" that is no longer struck; the unused piano of course points to the score that is no longer played but ought to be executed differently (modestly?) by a different musician.

Both Foucault and Latour speak of critique as an attitude, but the later thinker is explicitly concerned about its disappearance. This prospect is brought home by the military metaphors:

> My question is simple: Should we be at war, too, we, the scholars, the intellectuals? Is it really our duty to add fresh ruins to fields of ruins? Is it really the task of the humanities to add deconstruction to destruction? More iconoclasm to iconoclasm? What has become of the critical spirit? Has it run out of steam? (Latour, "Why" 225)

Unlike Foucault, Latour does not wish to see the critical attitude from the perspective of the hermeneutics of the self; but even though he favors a model of radical relationality (Actor-Network Theory) which eradicates the notion of the subject, he still links critique to a subject, a collective subject: "we, the scholars, the intellectuals." The crisis of critique might refer to the crisis of a group identity: critique "has run out of steam" because a certain collective subject and the self-representation of a group has run out of steam. The language here suggests the old subterranean entanglement of critique with the figure of the public intellectual who is given the task to think and orient the masses. It speaks to literary studies and the ambition of the scholar to take on such a role.[19] We might wish to find out what we mean by this collective subject, and whence the necessity of designating a group whose work is mental activity, as well as the ways in which we distribute intellect and human faculties like language and thought. The sense of this submerged class of intellectuals to whose destiny the literary critic owes his or her survival or disappearance plays a role in the current perception of critique, though, as suggested in the Introduction, there are other factors to take into account, especially the increasing precariousness of academic life. The unstable identity of the critic will be discussed at length in Chapter 3.

Notes

1. Foucault, "What is Critique?" was originally a lecture given at the French Society of Philosophy on 27 May 1978, subsequently published in *Bulletin de la Société française de la philosophie*, vol. 84, no. 2 (1990): 35–63. Page numbers are from "What is Critique?," trans. Lysa Hochroth, in *The Politics of Truth*.
2. Jean Laplanche and Jean-Bertrand Pontalis define the "imago" as "an 'unconscious' representation," the center of an imaginary set rather than an image: "a stereotype through which, as it were, the subject views the other person. Feelings and behaviors, for example, are just as likely to be the concrete expression of the imago as are mental states" (211).
3. Deborah Cook helpfully points to the less pessimistic traits of his work (116).
4. While the English text uses the verb "hem in"—"Capitalist production hems [the consumers] in so tightly, in body and soul, that they unresistingly succumb to whatever is proffered to them" (Adorno and Horkheimer, "Culture Industry" 106)—the Italian translation has "incatenati," chained body and soul (Adorno and Horkheimer, "L'industria culturale" 141).
5. Adorno and Horkheimer, however, clarify that they are not arguing for a "cultural lag" between America and Europe: "The belief that the barbarism of the culture industry is a result of 'cultural lag,' of the backwardness of American consciousness in relation to the state of technology, is quite illusory. Prefascist Europe was backward in relation to the monopoly of culture. But it was precisely to such backwardness that intellectual activity owed a remnant of autonomy, its last exponents their livelihood, however meager" ("Culture Industry" 105).
6. For a discussion of the continuity between Adorno's scenario of guilt and debt and Judith Butler's thought, see Stimilli 172–86.
7. What During calls critique sounds like theory in the traditional sense of a "heroic activity," with "the successful theorist" seen as "someone who manages to explain the hidden principles or forces that account for even our most mundane activities" (Moi 81).

8. For a similar reading of Nietzsche, see Agamben, "What is the Contemporary?"
9. See Foucault, "What is an Author?," which was originally delivered as a lecture before the Society at the Collège de France on 22 February 1969 and appeared in the *Bulletin de la Société française de Philosophie*, vol. 63, no. 3 (1969): 73–104.
10. Dieter Freundlieb expands: "The teaching of literature would no longer be considered the transmission of culturally important, perhaps even timelessly valid, truths contained in canonical texts and brought to light by a methodologically controlled process of interpretation; instead, it could be seen as an ethico-political training and a disciplinary formation of subjects under the guise of a search for truth in literature. Literary criticism, particularly within a pedagogical context, could be regarded as working on the 'soul' instead of on the body, and as part of an apparatus of ethical surveillance and normalization, including self-surveillance and self-fashioning, similar to that which operates in religious practices" (330). For further discussion, see During, *Foucault*.
11. The historical frame of Foucault's discussion of course matters. He is led back to critique by the postwar political impasse, with power maintaining itself through forms that "resemble one another like brothers" ("What is Critique?" 8). This "inertia of power" (7) is illustrated by the symmetry of ideologically different yet equivalent authoritarian regimes like Fascism and Stalinism, and this climate played a crucial role in the focus on the intersection of truth, knowledge, and coercion (8).
12. The unity of intent of mind and body in a movement of disengagement, that is slight, not excessive, that abandons something that weighs on everyone else, but only slightly, may be considered from the vantage point of what Foucault calls the hermeneutics of the subject, as one of the practices aimed at the transformation of the self. Foucault looks at history from antiquity to the present as traversed by "a veritable development of the 'culture' of the self." The centerpiece of his hermeneutics is the study of those effects "linked to practices, forms of life, and modes of experience of individuals on themselves and with themselves"; it is, in brief, the transformation of the self finalized to access truth. When the critical attitude is seen as part of these practices, the focus shifts to the critic. The critic becomes an example of the hermeneutics of the self, of a practice on the self and with the self (Foucault, *Hemeneutics*, lecture of 3 February 1982, first hour; I am working with the Italian version, *Soggettività e verità*, and all translations from it are mine).
13. Susan Sontag, Susan Sontag Papers, Box 128, Folder 1, Charles E. Young Research Library, Special Collections, UCLA.
14. For a detailed discussion of Benjamin's idea of interpretation, see Chapter 2.
15. Benjamin calls the field of intelligible things the "constellation."

16. In the quote above Benjamin goes on to compare the commentator of a text to a chemist and the critic to an alchemist: "Whereas, for the former, wood and ash remain the sole objects of his analysis, for the latter only the flame itself preserves an enigma: that of what is alive. Thus, the critic inquires into the truth, whose living flame continues to burn over the heavy logs of what is past and the light ashes of what has been experienced" ("Goethe's Elective Affinities" 298).
17. This point will be discussed in greater detail in Chapter 2.
18. Like philosophy, literature (but these terms with Benjamin suddenly become inadequate, obsolete) "threaten[s] to lose contact with extension in time" and "pass over" instead into a timeless surface of creative/critical gestures. On the one hand, this letter may be said to further Benjamin's thought beyond the standstill of the question in the essay on "The Concept of Criticism": "How is knowledge of objects possible?" There, he had to answer that, "on the principle of Romantic thinking, it is *not* possible" (146; original emphasis).
19. An important chapter of this ambition has been written by the great modernists who thought about the question of criticism, like T. S. Eliot (see von Hallberg).

Chapter 2

Theory: Thinking with Literature

Overview

In the preceding chapter we have been on the trail of the muse of critique, discovering how resilient it is, how desired and pursued even by thinkers of the present who, rejecting any hermeneutics of the subject, still seem to be receptive to this human figure and its gentle way of turning from established norms. Far from amounting to a clumsy againstness, this movement, as Judith Butler suggests, is contiguous with a moral question—something that the intellect ought to do. In the process, a theme has emerged that now requires proper attention, and that is the contact between literature and philosophy. We have actually seen that part of critique is the defamiliarization of philosophy outside the recognizable boundaries of a discipline with the aim of building conceptual systems. The three types of indocility proposed in the first chapter share a common trait: they shift to a border zone that is neither properly outside philosophy nor inside it. We have seen that for Foucault the question of critique rises at the margins of philosophy, as if to mark those margins, in the neighborhood of the non-philosophical ("What is Critique?" 42); it is a "project" that does not "cease to take shape, to persist, to be reborn on the frontiers of philosophy—quite close to it, quite against it, at its expense, in the direction of a philosophy yet to come, in the place perhaps of every possible philosophy" (42). Adorno's point in hanging onto a scenario of guilt and debt is the insufficiency of philosophy understood as the realm of the conceptual. Adorno pursues a type of reflection that comes belatedly after philosophy's missed realization of "the nonconceptual in the concept," lamenting that "no philosophy can paste the particulars into the text" (*Negative Dialectics* 12, 11). It is Adorno who explicitly addresses the contact between philosophy and literature, through the larger realm of art, when he construes each of the two fields as the productive outside of the other. For Adorno the immediate outside of philosophy is art, but "both keep faith to their substance through their opposites," art by resisting its meanings and philosophy by "refusing to clutch at any immediate thing" (15). "What the philosophical concept will not abandon is the yearning that animates the nonconceptual side of art," he writes (15). The desire coming from outside a discipline influences the constitution of another. As for Benjamin, we have seen that he probes what Foucault, after him, would call "the outer limits of philosophy" and tarries in that region long enough to be reprimanded by Adorno himself, who in a letter dated 10 November 1938 tells him that his "wide-eyed presentation of mere facts" attributes to particulars a "power of illumination which really belongs to theoretical construction alone" (Adorno and Benjamin 291, 284). In his reply of 9 December 1938, Benjamin openly thematizes the tension between philosophy (the moment of theoretical construction) and the linguistic and literary dimension of thought, calling it an "an antagonism of which I would not wish to be relieved not even in my dreams" (Adorno and Benjamin 291). In his introduction to the *Trauerspiel* book (1925), which did not earn him his Habilitation to university teaching, Benjamin defends what might have seemed "paradoxical" in his time, and that is the notion of a philosophical style (*Origin* 8), calling greater attention to "the symbolic character" of words, that quality whereby "the idea attains a self-transparency that is the opposite of an outward bound type of communication" (12). Benjamin is concerned with the relation, which is too often a divergence, between knowledge and representation. In his view, a greater attention to language enables the appearance of ideas that are released from the intentionality of human consciousness and rise as if at a neutral point.

As we have seen from the thinkers discussed in Chapter 1, an important aspect of critique is its capacity to raise the question of the distinction between philosophy and literature; in fact, it seems coeval with that question. The question of the contact between philosophy and literature has of course been and remains one of the shaping forces of literary criticism. In this chapter we shall understand Theory as a name for the shaping force of that contact. The keyword for this chapter is therefore "theory": "Theory" with a capital letter when it is understood as a stage in literary criticism delimited in time, and referring to a transatlantic transmission of ideas whose evaporation has led to talk about the crisis of critique; and "theory" with a lower case letter when it is understood as an approach to texts that, as Raymond Williams advised in Chapter 1, moves beyond their governamentality. I will trace the degree to which critique depends on the question of the contact between literature and philosophy through the example of Fredric Jameson. I choose Jameson because he was a pioneer of that transformation of criticism that in American academia became known as "theory."

"Reading literature, not theory"

Generally, we affirm that interdisciplinary work is desirable. Yet, today the movement of ideas across disciplinary borders is far from having consolidated into a safe and established legacy. Both within and without the Humanities, the translation of ideas across different fields of knowledge is not yet a given; the division of labor among the disciplines seems to be newly enforced. According to Carolyn Lesjak, the rigidification of disciplinary divides is reflected in the contemporary climate of postcritique, which pits reading against theory: "theory is on its way out; reading is (back) in" (17). She is joined from the philosophical camp by Graham Harman, who argues that "neo-Moderns" are "enforcing ... a division of labor" among the disciplines in order to "fend off" the dangers that arise from "the work of de-taxonomization" (*Dante's* 234).[1] There are signs of what Lesjak describes as "the increasingly conservative mood within literary criticism and its key theoretical gestures," with the demand inside and outside academia "for reading literature, not theory" (20). The question arises: What does "reading literature, not theory" mean? If by "theory" we mean understanding the text within a larger vision, then is it possible to read literature without engaging ideas? What do we mean when we talk about theory?

Lesjak responds to the conservative backlash by returning to Fredric Jameson. Here, I am not interested in presenting Jameson's dialectical thought as an antidote to the conservatism of the present, because that conservatism is only the partial story of critique. I will instead present Jameson as an interesting case because, even though he may be regarded as one of the founders of theory, he intends the term (with the lower case letter) to mean a critical practice, not a periodization, a movement, or a school. He is a particularly good example because in his work one hears that urgency of the neighborliness of disciplines as a defining aspect of critique, one which today is thought to be endangered. From the beginning, Jameson's work advocated an active transcoding and translation across disciplines, in particular literary criticism and philosophy. This form of translation understood as a migration of ideas continues to raise the question of what we mean when we speak of "reading literature" while also resonating with the power currently wielded by the idea of migration. "How do ideas move?" "How do cultures adjust to the migration of ideas?" These are questions at the center of the production (and definition) of knowledge at institutions of education.[2] It is important to attend to these questions while gauging their relationship with the question of the new. In Chapter 3, we shall see that the new is no longer tied, as it once was, to models of rupture. This chapter prepares that discussion using Jameson's career as a case study. The aim is neither to offer new insights into Jameson's work—an impossible task given the abundance of excellent literature on this theorist—nor to revive dialectical thought.[3] Instead, the chapter focuses on Jameson's invention of a new figure of the critic. We shall see that in doing so, his example helps us understand critique as a dynamic and wider movement not limited to adversarial gestures.

"Not philosophy but a preparation for literary criticism"

As a literary critic, Jameson begins with a strong interest in the neighborliness, within difference, of literary criticism and philosophy. This proximity proves attractive because it invites an incessant transcoding, an ongoing intellectual and cultural transfer. His version of critique—what he means by "theory"—is based on an enhanced reciprocity of the two realms, on a back and forth between the two. In *Marxism and Form* (1971), he calls this type of movement "learn[ing] to think dialectically" (x). Despite presenting the enterprise as "relatively modest and straightforward" (modesty again), Jameson actually inaugurates a new breed of literary critic who transfers other intellectual traditions, foreign to the Anglo-American tradition (xii). This transmission certainly implies the literal activity of translation from one language to another as ideas from German philosophy or French thought are set in motion and recontextualized along their transatlantic trajectory. Jameson, however, is more interested in the overall "exciting" and "liberating" effect of geo-linguistic displacements because they promise to take criticism to a level above "sheer *opinion* only" (xi; original emphasis). The transatlantic transmission relocates the critic beyond "non-reflective thinking" (307).

Boundaries and constraints lose their hold as the critic turns his back on what Jameson calls "object-oriented activity," another way of suggesting thematic exegesis (*Marxism and Form* 308). A sense of potentiality sets in:

> It is, of course, thought to the second power: an intensification of the normal thought processes such that a renewal of light washes over the object of their exasperation, as though in the midst of its immediate perplexities the mind had attempted, by willpower, by fiat, to lift itself mightily up by its own bootstraps. (Jameson, *Marxism and Form* 307)

The critic senses a vacuum between criticism and thought but also realizes that the vacuum separating criticism and thought has been bridged, and this is elating. Jameson reports "a breathlessness" comparable to "the sickening shudder we feel in an elevator's fall or in the sudden dip in an airliner" (*Marxism and Form* 308). The position at the crossroads of literary criticism and philosophy (in Adorno's inflection as critical theory) comes as a "shock" experience that "recalls us to our mental positions as thinkers and observers" (308). In the preface to *Marxism and Form*, Jameson announces a new kind of literary criticism: "What follows is, however, not philosophy but literary criticism, or at least a preparation for literary criticism" (xi). The preface is an important document for anyone wishing to understand the phenomenon of Theory in the U.S. Notice here that Jameson is defending the claim of the literary critic to interdisciplinary freedom, to curiosity, and to wonder with regard to areas of knowledge that are outside the established discipline of literature. He is setting an example for the critic's dependence on the neighbor as a good rule for reading. What does reading mean for Jameson?

Jameson turns from the assumption lodged deeply in the discourse of literary criticism that the critic is just a reader. We mentioned the reader/critic tension in the Introduction; it constitutes a fascinating topic in our field and runs like a *fil rouge* through critical texts and schools. From New Criticism and its core textbook, Brooks and Warren's *Understanding Poetry* (1938), to Renato Poggioli's *Theory of the Avant-Garde* (1968), from Wolfgang Iser and reception theory to Roland Barthes's "lover's discourse," and various refusals of theory, the critic ambiguously desires to be just a reader, comforted by Wolfgang Iser's insight, in *The Act of Reading* (1978), that "an interpreter can no longer claim to teach the reader the meaning of the text" (19).[4] Yet, from a certain perspective, this central assumption of literary criticism seems naïve. Of course, the critic is a reader, but as a professional reader she needs to consider what she does to and how she uses a literary work. In response to these responsibilities, Jameson wants to read by occupying the position of "observer[ ] and thinker[ ]" (*Marxism and Form* 308). The two levels of the cultural past and of the mystery of signs overlap. In the process, reading in order to understand a text can be described in terms similar to translation: signs beckon to us; they call us, converse with us; they speak to us like distant and foreign texts in a language that we must attempt to translate always in hostile circumstances. From this point of view, Jameson shares Paul Ricoeur's view of interpretation as steeped in the problem of "the signs of man" (Ricoeur, *Freud* 46) and how to decipher them:

> The ultimate root of our problem lies in this primitive connection between the act of existing and the signs we deploy in our works; reflection must become interpretation because I cannot grasp the act of existing except in signs scattered in the world. (Ricoeur, *Freud* 46)[5]

Interpretation and reflection are bound in an unavoidable confusion of tongues. In *The Political Unconscious* (1981), at the height of that displacement of European philosophy to the U.S. which was called poststructuralism, in response to the proliferation of critical approaches—"the psychoanalytic or the myth-critical, the stylistic, the ethical, the structural" (17)—Jameson proposes a "rival hermeneutic" that does not shy away from a leap that must be taken, from a distance that must be bridged (21). It is a question of "respecting the specificity and radical difference of the social and cultural past while disclosing the solidarity of its polemics and passions, its forms, structures, experiences, and struggles, with those of the present day" (18). Jameson cautions against the nullification of the problem of the past, and, in the early 1980s, takes his distance from *écriture* (later French Theory)—a cluster of authors as diverse as Roland Barthes, Hélène Cixous, and Jacques Derrida—because of what he saw as the latter's a-historical tendency to translate every kind of past into the present, a concern that, we might add, he shares with Benjamin, in favor of an idea of the text as action and expression (34).[6]

If texts, exhibiting what Ricoeur called the "signs of man" (*Freud* 46), are not inert but action and expression, the same is true of the past. History, or, as Jameson liked to call it after Joyce, the "nightmare of history," meaning "the dizzying accumulation of violence and cruelty" (*Valencies* 550), demands that we treat texts as if they were written in a language that we do not understand. Jameson laments the fact that the "modern reader" is an impatient translator: she turns away from "that dry and intolerable chitinous murmur of footnotes reminding us of the implied references to long-dead contemporary events and political situations in Milton or Swift, in Spenser or Hawthorne," but she ought not to "desperately . . . brush away" the estranging murmur of "the cobweb of topical allusion" (*Political Unconscious* 34). The rare word "chitinous," a term from biochemistry (it comes from "chitin," the substance that makes up the exoskeleton of most insects), is etymologically related to the word for marine mollusk, and both words derive from the Greek word for tunic (χιτών). In Jameson's use, the word helps to suggest a past that presses on as if in humanity's biological fold, and seems to issue an almost hallucinatory call from all the dimensions of the living. The modern reader's resistance to this primitive murmur is comparable only to our resistance to the unconscious but Jameson expects the critic to know better; she ought to know that the law of literature is the paradox of the inexpressible in the expressed: "The informing presence of society within art and language is all the greater when it is indirect and invisible" (Jameson, *Marxism and Form* 188). Insofar as literary criticism might be willing to deal with this indirectness or invisibility, the paradox prevents it from becoming *a* philosophy, that is to say, a conceptual concatenation and a fixed terminology.

Jameson formulates a reparative view of criticism and this is clear when he offers the example of modernism. The critic's task, he writes, is

> rather to demonstrate the ways in which modernism—far from being a mere reflection of the reification of late nineteenth-century social life—is also a revolt against that reification and a symbolic act which involves a whole Utopian compensation for increasing dehumanization. (*Political Unconscious* 42)

The reparative view helps him elaborate on the difference between the philosophical and the aesthetic. Adorno had warned about "the illicit attempt to transform bodily immediacy into more 'spiritualized' and idealistic forms of abstract thinking" (Jameson, *Late Marxism* 158). Similarly, Jameson thinks of the relation between literary criticism and philosophy as a way of interrupting the reduction of immediacy to abstraction; instead of this reduction, the flow of ideas between the two gives place to another discourse that is "not philosophy" (*Marxism and Form* xi). In the movement back and forth between the two, a critical discourse appears which specifically thematizes "a mind-oriented, philosophical dread of what cannot, in aesthetic experience or elsewhere, be philosophized" (Jameson, *Late Marxism* 158). In Jameson's words, theory is "the momentary and ephemeral act of unification in which we hold multiple dimensions of time together for a glimpse that cannot prolong itself into the philosophical concept" (Jameson qtd. in Lesjak 21). Philosophy and literary criticism are separated by an empty space, and in that gap Jameson glimpses the kind of criticism that he aspired to introduce in the Anglo-American tradition to release the critic not only from "mere opinion" or thematic commentary but also from the confines of literary periodization. What does Jameson mean when he says that aesthetic experience cannot be philosophized? In which sense is the "rival hermeneutic" that he proposed in *The Political Unconscious* theory?

Echoing somewhat Benjamin's antagonism between facticity and theoretical construction, which was mentioned at the start of this chapter, Gerald Bruns argues that interpretation becomes hermeneutics because of the observer's "fascination with particulars" (*Hermeneutics* 16). When Jameson speaks of theory, he might have in mind the details that escape the conceptual system. His idea of theory changes the figure of the critic. When he talks of theory as a "glimpse" that, in aesthetic experience, "cannot prolong itself," he generalizes the figure of the critic, who sheds any special trait in favor of the more anonymous identity of "observer and thinker." This identity allows for the freedom to focus attention outward, toward what is given and the surrounding environment. As energies migrate from literature to other cultural artifacts—for example, architecture—the observed or the given empowers the thinker, as in a ritual of truth-verification, giving him words for something that cannot be a philosophical system. One such word is "postmodernism."

Postmodernism

Objects like the Bonaventure Hotel in downtown Los Angeles, designed by architect and developer John Portman, afford the opportunity for the kind of transcoding that replaces the critic's traditional task of literary periodization. If modernism relied on "expressive correspondence"—the interior projects outward to the outside with "plastic lines" that change walls into an aesthetic pliant skin of the "realities within" (Jameson, *Postmodernism* 135)—the present speaks of the inverse procedure: it presents us with an outside that transcodes the inside. The critic is not immune to the procedure. With the term "postmodernism" Jameson indicates a "condition," suggesting the individual alignment with and the unavoidable consent to the surroundings. It names a waning of introspection similar to that observed by Adorno in relation to the late stage of industrial capitalism, when, as the German philosopher wrote, an "immense expansion of society" had brought on an epistemological disorientation, and the "conceptual shells that were to house the whole according to philosophical custom" had come "to seem like relics" (*Negative Dialectics* 3).

Adorno himself knew that the introspective thinker was already an anachronism at the time of Goethe, who talked of "seedy scholars feasting on subjective speculation," but the culture industry represented the end-station for the introverted thinker, who, as we saw in Chapter 1, was pushed to the outer border of "the phantasms of profundity" (Adorno, *Negative Dialectics* 3, 17). Adorno cautioned against such phantoms and advocated an exodus that leaves philosophy to its incompleteness and its dependence on the outside. Philosophy and art are bound in a reciprocal outsidedness (whereby art eludes the concept and philosophy eludes particulars), which not only accelerated the thinker's definitive exodus from introspection in late capitalism, but, more importantly, caused a loss of method. This loss is conveyed all the more by the replacement of the obsolete "introverted thought architects" with "extroverted technicians" (2).

Jameson's postmodernism affectively retraces the experience of such a loss. While it is presented as a weave of "intensities,"[7] postmodernism essentially raises the question of the critic's access to impersonal and collective feelings that have become unanchored and "are now free-floating"; it points to the critic's shift toward a zone that "tend[s] to be dominated by a particular kind of euphoria" (Jameson, *Postmodernism* 16). Above all, the term suggests the successful suspension of a familiar conceptual support, naming less a method for criticism and more a criticism of subjective involvement. Alien surroundings that nevertheless provide a desirable anchorage seem to yield to an exodus from introspection that is much greater than Adorno had suggested, with spatial estrangement and vertigo bringing about a reawakened encounter with history. History is felt as symptom, that is to say, in the extreme, abridged version of material elements that overwhelm the observer. The architectural object that Jameson analyzes in the overture of *Postmodernism, or, The Cultural Logic of Late Capitalism* compresses, in the objecthood of the building, what in *The Political Unconscious* was history's murmur and the call of texts to be restored to "life and warmth" (Jameson, *Political Unconscious* 19).

The Bonaventure Hotel represents a disorienting environment and occasions a barely veiled Dantesque descent that enables "cognitive mapping" (Jameson, *Postmodernism* 51). The gate of the building is uncannily invisible: access to it is figured as dispersed, multiple sovereignty. There are three entrances, all of them "lateral and backdoor affairs" (39). Vertical, hierarchical relations of power are altered in favor of a "populist insertion into the city fabric" (39). In order to enter, the visitor does not climb up but takes an escalator from the second floor down to the main registration desk (39), admitted to a "minicity" that aspires not to be a part of the city but "rather its equivalent and replacement or substitute" (40). The miniature effect affords a different kind of warmth, with the critic admitted to "a new total space" (40). The transit unexpectedly restores the critic's interpretive powers in the presence of the beloved object: the collective. Jameson records the auroral apparition of "a new collective practice," a "new mode in which individuals move and congregate, something like the practice of a new and historically original kind of hypercrowd" (40). He can then return to Marx: a true "dialectical view of historical development" would consist in

> do[ing] the impossible, namely, to think this development ... positively and negatively at once; to achieve, in other words, a type of thinking that would be capable of grasping the demonstrably baleful features of capitalism along with its extraordinary and liberating dynamism simultaneously within a single thought. (Jameson, *Postmodernism* 47)

Ascending and descending; we must "lift our minds," Jameson had said in *Marxism and Form*. In that early work, theory, a new form of literary criticism which is "not philosophy," was captured by the dread and elation of a descent, as when in flight. The "dialectical thought" he had wanted to transfer to American literary criticism amounted to the heightened sensation of being closer to thought. Re-experiencing the elation twenty years later, the same sensation inaugurates the "postmodern era" (Jameson, *Postmodernism* 47).

In Jameson, the boundary between dialectical thought and the problem of conceptual invention thins to the extreme. Dialectical thought appears to become part of what Donald Pease and Robyn

Wiegman, reviving an expression of Gene Wise, call "paradigm dramas," referring to the sequence of symbolic acts that, imposing order on chaos, determine the foundation and formation of a field. Speaking for American Studies, Pease and Wiegman look at Perry Miller's classic *Errand into the Wilderness* (1956) as a paradigm drama or an attempt to impose order on chaos and thus organize intellectually a disparate heterogeneity (Pease and Wiegman 6). In Miller's case, the founder's act organizes an academic field around a "substantive consensus on the nature of American experience and a methodological consensus on how to study that experience" (Pease and Wiegman 6). Paradigm dramas imply an ordering that relies on breaks and ruptures, with breaks marking the onset of a decline from the point of view of the founder which, however, the newcomer judges positively. More specifically, Pease and Wiegman discuss the breaks from Miller's founding paradigm: the first break in the mid-1960s, when the ordered materials appeared to enforce the dominant culture, and the second break in the 1970s, when the critique from social movements outside the field resulted in a proliferation within the field (African American Studies, Latino Studies, Asian American Studies, Native American Studies, Gay and Lesbian Studies, and Women's Studies). While Gene Wise saw these breaks as the onset of a decline, Pease and Wiegman judge them positively. Similarly Jameson's paradigm drama, too, relies on a sense of the decline implied in the modernism/postmodernism rupture (Van Gogh/Warhol) that scholars after him will judge positively.

In Jameson's reading of the Bonaventure Hotel, after the "dramatic" descent into the "confusion of the place" (*Postmodernism* 43), literature and the architectural object merge to become part of the same space. At that point, the critic can gain insight into the present:

> So I come to my final point here that this latest mutation in space—postmodern hyperspace—has finally succeeded in transcending the capacities of the individual human body to locate itself, to organize its immediate surroundings perceptually, and cognitively to map its position in a mappable external world. (Jameson, *Postmodernism* 44)

Postmodernism offers an example of the experience of theory: the mind stalls, glimpsing something that cannot prolong itself into the philosophical concept. Jameson stresses "the incapacity of our minds" to grasp a vaster global plane (*Postmodernism* 44). He describes this plane as "the great global multinational and decentered communicational network in which we find ourselves caught as individual subjects" (44). Unlike Roberto Esposito's plane of coevalness, which will be discussed in the next chapter, Jameson's global plane is not beneficial. It is vast, but it is also an imprisoning space. It is a shell of opacity effected by the extraordinary adherence of the social and political dimensions of "multinational" capitalism, on the one hand, and the vaster cultural dimension, on the other. The adherence locks in and chases away to the furthest distance texts as expression and action, as signs that call us. For Jameson, deconstruction's decentering of meaning, with the severance of the bond with hermeneutic depth, shores up the imprisoning shell.[8] The global plane called "postmodernism" feels like a *dispositif* of preservative repression which seals hermetically the "life and warmth" of history (Jameson, *Political Unconscious* 19). If postmodernism is a test for theory (that kind of reflection that does not settle into the philosophical concept), the global plane informs us that the challenge of theory is the suppression of life. Jameson himself observes that while everything has become cultural it also remains "untheorized" (*Postmodernism* 48).

I-experience

When Carolyn Lesjak advocates a return to Jameson's dialectical thought, she voices the discomfort of many scholars for what must surely feel like a strange imperative of scarcity: what does "reading literature, not theory" mean? What advances in these arguments is the specter of a naked literature, self-sufficient and cut off from the world. We assume that, as we said in the Introduction, this is the opposite of what postcritique wants. Although it is not clear why Lesjak qualifies these imperatives as "catholic" (21), the return to Jameson interests us not because it asserts the need for "a Marxist literary criticism and of a dialectical Marxist criticism" (21) but because it reacts to the reinstatement of disciplinary boundaries, while also opening to interesting methodological questions. Lesjak includes Jameson in an arch of "reparative reading" (35) along the lines indicated by Eve Kosofsky Sedgwick. In Lesjak's view, reparative reading remains secondary since reading is "by necessity overreading ... political rather than historicist; highly interpretive rather than descriptive," and she defends a form of "perverse or ardent reading" in opposition to "commonsensical reading" (32). While Jameson is of course interested in the question of reading, and while his work, as Lesjak rightly points out, cautions us against reductive images of critique in the current postcritical climate, Jameson's main concern lies with the ambiguity surrounding the role of the critic in literary criticism. If traditionally the critic has fluctuated at will toward the more "commonsensical" position of the reader, Jameson, as we saw in the excursus above, invents another critic, parallel to the reception of critique in the U.S., one who reveals his explicit ambition to be an "observer and thinker." Jameson begins with the mystery of the cultural past, with the task of "mak[ing] time and History appear" (Lesjak 19), but it soon becomes clear that the "life and warmth" he seeks to restore are entangled with the problem of the literary critic's self-authentication. In other words, by the time he comes to articulate the multinational membrane of postmodernism, Jameson realizes that the order imposed on chaos has too often been dictated by the critic's need for truth certification within his or her disciplinary fields.

As Jameson intends it, theory responds precisely to the problem of truth certification within disciplinary fields, as a space outside "compulsory rationalizations":

> the emergence of theory in the past years has seemed to offer a space outside the institutions and outside the rehearsal of such compulsory rationalizations, and it is the claims of theory (if not its achieved realities) which allow us to grasp the limits of philosophy as such, very much including dialectical philosophy. (*Valencies* 9)

Thus, Jameson grasps theory "as the perpetual and impossible attempt to dereify the language of thought, and to preempt all the systems and ideologies which inevitably result from the establishment of this or that fixed terminology" (*Valencies* 9). Theory suspends two connected tendencies: the tendency of a disciplinary field to close in on itself ("dereify the language of thought") and the tendency to build conceptual systems that become esoteric terminology, the problem pointed out by Toril Moi in *Revolution of the Ordinary*, as we shall see in Chapter 3. The mutability of its language is one of theory's prime attributes: "undoing terminologies," this is what theory does (Jameson, *Valencies* 9). It prevents a system or an ideology from being one.[9]

The undoing of which theory is capable may not be too far from the dialectic as a movement of thought (as a moment of thought, as Jameson prefers to say in *Valencies of the Dialectic*). Jameson describes it thus:

> And indeed, the dialectic is just that inveterate, infuriating perversity whereby a common-sense empiricist view of reality is repudiated and

undermined: but it is undermined together with its own accompanying interpretations of that reality, which look so much more astute and ingenious than the common-sense empiricist reality itself, until we understand that the interpretations are themselves also part of precisely that "first impression." (*Valencies* 59)

Like dialectical thought, which is premised on a negation of common sense that seems an "inveterate, infuriating perversity," theory treats first impressions as mental objects that, like the text in *The Political Unconscious*, incorporate the hallucinatory murmur connecting the literary scholar to the warmth of history. In *Marxism and Form*, the dialectical method starts in discomfort, in a fragmented vision; it amounts to the act of straining to see. Invoking a comparison with the sciences, Jameson speaks of "the thinking mind" that "remains cool and untouched, skilled but unselfconscious," and "is able to forget itself wholly in the content and problems offered it" (*Marxism and Form* 45). In *Valencies* he returns to the dialectic, defined as "that inveterate, infuriating perversity" (59)—with the adjectives here somehow carrying the passage of time and critical schools—whereby things as they are are negated and undermined; but, while earlier on the dialectic might have been easily confused with a philosophical system, in *Valencies* it "belongs to theory rather than philosophy" (59). The dialectic continues to be what it was in *Marxism and Form*, "a thought to the second power, a thought about thinking itself" (*Marxism and Form* 45), but the stress falls on the particulars, on the discovery of the nuances of a "first impression":

> This is why the dialectic belongs to theory rather than philosophy: the latter is always haunted by the dream of some foolproof, self-sufficient, autonomous system, a set of interlocking concepts which are their own cause. This mirage is of course the afterimage of philosophy as an institution in the world, as a profession complicit with everything else in the status quo in the fallen ontic realm of "what is." Theory, on the other hand, has no vested interests inasmuch as it never lays claim to an absolute system, a non-ideological formulation of itself and its "truths," indeed, always itself complicit in the being of current language, it has only the never-ending, never-finished task and vocation of undermining philosophy as such, of unraveling affirmative statements and propositions of all kinds. (Jameson, *Valencies* 59)

The contact between literary criticism and philosophy is the leitmotif of Jameson's career and it seems to intensify over time. If I dwell on it here, it is because at this point of the discussion we may see that theory, as the name of the question of that contact, responds to the problem of truth verification linked to the authority coming from belonging to a discipline (Jameson, *Valencies* 9).

If what we said here about the metamorphoses of the critic in Jameson's work is reasonable, theory is also a kind of I-experience, and what Jameson calls the dialectic is something akin to what Foucault calls I-alethurgy. By I-alethurgy, Foucault means a veridiction or an attestation, an authentication of the truth via presence—"'I was there myself,' 'I myself saw,'"—and the words spoken on the basis of having been present (*Government* 48). In the case of Jameson, presence is to be understood in terms of his steady connection with history as symptom, that is to say, in terms of his willingness to encounter history (much like Benjamin) in haunting images that keep the I of the literary observer and thinker tied to speech so that the latter may be restored to warmth and life in hostile surroundings.[10]

It was actually art critic and feminist philosopher Carla Lonzi who was to suggest the centrality of the problem of truth authentication in our time and was to discuss the appearance of a new critical practice as a type of what Foucault would term I-alethurgy, in an extraordinary essay entitled "La solitudine del critico" (The solitude of the critic), already mentioned in the Introduction of this book. Taking her cue from avant-garde art, Lonzi argues that it exemplifies an "operation of truth," whereby each viewer/reader (seen as a member of society) is invited to accept as truth "what flows from a spontaneous constitution of consciousness" ("Solitudine" 356). For Lonzi experience is the basis for the critic's truth authentication (356). In her case, this caused a rift with established criticism and the rise of feminist theory.[11] The I-experience was for Lonzi at the origin of theory in the sense that Jameson intends theory, as a space "outside the rehearsal of such compulsory rationalizations" by which he means the rituals of truth verification linked to the authority coming from belonging to a discipline (Jameson, *Valencies* 9).[12] These rituals jar with a modernity that, through the word "postmodernism," Jameson came to perceive in terms of an overwhelming multiplicity charged with bringing order to chaos, much as, through abstract thought and universals, the Greeks tried to "order the chaos of an older 'pensée sauvage'" (*Allegory* 344).

Méconnaissance and Denkraum

We have seen that in the attempt to order chaos, Jameson's critic, as "observer and thinker," inaugurated the postmodern plane. This section will take a closer look at the postmodern plane: a cultural plane of untheorized experience. A comparative discussion with Aby Warburg's cultural plane of *méconnaissance* will prove particularly helpful to illuminate the role of the postmodern plane in the current demise of rupture as a desirable model of critical practice.

Our overview of Jameson's work has shown that theory regards the institution of fields and disciplines; it regards the acts of intellectual order that found and transform fields and disciplines. As we have seen, Jameson's critic is concerned with the "mystery of the cultural past" and wants to allow the past "to deliver its long-forgotten message in surroundings utterly alien to it" (*Political Unconscious* 19), but ends up discovering that the utterly alien surroundings constitute the very condition of speech: acts of understanding thrive on an element of misunderstanding. We understand because we recognize something in misrecognizing it. Perhaps this is what Lesjak means when, by returning to Jameson, she finds that reparative reading is "ardent" reading.

The fact that acts of understanding hinge on an element of misrecognition amounts to a lot more than a subjective failure in the field practitioner; it constitutes the very condition of illumination. If, as Lacan affirms, there is no speech without a reply, it is also true that a speech act is, somehow, always a call for recognition, even in the absence of another ("Function"). The fundamentally divided condition of the linguistic subject and the dialogic nature of speech (I–you) imply identities and ideas formed through speech and recognized in the act of naming; but insofar as they are formed in and through speech, they are also constantly misrecognized. The act of grasping something is grounded in the fact that that something which becomes available for recognition ("acknowledgment," Moi would say, drawing on Cavell) will come forward, appear, and become meaningful (i.e. conceptually accessible) *in* something else, *as* a familiar unfamiliar.

In psychoanalysis, the standard account of *méconnaissance* is Lacan's Mirror Stage. The child's jubilant moment of self-apprehension is simultaneously a moment of misapprehension, when, from body-in-fragments lacking any motor coordination, the child recognizes himself in the idealized, unified mirror image over which he is the master. It is possible, however, to point to an alternative account that, perhaps, even more poignantly illustrates the intimate link of *méconnaissance* and the power of symbolic acts.

My example will be a fragment by Aby Warburg (1866–1929), the founder of iconology (Binswanger and Warburg 153–6).[13] Warburg suffered from depression and symptoms of schizophrenia. He was hospitalized in Ludwig Binswanger's neurological clinic in Kreuzlingen, Switzerland, in 1921, and was cured and released from the clinic in 1924. The autobiographical fragment I will read was written during his stay at the clinic and dated 1922. Like the Mirror Stage text by Lacan, Warburg's text deals with the force of images, and is particularly relevant to our discussion of Jameson's apprehension of the vaster plane of postmodernism.

Like Lacan's account, Warburg's fragment features a child seduced by overpowering images, but this time the seduction is explicitly made to prefigure the adult's capacity for forging paradigms and imposing intellectual order on chaos. Remembering the time when he fell ill with typhus, Warburg writes:

> From that time my mind still retains the images created by the fever with such clarity. They well up, as if they had just been impressed in my memory this very moment, combined with olfactory sensations which, since that time, have caused me to suffer from an unpleasant overexcitation of the olfactory organs. I remember exactly the odor of the toy gun that I used to hold as a child, the soup bowl and the soup it contained, even the texture and the odor of the wool that our old governess used for her knitting (the reason why today I still have a marked aversion for certain shades of yellow). (Binswanger and Warburg 154)

The most beautiful moment of the fragment comes when Warburg relays his vision of a small coach or carriage:

> At the time of the fever-induced delirium, I also had visions of a small horse-drawn carriage moving forward on the window sill, a memory derived, I later realized, from an illustration in a book by Balzac which, as a child, I always sought to touch without, however, understanding the written text. (Binswanger and Warburg 154)

Warburg speaks here of images that exert a prelinguistic force even before the child can read and understand. It is to this force that he traces the adult's capacity for new intellectual paradigms and founding acts of order, suggesting that the discipline he created as an adult researcher, iconology, originates precisely in his visual memories, particularly in the anxiety evoked by the visual chaos. Tellingly, Warburg muses on "the tragic infantile attempt of the thinking man" (Binswanger and Warburg 154).

The child of Warburg's fragment begins to think of the events around him in terms of an uncontrollable, material power that makes itself felt through "the illogical supremacy of colors, odors and sounds" (Binswanger and Warburg 154). He manages to outline a fatal weave of intellect and environment: "The fever-induced delirium isolates and emphasizes the memory image, which is suddenly brought before us in its unbounded singular power" (154). The image triumphs in a face-to-face with the child-observer, in a way that makes him feel decontextualized from the rest of the environment. Later on, describing his feverish state, Warburg explicitly refers to the "effect of an environment" (154); the expression is key because it indicates that the illogical sovereignty (colors, odors, sounds) that has him in its grip is no subjective concoction. The power of images is not the momentary delusion of the feverish child but concerns his place in the community, and, what is more, it prefigures something irreparable in the conjoining of intellect and community, of individual psyche and national character.

As the fragment progresses, Warburg gradually focuses the link between the uncontrollable force of certain images and the problem of community (in terms of the ambiguous link of burden and gift at the core of *communitas* which will be discussed at length in Chapter 3). Warburg informs us that he tried to contrast the illogical force of the image with integration in "a normal community ready to act and impose order on chaos" (Binswanger and Warburg 154). He goes on to relate his vicissitudes in public schools, his necessity to change communities and adjust to new groups of peers, his experience of being brutally beaten on his fingers with an iron ruler by an anti-Semitic theologian, and other violent rites of excluding inclusion that underpin the mythology of community as communion. Warburg eloquently relays the drama of the ambiguous conjunction of a being-with-others and the preservative defense from others, all the while suggesting that the enigmatic link of gift and burden is inseparable from the subjective agony of symbolic activity.

The fragment marvelously stages intellectual invention as the alternation of the child's retreat to his cocoon, which is emphasized by his illness and delirium, and the pressure of belonging, which is associated with the discomfort and outright violence at school, sovereign symbol of the much wider *dispositif* of community. The word "environment," then, suggests a nuanced complex, and the work of the fragment is to show the child's attempt to become unmoored from it, reflecting his, as well as our own, unease at that kind of belonging. Warburg mentions his struggle to become included in an "already ordered mass," a torment that was ended by Dr. Cohen's intervention and the child's withdrawal from school. The point of Warburg's fragment is that intellectual work issues from the pressure of the communal mechanism; from the perspective of Warburg's child, the "thinking man" cannot become unmoored from the burden of community; this remains residual to language, which means, in his case, that it casts the problem of method and of new disciplines in terms of that impossibility.

In Binswanger's clinic, Warburg was given the opportunity to prove his sanity with a public conference in 1923. He chose to speak on the Hopi people, a Native American tribe, and his talk was on their rituals. It became known as the "Schlangenritual" text but remained unpublished, in accordance with his wishes, in his lifetime.[14] The talk's manuscript begins with an epigraph that plays on the book-of-the-world metaphor: "Es ist ein altes Buch zu blattern, / Athens-Oraibi, alles Vettern" (Warburg qtd. in C. Johnson 30) (It is to leaf through an old book, / Athens-Oraibi, all cousins). The question of the world is put in terms of a space of thought, an environment of thought or *Denkraum*, that ensures the world. Every thinker's secret dream is "to move the world" (Sontag, "Idea" 286). For Warburg, it means shuffling the images that compose the book of the world. The real challenge is to take oneself, in a willed and certainly costly manner, out of one's own location. That seems to be what Warburg fought for. In the lecture that was to prove the reparative work he had done in Binswanger's clinic, he wrote: "The synchrony [*Nacheinander*] of logical civilization and fantastic, magical causation show the Pueblo Indians' peculiar condition of hybridity and transition" (Warburg qtd. in C. Johnson 31). Warburg reassembles the pages of the world. However, in doing so, he is not interested in the globe; he invents a vast plane of connections and *méconnaissance*, "an immense network of discourses" (C. Johnson 19).[15]

Christopher Johnson, one of Warburg's best explicators, accuses the iconologist of rashness in recognizing analogues of Hopi rituals in classical Greece and in his own culture, as well, but Warburg's method relies precisely on seeing forms as if they were repeated in translation, against the moving background of a strange neighborliness of cultures in time and space. Distance generates the sensation of a nearness that ensures Warburg's extra-disciplinary truth verification ritual (he became the first iconologist). Georges Didi-Huberman brilliantly refers to Warburg's self-verification with the notion of "dislocated genealogy," adding that it "makes of his 'contortion' a construction (which every historian should learn from)" (338). In the Kreuzinglen lecture, the problem of method, of fields and of ordering, becomes reflected in the hybrid style of the cultural historian, in the miscellaneous and heterogeneous elements, all of which address the problem of the unevenness of historical temporalities, of a plane that is always the historicization of the non-historical. In a letter to his family dated 26 December 1923, a few months after he had proven his sanity, Warburg tries to explain that the goal of his work is the "inclusion of the irrational drives in the investigation of historical development" (Warburg qtd. in C. Johnson 29).

The Notebooks from the years between 1919 and 1924 bear the trace, in pencil, of the upheaval, of the flux of energy and writing that led to Warburg's method. On one of the pages of a notebook, scribbled in block letters, we find the word "FASTEN," the verb "to fast" in German. Might Warburg mean the fasting of the one who devours signs? The "constructed space" that his scholars acknowledge is inseparable from a psychic world shattered to pieces, but Warburg's example informs us that the pieces and the construction are the essence of method. In Didi-Huberman's formulation, they are "a fundamental experiential structure," a "vital global fact" (349), in brief, Warburg's own discourse on method.

Warburg's extraordinary fragment ties the logic of *méconnaissance* to the problem of founding acts that impose order on chaos and thus organize intellectually a disparate heterogeneity. Eve Kosofsky Sedgwick would refer to these paradigm dramas as "paranoid reading" ("Paranoid Reading" 1997). The acts determine the vitality of a field. At times, they may result from the anxiety about the field's lack of an inner unity.[16] Jameson's thinker, who seeks to clear new ground in literary criticism, is similar to Warburg's iconologist. We have seen that in his encounter with what he would call "postmodernism," Jameson's critic, like Warburg's iconologist, is overwhelmed by the power of images that exceed his capacity to domesticate them. In both cases, *méconnaissance* (the overwhelming power of images and the founding theoretical acts to which that power is a prelude) is governed by the pressure of the clash of gift and debt in the collective dimension. Jameson's "rival hermeneutic" defends the warm meanings of the past against the neutralizing blows of poststructuralist *écriture*; it helps to keep at bay the melancholia of community, the *nihil* at its core. It is like the *Pathosformel* of the nymph in Warburg: a diaphanous appearance, "a peculiar accumulation of power, a pulsing concentrate in [poetic] and iconic space" (Baert 68). The collective past visits Jameson's critic like a murmur that asks to become clear speech. Jameson's critic seeks to translate this auditory hallucination into reparative speech. For Warburg's child and for Jameson's critic the visual-auditory hallucination resolves itself in paradigmatic symbolic acts. In the next chapter, Roberto Esposito's new plane of coevalness will bypass the heroic dimension behind Warburg's and Jameson's paradigm dramas. The stress will fall neither on recognition nor on estrangement but rather on the vastness itself, on the fact of a *Denkraum*, to use Warburg's term, that appears and is "much wider than a local or national one" (Esposito, *Pensiero vivente* 3).

Notes

1. Harman's reference is to the work of Quentin Meillassoux.
2. European-based scholars have increasingly approached translation in terms of "migration." In its ordinary use, the term "migration" indicates a social wound in Europe. When it becomes an object of research, it retains an aura of urgency while enabling to gesture simultaneously toward intersemiotic migration from one medium to another (and the migration of the collective imaginary across different media) and a broader view of thought and culture that is predicated on the circulation of ideas (Guglielmi).
3. The list would be too long. By way of introduction, see Buchanan; Irr and Buchanan; and, more recently, Duncan, who reconsiders Jameson's postmodernism after the affective turn.
4. I am thinking of the kind of theory refusals illustrated by Valentine Cunningham's *Reading After Theory*.
5. I return to a more detailed discussion of this point and of Ricoeur in Chapter 6.
6. Thesis 2 in Benjamin, "Concept of History" 389–90.
7. Jean-François Lyotard would use the same term to expound on the postmodern condition in *Libidinal Economy*.
8. For examples of the severance of the bond with hermeneutic depth, see Derrida, "Différance" and "Signature Event Context" 1988.
9. In *Valencies of the Dialectic*, Jameson cautions about deconstruction becoming fixed terminology: "Deconstruction is thus the very paradigm of a theoretical process of undoing terminologies which, by virtue of the elaboration of the terminology that very process requires, becomes a philosophy and an ideology in its own turn and congeals into the very type of system it sought to undermine" (9).

10. I have written on history as symptom in Benjamin in Mitrano, "Voglia di realtà."
11. In Lonzi's "La solitudine del critico" (The solitude of the critic), Foucault's I-alethurgy for Lonzi will be in open conflict with the authority of the *patres*, the plural of *pater*, the Latin word for father, which therefore means a male patriarch but has many more resonances, meaning also forefathers, elders, and thus connoting something at the origin and family-related, the domestic origin of the origin. Because *patres* were also the selected members of the confederated board of elders that would become the Roman senate, it also connotes the imbrication of domestic familial origin and the political sphere (355).
12. In *Valencies of the Dialectic*, Jameson speaks of philosophers and other practitioners (literary critics included): "those of us in other institutional disciplines," who "waste their time" in "institutional self-justifications" (9).
13. All translations from Binswanger and Warburg, *La guarigione infinita* are mine. To my knowledge, no English edition exists.
14. W. R. Mainland loosely translated the text as "A Lecture on Serpent Ritual," *Journal of the Warburg Institute*, vol. 2, no. 4 (1939): 277–92, subsequently published in *Images from the Region of the Pueblo Indians of North America*. For a long time, this was the only text by Warburg available in English (Didi-Huberman 337).
15. Christopher Johnson's definition of Warburg's *Mnemosyne Atlas*.
16. For example, Pease and Wiegman mention Gene Wise's concern about American Studies being a "parasite field," living off the ideas of others. In response to Wise, Pease and Wiegman pose the field as a "hybridized borderland," a conceptual zone where "the emergent inhabits the residual," whose focal point is the recognition of "the unsayable" within the cognitive parameters of the discipline (21).

Chapter 3

What is a Critic?: Weak Thought, Weak Theory, Italian Theory

Overview

Thinkers from different positions and disciplines linked to a variety of critical and philosophical orientations (postcritique, realism, Italian Theory) converge on a momentous cultural shift from rupture to a vast plane of ideas. The shift may be formulated using different lexicons, with Italian theorists perceiving an exit in a vaster world,[1] while transnational scholars and realists and speculative philosophers alike may prefer to speak of a radical relationality (Elias and Moraru; Shaviro). Nevertheless, across the differences, a figure begins to emerge, that of a plane of coevalness. Aby Warburg's and Fredric Jameson's paradigm dramas in the previous chapter have prepared us for discussion of this new figure which, in this chapter, will be studied through the work of political philosopher Roberto Esposito. I choose to focus on Esposito because his plane of coevalness not only enters into conversation with a similar figure in Felski's work but also results from a reorientation of the problem of the new. It replaces (or displaces) the logic of the avant-garde with a logic of circulation, and, in so doing, Esposito argues for a new that need not arise from rupture. Unlike Felski, he therefore feels compelled neither to reject modernism nor to conceive of its temporalities as based on an adversarial stance. Quite the contrary, as we shall see, Esposito's Italian Theory carries modernism all along; it reactivates the central conflict of Life vs. Form, embedded in the concept of modernism, and thereby moves beyond the sovereignty of language decreed by the linguistic turn. In this chapter the actualization of the anglophone concept of modernism will imply a revision of its meaning. With the help of Esposito, we will zoom in on the nexus between modernism and theory as disciplinary areas to see how differing ordering principles and different temporalities emerge which ultimately raise the question of the boundaries of a field and cause us to reflect on how we conceive a disciplinary field. The keyword in this chapter is "critic." Esposito's work will throw into relief the development of recent theory, especially the so-called Weak Theory as a discourse on the profoundly altered self-representation of the critic. Emancipated from the exigencies of pluralism which, in the second half of the twentieth century, had demanded the notion of a rhetorical communion between authors and readers,[2] freed from the need to counter the skepticism of deconstruction with the notion of a "discursive community,"[3] the contemporary critic has evolved beyond the task of producing persuasive readings and is instead concerned with his or her epistemic stance. Having disentangled his or her mission from the demands of argumentation, the critic is interested in a practice that feels less like a procedure and more like the wonder one associates with genuine moments of thought. Discussion begins in the section below by detailing this shift through the work of Wai Chee Dimock.

Reading and democracy

In her 2013 influential essay "Weak Theory," Wai Chee Dimock champions a decentered literary field, "a nonsovereign field with . . . a variable ordering principle, so that what appears primary in one locale can indeed lapse into secondariness in another" (738). Dimock's essay, in fact, reveals the predicament of a literary critic who is mired in a practice that seems estranged from knowledge, for whom reading has come to feel like the exertion of a "sovereign knowingness" (744). Consequently, Dimock draws the portrait of a critic without certainties, who wishes to withdraw from the theoretical criticism of the recent past. The background is the sense of loss brought on by the presumed end of Theory, understood as a period of U.S. intellectual life, that, as we saw in the discussion of Rita Felski's *The Limits of Critique* in previous chapters, seems to have resulted in a rote and ineffective exercise. Like Felski, Dimock's weak critic reacts to this state of affairs, though she refrains from equating critique to an adversarial attitude. What prevails, instead, is a certain restlessness: Dimock's critic wants to be elsewhere, but this elsewhere is not a geographical position. The previous chapter on Jameson, a pioneer of Theory, helps us understand this restlessness. Dimock's critic inherits from Jameson's theory the problem of a genuine affinity for thought. As we saw in the previous chapter, Jameson called theory a preparation for criticism. In his vision, criticism is a moment of "thought to the second power" (Jameson, *Marxism and Form* 307). The old problem of criticism's neighborliness with thought resurfaces in Dimock's impasse, and, once it is understood in this sense, her "weak theory" builds bridges between the past of theory and contemporary generations of scholars for whom the problem is not the rejection of critique (the hermeneutics of suspicion) but a "kind of criticism . . . deliberately oriented toward the ongoing labor of thought" (Dabashi 950).[4]

Twenty years prior to "Weak Theory," in another essay entitled "A Theory of Resonance" (1997), Dimock had argued for the role of criticism in transforming literature into a more inclusive, "democratic institution" ("Theory of Resonance" 1060). At that time, she had associated reading with the purposeful decontextualization and relocation of texts outside their usual temporal and geographical boundaries. The task involved redrawing key terms in the field, like "text" and "literary history." In the earlier article, Dimock redefined texts as traveling objects, whose semantic texture exists through its changes in time. She replaced the notion of a literary history understood as a linear, national chronology with the plane of traveling texts (1061). This plane recalls quite closely Walter Benjamin's "intensive" plane of interpretation, which we discussed in Chapter 1. It will be recalled that, for Benjamin, texts are taciturn and enigmatic objects that are nevertheless linked to each other in an "intensive process of interpretation" ("Letter" 388). Following up on Benjamin, Dimock dispersed literary history, but she also refined the predecessor's concept of interpretation. In the earlier essay, her plane was not only "intensive" but also diasporic, with texts dispersed across different geographies. The dispersion projects an open exchange of thoughts between texts and readers that suggestively conveys the idea of literature as a democratic institution.

It is, in fact, possible to think of Dimock's plane in terms of Claude Lefort's notion of "collective discourse." Lefort would say that literary works strike us as taciturn and enigmatic when they do not easily fit any disciplinary boundaries (he offers the example of Machiavelli's *The Prince*). In such cases, the literary work comes into existence "on condition of the gift of our thoughts," he says: "the work has never had any other form of existence except in an open exchange" of the kind that generates ever new questions, through "the institution of a collective discourse" in which the readers' thoughts become articulated among themselves "at the same time that they determine the advent of the work" (Lefort qtd. in Esposito, *Pensiero istituente* 198). Lefort uses the word "institution" to name this exchange—this giving of thoughts—and concludes that when "we interrogate this exchange, this institution," not only does our work include us in it but "we are already interrogating the literary work" (Lefort qtd. in Esposito, *Pensiero istituente* 198). In Dimock's earlier essay, we hear something like Lefort's "collective discourse," especially when she proposes that, with each relocation, each text requires a response that "alters" its semantic fabric ("Theory of Resonance" 1060). Notice that Dimock's readers do not seek the certainty of meaning; they treat the text as action and expression, and they feel addressed by it. The difference with Lefort is that Dimock's emphasis is less on the giving (the gift of our thoughts to the literary work) and more on intention: "Across time, every text must put up with readers on different wavelengths, who come at it tangentially and tendentiously, who impose semantic losses as well as gains" (1061). These readers cross paths with the text "tangentially," but their acknowledgment of the text happens "tendentiously," that is, by applying to the text the pressure of their own expectations. They enter the collective discourse of interlocked questions and answers which, as Lefort contends, is not peripheral to the text but institutes it, with those pressures. These readers acknowledge the text in the expectation of a response *from* the text. In short, reading holds the possibility of recognition.

I am using recognition in the sense that Toril Moi uses acknowledgment, but with a difference. Moi builds on Stanley Cavell's notion of acknowledgment, which he introduces in relation to the problem of imagining others ("how I can know what another human being is thinking, feeling, sensing") (Moi 205). From this perspective, acknowledgment "is not an operation a subject performs on an object and its goal is not scientific certainty" (208); on the contrary, it "includes knowledge, but in its insistence on response, on action and self-revelation, it moves beyond epistemology to raise questions of ethics and morality" (208). Like Moi, Dimock thinks that "the category of 'certainty' is no longer the relevant dimension in which to assess the kind of knowledge a literary critic has of a literary work" (Moi 208). On the one hand, Dimock may be said to emphasize the specificity of the response—just as "[e]ach case, each human situation, requires a specific response" (Moi 208–9), so does each text—but, on the other hand, like Lefort, she is ultimately interested in the collective discourse in which the readers' questions and answers become interlocked and generate new ones.

Thus, in this earlier essay, Dimock's critic (like Moi and Cavell) moves beyond epistemology to raise questions of ethics, and does so by including literature in a transnational web of resonances. She redesigns literature's global orbit, turning outward, toward other regions and toward others. Over the years, the critic's enterprise is caught up in the problem of the nexus between literature and knowledge, the problem specifically addressed in the later essay on "Weak Theory." Here, Dimock becomes preoccupied with literature's connection to "sovereign knowingness" rather than knowledge. Dimock's critic finds that she wants to be somewhere else, where ideas happen and "other meanings" are ("Weak Theory" 744). Having undone the center/periphery divide, having included texts in larger structures (systems), and having known the urgency to weave great cultural narratives, she now wishes a "retreat from a strong claim," and the "trying out instead of a . . . lower-level kind of theorizing" (733), the pursuit of "lateral planes of meditation" and "wayward lines of association oblique to any existing system" (736). These lateral, wayward, and episodic threads are expected to bring some relief from the "invariance of power" which seems to govern meaning making (734). Hence the expectant mood for a less forceful critical practice: "what can be said for a critical practice that does not even try to clinch the case?" (735). The term "clinch," a variant of "clench," when it is a noun indicates the action of clenching as in a grab, a grip, a clutch, a tight closure, a secure fastening. It renders figuratively the conclusion of an argument. When it is a verb, clinch means to fix as in fix a nail or bolt securely, by bending and beating back or flattening the point or the end which has passed through a plank or plate of any kind; it means to make fast by such means. Understood as this enterprise, theory no longer has the critic in its thrall. Paradoxically, Dimock's withdrawal suggests that her critic misses the feeling of thinking with literature.

Dimock suggests what thinking with literature might entail when her account of theory leads up to the problem of the boundaries of disciplines, to the fundamental question of how something like the literary field might arise. She questions the notion of "field" and the idea of literary history through a reading that connects three different writers across time: two modernists (Henry James and W. B. Yeats) and a contemporary (Colm Tóibín). A field, she considers, is organized by dominant forms, therefore it is structurally given and "permutationally finite" ("Weak Theory" 734). "To insert any work into such a field," writes Dimock, "is rather like assembling the pieces of a jigsaw puzzle—a completable task with preassigned limits" (734). This is why critical practice is inevitably incomplete: "It is not so easy to clinch the case, *to cover the entire field* with a single causal agency" (735; my emphasis). The phrase "clinching the case," therefore, not only refers to an aggressive style of reading but it tells us that aggressive style is the consequence of a limited idea of theory which consists in imposing a method borrowed from the sciences, thus reviving the crux of critical method first explored by Hans-Georg Gadamer.[5]

Dimock is concerned with what Moi calls the "curious formalism" of theory (65), when by theory we mean a "commitment to rigorous and scientific concepts" that "should be able to predict future cases and have explanatory power" (68–9).[6] Dimock seems to think that even if one were to expand the field to planetary dimensions, it would not be possible to make arguments, classify, invent categories that cover the entire field. Yet, theory understands power "to be the ultimate determinant, the ordering principle that unfailingly structures the sciences as well as the arts" (Dimock, "Weak Theory" 734). She thus foregrounds the tension between the two terms "thought" and "theory." Her critic resumes the interdisciplinary dialogue with philosophy on the formalist meaning of theory, which we discussed in the previous chapter with the example of Jameson. But something happens when we call theory "weak theory": it intercepts a trajectory that had up until then been foreign to the widely accepted narrative of theory as discussed in the Introduction to this book and in the previous chapter on Jameson.

Weak thought/weak theory

Dimock's phrase "weak theory" was circulated a year after the publication of *Weak Thought*, the 2012 translation by Peter Carravetta of *Il pensiero debole*, first published in Italian in 1983. This is no negligible detail. The temporal arch that goes from weak thought to weak theory indicates, at the very least, that the notion of weakness has persisted over time, across different cultural climates and across different disciplines, pointing to an ongoing contact between literary criticism and philosophy. *Weak Thought* contains contributions by major Italian philosophers. Here, for the sake of discussion, I single out the work of Pier Aldo Rovatti because not only is his understanding of weak thought close to Dimock's weak theory, it also enters into conversation with anglophone postcritique.

When it began to circulate in the early 1980s, the phrase *pensiero debole* was meant to suggest a different style of knowing (Rovatti, "Trasformazioni" 42), one in which the thinking subject and the object of thought are no longer "locked in specular correspondence" (29).[7] Rovatti speaks for a weak subject that departs from the meaning of theory in standard philosophy as a model that can predict future cases. He argues for metamorphosis rather than theory. Relying on Kafka's well-known novella, *The Metamorphosis* (*Die Verwandlung*), Rovatti champions the discovery of reality rather than an adaptation to it. The weakness of "weak thought," then, rests on a "neighborliness to things" (34). Rovatti uses the image of the observer "sitting on the grass" to describe a style of reflection that he calls "just perceiving," when consciousness becomes accessory and "[w]e can be 'next to' things" (34). He asks: "What happens then?" (34).

Both weak theory and postcritique, as represented in this discussion by Dimock and Felski, follow up on Rovatti's question. Rovatti is concerned with our tendency to treat reality as a construction: "if by reality we mean a reality to which the model must adhere perfectly, that is itself a construction" because "it has been already predisposed for a model and it is to be considered a symbolic redoubling" ("Trasformazioni" 42). Felski is inspired by a similar problem, and her language resonates with the metaphors used by Rovatti to describe the task of the thinker. So, for example, disapproving of what he calls "the flight of the eagle," Rovatti turns to the viable alternative of "learning to adhere to the earth, like the serpent," referring to an image from Nietzsche (34). Similarly, Felski invites the critic "to trudge along . . ., marveling at the intricate ecologies and diverse microorganisms that lie hidden among the thick blades of grass" (*Limits* 158).[8] Of course differences remain. Weak thought aims at a desirable transformation of the relation between subject and object, knower and known, without necessarily championing a radical relationality. It counters "theory" in the same way that Moi objects to it, that is to say, as a unified model of knowledge—"the constraining force of unity"—and tips the scale toward "the idea that we have, and to which we hold, of reality and of ourselves" (Rovatti, "Trasformazioni" 62).

By Rovatti's own admission, weak thought does not want to replace the notion of the subject with an unavoidable relationality among all agents, but it wants to erase the precise contours of the subject, in the attempt to sever the concept from the face-to-face with the other in which it is lodged by Hegel's master–slave combat model of recognition. He describes the fading contours of the subject, its increased opacity, but not its disappearance; the concept of the human subject contains in itself a structure of recognition that Rovatti does not wish to let go. I have chosen Rovatti because he insists on the importance of recognition. In this, his weak thought connects with Elaine Scarry's concern, mentioned in the Introduction, with our capacity to imagine others. Rovatti's weak thought is propelled by that concern. It assumes a human subject, whose neutral mold has rightly been under attack (Cavarero), but applies a turn to it that is quite distinct from Foucault's modest indocility discussed in Chapter 1. Rovatti's thinker turns, but the motion of the figure this time is neither a refusal nor a conversion; in disengaging from the face-to-face with the other, the subject still turns toward another, with the expectation of a returning gaze. Rovatti leans toward a more impersonal dimension when he relocates the human subject amidst transgenerational forces that do not remain alien to it because they cannot be easily neutralized. In particular, he puts into play the notion of *pietas* to indicate a solidarity between generations, a non-antagonistic relation to the past.

From the distance of time, in a historical reconstruction of 2011 (*Inattualità del pensiero debole*), Rovatti explains that the weakened subject of weak thought was aimed at countering the society of the spectacle which makes visibility dependent on the spectacularization of life. To put it differently, he contrasts the reduction of life to surfaces. In the face of this reduction, weak thought suggests a practice of modesty or restraint (*pudore*) that contrasts with the "arrogance" (*prepotenza*) of cultural surfaces. Like Dimock's weak theorist, then, Rovatti's weak thinker withdraws, but, more overtly than Dimock, his weak thinker is careful to withdraw from the endorsement and celebration of surfaces that would smooth out any gap between what can be articulated and what remains unsayable (*dicibile e indicibile*).

When compared with Foucault's reflective indocility, Rovatti's weakness may seem a clumsier movement, a withdrawal resembling renunciation and even an implosion. His weak thinker is not to be confused, as Rovatti underlines, with the postmodern freewheeling subject; weakness is a kind of fortitude required by the refusal of the triumph of surfaces and the related command to be visible, to appear publicly (*Inattualità* 59). He argues that the regime of surfaces—the spectacularization of life—cannot adequately address and respond to the "need for a socializing recognition"; if anything, the society of the spectacle makes the need for recognition even more acute since visibility is given "within a 'public' language that can distort visibility itself into a false sense of recognition" (60).[9] This is why he speaks of a turn in the direction of the other: weak thought is "a way of listening to the other" (11). At the same time, this way of listening requires a withdrawal, an implosion with regard to forms of available expression, a form of modesty (*pudore*).

What Rovatti calls *pudore*, modesty, bears emphasizing. The word activates a range of meanings spanning from discretion to introversion, from renunciation to shame; it is a state that connotes an alternative epistemic attitude, introducing that particular weakening of the subject/object duality that does not aim at a disappearance of the subject but its reorientation to make it more capacious, to reinvent its capacity for the recognition of another.

When Rovatti contrasts the effect of cultural surfaces with modesty, he reminds us that moods and affects are an integral part of our epistemic endeavors. This insight opens to that strain within the postcritical movement which follows from the pioneering work of Eve Kosofsky Sedgwick and has coalesced in affect theory.[10] Affect theory represents a departure from standard theory understood as a conceptual model, as the heroic belief, common to the hermeneutics of suspicion and versions of critique such as deconstruction and poststructuralism, that "the successful theorist manages to explain the hidden principles or forces that account for even our most mundane activities" (Moi 81). From this vantage point, Rovatti's modesty is amenable to the non-descriptive model favored by affect studies scholars, who champion a critical practice understood as "a matter of accounting for the progressive accentuation (plus/minus) of intensities, their incremental shimmer: the stretching of process underway, not position taken" (Gregg and Seigworth 11).

It is interesting to consider affect studies in relation to Rovatti's weak thought, especially as we see the latter as a preparation for the current phenomenon of Italian Theory. Affect theory, in fact, reactivates work alongside the linguistic turn; Gregg and Seigworth refer, among others, to Raymond Williams's "structure of feelings," Franz Fanon's "third person consciousness," and Benjamin's non-sensuous similarities (8). In this sense, it is contiguous to Italian Theory, which does not reject the linguistic turn but presents itself as both ahead and behind it, as a latent line of thought in excess of the linguistic turn, as we shall see in detail in the second part of this chapter. This off-position is highlighted by the editors of *The Affect Theory*

Reader (2010), who return to Barthes and champion the "immanent neutrality" of what the French critic called "the affective minimum" as a way of outplaying "oppositions and negations by referring to 'intense, strong, unprecedented states' that elude easy polarities and contradictions" (10).

The editors rightly highlight Barthes's "lateral choice" of a critical practice that might allow for a way of "being-present to the struggles of [his] time" through supple annotation in the genre of "an inventory of shimmers, of nuances, of states, of changes" (Barthes qtd. in Gregg and Seigworth 11). Like Rovatti's modesty, Barthes's "affective minimum," with the writing of nuances that it brings in its train, represents a renunciation aimed at weakening the valence of a concept (subject) and the divide that ensues (subject/object). Similarly to Barthes's lateral choice, Rovatti's modesty champions the exertion of critical attention against the universalizing vocation of philosophy (see Rovatti, *Etica*), but more pronouncedly than Barthes, perhaps, Rovatti has a stake in the notion of the subject insofar as it preserves within itself the possibility of recognition.[11] The fact that cultural surfaces still cannot prevent the creation of the unsayable (*indicibile*) makes it necessary to actualize recognition.

Dimock picks up from Rovatti's problem when she stages a critic who, despite the forward thrust of the extended surfaces of transnationalism and world literature, finds herself stranded in a zone of "noncommunicability" ("Weak Theory" 751), where unsayable "peripheries" still remain hidden (752). She reacts to the folds that shimmer within the global surface of literary studies by mobilizing a profound skepticism about the notion of "field." Like Rovatti's weak thinker, Dimock's weak theorist comes to resist the heroic belief in a formalist view of theory but, lured by Bruno Latour's relational ontology, she prefers to dissolve the literary in a vaster plane of dispersed episodic webs, of centrifugal "long networks" that permit to "undo any naturalized hierarchies" (737, 736). Dimock concludes that a field "as a fully integrated and fully rationalized entity, simply does not exist" (737). I would define her centrifugal lines as diasporic because they flow from the removal of centers to marginal locales, from a tradition of places between what counts and what does not; what takes on thematic significance and what does not make sense and remains opaque. It is a "site-dependent form of ordering" (737), which makes it "an open question what is primary, what is determinative, what counts as the center and what counts as the margins" (737). From this vantage point, literary studies is no longer a question of classifying writers according to an ordering principle (e.g. T. S. Eliot as a canonical, or even hyper-canonical, modernist); the main question raised by the weak theorist seems to concern neither lineage nor tradition but a desirable critical practice that is expected to feel more like the "intensity of an act" (Badiou 23).

Dimock's withdrawal from grand theoretical models may be said to recall Rovatti's modesty, but the temptation of an epistemic position on the side of modesty in the two cases unfolds differently. For Rovatti it represents the possibility to restitute recognition, which entails redrawing the philosophical problem of consciousness, while in Dimock's case it poignantly suggests a profoundly altered self-representation of the critic over the longer arch of Theory. Her critic has come to share Rovatti's distancing attitude from the surfaces which she nevertheless has contributed to spinning. But when Paul Saint-Amour extends Dimock's weakness to modernism, weak theory's temptation of modesty disappears, and Dimock's impasse is understood in terms of its potential for radical skepticism. Saint-Amour wonders whether "it might be time to think about dissolving" the field and "reconstituting around some other term or concept" (455). The term or concept in question is modernism, and the question insinuated is: What keeps a critic and a scholar in a field? More than questions, Saint-Amour speaks of specters that haunt him as a field practitioner. Modernism, in fact, more than other fields (e.g. American Studies), indicates an unsteady concept, one that has vanished and been resurrected. As such, modernism is not foreign to the fundamental question of what holds a field together. In the anglophone world, the concept declined in the early 1980s because it seemed to lack the necessary "semantic openness" and "mobility." These qualities would be "read back" into the concept two decades later, in the early 2000s, with the concept's "broadening" (Liska 80) thanks to the rise of the New Modernist Studies. After the reconstitution of the field, the specter of dissolution comes back to haunt its practitioners, and this time, as it transpires from Saint-Amour's language, it is inseparable from an unworked through mythology of community.

Saint-Amour compares the field practitioners to companion travelers "trying to warm our hands at a fire that's gone out, as fires do," tacitly convinced that "we'd all be better off moving on" (455). Weakness is no alternative route; rather, it literalizes into impotence: here is the crepuscular image of a community that discovers the *nihil* at its core, the nothing that binds it. Saint-Amour apperceives the heroic shaping of the field of modernism. This is no irrelevant factor since, traditionally, a confusion of tongues has been established between modernist aesthetic experimentation and the theoretical expansion of literary criticism, a confusion of tongues that has resulted in the field's reliance on "the critic as heroic demystifier of ideology" (439). The maintenance of the figure of a critic primarily associated with the partial view of critique as demystification has been made possible also by an unworked through concept of community. The mutual link of aesthetic innovation and critical demystification seems to have produced its own temporality, with a modernism that comes after weak thought, while it also looks back to catch up on it.[12] From another point of view, however, the mutuality of modernism and theory has resulted in disconnected temporalities, each blind to the other but collaborating, and rejoined at the crepuscular moment of modernism's dissolving. As we shall see in the second part of this chapter, weakness carries with it an analysis of community that was never really a question with modernism before. This analysis alters modernism's "adversarial schemes," in Felski's phrase ("Introduction" 217), producing an anti-heroic effect within the field as well as a shift from rupture to a more affirmative mood.

The analysis of community

It is the analysis of community that will lead to the notion of a plane of coevalness with Esposito. While, as we shall see in the rest of this discussion, Esposito's plane of coevalness is somewhat reminiscent of Dimock's diasporic plane, it also differs, providing an alternative both to the aestheticized radical relationality championed by the new speculative materialism and realism and to the revival of an unproblematically cohesive subject inherent in the planetary bonded multitudes that are sometimes celebrated by transnationalism (Elias and Moraru xviii).

The analysis of community has a longer history than can be relayed here. The debate develops along a line of texts and authors—Georges Bataille, Maurice Blanchot, Jean-Luc Nancy, Giorgio Agamben, Jacques Derrida—that steer away from historical and ideological perspectives on community. At a decisive moment, in *The Inoperative Community* (1990), Jean-Luc Nancy speaks of the "myth of community" and clears a space for "the exposure of singular beings" outside ideological and historicist constraints (57, 62). The focus of critical inquiry shifts from the social tie to another sort of bond, a being-in-common that is the real enigma of community and occupies critique in both its psychoanalytic and deconstructive inflections, with Mikkel Borch-Jacobsen speaking of "an *ethical* beyond of the subject" ("Freudian Subject" 110; original emphasis) and Jacques Derrida of the "an-economic exposition to others" (*Specters* 23).[13] This theoretical line culminates with Roberto Esposito's analysis of community and the rise, in recent years, of something called "Italian Theory."

Coming from the modernist and poststructuralist heroic narrative of "the critic as demystifier of knowledge" (Saint-Amour 439), the first encounter with Italian Theory can be quite disorienting and destabilizing. It is as if everything one had learned from anglophone feminism, psychoanalysis, and theory—embodied experience, subjectivity, the unconscious—were suddenly nullified. This impression is especially true of the encounter with Roberto Esposito's *Terza persona* (2007), which is in many ways a transitional text because it inaugurates a process of *translatio* of the U.S.-based concern with deconstruction. Esposito resumes the central question of deconstruction of a radical opening to otherness in terms, however, that seem to reverse time and throw us back into some sort of wilderness or antecedent conceptual chora. Esposito veers toward life, but life in its impersonal dimension, understood as a virtual spark, as "a kind of preindividual or transindividual biological substance" (Lisciani-Petrini 45; my translation). Throughout, the object of research remains the possibility of humanization beyond the cruel dynamics of "being desired by the gaze of the other" (*Terza persona* 135),[14] but what comes to the fore is a biological datum that evokes archaic or primitive social orders while the notion of mere life, which emerges as a strong motif not only in Esposito but also in Giorgio Agamben, in *Terza persona* implicitly suggests a cultural tabula rasa.[15] Esposito's third person is the non-person, the concept through which the thinker reacts to the discourse on the other, a discourse that can valorize but still remains within the limits of an oppositional structure, within the terms of the subject/object combat. Esposito thinks of the non-person as the locus of true plurality (*Terza persona* 140), yet the notion can be quite destabilizing. The human body loses its contours; it becomes "extended and externalized" in ways that recall the modernist paintings of Francis Bacon (1909–92) (Lisciani-Petrini 45; my translation).[16] It is at this point that something called "Italian Theory" begins to emerge as the sense of a parallel theoretical temporality to the heroic modernist-friendly demystification. While the two temporalities remain blind to each other, as we shall see, they may also be said to collaborate. Esposito completes Rovatti's weak thought, further blurring the contours of the subject, actually taking the notion as if to the furthest outpost of thought, where it fades in the physical datum of flesh. The notion of the impersonal rises to indicate a limit zone of thought. Once the analysis of community is taken into account, Esposito's impersonal appears as an attempt to counter the thanatological legacy within the idea of modernity.

Esposito takes a distance from substantivist notions of community by steering the analysis of community in a semantic and etymological direction. His analysis is propelled by the interweaving of both the idea of gift and obligation contained within the word "communitas," *cum* + *munus*. Since the work of Jean-Luc Nancy from the 1990s had made it no longer tenable to emphasize the "cum," the "with" indicating the collective dimension, Esposito focuses on the meaning of the "munus" to clear new theoretical ground. Referring simultaneously to the gift and the debt that ties us to others, the *munus* in *communita*s indicates "that relation which, committing its members to the obligation of a reciprocal gift, endangers their individual identity" (Esposito, *Bíos* 47).[17] Once it is reconnected to its etymological matrix, community is shown to be interwoven with the question of immunity, "the condition of dispensation from such a bond or obligation and therefore a defense with regard to its effects of expropriation" (47). Esposito's etymological analysis, in fact, reworks the nexus of power and life that Michel Foucault had called "biopolitics," but with a difference. While Foucault had applied the term generically from Plato to the present to mean politics that is always, in one way or another, aimed at life,[18] Esposito's semantics of immunity delimits the phenomenon to contemporary modernity, to target especially the period that has been called the postmodern (49).

The necessity of self-preservation—increasing, preserving, and perfecting life—not only belongs to our time but it constitutes, Esposito argues, its "most intimate essence," to the extent that one might assert that "it was not modernity that posed the problem of the self-preservation of life, but the latter put in place, that is to say 'invented', modernity as a historical-conceptual apparatus capable of solving the problem" (*Bíos* 52). The analysis of *communitas* uncovers what is always borne by and through the word "community," and that is the threat presented to the singular individual and the related mechanism of "repressive self-preservation" (Bazzicalupo, *Biopolitica* 115).[19] There is, however, another aspect to community, and this aspect is brought out by Saint-Amour's dissolutive extension of Dimock's weakness to anglophone modernism, where it gives rise not to the productive emergence of a diasporic plane but to the specter of the nihil at the center of the field. As Esposito observes, community has a "constitutively melancholic character" ("Melanconia" 81).[20] The original foundation of the *cum-munus* is not a center in a subject but a "being-in-the-world" that is an "inter-being" (Esposito, *Communitas* 91). Community, like language, represents the relation that defines the human condition: "a belonging to men's being with one another" (Heidegger qtd. in *Communitas* 91). All that exists coexists. The essence of existence is "with" (*Communitas* 93). Thus, community is impossible to make because it already is: "what human beings share is just this impossibility to 'make' the community that they already 'are,' which is to say the ecstatic opening that destines them to a constitutive lack" (*Communitas* 95). Such an opening can only be in the privative modality of Lacan's "manque à être" ("Melanconia" 80).[21] My point is that this analysis of community alters the modernist idea of modernity. Twentieth-century modernity meets us as the baffling nexus of the protection of life and its negation.[22] Modernity becomes "a historical and conceptual apparatus" (*Bíos* 52), the conceptual mechanism invented by the will to achieve community, that is to say, the illusion to identify the community with itself, to dress the wound and free community from its nothing ("Melanconia" 81). The *munus* of community, however, prohibits its achievement ("Melanconia" 85).[23]

The analysis of community enables us to posit "another modernity" (Esposito, *Pensiero vivente* 23). This other modernity is still connected with the notion of modernization and does not deny the "heuristic productivity" of the most familiar and consolidated models at the basis of modernist studies, such as rationalization and secularization (Esposito, *Bíos* 47),[24] but, within these more familiar models, it is shaped by a perspective that might seem temporally askew or anachronistic and anatopic but is, in fact, alternative to the post-Saussurean linguistic turn because it "has developed as a knowledge about life, about the body, about the world" (Esposito, "German Philosophy" 109).[25] I have dwelled at some length on the analysis of community because, through that route, we can begin to see that the phenomenon that goes by the name of "Italian Theory" marks both a continuity with and a departure from the Anglo-American reception of critique. It is a different kind of poststructuralism; a poststructuralism that moves at an eccentric pace.

"Italian Theory"

The phrase "Italian Theory" has emerged in recent years as a result of the influence of a cluster of Italian philosophers outside of their country of origin. This influence is manifest in a number of international conferences, the first of which took place in September 2010 at Cornell University, and in high-profile international publications, including two volumes of *Diacritics*.[26] At the 2014 international symposium in Paris, whose proceedings have been published in a volume called *Differenze italiane* (2015), participants actually wondered whether an "Italian Theory" really exists. Discussion outside Italy was followed by a conference in Naples (Institute of Philosophical Studies and Istituto di Scienze Umane), an international symposium at the University of Salerno (October 2015), and by a seminar in Pisa (Scuola Normale Superiore, January 2016). These events culminated in the constitution of a new research Network on Italian Thought and European Philosophies (Workiteph) in March 2016, later renamed Italian Thought Network (ITN). The Network's manifesto speaks of events that have resulted in a "new theoretical paradigm" (Italian Thought Network).

As mentioned in the Introduction, Esposito argues that "Italian Theory" makes apparent a movement of deterritorialization that has propelled European philosophies outside their boundaries ("German Philosophy" 105). The movement is relevant insofar as it no longer confines us to operating with concepts such as identities and nationalities but allows us to think in terms of the circulation of ideas. What has been called "Italian Theory" continues the movement of deterritorialization, but, when compared with the preceding waves, it adds a different emphasis: "The 'outside' that propels Italian Thought [the formula preferred by Esposito, and we shall see later why] is neither the social dimension of German Philosophy nor the textual dimension of French Theory, but the constitutively conflicting space of political practice" ("German Philosophy" 107). The difference does not mean that this wave of theory does not share with the previous waves an emphasis on language (Esposito, *Pensiero vivente* 7), but the question of language, therefore of its power to mediate experience, is "situated on a vaster horizon" (*Pensiero vivente* 10).

The question of the name is overdue here. Certainly one of the interesting traits of the new wave of theory is that its name comes from the outside, given, that is, within an anglophone context (Italian Theory is called by its English name even in Italy). It is, however, a strange name. At first sight, it might be taken to signal the unpleasant idea that thought has a nationality. The adjective of nationality in fact is there to do something. It retroactively makes past instances of theory—French Theory or German Critical Theory—sound strange: they call attention to the Anglo-American assimilation of bits of national traditions in the linear sequence called "Theory." Esposito seizes on the name "Italian Theory" to merge Theory with a vaster horizon. For this reason, he shifts to the phrase "Italian Thought," which, in turn, becomes "living thought."[27]

What Esposito calls "living thought" extends to an international tradition and englobes feminism.[28] It points to a line of reflection that "assumes the notion of life as its own semantic horizon" (Esposito, "German Philosophy" 108) and "understands life neither in a biological or metaphysical sense" but always "in relation and in tension with the categories of history and of politics" (Esposito, *Pensiero vivente* 32). When he proposes that the difference of living thought lies in its engagement of the "inadequacy of the linguistic horizon with regard to something that is irreducibly corporeal" (*Pensiero vivente* 10), Esposito re-energizes feminist thought, with its emphasis on embodied knowledge, but also psychoanalytic knowledge, which builds on the remarkable conjunction of the body and the experience of speech. What is labeled "Italian Theory" looks back favorably on these fundamental resources; it returns to them, and, from this point of view, it preserves the linguistic turn, while crucially shifting from the dominant paradigm of rupture to the other "paradigm of life" (*Pensiero vivente* 10). It is a shift in pace, in tonality, and it entails an idea of critique conceived as a movement of geographical and intellectual displacements, part of simultaneous and interconnected phenomena, among which we might include the regionalization of Europe, the relocation of America, and the postcolonial erosion of the unevenness of cultures.

As it is presented here, therefore, the narrative of Italian Theory interrogates the periodization of Theory to give expression to a line of reflection that has remained in the folds of poststructuralism, eccentric to it. At first, Esposito captures the difference with poststructuralism through tonality. He speaks of a thought with an affirmative tonality, in contrast with the negativity of German Critical Theory and the neutralization of French Theory.[29] Perhaps, however, the metaphor of the body in motion seems particularly felicitous, as when Esposito describes a thought that "steps along" differently, suggesting a style of moving and advancing (*assume una movenza*), almost in Gradiva-like fashion, that places this wave of theory in an "eccentric" relation to "analytic, hermeneutic and deconstructive philosophies" (*Da Fuori* 161).[30] Living thought simultaneously precedes and exceeds the linguistic turn and those thinkers that define themselves around the axis of language. This does not mean that it denies the linguistically mediated character of experience, but, in including the linguistic turn within the wider semantic horizon of life, it reshuffles the narrative of Theory to which we have been accustomed in the recent past.

A dynamic, self-transforming, ampler arch of reflection appears whose defining trait is a movement toward an outside "that is wider than a local or national one" (Esposito, *Pensiero vivente* 3). The shift from the paradigm of rupture to the paradigm of life implies this rotation of critique so that it consists neither in acts of unmasking and dismantling nor in the scrutiny of surfaces, but in an exit—in the expectation of an exit—in a vaster space where ideas appear in their force and novelty because they have been inaugurated somewhere else:

> As is often the case (in the circuit of ideas), what seems proper to a given conceptual horizon, determining the autonomy of that horizon, also comes from a labor of contamination and the result of strands of thought already inaugurated elsewhere but which only within the new tonal register can find the thematic stability and the descriptive (conceptual) force that are necessary to their appearance in a scenario that is much wider than a local or national one. (Esposito, *Pensiero vivente* 3)

New ideas do not appear against something; rather, they reach us from an uncertain elsewhere. They make sense, are given credit, and become valuable at a particular time, on certain conceptual horizons.

A latent body of thought becomes meaningful only belatedly. The most cogent example offered by Esposito is the reception of the biopolitical category, the life and power nexus identified by Foucault in the mid-1970s, which remained inactive for twenty years before acquiring conceptual force in the 1990s. Another example would be the one discussed at the beginning of this chapter, weak thought, which is reactivated twenty years later by the English translation and by Dimock's realignment of the critic with weakness. One of the effects of the label "Italian Theory" is to suggest a sort of theoretical lag, a "reserve" within poststructuralist thought (yet another summary label) that now acquires significance, a philosophical-critical body which seems to have remained inoperative but takes on transnational resonance belatedly, when it can be understood as particularly attuned to the "dynamics of globalization and immaterial production that are typical of the postmodern phase" (Esposito, *Pensiero vivente* 5).

Living thought

With the notion of living thought, Esposito retells the story of Theory, a term which stands for the transatlantic transmission of critique. Living thought suggests a line of reflection that never really begins, that has always been there, dormant. When it awakens, we find it already mixed with the logic of circulation described above, according to which ideas that seem "new" against certain conceptual horizons come, in fact, from strands of thought already at work elsewhere. There are similarities between Esposito's plane of circulation and Dimock's diasporic plane. Before specifying them, it is necessary to understand Esposito's notion. As anticipated in the Introduction to this book, the cultural plane of circulation is engendered by a different angle on modernity and on the central question of modernity: the new. We have addressed the question, directly and indirectly, through the types of indocility discussed in Chapter 1. Esposito uses the example of European philosophies to disentangle the appearance of the new from the logic of rupture. As mentioned in the Introduction, Esposito analyzes the production of new knowledge in European philosophies and concludes that this has been made possible by "the construction of a threshold—whether anthropological, epistemological, or institutional—which shelters from something primordial and constitutive, that cannot be governed by reason but instead threatens reason" (*Pensiero vivente* 24). He calls this "something primordial and constitutive," which is deferred but always returns aggressively, a "pre-reflexive magmatic substance" (*sostanza magmatica pre-riflessiva*) (24). It is sometimes identified with an "anthropic margin that is still too contiguous with the animal dimension" and, at other times, with the language of magic and myth (24). It is this magmatic pre-reflexive substance that he refers to as the "origin" from whose spectral returns the thinker must defend herself in search of new beginnings. (Esposito names Descartes and Hobbes as examples, but he might have included Adorno's negative dialectics, which is involved in the archaic anxiety emanating from ossified history and from conventions that have hardened into an unquestionable origin.) Thought becomes a matter of tonality, of affective shades, of kinetic possibilities, all related, in turn, to the possibility of displacing the immaterial force of a spectral origin. By cutting off the affective bond with the anxiety of a spectral origin, thought exits into the vaster dimension of a shared beneficial space: the outside. The outside is the plane of coevalness or of living thought. It is beneficial because, in alternative to rupture, "the origin is made available as a resource rather than something to be subjected to as if to a spectral return" (25). We begin to see that the question here is not to reject the hermeneutics of suspicion but rather a theoretical labor on the destructive element which finds its concrete expression in the critical gesture of reorienting it, so that interpretation may open to new meanings, in a "latent manner."[31]

Moreover, Esposito's plane of coevalness is beneficial in that it corresponds to a cross-temporal logic of circulation (*Pensiero vivente*). From this point of view, it might be said to bear similarity with Dimock's diasporic plane. Indeed, the two planes may be studied as an example of the contact between literature and philosophy. As we saw in an earlier section of this chapter, Dimock is of course specifically talking about literary texts and their readers, wishing to extend the reach of the texts and enlarge the circle of their readers through the tools of theory, that is to say, by connecting the text to a larger structure.[32] Unlike Dimock, of course, Esposito is concerned with the production of knowledge in the context of philosophy, but the production of knowledge within European philosophies happens to be a matter of concern for literary critics because Theory, as a transatlantic traffic of ideas, has mostly meant criticism's own assimilation of different philosophical traditions. Simultaneously, it has resulted in a questioning of the meaning of "theory," with the lower case, understood as critical method. The literary critic has developed a concern with the extent to which the concepts produced are used as models to understand a variety of differences. This *modus operandi*, as Toril Moi argues, reflects a standard notion of theory according to which the concepts produced "should be able to predict future cases, and have explanatory power" (69). Moi usefully offers the example of deconstruction and Jacques Derrida. She presents Derrida as a traditional philosopher with a classical understanding of concepts, a thinker who wants concepts to be "'scientific and rigorous'" and "have a sharp boundary" (Moi 68, 73). Derrida displays the indubitable capacity for creating new, previously unheard-of concepts, but his concepts all conform to the requirements of the standard model of theory. When Dimock's critic vacillates as she acknowledges the practice of a literary criticism transformed, over the arch of Theory, into "sovereign knowingness," she, like Moi, poses the problem of theory in the standard sense, as "a general account that can predict all anomalies, mistakes, misunderstandings in advance" (Moi 70). For Dimock's critic, weak theory means a withdrawal from theory in this sense. Withdrawal, however, cannot solve the problem of method, which concerns deciding what the best way of relying on concepts might be when deciphering individual literary works. Dimock's solution is to disperse texts on a diasporic plane which closely recalls Benjamin's intensive plane, where texts are in contact like so many monads in relation. And this, in Benjamin as in Dimock, gives rise to a critical discourse consisting in their reciprocal "consummation" (later echoed by Lefort's gift of the readers' thoughts to the texts). Esposito's plane of coevalness differs in that it introduces us to a different environment of thought where, as anticipated in Chapter 2, the logic of circulation seems indistinguishable from the logic of *méconnaissance*. The plane of coevalness (under the heading "Italian Theory") specifically thematizes the problem of temporalities, with occluded, eccentric lines of thought hosted in the folds of an ongoing critique, which can only fully emerge in the present. Critique becomes the style in which it moves; it becomes the problem of enabling conceptual horizons.

Moreover, the beneficial plane of coevalness does not have an argument with human history and human agency; it capitalizes on the past. Time folds. The past and the present become coeval. The exit in a vaster world causes the present to fold back onto the past and acknowledge what has developed in an eccentric relation to dominant concerns. Like the diasporic plane, the plane of coevalness takes stock of what Dimock calls the "invariance of power" ("Weak Theory" 734) in the fact that geography creates an order of ideas and invents their force, but it is more interested in ways of "feeling the historical" (Freeman, *Time Binds* 103). The phenomenon that has been labeled "Italian Theory," which slides into *pensiero vivente/* living thought, is contiguous to queer and postcolonial visions of time, as well as to postcritique. Queer Theory has a special interest in "how time wrinkles and folds" (Freeman, "Introduction" 163), while postcolonial scholars have described the feeling of "the overlapping, disadjusted, and noncontemporaneous nature of time," with its "whirls and eddies" bracketed in the folds of "a contemporaneity that carries along various things even as it is not fully cognizant of itself" (Aravamudan 347). For her part, Felski speaks of "[c]rosstemporal networks" that "mess up the tidiness of our periodizing schemes" and "force us to acknowledge affinity and proximity as well as difference, to grapple with the coevalness and connectedness of past and present" (*Limits* 159). These are all examples of an intervention on what Esposito would call the "chronological order of succession," and assume, as living thought does, that human history unfolds in a "multiplicity of times" (*Pensiero vivente* 27).

Esposito argues for the "structural absence" of a generative moment of history; the past can always be reactivated in a "latent manner" and is always "coeval" to any other historical moment (*Pensiero vivente* 25). When not reduced to time, history affords a theoretical openness; the thought process can include what does not seem historical, "the historicization of the non-historical" (27), or what appears at odds, awkward, or in contrast with historical and social orders, like corporeality for example (25). The relation to the past is grasped as "a structure of feeling," as Raymond Williams would say; it is made of intertwined cognitive and affective dimensions which sense the "opaque, semi-natural, historically intractable" aspect of chronological temporality (Esposito, *Pensiero vivente* 29). From this perspective the term "theory" (with lower case) changes meanings: it begins to refer less to the standard conceptual model that predicts future instances, and more to an ongoing renaming of concepts within an incessant process of recuperation and reparation.

This shift in meaning informs us that the problem of method remains central to the Humanities, for theory in the lower case, as Moi's discussion makes clear, bespeaks that very problem. It was Hans-Georg Gadamer who first cogently raised the question that in literary studies today Moi calls the question of reading. Gadamer saw the problem of assimilating the Humanities to the standard notion of theory borrowed from the sciences, and he spoke against this assimilation. In *Truth and Method* (1960) Gadamer details the attempts at assimilating what were once called the sciences of the spirit (*Geisteswissenschaften*) on the ground that the only valid method is that of the experimental or natural sciences, according to which it would be a matter of identifying "the uniformities, the regularities and the conformities to laws/rules that make possible to foresee (or predict) certain phenomena and processes" (26). He argues that the criterion of a surfacing of general laws cannot be applied to the Humanities. To the inductive procedure of the natural sciences, he opposes a "historical knowledge" whose aim, he writes, is not "to grasp the concrete phenomenon as a specific case for the general rule" (26). The singular individual case should not be used to validate a law or a model on the basis of which to comprehend other specific phenomena or processes. The aim of this knowledge, which Gadamer calls historical but concerns us as literary scholars insofar as we deal with literature over time (periodization), is rather, he proposes, "to understand the phenomenon itself in its unique and historical concreteness" (26–7). We will say more about Gadamer in Chapter 6, devoted to "Text and Method." Here I mention him because the historical knowledge that he proposes is somehow validated by Esposito's "living thought." In its guise as "Italian Theory," living thought both continues the movement of Anglophone Theory (disproving once again the death of Theory) and questions the standard notion of theory within the movement. Esposito uses the phrase "living thought" to affirm, besides the more properly philosophical critique of political theology ("German Philosophy" 110), an immanent plane and a certain predisposition to perceive what Gadamer would call "the singular individual case" and Esposito understands as the ways in which life exceeds fixed forms and rigid grids. As we shall see in the next sections, the plane of coevalness acts on the temporality of Theory, as well as on its assumed intimacy with the concept of modernism. It creates the effect of a movement forward and backward, which is more than a mere prosecution of Theory but re-envisions it as an ampler movement forged by the anachronism and anatopism that ensue from the notion of another modernity.[33]

Modernism/modernity

In Esposito's double-focused discussion of "Italian Theory," from the inside and from the outside, the activity of critique, more than originating somewhere, means the reawakening, within a given intellectual climate and geographical location, of concerns that have remained incompletely resolved in other intellectual-geographical locations. This is why Esposito uses the term "horizon" more than once and speaks of strands of thought that were already at work elsewhere and take on "thematic stability" and the necessary conceptual force only in "a new tonal register," in an "ampler context" (*Pensiero vivente* 3, 5). The plane of coevalness has an effect on the concepts that we employ. The "other" modernity, for example, calls directly into question the concept of modernism. Running "parallel and perpendicular" to the prevailing views of modernity, the "other" modernity keeps intact and vital the capacity for a "reversal of meaning" when the dominant view of modernity can no longer address the questions and conflicts out of which it had been forged in the first place (23). What Esposito calls the "other" modernity consists less in a set of contents and more in a perspective from which questions and problems "take on a different import and thus become available for a new interpretation" (24). The new interpretation concerns basic terms and methodological questions that extend to literary studies, with the relation of modernity/modernism in the forefront.

Susan Friedman once explained the meaning of modernism as follows:

> Modernism, for many, became a reflection of and engagement with a wide spectrum of historical changes, including intensified and alienating urbanization; the cataclysms of world war and technological progress run amok; the rise and fall of European empires; changing gender, class, and race relations; and technological inventions that radically changed the nature of everyday life, work, mobility, and communication. Once modernity became the defining cause of aesthetic engagements with it, the door opened to thinking about the specific conditions of modernity for different genders, races, sexualities, nations, and so forth. Modernity became modernities, a pluralization that spawned a plurality of modernisms and the circulations among them. ("Musing" 474)

Along these lines, our perception of modernity has been shaped by the Baudelaire–Benjamin axis, which privileges architecture, topography, memory, childhood, and history and, importantly, is associated with what Mauro Ponzi calls "the negative path of method" (201). In this tradition, Ponzi argues, method implies the cathartic role of evil: the "negative path means overcoming the lure of evil through the cathartic value of the indecent, the immoral, the transgressive" (201). In this view of modernism, technology and the mythological and archaic past are linked in the attempt to understand the new organization of labor (the assembly line) and the mechanization of tasks. This familiar narrative understands modernity as a "condition of the individual subjected to the shocks of the experience of the new who feels dislocated from nature and isolated in the labyrinth of the metropolis" (201). By contrast, Esposito proposes an alternative account in which modernity emerges as "the paradoxical project that wants to preserve life through power, denying precisely the vital power of life" (Bazzicalupo, *Biopolitica* 114). What becomes of modernism in this account? Especially, what becomes of modernism *and* the avant-garde in this account? The two names have been often pronounced in the same breath because each has the power to reinforce in the other a certain capacity to mean and amplify an explosion of vitality in language and in culture. What happens when we see them in relation to the repressive conceptual apparatus of modernity? The insight into modernity as a conceptual apparatus of "repressive self-preservation" (Bazzicalupo, *Biopolitica* 115) might cause us to re-evaluate some of the basic terms of a shared and cross-disciplinary lexicon. We have already looked at the example of community. In that case, the linguistic work reveals immunity to be the intimate essence of the postmodern condition, which then begins to display affinities with past accounts of the social tie.[34]

Thinkers of the postmodern condition like Jean-François Lyotard have upheld desire as the alternative to the mercantilist and economic logic of exchange (Lyotard, *Libidinal Economy*). In contrast with this construction of the postmodern, Italian Theory confronts head-on the confusion of desire—in the *longue durée* of modernism—with the anarchic autonomy of economic phenomena that shape people's lives in late modernity (Bazzicalupo, "L'economia" 26).[35] A configuration of individual vectors begins to emerge, each guided by his or her own interest, which brings into focus a specific object of research: life and how life manifests. Examining the configuration, Laura Bazzicalupo writes:

> Life manifests as movement, singular, concrete motivation directed toward its own satisfaction.... The inner direction of the movement is one and only one: it is interest, *desire*. Its pursuit by each and every living being constitutes the ontological premise of any economic work. Scarcity and lack no longer inhere to the world out there, but become constitutive of subjects: it is hunger, hunger for eudaimonia. This desire—the same libidinal principle at work in Foucault's notion of subjection, or in Freud's notion of psyche, as well as in the social movements of the 1960s and 1970s—is the new empirical dimension of bios. The dimension of life is the mechanism of drives in movement toward self-realization, eudaimonia ... ("L'economia" 27)[36]

In the scenario of "subjective vectors, guided by instrumental logic," constituted by the "spontaneous intersection" of "flows of desires" and by an interweaving of "immanent powers," relationality is no longer necessary; neither is empathy, since they are not functional: "There is no common aim: the only measure of value is individual subjectivity, always different, always anarchic" (Bazzicalupo, "L'economia" 27). The isolated singularities, each pursuing his or her libidinal vectors, suggest that Hobbes's state of mutual appropriation and suppression of goods and lives keeps hovering in the background of our present, in the fashion of an archaic aggression that insists in modernity (Bazzicalupo, *Biopolitica* 113). The archaic threat only amplifies Esposito's notion of the "other" modernity. From his vantage point, for example, the phenomenon of "hypertrophic virtual communication" connected with globalization might be read as the sign of a generalized immunization in a way that continues, without simplifying it, Rovatti's argument against cultural surfaces and for the need for recognition in regimes of externalization while problematizing Steven Shaviro's celebration of surfaces and the assumption that nothing is hidden.[37]

Amor vitae (Life vs. Form)

I have suggested that the paradoxical project of modernity—preserving life by denying its vital power—raises questions about the concept of modernism. In this final section I propose that living thought encourages literary scholars to consider the beauty and appeal of modernist forms in conjunction with their questionable fascination with grids, repression, and rigidification (Sontag, *Consciousness* 495).[38] Esposito himself turns to a modernist literary critic, Adriano Tilgher (1890–1941), whose reflection centers around the "radical conflict" between Life and Form. Tilgher, as we shall see in this section, enables the philosopher to specify an affirmative strand of critique, which must deal with life as something "undifferentiated": "a force that exceeds the limits of any economy" (Esposito, *Da Fuori* 165).

Tilgher was the first to appreciate Pirandello's drama, and he drew on the writer to elaborate his critical poetics based on the Life–Form polarity (Tilgher, "Teatro").[39] For Tilgher, the polarity is inherent in the notion of life: life oscillates between flow and stasis, between becoming and form, in the metaphysical sense of form as something finite and concrete, different from the aesthetic meaning of form as something fixed and rigid. His positions differed from those of his more renowned contemporaries, especially Croce, who had argued that art entertains an intuitive and cognitive relation to its object. Croce's aesthetic theories were rife with Hegelian influences. Unlike Croce, Tilgher takes art outside the dialectical setting, and defines artistic experience as "immanent life," as "productive activity" that stands in open conflict with lived life.[40] Art opposes life; it is a type of productivity that exceeds the aesthetic meaning of form and neither can it be contained within the Life–Form dialectic. As Tilgher argues in *Estetica* (1931), art is a special productivity, sufficient unto itself, and "rests in its own immobility": "it is there because it is there" (Tilgher qtd. in Faraone 265).[41] This does not mean that art negates life, quite the contrary. The special productivity is a *sui generis* kind of life that Tilgher calls *amor vitae*. If lived life is dominated by object love ("amor rei"), which makes us lean toward the outside and destines us to a structural lack without end, aesthetic productivity is *amor vitae*, love without object: it elects life to be its own sole object. In the same 1931 treatise on aesthetics mentioned above, Tilgher rejects the idealistic confusion of art and life and defines aesthetic life as *forma formante*, a productivity that "engenders its content and does not presuppose it as given" (Tilgher qtd. in Faraone 266). In a later work, *Il casualismo critico* (1942), he would apply this formula to thought itself. Thought is "activity, potentiality, energy" (Tilgher qtd. in Faraone 283).

A look in Tilgher's archive will reveal among his influences the Spinoza–Nietzsche axis. With the interesting addition of the American philosopher Emerson, these influences emphasize the plane of immanence that catalyzes his interests. In one of his articles on Nietzsche, Tilgher translates his notion of *amor vitae* with the German philosopher's term "affirmation": "He has seen very well that art is 'essentially the affirmation, the benediction, and celebration of existence,' or, as I prefer to say, life that loves itself, taking joy in its own pure vital rhythm."[42] Tilgher's notion of a *sui generis* productivity is akin to Nietzsche's idea of aesthetic life, a state of "potentiality, of ascending force, therefore of pleasure and joy."[43]

Recovering Tilgher, Esposito annexes to the third wave of Anglophone Theory the modernist critic's "subterranean fire that englobes all determinations and negations" (*Da Fuori* 165). Tilgher's Life–Form opposition is raised to an example of living thought, the alternative line of reflection eccentric to the linguistic turn.[44] The modernist's living principle "that has neither aim nor end" and exceeds "the fixity of forms" (166) becomes the trace of "a bios that cannot be contained within artificial limits" (*bios che non si lascia imprigionare dai limiti artificiali*) (165).

The recourse to Tilgher illuminates an important aspect of living thought: like weak thought, it is unwilling to get rid of the notion of the subject. What Esposito means by "living thought" emphasizes the intersection of being, life, and history, with the subject firmly planted at that intersection, in a dimension that is no longer dominated by the unavoidable polarity of positions (subject/object) but resembles a dynamic achievement. A different figure advances, in another kind of relation to the world. The movement and the pose are affirmative, captured in Tilgher's formula *amor vitae*, which suggests "an equilibrium and a serenity that the confrontation with the world does not allow for" (Faraone 269).⁴⁵

Tilgher's *amor vitae* of course could not be further from Adorno's critical theory and suggests a different affective scenario for critique. If we take as an example Adorno's much-quoted essay on "The Culture Industry: Enlightenment as Mass Deception," co-authored with Horkheimer and discussed in Chapter 1, we realize that the central event in that essay is the rise of the subject *as* form. The seamless continuum of "represented world and everyday perception" matches the equally seamless continuum of interiority and cultural production. Individual consciousness transforms into the reified consumer (Adorno and Horkheimer, "Culture Industry" 99), and the two poles of the particular and the universal "touch": they "become a murky identity in which the general can replace the particular and vice versa" (102). The essay maps the closure of an imaginative and intellectual terrain as two poles without distance become substitutive models for one another. The closed space inaugurates the rise of the subject as substitutive model as well, the subject as fixed form or grid. It is this event that engenders a new breed of thinker, the critical theorist, who shifts the attention to unheard, suppressed life (137), to life "made indistinguishable" from its cultural production (99). However, the fact that subjectivity becomes formulaic does not mean that it should be discarded; it rather prompts the thinker to walk unbeaten paths.

In Tilgher (and Esposito), the figure of a subject turned toward the world does not exclude the linguistically mediated texture of existence. If anything, Tilgher stresses the symbolic factor when he thinks of life and the instability of meaning as two intertwined concepts: language is shaken, he writes, by "the inner tumult of life."⁴⁶ The example of Esposito's recourse to Tilgher informs us that "Italian Theory" does attempt to name something different from the linguistic turn (*Da Fuori* 216). It attempts to address the incompleteness of language-centered thought with its shadow areas, one of which regards the tension between Life and Form. "Italian Theory" extends this tension to the literary debate, but in doing so it also causes Theory to fold back. A prime modernist motif, the conflict between Life and Form creates something like a "temporal modernism" within the established narrative of Theory, by which I mean an incomplete temporality of occlusions that manifest in the disorienting gaps of the theoretical temporalities of the present.⁴⁷ Chapter 5 will begin to consider the effects of these uneven theoretical temporalities. Before we get there, I would like to use the next chapter, Chapter 4, to expand on the eccentricity of Italian Theory with regard to the linguistic turn by focusing on the return to Saussure and the reformulation of the problem of language.

Notes

1. Virno, *Grammatica della Moltitudine* 19. Hereafter abbreviated as *GM*. All translations are mine. For the English version, see Virno, *Grammar*.
2. On the "rhetorical bonding" between authors and readers, see Booth, *Rhetoric*, and "My Life." On Booth, see chapter 8, "Literary Criticism and Rhetorical Invention: Wayne C. Booth's and Stephen Greenblatt's Marvelous Possessions," of Olmsted (116–26).
3. On the notion of "discursive community," see Fish.
4. Pardis Dabashi is quoting the authors of the *Ferrante Letters*, returning to or reminding us of the vocation of theory or critique as expressed by Jameson.
5. In *Truth and Method* (*Warheit und Methode*, 1960), Gadamer helps us see that thinking about method means thinking about the construction of the Humanities. This point will be discussed later on in this chapter, while discussion of Gadamer's work will be resumed in Chapter 6.
6. The problem of the field of cultural production has concerned early theorists of the avant-garde who grappled with the question of the inclusion of an individual aesthetic object in a series while keeping the order or the series dynamic and doing justice to the "singularity of the real and the uniqueness of the concrete" (Poggioli 283).
7. All translations from Rovatti, "Trasformazioni nel corso dell'esperienza" are mine.
8. In Rita Felski's *The Limits of Critique*, Nietzsche's snake is displaced by Latour's ANT, but both the snake and the "ant" serve to delimit an arch of critique that closely interrogates the link between thought and reality.
9. Building on the position of Rovatti, Giorgio Agamben, in the section "Schechina" of *The Coming Community*, talks of the entire transformation of politics and social life into "a spectacular phantasmagoria," with "mercantile economy acceding to an absolute and irresponsible sovereignty over social life" involving everything, including communication (65). Agamben moves beyond the analytic instruments of Marxism to point out that the question today is not only the "expropriation of our productive activity" but also "the alienation of language itself," of "the linguistic and communicative" nature of the human (64).

10. See Eve Kosofsky Sedgwick's influential essay "Paranoid Reading and Reparative Reading, or, You're So Paranoid, You Probably Think This Introduction is About You."
11. This notion has assumed an even greater centrality in Italian Theory with Paolo Virno's critique of the poststructuralist sovereignty of language. For Virno, language destroys an impersonal prelinguistic area of biological empathy. This aggressive labor on the human subject is illustrated by his research on negation; language accounts for our anthropological disposition, Virno argues, to deny the other. In propositions like "This is not a man," or "This is not a human being," the structural element "not" illustrates the radical human capacity to deny the recognition of another human. After Virno's work, Rovatti's investment in recognition seems to increase (rather than decrease) in relevance (Virno, *Saggio*).
12. Thus opens Paul Saint-Amour's "Weak Theory, Weak Modernism": "*Weakness*: not a word that would seem, at first blush, to have anything to say to modernism" (437).
13. An important text in the debate on community is an article co-written by Philippe Lacoue-Labarthe and Jean-Luc Nancy, "La Panique Politique." Although the volume came out in English in 1997, the materials included originally appeared in 1979, 1981, and 1983. Nancy himself first commented on the consequences for literary studies when he sketched a theory of literature whose fulcrum is no longer resistance but, as he puts it, "the courage of interruption," which "consists rather in daring to be silent . . . in *allowing to be said* something that no one—no individual, no representative—could ever say" (*Inoperative Community* 80; original emphasis). Nancy's courage of course echoes Rovatti's modesty.
14. I am working with the Italian edition, *Terza persona*, and all translations from it are mine; for the English edition, see Esposito, *Third Person*.
15. See also Agamben, *Homo Sacer* 1998.
16. Lisciani-Petrini places Esposito in dialogue with Gilles Deleuze and Gilbert Simondon.
17. I am working with the Italian edition, *Bíos: Biopolitica e filosofia*, and all translations from it are mine; for the English edition, see Esposito, *Bios: Biopolitics and Philosophy*.
18. See the 1979–80 course at the Collège de France published as Foucault, *The Birth of Biopolitics*.
19. All translations from Bazzicalupo, *Biopolitica* are mine.
20. All translations from Esposito, "*Melanconia e comunità*" are mine.
21. In *Communitas*, Esposito writes: "The community isn't before or after society. It isn't what society has suppressed, nor the goal that society has to place before itself. In the same way, community isn't the result of a pact, of a will, or of a simple demand that is shared by individuals,

nor is it the archaic site from which these individuals originate and then abandon for the simple fact that there are no individuals outside their being-in-a-common-world" (92).
22. The nexus between the protection of life and its negation is exemplified in its extreme variant by the Nazi camps of World War II.
23. The prime figure of community remains language, which Esposito, following Heidegger, sees not as the figure of a relation to something but as the figure of relation itself, "a cum-munus" whose original foundation is not a center in a subject but presents itself as a "being-in-the-world," that is, an "inter-being" (*Communitas* 91).
24. Esposito mentions three models: "'rationalization' (Weber), 'secularization' (Löwith) or 'legitimation' (Blumenberg)" (*Bíos* 47).
25. To clarify for my readers, let me offer an example once again taken from my research for my previous book, on Susan Sontag. While researching in her archive, I found that she was in conversation with the most influential theorists of her time, from Jameson to Derrida, from Lacan to Deleuze and Foucault, but she did so with the mediation of Benjamin, treating Benjamin as the theorist of *her* time, as her contemporary, and thus appearing "off" with regard to the phenomenon of "Theory." At the time, I talked of an "unwritten theory" and meant by that an angle of vision that is in conversation yet withdrawn.
26. The conference held at Cornell, 24–5 September 2010, was entitled "Commonalities: Theorizing the Common in Contemporary Italian Thought." See *Contemporary Italian Thought*.
27. As we shall see in the rest of this chapter, Esposito embraces the logic of circulation, which implies that thought has no nation. At the same time, it would be wrong to ignore the potential nationalist leanings that might inhere in something called "Italian Theory" or "Italian Thought." As I research the field, I am made nervous by discussions of "italianità" whenever they crop up. The notion itself of an "Italian difference" may be strategic and, as such, productive in the process of understanding the development of theory over time, but remains questionable. For work that has a productive angle on these concerns, see Claverini, especially chapter 2 on the work of Bertrando Spaventa, who theorized the non-national core of Italian philosophy, understanding Italian thought within the logic of the circulation of ideas, and chapter 5, on Esposito and Italian Thought. By the same author, see also "Localizzare il pensiero. Filosofia italiana e migrazione delle idee."
28. It has been observed that "Italian Theory" names a thought of immanence that unties Spinoza from Nietzsche, and both from Deleuze and Foucault (Gentili and Stimilli).
29. The term "affirmative" refers to a new ontology that shifts the focus from resistance, conceptualized in the negative, to creativity. Thus, Bazzicalupo speaks of "the affirmative quality of creating, recreating

and transforming situations, and being actively involved in the process" so that "life and the living become matter that resists and creates new forms of life" (*Biopolitica* 92).
30. I am working with the Italian edition, *Da Fuori*, and all translations from it are mine; for the English edition, see Esposito, *From the Outside*.
31. Esposito's "living thought" is not exactly a tradition, although in *Pensiero vivente* he offers compelling readings of Italian thinkers, including Vincenzo Cuoco and Giacomo Leopardi.
32. See my discussion of theory in the sense of Judith Butler and Simon During in Chapter 1.
33. I would like to recall the centrality of Walter Benjamin in this redrawing of modernity. One of the key texts is Benjamin's "On the Concept of History," previously known as "Theses on the Philosophy of History," with its critique of the notion of time as "a flat plane on which events march forward in sequence" (Freeman, "Introduction" 163). This other modernity is shared by different disciplinary areas. Here I will limit myself to mentioning the examples of Queer Studies and Postcolonial Studies. Benjamin has inspired Elizabeth Freeman's "queer vision of how time wrinkles and folds" ("Introduction" 163). At a roundtable on queer temporalities, speaking as a scholar of medieval author Margery Kemp, Carolyn Dinshaw said: "I'm yet another subject of anachronism, experiencing a kind of expanded now in which past, present and future coincide" (Dinshaw et al. 190). Similarly, following up on Benjamin, postcolonial theorist Homi Bhabha has argued that history seen as the teleology of time "tips over into the 'timeless' discourse of irrationality" (Freeman, "Introduction" 163).
34. For example, the "natural state of mutual annihilation and appropriation of life and goods," which political philosopher Thomas Hobbes used to justify the institution of a transcendent power (sovereign power) (Bazzicalupo, *Biopolitica* 113).
35. In "L'economia come logica di governo," Bazzicalupo explains it in terms of the passage from classical economy (Smith, Ricardo, Marx), which was not yet a form of government, to the anarchic autonomy of economic phenomena which governs people in late modernity (26).
36. All translations from Bazzicalupo, "L'economia come logica di governo" are mine.
37. See the Introduction to this book.
38. A similar insight into modernism's excessive preoccupation with form led Australian art critic Bernard Smith to coin the term "formalesque" (*Formalesque*).
39. For a fascinating account of the mutual influence that Pirandello and Tilgher exerted on each other, see Tilgher, "Le estetiche di Luigi Pirandello." I have read the text of this essay from the proofs in Tilgher's archive.

40. National Central Library of Rome, A.R.C. 9. E. III. 1, Archivio Tilgher, early writings on aesthetics (1911), autograph page (Page B); my translation. Tilgher discusses his affiliation to and difference from Croce's philosophy in "Immagine e sentimento nell'opera d'arte."
41. All translations from Faraone, *Adriano Tilgher* are mine.
42. "L'ultima estetica di Nietzsche," National Central Library of Rome, A.R.C. 9. E. VI. 1, Archivio Tilgher, "Studi di poetica," proofs with autograph corrections, p. 66. See Tilgher, "L'ultima estetica di Nietzsche," in *Studi*, 177–83 (179; my translation).
43. "L'ultima estetica di Nietzsche," National Central Library of Rome, A.R.C. 9. E. VI. 1, Archivio Tilgher, "Studi di poetica," proofs with autograph corrections, p. 66. See Tilgher, "L'ultima estetica di Nietzsche," in *Studi*, 177–83 (179; my translation).
44. In *Adriano Tilgher: Tra idealismo e filosofie della vita*, Rosella Faraone has been careful to distinguish his living principle from the currents of irrational vitalism that held Italy and Europe in their grip, especially in the early decades of the twentieth century (267). Esposito's return to Tilgher confirms this; however, Antonio Negri, in a review of *Da Fuori*, assimilates Esposito's argument to the horizon of vitalism and accuses him of not moving beyond the "rhetorical proclamation of vitality" (n.p.; my translation) See Esposito's reply, "Il sintomo".
45. Esposito, as we have seen, had drawn on Benveniste before; here there is a spatial and dynamic dimension to the new figure that recalls the affirmative pose of Benveniste's subject before the world, a speaker who steps forth "to situate himself ... in relationship to the world" (Sebeok 227). Despite their difference, both thinkers—Benveniste and Tilgher—insist on a human figure turned toward the world whose motion bespeaks well-being. Moreover, Esposito's notion of the "impersonal" bears the stamp of Tilgher's dissident vocabulary. Tilgher defines reality as a "universe of living beings" with each as "a peculiar tonality" of the same transindividual vital principle (Faraone 283).
46. "Inesprimibilità," National Central Library of Rome, A.R.C. 9 E. VI. 1, Archivio Tilgher, "Studi di poetica," proofs with autograph corrections. See Tilgher, *Studi* 268–9, 268; my translation.
47. I am adapting Elizabeth Freeman's idea of "temporal drag." As for the Life–Form conflict being a prime modernist motif, see Tonning 8.

Chapter 4

Language: The Return to Saussure

Overview

In the previous chapter we went through Esposito's analysis of community. We saw that it was instrumental in overcoming an oppositional analytical framework mainly rooted in the primary combat-like confrontation of self and other. In its turn, the analysis of community made possible the sense of an exit in a world that is much vaster than the local or national dimension and encouraged us to think of culture in terms of a logic of circulation. This chapter expands on the principal figure of community: language. It will examine the consequences of the analysis of community on the dominant idea of language. The idea of language that has prevailed in the twentieth century and has climaxed with the phenomenon of poststructuralism establishes the centrality of language: language, it is assumed, always mediates experience. Following a parallel line of investigation, which to some extent converges with the ideas of Émile Benveniste, Esposito stresses that in the twentieth century, language became the dwelling of being understood in the non-metaphysical sense of being-with (Benveniste 223; Esposito, *Communitas* 88). As we saw in Chapter 3, Esposito shows that this being-with is the condition of community, and making community shows the latter's impossibility, or chronic melancholia, since we always exist as *cum*, bound to each other by a simultaneous gift and obligation from which we defend ourselves. In this sense, community is impossible because it is experienced as a lack in common. Given the impossibility of making community, and given, too, the status of language as the main figure of the human community, one might ask whether any form of well-being is lodged in language. This chapter enlists the return to Saussure, especially through the work of Paolo Virno, to explore this question. The inquiry will lead us to formulate the notion of language as attachment.

The chapter's aim is to try to illuminate the notion of a beneficial resource in language that subtends our attachment to it. Building on Virno's return to Saussure, I glimpse in the background of Saussure's theory the figure of the accepting receiver that poses the question of a beneficial part-taking stored in language. But taking cognizance of a beneficial resource in language will mean coming face to face with the twin question of the many: the question of human multiplicity. In the work of Virno and of Jean-Luc Nancy this motif will appear as an incomplete modernist motif. While not arguing that modernism amounts to a return to Saussure, this chapter proposes that the return to Saussure in contemporary thought entails a view of language that departs from the poststructuralist view, a fact that has consequences for the concept of modernism and for the intimate tie between modernism and critique. Lingering on in contemporary theory, further enhanced in thinkers like Virno and Nancy, the modernist motif of the many reveals the split temporalities of critique mentioned in our discussion of Italian Theory in Chapter 3. Freed from the poststructuralists, Saussure appears as a modernist thinker for the present, and this prompts us to rethink further what we mean when we speak of the intimate tie of modernism and theory, with the re-reading of Saussure offering a good example of disconnected temporalities blind to each other but also collaborating with each other.

Euēmeria: the natural delight of ur-attachments

We are inclined to believe that language belongs to everyone; we are not mistaken since language is a common good. There are moments when we realize that being able to use something common brings a temporary but irresistible sense of well-being. The prospect of a similar kind of well-being also appears whenever we think about language. This might be because, as Paolo Virno observes, speaking, like breathing or living, is an action in itself without aim; even though we may think of language as a means of communication, a mistaken assumption already refuted by Benveniste (224), we do not speak, as Virno reminds us, "because we have found out that the use of language is advantageous; just as we do not live because we think that life is useful" (*Quando* 18).[1] Drawing on the musical metaphor used by Saussure, who compared language to a symphony, Virno thinks of the language user as a performer before a score, with the difference that the speaker's "paradoxical score" is the potential to speak (25). Virno distinguishes two types of potential-score: the historical-natural language and the faculty of language. Here, we will be focusing on the second, what Virno calls the "faculty-score," which manifests in the simple verbal action itself, in breaking silence, in the fact that one speaks (26). This potential for language is given and received; it is an endowment at the disposal of the human species, that is to say, something in common. In this sense, speech comes to us with an affirmative feeling, with a sense of well-being that may account for our attachment to language.

If language as a faculty-score, like breathing and living, unites all human beings without distinction, we can begin to think of it as an attachment along the lines of the basic kind of attachment that Aristotle discusses in relation to life. In *Politics*, he distinguishes between *bios* and *zoē*. Both terms mean "life," but while the first refers to the social life of the public and political sphere, the second comprises the mere life of all living beings, not only humans but also animals and other creatures. It is therefore the simplest and most basic meaning of life, yet he observes that most men cling to mere living as if there were in it a kind of gladness or natural sweetness (*euēmeria*):

> It was said in our initial discourses, where household management and mastery were discussed, that man is by nature a political animal. Hence [men] strive to live together even when they have no need of assistance from one another, though it is also the case that the common advantage brings them together, to the extent that it falls to each to live finely. It is this above all, then, which is the end for all both in common and separately; but they also join together, and maintain the political partnership, for the sake of living itself. For there is perhaps something fine in living just by itself, provided there is no great excess of hardships. It is clear that most men will endure much harsh treatment in their longing for life, the assumption being that there is a kind of joy inherent in it and a natural sweetness (Aristotle Bk. 3, sec. 1728b, 94)

Even though mere life is the rawest form of life, Aristotle suggests that it be considered political because we make community around it through our attachment to it. Something similar might be said for the faculty of language. We experience the same simple delight, the same kind of sweetness in the potential of using and partaking in something in common, something in which everyone else partakes.[2] We may think, for example, of the most basic conventions of politeness, like salutation formulae—"good morning," "hello"—as the most ordinary manifestation of that simple delight at partaking. We cling to language as if it held something beneficial in reserve.[3] Hannah Arendt was perhaps thinking of a beneficial attachment to language when she wrote of Rahel Varnhagen and her quest for "the great opportunity to confide ... in language" (*Rahel* 248), and in *The Human Condition*, Rahel's confidence translates into the possibility to "make [our] appearance explicitly" (199).

In the previous chapter, we have seen how the debt or obligation (*munus*) lodged at the heart of community (*cum-munus*) implies a mechanism of preservative defense that places each in relation to the other. The preservative defense concerns those faculties and potentialities that, while seeming more than mere life, might be defined, with Eric Fromm, "essential attributes" of the human: attributes, as Fromm puts it, that "belong to man qua man" (76). Like Virno, Fromm affirmed that these attributes include language (and thought): "reason ... and the capacity for symbol making" (76).[4] Can language, as a faculty-score or essential species attribute, counteract the mechanism of preservative defense? Can it resist the repression of life that, according to Esposito, inheres in community?

Esposito's line of argument suggests that language may be the principal figure of community, but it is also eccentric to it. As an example of this eccentricity we might point to the awkward transaction with the having mode. Language and the verb "to have" do not agree well. One can have a good knowledge of a language, a good mastery of linguistic skills, but one cannot really be said "to have language." Language—through its concrete specification in a plurality of language*s*—asks the question of having not in terms of a possessing but in terms of a proximity, a fact that psychoanalysis understands. In the analytic situation, the two agents, the analysand and the analyst, enact a being-in language that is simultaneously a being-with language, a co-substantiality effectively rendered by Lacan's word *parlêtre* (speaking-being). The coinage indicates that being does not disappear in speaking, but they are joined; it reminds us that language is a condition shared by everyone. For Lacan, language is like a used coin that is passed from hand to hand, but not with anyone's particular gain. This means that, in its manifestation as speech, language is a common good in which everyone can partake.[5] In fact, it is only through *a* used coin (because we can only use a language at a time), that we can give a presentation of ourselves, that we can make ourselves known, or, as we might say, let ourselves be acknowledged. When Lacan says that "there is no speech without a reply" ("Function" 40), this also means the fact of something reaching us, finding us, on our end. Something is given to us. Thus, we might say that we have something through speech, but this having mode amounts only to the simple potentiality of speaking; it amounts, in Virno's lexicon, to the mere potentiality (*mera potenza*) of the most generic performer before the most generic of scores (*Quando* 25). One of the most fascinating features of language of course is that it admits proximity to this mere potentiality. Most of us would undergo all sorts of troubles to experience the part-taking in that proximity. In itself, it becomes a common good, and a sense of well-being in reserve.

Yet, taking cognizance of this beneficial resource in language means coming face to face with the question of the many, the problem of human multiplicity. This will be the topic of the next section.

The many

> A crowd flowed over London Bridge, so many
> I had not thought death had undone so many.
> T. S. Eliot, *The Waste Land*

The fall of the myth of community in contemporary theoretical and critical discourse results in heightened attention to the problem of plurality understood as the sense of our place in a multiplicity of others. Esposito's analysis informs us that this experience of plurality is unavoidable, but also that it is necessarily melancholic, based on a shared lack. The fall of the myth of community imagined as a wider subjectivity, as a communion of individuals forming a whole held together by a common will, foregrounds the exigency of thinking the sense of "being-with." The question arises of "what holds us in common" beyond, that is, those social rites, values, and identities around which we bond politically (Butler, *Undoing Gender* 35). The problem of plurality, the realization that there are many of us in the world, and, above all, the urgency surrounding this realization, is not new of course. It constitutes the experience of modernity for canonical writers like T. S. Eliot. Eliot's crowd is an example of the many. The image is especially meaningful because it encapsulates the unique pursuit of a thinker who, having started out in philosophy, turns to poetry in the hope of better attuning himself to the shadowy existence of the individuals forming the many. What is striking is that Eliot's concern with the many returns in our time, manifested through the same mixture of bafflement and wonder that one hears in his poetry. It is as if the many were an incomplete strand of thought. This impression is particularly strong in one of the most original responses to the structuralist revolution, Jean-Luc Nancy's *Corpus* (1992). *Corpus* reads like the intellectual diary of an author who awakens to the reality of the many: "the exposed body of the world's *population*" (13; original emphasis). The world's many demand that we redefine language and thought; names need to be found; kinds of writing need to be invented.

Nancy takes stock of the world after transnationalism: "a world that is no longer 'international' but something else" (*Corpus* 41). The salient note here is that this world-as-something else affords one the impression of having finally exited *in the world*. It is interesting to notice that the expression used by Nancy to describe the exit in the world experienced as a vaster world, "a word-wide world," does not depart too drastically from Eliot's modernist "many"; rather, it is as if Nancy's "world-wide world" uncannily picked up from Eliot to reintroduce the problem of the many, marking it, as one might mark or underline the words or sentences of an author when reading: "in the world bodies multiply more and more" (9). Eliot's crowd, forged in Dante's classical fire, translates into Nancy's "prodigious press of bodies" (41). The problem of the many changes the meaning of "world": it is now a "place of real extensions," the place of "the spacing of our bodies" (41). When the world is revealed as the "press" of bodies and the "spacing" of bodies, what does it mean to see a body? To see a body is not to penetrate a mystery; it is to see, writes Nancy, a *"naked image"* that is foreign "to any interpretation" (47; original emphasis). But the return of the unfinished modernist motif of the crowd in Nancy's bodies is linked to the particular problem of the limits of language. Nancy's concern is to prevent the body from disappearing under the weight of signs ("signifying imprints"), reduced to a texture of signs, to a semantic vesture (51). *Corpus* rejects the structuralist concept of the sign, claiming that it has "ex-written" the body, expelling the body in advance from any writing.[6] To this end, he proposes that interpretation—("deciphering") (47)—be replaced by touch, while the displacement of time by space stresses "the body endlessly multiplied" (9). How to think the non-thinking and unthinkable "hard strangeness of this *body*" (17; original emphasis)? Where others would probably talk of a planetary turn or of multitudes, Nancy prefers to attend to the fact of the world becoming larger: an "areality" of bodies (43).

It should be remarked that Nancy's thinker is turned toward the world. In other words, he assumes the posture that is reputed as most desirable in contemporary critical discourse (including postcritique), but, in that posture, he does not see, like William James and Alfred North Whitehead, favored by the realists and by the speculative philosophers, a buzzing democracy of relations; neither does he see, like Parmenides, "the well-rounded Truth" nor, like the stoics and Marcus Aurelius, the "external world," with "the most tenuous and minute texture of things."[7] He sees what Paolo Virno calls the "social and political existence of the many as many" (*GM* 10). And he stays as close as possible to that problem. His example demonstrates that, as Virno argues, the motif of the many, far from being a thing of the past, "*persists as such* on the public scene," in a form that "is permanent rather than episodic or interstitial" (*GM* 10; original emphasis).

When we look at the modernist past, we find that for Eliot and his colleagues, turning to the world meant what Vladimir Jankélévitch grasps as a perilous oscillation between ipseity and "almost-nothing" (*Il non-so-che*). Standing before a gray ocean of interchangeable others, Jankélévitch sees a vast aphonic space that persists before language and conceptuality. Both Eliot and Jankélévitch see what Nancy, after them, would call an "areality." Nancy's "areality" resembles the modernists' desert of broken correspondences, of delays and missed occasions, of deferred recognition, of misrecognition, of recognition turned into anachronism. Jankélévitch offers the example of Golaud and Mélisande: a fraction of a second would be enough, and they would never meet. What is brought to the fore is the mystery of the occurrence, the instant of an aleatory coincidence and convergence of factors combined into an availability to receive something gratuitously given (Jankélévitch, *Music* 125): "Da/Datta: What have we given?" writes Eliot in *The Waste Land* (*Complete Poems* 74). We are all turned into so many hunters of the occurrence, of the propitious occasion, proposes Jankélévitch. Eliot's and Jankélévitch's version of the vaster world has an effect on ideas of the human subject. It prepares the transition from the notion of a subject forged in abstract thought, in that face-to-face that is the battle of self and other (via Hegel and via linguistic theory and the dialogic I–you), to a third person that remains external to the plane of interlocution (*Terza persona* 141). The aphonic space of others creates the precondition for the appearance of Esposito's impersonal, the impersonal and acephalus third that replaces the pronouns "he" or "she." Quoting Jankélévitch, Esposito defines the third as "a person without a face," "a person that is a non-person," an absent one excluded "from any and every affective, imperative or aggressive allocution" (Jankélévitch qtd. in Esposito, *Terza persona* 144).[8] Like Esposito's impersonal, the modernist many overshadow the world and shape our relation to language and thought as always incomplete. Jankélévitch speaks of an insistent "invisible presence," "inexplicably absent," that seems the only thing worth saying but remains before the threshold of language, in the region of wonder and exclamation (*Music* 5).

In an extraordinary piece, originally published in 1969, "From Moby Dick to the White Bear," writer Anna Maria Ortese (1914–98) follows up on Jankélévitch's atmospheres. She associates the many with a "great sadness" (*tristezza grande*). Like Jankélévitch, Ortese introduces us to the question of bodies through the image of a vastness "full of noise, but simultaneously taciturn, unknown to the Word" (99).[9] Her observer recalls Adorno's individual in the culture industry, which Ortese translates with the phrase the "triumph of the useful" (*trionfo dell'utile*) (98): he is anxious to rebel against the "false security of associated life" (100). Ortese takes her protagonist to the edge of the sea on a typical summer day and stills him in a pose of wonder, expectation, and surprise (reading her, one is put in mind of Carpaccio's two women on a Venetian *altana*) at a world of multiplying bodies: "What multitude of bodies, everything is body, only body, immobilized body" (101).[10]

Our examples all wonder about human plurality, and in so doing they raise the question: How to imagine others? Their wonder calls attention to the fact that the term "others," as Elaine Scarry argues, should not be reduced to the singular ("other"), but understood in the sense of a true plurality. In the Introduction to this book, we have seen that Scarry defended the labor of imagining others (45). Jean-Luc Nancy argues that signs impede it. Remaining impenetrable to interpretation, the many dull deciphering and diminish our trust in language. Following up on Nancy, Virno tries out a more affirmative position and thinks of Nancy's multiplying bodies as a new subject: the multitude. The multitude is a plurality that persists "without converging into a One, without evaporating in a centripetal movement" (*GM* 10). The multitude is a fundamental element of the "grammar" of the present, but it seems harnessed to a political utopian project; I am less interested in that dimension and more in Virno's theoretical work. This work is compelling because, in the process of theorizing the multitude, Virno shows the intimate link between the problem of imagining others and our idea of language by returning to Saussure. Discussing Virno's return to Saussure will be helpful in pursuing this chapter's aim, which is to try to illuminate the beneficial attachment to language presented in the previous section.

From small world to vast world

> With modern transport, everywhere you go
> The whole world is an archipelago,
> each place an island in a void of travel
> Les Murray, "Kimberley Brief"

Virno refers to his work as a form of cultural anthropology which aims at decoding the present. His writing seeks to map collective moods and sentiments, first and foremost the shared sense of a transition from small world to vast world. From this vantage point, it may be said to bear affinities with the aims of affect theory. Like other orientations within Theory, affect theory is a consequence of the deconstruction of the subject and represents the subsequent expansion of the range of objects of study from a heterogeneous approach that resists a standard generalizable model of theory. What seems to distinguish affect theory is its capacity to make inroads into different ways of writing about perceptions and experiences that are not easily describable even though they make up an indubitable part of reality (Di Leo; Gregg and Seigworth). Similarly, for Virno, the promising concept of an exodus or an exit into a vaster world is a matter of perceiving and mapping mounting states of fear and anxiety. In the case of his work, the "affective" decoding results in the glimmer of familiar modernist atmospheres, only intensified. Virno describes a human condition without shelter, a homeless condition progressively brought on by the dissolution of local community and by the escalation of what in the past was perceived as fear (the fear, for example, inherent in the loss of human attachment to small local worlds) into a state of anxiety linked to the phenomenon of becoming worldly in the sense of Nancy. The traction of Virno's thought depends on his mapping of an intensified exposure to the world. From a certain point of view, the centrality of this affective state may be explained, at least in part, as an effect of the regionalization of Europe. Virno, however, never mentions the phenomenon; his attention is magnetized by a movement, within European thought, which he refers to as exodus and it indicates the completion and exhaustion of the concept of alienation ("Virtuosity"). Virno's exodus is less a discourse on the decentering of Europe and more a planetary extension of the affective make-up of community in Esposito's sense, that is to say, of the impossibility of community: "No feeling is more shared, more public, than that of not feeling at home" (*GM* 21). This unsheltered condition is tantamount to the familiar notion of a modernity readily associated with the Marxist concept of alienation and its critical-literary branchings. An intensified state of *Entfremdung* now makes its apparition in the open of a vaster homeless world; it becomes, in Virno's phrase, "more public." Unlike Felski's strand of postcritique, Virno's cultural anthropology does not conclude that we need to dispose of modernist adversarial temporalities: periphery vs. center, small vs. large, inside vs. outside, to name the most obvious ones; his approach externalizes them. Virno's point is that those adversarial temporalities concern everyone. Thus, he speaks of "the anxiety-ridden experience of estrangement that eludes the public sphere," and, precisely in eluding it, calls for deciphering (*GM* 28).

This world-wide *Entfremdung* accounts for the distinctive trait of the multitude (*GM* 21), a collective subject that shares in a lingering modernist imaginary of fear and thresholds (domestic vs. public; community vs. world). The extended and intensified unsheltered condition that captures Virno's imagination may, at first, seem to be propelled by an archipelagic view of individual locales converging in one common cultural surface, but if compared with other archipelagic views, a key element stands out in Virno's deciphering, and that is the belaboring of something residual from the past. If, for example, we think of the archipelagic view offered by Australian poet Les Murray in the epigraph to this section, we will notice the difference with Virno's idea of world. Murray describes a synchronous arrangement of interconnected regions separated by a vacuum; "everywhere you go," the regions are synchronous with the world, with no outer rim. In Murray's poem, before one even realizes it, the sheltered community, which from Virno's perspective fears the vast world, is superseded by a plane without memory of access, shelter, and exclusions, a great expanse that Murray calls simply "a void." Like Virno, Murray is saying that it is no longer possible to speak of "substantial communities" (*GM* 19), but, from the other side of the world with respect to Europe, the poet does not focus on the fading of a local periphery into a vaster world, neither does he concentrate on the transmutation of inside into outside. His archipelago does have local connotations of course, its immediate reference being the Kimberley region in Western Australia, and the poem's beginning evokes the traversal required to get there from other, perhaps more urban parts of Australia. But the point is that, seen from above, the land is both a site-specific, Australian locality *and* a more rarified, abstract landscape: a "void of travel." The image suggests an expanse in which the different "islands" or enclosed communities of the world are united in a similar state of mind. Becoming worldly appears as a shared resource; it is presented as a shift that teaches us to perceive in terms of clusters rather than oppositions. I mention Murray here because he provides an alternative narrative of Nancy's feeling of becoming worldly. For the poet, this is synonymous with a different exigency of thought, a different triangulation of subject, intellect (faculty of language, thought), and expanse (land, environment). It is as if his archipelago voided the center vs. periphery imbalance and other related dichotomies. While its concrete reference is the aerial view of Western Australia, Murray's archipelago does suggest, like Dimock's "weak theory," the erosion of certain tools for thinking the world.

By contrast, Virno's gradual passage from small to vast world, and from community to multitude, has the specific function of belaboring something residual from the past. Virno wants to move beyond the radical impossibility of community. He takes his cue from the modernist wonder, bafflement, and surprise elicited by the sight of the many, and responds by expanding the notion of the subject, inflecting it with a type of agency that might prevent it from sinking under the weight of fractured cultural geographies. The multitude is the outcome of such a revision, and it is indebted to Saussure. Freed from the poststructuralist armature, Saussure's idea of language can display an affirmative resource that we had not seen before.

The return to Saussure (language as a social fact)

Virno's return to Saussure does not stress negativity. This is not to be misunderstood; the idea, of course, that there is nothing substantial in language but only differences remains the fundamental law of language. But in re-reading Saussure, Virno is focused on the preindividual and suprapersonal dimension of language and the fact that language concerns each user only insofar as he or she is part of a collective of other users ("Pensare" 42). Thinking about language is thinking about the many, since language exists only among the members of a collectivity. Virno makes the claim that there is a new publicness of language. He builds on the Marxist notion of labor-power and sees labor-power as pure potentiality (dynamis), "something that is sold only as a possibility," that is, therefore, not present but depends on demand and offer to become act (*GM* 76).[11] It follows that life "takes on a specific importance as the tabernacle of dynamis, of mere potentiality" (*GM* 77),[12] with language as part of this tabernacle of potentiality since it is one of those faculties that make for labor power (*GM* 77). Following Marx, Virno uses "subjectivity" in the sense of the living body understood as "simulacrum of work" (*GM* 78), hence as a sum of faculties, and concentrates on the role of language as potentiality to be governed. While his aim is to show that creativity and cultural content are incorporated in capital (Brouillette 97),[13] we are interested here in the capacity of his analysis to reveal the impact of Saussure's modernism on the present.

Saussure bases his idea of language on the analysis of the sign to argue that language equally eludes individual and social claims to possession. In the *Course in General Linguistics*, Saussure posits that language belongs neither to the individual user nor to society, "[f]or the distinguishing trait of the sign—but the one that is least apparent at first sight—is that in some way it eludes the individual or social will" (17). In Virno's reading, Saussure's sign opens to a preindividual realm that each user has in common, and through which each is individuated. He includes language in this preindividual realm, which is the real object of his study and comprises a variety of elements: the biological element (sensory perception), public and intrapsychic traits of language (mother tongue), productive cooperation and General Intellect, a notion that he takes from Marx's *Grundrisse* (1858) (*GM* 72). Through the process of individuation, the individual takes from the preindividual realm that immaterial labor force, that ensemble of productive forces that will become the object of biopolitical negotiation. Language is the centerpiece of the ensemble,[14] and Virno explicates its role in the biopolitical negotiation through the example of enunciation (*GM* 60). He argues that enunciation determines the I as "my own I." The appropriative process inherent in enunciation informs us, Virno says, that some preindividual linguistic dimension exists where language belongs to no one and everyone. If, as Saussure affirms, language is neither an individual nor a social possession, then language presumes a preindividual layer that Virno can enlist as a shaping force of subjectivity in advanced capitalism.

His reading highlights three points in Saussure's theory of language: (1) Language sheds light on the social fact of a tie between individuals; (2) Language is an imperfect property, a possession that we cannot have; (3) The movement, in the background of Saussure's theory of language, of something like the shadowy continuum of a preindividual dimension from which Virno draws the force of his argument. I would like to concentrate on the third point. I am interested in the fact that, although Virno uses Saussure to prove that creativity and language are incorporated in capital, his reading reveals that Saussure's idea of language comes from that state of bafflement, wonder, and exclamation with regard to the many that we have discussed above. I will now expand on this point with a reading of Saussure.

What attracts Saussure to "the linguistic phenomenon" is its irreducible doubleness; language "always has two related sides, each deriving its values from the other" (8). The two parts are mutually sustaining and value-giving: they are, on the one hand, the "acoustical impressions," perceived by the ear, and, on the other hand, "oral articulation" (8). Such a description foregrounds the body and its parts: the mouth, the ear, the muscles of phonation. The micro-unit of the linguistic phenomenon in its speech manifestation (the circuit of *parole*) is constituted by two speaking subjects, alternating in the use of the mouth and of the ear (11).

Even though Saussure emphasizes the oral-acoustic dimension of language (speech), he is struck by the fact that "the thing that constitutes language is . . . unrelated to the phonic character of the linguistic sign" (7). He realizes that "language is a social fact" (6).[15] Even after analyzing the essential elements of the speaking circuit—the physical parts (sound waves), physiological parts (sound articulation and auditory dimension), psychic parts (word-images and concepts) (12)—Saussure does not cease to wonder at the "social crystallization" of language (13), at what causes the individuals to be connected among themselves by and through language. He marvels, in other words, at "the social bond that constitutes language" (13).

The two figures in Saussure's diagram of the speaking circuit represent *in nuce* the social bond of which language is a repository. He speaks of "impressions that are perceptibly the same for all" that are "made on the minds of the speakers" (13); he speaks of a "treasure" deposited in the practice of words by "the subjects belonging to the same community," a system that, existing virtually in every brain, exists also in the many, "[f]or language is not complete in any speaker; it exists perfectly only within a collectivity" (14). Yet, while insisting on the collective dimension, on the system as a common possession, he also marvels at the capacity of the individual act of speaking: a "wilful and intellectual" act to counterbalance the system (14).[16] He emphasizes a zone of conflict between the collective system and the individual act, suggesting an uncertain, slippery conceptual area that the system actually delimits. The sign itself may be taken as an introduction to this uncertain zone. The dual nature of the sign (66) alludes to a dense space of vagrant sound-images in search of concepts. His description evokes a background of moving shadows delimited by the system: both parts of the signs that form the system are "psychological." Signs are associative formations, yet they are not "abstractions" but "bear the stamp of collective approval" (15). But the sign eludes, and its elusiveness—the bedrock of Saussure's theory—informs us that, far from harmonizing individual and collectivity, his idea of language questions other immediately contiguous concepts, like community, collectivity, and the social bond. The *Course* oscillates between the idea of community, evoking a cohesive group, and an idea of collectivity (at times masses) that suggests instead a more inhomogeneous whole. Certainly he stresses the sovereignty of the system "outside" the individual user who is inside it: language is "the social side of speech, outside the individual who can never create nor modify it by himself" (14). But, at times, the impression is that part and whole, inside and outside, form an indeterminate background.

Nowhere is this impression stronger than in the section on "Phonology," where Saussure uses one of the most beautiful metaphors in the *Course*, that of a tapestry, to illuminate "the problem of language" (33): "It is a system based on the mental opposition of auditory impressions, just as a tapestry is a work of art produced by the visual oppositions of threads of different colors" (33). The simile lends an aesthetic edge to his reflection on language. Clearly the task of the linguist remains the analysis of the spoken chain, the analysis of its parts—"there should be one symbol for each element of the spoken chain" (33)—and the rigorous representation of the articulated sounds to "rule out any ambiguity" (33), but Saussure's admiration for the tapestry suggests something else beyond the fundamental law of language, which is difference therefore conflict. The back of the tapestry shows the different strands, exemplifying that "the important thing in analysis is the role of the oppositions, not the process through which the colors were obtained" (33), but, while concentrating on difference, Saussure's observer is also drawn to the transition from conflict to form; his attention is concentrated on that dynamic achievement. Conflict foregrounds the unruly, raw phonic matter that the textured work of the tapestry mitigates. The tapestry introduces another sensory level, the tactile, which accrues to the main acoustic/auditory sensory level, adding the suggestion of a visual pleasure linked to the transition from unruly matter to the unambiguous representation of articulated sounds. This element of pleasure of course remains negligible in the linguist's analysis, which should be oriented by the conflict and the oppositions subtending the achievement of the spoken chain. But the simile of the tapestry does allude to the imaginary underpinnings of the system, which are present even though they can never be fully part of its description. It is as if there were a supplementary task for the linguist in Saussure's admiration for the mass of indeterminate sound agitating, in its pure unresolved state, in the background of the system. These imaginary underpinnings lend Saussure's meditation a special force.

Writing, Saussure explains, gives us the possibility of objectifying "the unmanageable mass," and therefore of taking a distance from the matter that it is, but, like the tapestry with its two faces, writing also constantly reminds us of it: "Whoever consciously deprives himself of the perceptible image of the written word runs the risk of perceiving only a shapeless and unmanageable mass. Taking away the written form is like depriving a beginning swimmer of his life belt" (32). The written word is the life of language; it protects us from the impact of the "shapeless and unmanageable mass." Before there is a unit, there is a shapeless mass; before there is a value, there is no meaning (96). His theory of language is a reflection on the eternal coexistence of these levels. This is the reason why Jacques Derrida, who built on Saussure's inconsistencies, can perceive his "quasioneiric" coherence (Derrida qtd. in Bennington 191). At best, "[e]verything in language is basically psychological" (Saussure 6); at worst, language, like Warburg's images, consorts with delirium.

Such moments in Saussure, together with the constant emphasis on difference and conflict, facilitate a view of the subject that is far from dualistic and reductive. Building on this view, Virno argues for a preindividual dimension which each user accesses through the individual performance. He can take from Saussure his plural subject—the multitude—by zooming in on the master's weave of "I" and "one" (*GM* 71), which Virno highlights as a "strong weave," as a "battlefield" (*GM* 72).

The hermeneutics of the subject

Reading Saussure in the wake of the return to Saussure can reveal the neglected side of his theory of language: the work of affirmative passions. Conflict of course dominates Saussure's contribution: it innervates the concept of the sign and governs the relation between system and individual act, but language is also a storehouse of affirmative passions, and it can be perceived as such when Saussure speaks of language as an institution.

Saussure presents language as a unique institution. Unlike other institutions, it can never be modified by individuals. Comparing it with matrimony, for example, he observes that, while the forms of the institution of matrimony can be discussed comparatively over time, debating monogamy and polygamy, when it comes to language, which is "a system of arbitrary signs," any solid ground for discussion is taken away from us: "there is no reason for preferring *soeur* to *sister*, *Ochs* to *boeuf*" (73). The consequence of the immutability of the institution is a certain inclination of the speaking subject to accept the language that he or she inherits. What begins to emerge in the folds of Saussure's theory is the figure of a human subject construed as a receiver, a subject who, in the particular natural-historical language he or she comes to speak, accepts what he or she receives. Even though briefly, the *Course* does manage to thrust into relief the exceptional trait of language (perhaps the most fascinating trait), and that is that language is given to us; it calls on us as receivers. In the section entitled "Mutability and Immutability of the Sign," Saussure writes that even if speakers were aware of the laws of language, which they are not, "we may be sure that their awareness would seldom lead to criticism, for people are generally satisfied with the language they have received" (72). Saussure meets us with the hypothesis of an affirmative disposition of the subject as accepting receiver. Although the figure of the accepting receiver remains enigmatic, the notion begins to appear of a beneficial resource in language, a source of well-being stored in the collective repository. This enigmatic figure now claims our attention and asks for a fuller understanding.

Considering the affirmative disposition of Saussure's subject who receives and is content with what he or she receives, considering also the natural delight procured by the attachment to the potential to speak, comparable to the attachment to mere life, one might perhaps go as far as positing a delectable speaker. As used here, the word "delectable," less common than "delightful" but echoing the contiguous Latin verb *delectāre*, delight, coterminous with *delectus*, synonymous with *amatus*, meaning chosen or loved, suggests the state of being influenced beneficially. The subject as accepting receiver and/or delectable speaker can appear because Saussure's idea of language is based on its missing origins. The sign is a dual entity; but its doubleness comes from the fact that any comprehensible link between concepts and sound images is missing; if there ever was a pact stipulated between concepts and sound images, that pact has been lost in mythological memory: "it has never been recorded" (Saussure 71), and it cannot constitute knowledge that the subject might accumulate. But, in language, the subject is given access to another kind of knowledge, the truth of being a receiver. And this takes us to our hypothesis about language as attachment. Saussure helps us understand language as a term of attachment within a hermeneutics of the subject that construes speech as a transformative practice of the self, as an action of the self on itself and with itself with the aim of becoming an accepting receiver. The satisfaction of the speaker *qua* receiver, which Saussure points out when he remarks that even if people were aware of the hidden laws of language, this "would seldom lead to criticism," is key, for it makes it possible to think of the speaker as a member of a social mass (language as a social relation), therefore as a subject defined by the relation to others, but, as such, also always in a potential proximity to a beneficial attachment.

Once it is glimpsed in the background of Saussure's theory, the figure of the accepting receiver raises the question of a beneficial part-taking stored in language, a part-taking that is pure potentiality (i.e. always available), and directs attention to the fascinating question of speaking: speaking as receiving. As receiving, speaking would also be a potentiality taken from the common good of the collectivity; this taking can be grasped as a prelinguistic faculty, a faculty that precedes the actual execution of language in any particular naturalhistorical form, a faculty that might be called taking-to-be able to (*prendere per potere*).[17] For language as a faculty implies exactly this potentiality to speak at the beginning. Virno observes that Saussure neglected language as a faculty in the sense of this potentiality, expelling its discussion from his scientific project because it had seemed to him a daunting tangle of physiological and biological elements (*Quando* 33). Revisiting the distinction between language as *langue*, or an infinite ensemble of acts, and language as faculty, Virno specifies the latter meaning as "a mere being able-to speak," which is never the same of course as a series of hypothetical linguistic executions (34). Our accepting receiver adds another layer to Virno's faculty. As mentioned a few lines above, speaking, understood as receiving, would be a potential taking from the common good of the collectivity. This taking specifies the faculty of language not only as the mere (*vuota*) potentiality to speak, but, even prior to that, as the faculty of taking-to-be able to (*prendere per potere*) speak. As such, it opens to the question of a beneficial attachment, a notion that perhaps can be best approached through feminism, when we get to Chapter 6, and psychoanalysis, when we get to Chapter 7.

In the remaining section, it is necessary to return to Saussure's meditation on language in the attempt to clarify how Saussure inflects Virno's deciphering of the present with its distinctive contiguity with modernist atmospheres. In the work of Saussure, contentment alternates with dejection. The contentment of the speaker *qua* receiver is counterbalanced by a social mass that has no sovereignty over the language that constitutes it as a mass. Saussure's admiration for the individual who, with intelligence and will, manages to express his individual thoughts is palpable, but it is also countered by the sadness for the individual's place in a collectivity that cannot exert its sovereignty, not even on a single word (71), and is subjected to the enforced law of arbitrary associations between signifiers and signified (sound-images and concepts) (71).[18] Saussure oscillates between the receiver's well-being and the privation of the many, who can exert no sovereignty over their common "possession," as if the idea of language itself emblematized that mechanism of preventive defense from the *munus* in community which we discussed with Esposito. This impasse in his linguistic theory resonates with portraits of the thinker that underline his melancholia or even his nihilism, traits that have become more pronounced in the recently discovered unpublished writings.[19]

Specters of Saussure: modernism

When Saussure speaks of the "delusions of writing" (33), more than berating writing he conveys the power of that slippery conceptual zone which he has attempted to describe through the tapestry, symbol of a formidable formless and unmanageable matter that defies study. The tapestry introduces us to the shadowy, elusive existence of signs that are always closer to the silhouette and contour of something missing, not quite there. From this perspective, Saussure's language invites comparison with the unconscious. Both are amenable to the notion of deposited imprints. As a matter of fact, the idea of a precipitate of impressions or traces stored in the cultural fold cuts across the three major disciplines whose foundations were laid in modernist times: linguistics, psychology, and sociology (Sanders 41).[20] Saussure stands out because of his capacity to frame language as an institution, while steering us toward the contradictions of this institution. While the oscillation between individual and the collectivity, gift and debt, benefit and loss may suggest the dynamic nature of the institution, the latter is also shown to be traversed by archaic forces. The *Course* bears witness to the traces of powerful archaic forces not only when it reminds us that language is an ungovernable, raw mass of phonic matter before it perforce becomes speech, but also in the fundamental law of arbitrariness. Arbitrariness covers over the unrecorded origins of language; lost in the mythological past, those origins are the proof of an archaic dimension that traverses the institution in the present and lodges in it the sense of an arrested time: Saussure speaks of linguistic signs as "a multiplicity," as a "numberless" multitude (73), implying that it would be difficult to change a system that is made of multitudes. In Esposito's terms, in Saussure's vision the past has not yet become coeval; the origin is still a specter. His emphasis on speech turns out to be another uncanny reminder of archaic forces within the institution.

The conflict between the system and the individual takes center stage because of Saussure's emphasis on speech. A particularly telling moment is when, to explain the psychological character of sound-images, Saussure offers the example of silent speech: "The psychological character of our sound-images becomes apparent when we observe our own speech. Without moving our lips or tongue, we can talk to ourselves or recite mentally a selection of verse" (66). One wonders what speech means for Saussure. Acoustic impressions are there, whether they are spoken (through voice) or not, and he points to a continuum of psychic impressions in which the sensory part (the acoustic image) englobes the whole (the concept) (85). Even after the terms "signifier" and "signified" are introduced in the attempt to mark a divide, the sense persists, in the auditory-visual environment that constitutes Saussure's psychic impressions, of a free signifier that continues to englobe the concept. But the power of the signifier is in striking contrast with the masses that use *langue*: "The masses have no voice in the matter, and the signifier chosen by language could be replaced by no other" (71). Finally: "the community itself cannot control so much as a single word; it is bound to the existing language" (71). Saussure's language does not consist of tools for thought, but of imprints, impressions, and traces that cling ambiguously to concepts, and can always ambiguously englobe—or, to use a psychoanalytic term, incorporate—concepts and thoughts. What persists in his meditation is the murmur of these englobing signifiers, a murmur only made more audible by the fundamental law of arbitrariness. His sign does not belong; it eludes. Against the aggression of a raw, archaic matter, there rises the speaker-as-receiver.

Saussure's speaker-as-receiver is bonded to masses without sovereignty by and through something that he or she does not possess. But receiving is not to be thought in the same breath as passivity or powerlessness; rather, it raises the question of another form of agency and, related to that, the interesting problem of how the receiver will fend off the spectral returns in order to keep as near as possible to a source of well-being.[21]

While Saussure is ostensibly theorizing the sign, his vocabulary reveals his engagement of the problem of the many, to the extent that we might think of his theory of language as a reaction to the bafflement and wonder of the sort that occupied Eliot, Jankélévitch, and Ortese. In this regard, the work of Carol Sanders is particularly helpful. Sanders draws a portrait of Saussure that steeps the thinker in the modernist wonder about the many, especially in her reconstruction of his Parisian years. By the end of the nineteenth century, Paris had been rebuilt and the city enjoyed a relative social stability within a flourishing Republic which, as of 1879, had its own national anthem and an annual national celebration. Setting the thinker against the background of the thriving French capital, Sanders speculates on the excitement that young Saussure must have felt "as he strolled down the thronging boulevards of what the Victorian writer Thackeray described as the 'wicked city,'" feeling part of an intellectual and artistic milieu that by far surpassed the life of "the Protestant and more parochial towns of Leipzig and Geneva" (43). Saussure's story, like Freud's, is the modernist story of a European claustrophobia overcome through conceptual inventiveness. It might not be farfetched to assume that the kind of excitement described by Sanders made its way into his academic life and the lectures that constitute the *Course*, a transcript by his students. Perhaps, traces of that excitement might be gleaned from the contradictions that are palpable in his students' transcription.[22] But those contradictions, too, would show his modernist story: his idea of language as a moment of internal (domestic) intellectual displacement.

The connection between modernism and the *Course* is more than a conjecture. Sanders herself begins to place Saussure's work in the context of a widespread reaction against realism and naturalism in literature and in the arts.[23] Mallarmé and Valéry challenged traditional ways of thinking about language and, as Sanders proposes, it is possible to find "some striking parallels" between Saussure's theory and "the practice of writers from the Symbolists to the Surrealists, as if the radical shift in the study of language found an echo in the beginnings of literary Modernism" (40). In particular, the unity of language and thought, a belief that joined Mallarmé and Valéry (Sanders 40), finds its way in Saussure's concern for a sensory fold of sound-impressions or psychic traces that englobe concepts. We could add to Sanders's list his interest in the weave of social institution and individual act. Perhaps, however, the most tangible connection with modernism is Saussure's well-known speaking circuit. The pair in the circuit is taken up and isolated from a vaster space of conflicting forces, and the body-centered diagram of speech governs the tension between individual and mass, a tension highlighted by the shifting terms that in the *Course* indicate the many (community, collectivity, masses). Saussure's version of the subject as a face-to-face encounter projects a reciprocity (preserving the abstract scenario of two neutral bodies, without gender, class, race, or other social markers) away from the conflicting threads of a larger whole.[24]

Virno works through the lingering modernist sentiments about the world in Saussure's *Course*, and restitutes Saussure, the modernist thinker, to the present. But in restoring the master's modernism, Virno also transforms Saussure into the capacious thinker of his own enhanced modernist version of the present, with the fear and anxiety which characterize the human condition in times of modernization simply changing in scale from local to planetary. While this narrative repeats, by intensifying them, Heidegger's sentiments at the opening of "The Thing" (1937),[25] differing significantly from Esposito's plane of coevalness, what interests us here is Virno's accent on the publicness of language as an attribute of mere life. Language is shown as one of the basic principles of a general intellect that becomes public and "appears worldly" ("Virtuosity" 206–7), it is part of a human potentiality always already encoded into the labor force, always available to pass into the act of production.[26] Virno's notion of the publicness of language builds on the Saussurean (and modernist) crucial link of language to thought; it makes the problem of how we become a subject of language *and* thought still matter.

Notes

1. All translations from Virno, *Quando il verbo si fa carne* are mine.
2. The idea of a shared attachment to language is found also in Heraclitus: "Although the word is common to all, most men live as if each had a private wisdom of his own." Helen Gardner uses the sentence by Heraclitus as an epigraph to chapter 3, "Poetic Communication," of *The Art of T. S. Eliot* (67).
3. Giorgio Agamben discusses *euēmeria* at the start of *Homo Sacer* 1998 (9).
4. Fromm includes work and society: "the capacity for production, the creation of social organization" (76). He distinguishes between having and being. The having mode agrees with the belief that man is historical and temporal (Marx, William James, Bergson, Teilhard de Chardin) while the being mode stands for an unalterable human nature.
5. This question seems to have attracted more psychoanalysis and theology. See discussion in Chapter 7.
6. The distance between the body and thought, which seems to become unbridgeable in Nancy, mirrors the question of immanence in Deleuze. Deleuze's immanence recalls Nancy's ex-written body, with the difference that the former talks about "A LIFE": "Immanence is not related to Some Thing as a unity superior to all things or to a Subject as an act that brings about a synthesis of things: it is only when immanence is no longer immanence to anything other than itself that we can speak of a plane of immanence ... We will say of pure immanence that it is A LIFE, and nothing else. It is not immanence to life, but the immanent that is in nothing is itself a life. A life is the immanence of immanence, absolute immanence: it is complete power, complete bliss" (27). With reference to Charles Dickens's novel *Our Mutual Friend*, Deleuze discusses the immanence of "singular life" in ways that are echoed by Nancy's discussion of the body in *Corpus*. Here is Deleuze: "It is a haecceity no longer of individuation but of singularization: a life of pure immanence, beyond good and evil, for it was only the subject that incarnated it in the midst of things that made it good or bad. The life of such individuality fades away in favor of the singular life immanent to a man who no longer has a name, though he can be mistaken for no other. A singular essence, a life" (29). I am not prepared here to take on the question of writing: Nancy speaks of "writing," not of speech; he speaks of an "ex-written" body.
7. Parmenides; Foucault, *Hermeneutics*, lecture of 24 February 1982, first hour. In fragment 1 of *On the Order of Nature* (Poem), Parmenides writes. "You must comprehend all: / the firm heart of the well-rounded Truth / and the appearances of mortals in which there is no true certainty" (49, lines 29–32).

8. In his "impersonal period" Esposito builds on Benveniste's discussion of pronouns to pave the way for an analysis of community that will lead to the notion of the "other modernity" identified with the simultaneous preservation and repression of life. See Esposito, *Terza persona*; Bazzicalupo, *Impersonale*.
9. All translations from Ortese, "Da Moby Dick all'Orsa Bianca" are mine.
10. Vittore Carpaccio, *Due Dame Veneziane* (Two Venetian Ladies), 1490, Museo Correr, Venice.
11. Virno quotes Marx from Book I of *Capital*: "The purchaser of labor-power consumes it by setting the seller of labor power to work. By working, the latter becomes actually what before he only was potentially, labor-power in action, a laborer" (Marx qtd. in *GM* 76).
12. With his focus on life as "pure and simple bios," Virno carries on Michel Foucault's biopolitical insight into the living as something to be governed; here I am particularly interested in one of the effects of that insight: the image of the body as the "tabernacle of dynamis."
13. In a good summary of Virno's contribution, Sarah Brouillette writes: "In the theory of immaterial labor, defined in part as the incorporation of information into production, but mainly as the post-factory work that 'produces the informational and cultural content of the commodity,' capital is busily orchestrating the incorporation of creativity into itself" (97).
14. In the fragment on machines and living labor in Marx's *Grundrisse* (1858), General Intellect indicates a social knowledge pertaining to human industry (the human capacity to transform natural materials into organs of the human will), which becomes a direct force of production (*GM* 72).
15. Speech presupposes at least two individuals, the "minimum number required to complete the circuit" (Saussure, *Course* 21). Saussure specifies that language concerns the expression of "facts of consciousness," and describes the process through which the concept from the brain sends to phonatory organs an impulse that is correlative to the image and how sound waves travel from the mouth of A to the ear of B, through a purely physical process, which can be prolonged in reverse order from B to A.
16. Virno may be using Saussure in lieu of psychoanalysis to point to a zone of transaction between inside and outside that is not only vital for the individual but articulates the individual to the public sphere. Without overt recourse to psychoanalysis, Virno seems to combine it with Gilbert Simondon to help articulate a "psychic" region understood as a presocial dimension that testifies to society's role in the process of individuation.
17. When read from this perspective, Saussure moves in a different direction than Freud did in *Group Psychology* (1921).

18. This mutual dependence has induced Virno to see in Saussure a correction of the positions of classic critical theory, especially of the Frankfurt School. Critical theory ascribes unhappiness to the fact that the individual must oppose the forces of industrial production. According to Virno, Saussure proves that the view of the individual banished to "a cold and dark corner" by the impersonal power of society is wrong. Unhappiness results, Virno argues, when the strong weave of forces which constitute Saussure's embattled subject "manifests as disharmony, pathological oscillation, or crisis" (GM 72).
19. Virno, "Pensare" 42; Gambarara 56; Esposito, *Politica* 15.
20. Sanders finds that it was Jung's notion of the "collective unconscious" more than Freud's notion of the individual unconscious that might have appealed to "the creator of the notion of langue" (42).
21. Before the advent of performativity, feminist theory has been preoccupied with well-being in language as is manifest by the recurrent motif of a threshold to cross and an access to gain in order to affirm a native tie to language and speech. See, for example, Anzaldúa.
22. These contradictions have been discussed exhaustively by Derrida, who began his public career as a philosopher and as public intellectual by taking on Saussure not so much as a modernist thinker but as the name for a certain dominant atmosphere of structuralism in France. As Geoffrey Bennington observes, Derrida, besides denouncing his phonocentrism (blind spot), also points to the resources of Saussure for our time. Derrida himself developed the "other gesture," the conceptual resources not to be found in Saussure's explicit claims (Bennington 188).
23. An overriding concern of the times was "seeking to escape from materialism, whether in the fin-de-siècle 'decadent' novel or in Catholic writing" (Sanders 40).
24. Saussure's speaking circuit emphasizes the expressive potential of the subject, language as articulation. Sanders quotes Valéry from his *Cahiers*: "Le Mot Moi n'a de sens que dans chaque cas où on l'emploie. Pas de moi sans parole—sin voce" ("The word 'me' only has meaning in each instance of its use. There is no 'me' without speech—sin voce" (Sanders 41). The interweaving of speech and the identity of the speaking subject, the idea that speech gives us a voice, has not only shaped our concept of modernism, as Sanders rightly suggests through the genealogy of Valéry, but has had a decisive impact on twentieth-century feminism and movements of emancipation and liberation.
25. Martin Heidegger expresses the same sentiment at the opening of "The Thing": "All distances in time and space are shrinking. Man now reaches overnight, by plane, places which formerly took weeks and months to travel. He now receives instant information, by radio, of events which he formerly learned about only years later, if at all. The germination and growth of plants, which remained hidden throughout

the seasons, is now exhibited publicly in a minute, on film. Distant sites of the most ancient cultures are shown on film as if they stood this very moment amidst today's street traffic" (163).
26. Building on Marx, Virno argues that intellectual labor, a kind of labor in which the product is not separable from the act of production, comprises "activities that find their fulfillment in themselves," with the performing artist becoming the prototype of waged labor today. Language and the ability to relate to "the presence of others" are included in the labor force, but virtuosity, in relating to the "presence of others," translates into personal dependence and a widespread modern servitude ("Virtuosity" 190).

Chapter 5

Tradition: Eliot and Work

> Between the potency
> And the existence
> ...
> Falls the Shadow
>
> T. S. Eliot, "The Hollow Men"

Overview

In Chapter 3 we discussed the latent thought without nation, alternative to poststructuralism, coexisting with it but also exceeding it, which Esposito calls "living thought." In that discussion, Esposito's turn to literary critic Adriano Tilgher (1890–1941) exemplified the annexation of the modernist motif of the conflict between Life and Form. Living thought reactivates the meaningfulness of that motif, directing the concerns of critique toward life as "a force that exceeds the limits of any economy" (*Da Fuori* 165). Living thought enfolds at least two different temporalities one in the other—that of modernism and that of poststructuralism—appealing to modernism in order to mobilize what remains lateral and undescribed under the agenda of poststructuralism with its belief in the power of language to mediate experience through and through. We have seen in the previous chapter how, with the return to Saussure, language itself remains an incomplete modernist motif. We said that the theory of language becomes compellingly interwoven with the problem of human multiplicity, which persists and is amplified as a concern of contemporary theorists. In this way, modernism and theory have emerged as disjunctive yet collaborative temporalities. Briefly said, this chapter enlists Eliot in living thought. We shall see how his theory of literature flows from the conflict of Life and Form, breaking down tradition as a temporal sequence of authors and works in favor of a plane of repetition and *méconnaissance*. This is not of course the same as Esposito's plane of coevalness but precedes it, as do Benjamin's and Warburg's planes discussed in Chapter 2.

To introduce the chapter in more detail, it is helpful to start with Eliot's distinctive trait, which is undoubtedly his turn from philosophy to poetry. To a certain extent, it meant a change in the focus of his attention from conceptual systems to the practice of the writing life. While the turn has been superbly illuminated by Jewel Spears Brooker, here we will concentrate on something that is part and parcel of the Eliot persona: his projection of himself as a practitioner of a writing life that overlaps with ordinary life. While his working and writing arrangements are usually considered as a biographical datum, here the connection and tension between writing and life will be treated as the seal of Eliot's privileged association with the conflict of Life and Form. To clarify, it will not be a question of thematizing the struggle to write, as for example in the heroic modernist iconography of the artist: the poet in the garret (Ezra Pound), the modernist saint (Gertrude Stein), the writhing ephebe (Wallace Stevens), or the artist as "exemplary sufferer" (Susan Sontag). We are all familiar with the mythology of Eliot as a man without qualities by day and a writer by night, the American expatriate with "a four piece suit," as Virginia Woolf described him during the first stages of their acquaintance, before she came to depend on his literary judgment.[1] The fact that the sustainability of the writing life is central to Eliot, the fact that the connection between his form of life and his writing practice is foregrounded as problematic or jarring in his public persona, makes the notion of form of life particularly relevant to approaching Eliot. It can shed light on a mode of action in which the stake was keeping himself in relation to language as if to "the potency," as he puts it in the epigraph to this chapter. Antonio Lucci used the same epigraph in a study of Giorgio Agamben's notion of *forma-di-vita*, practice of life (80). With the phrase, Agamben means life that is constituted "in an inseparable context as form-of-life," with thought acting as a shaping nexus between context and life, that is to say, not as the individual exertion of an organ or of a faculty but as an "experimentum that has as its object the potential character of life and of human intelligence" (*Means* 9).

Commenting on Agamben, Lucci distinguishes the notion from "a subjective *metanoia* induced by technologies of the self" and explicates it as "the relation to a practice" (70; my translation). The same applies to Eliot, in whose case it would be limiting to understand the relation of life to writing in terms of a discursive practice through which the subject creates himself, though of course this is not to be ruled out, as the care he took in projecting his persona through both the photographic image and his voice would nevertheless indicate (Jaffe). Rather, we shall see how the conflict of Life and Form is meaningful in Eliot because it indicates a practice of life aimed at ensuring a relation to language as pure potentiality.

"Experimentum" (literary history)

Eliot's idea of criticism seems to consort with destruction. One of his most celebrated essays, "Tradition and the Individual Talent," attests to a destructive force that is at work even more clearly in other essays, such as "Reflections on Contemporary Poetry [IV]" and "The Method of Mr. Pound."[2] He opposes the dull surface of common sense with the labor of the negative: he disassembles traditional literary history, understood as a procession of authors, and collapses the idea of literary linearity in favor of a coeval plane of writers: "you must set [the poet], for contrast and comparison, among the dead" ("Tradition" 106). Recalling in part Hegel's notion of understanding as an activity of dissolution, where the idea is lost to "the unreal, 'death'" (Day 18), and in part Benjamin's "method of ... consummation" ("Goethe's Elective Affinities" 153), Eliot's own notion of understanding is concerned with the potential of a thought activated through the past. This is the reason why he was critical of an "archeological" (his word) view of tradition which, while aimed at the reconstruction of the past, remains unconcerned with its living potential ("Method" 145 n.2). From this point of view, he revises literary history, a revision that has become known as the doctrine of impersonality. One of its cornerstones is the "progress of the artist," which Eliot described as self-sacrifice: "The progress of the artist is a continual sacrifice, a continual extinction of personality" ("Tradition" 108). How is this extinction to be understood? Eliot's phrase the "progress of the artist" might suggest a type of self-fashioning based on a series of practices or technologies of the self specifically targeting becoming an artist. But Eliot himself seems to withdraw from the prospect of identity: he resists becoming an artist, that is to say, he resists being reduced to the work of the artist.

Before we get into a fuller discussion of Eliot's form of life, it would be helpful to take note of the fact that his criticism, in fact, dethrones the artist to a more anonymous status. This, it may be argued, is not unusual for modernist writers; part of the attractiveness of fellow artists like Gertrude Stein or Ezra Pound lies in the temptation that anonymity and ordinary life represented as a gateway to saying something new or authentic, to a writing that would be something other than blank writing. Eliot, however, mobilizes this idea of the artist in the attempt to grasp a transition—he uses the word "transmutation" ("Method" 141)—from an individual to a public dimension. The ideal method of the artist, he argues in the essay on Ezra Pound, is based on "the fusion and transmutation of elements" (141), whereby the "constituents [of the past] fall into place and the present is revealed" in a moment of illumination that is like a "convulsion" (142). Pound is divested of everything except an original debt to the past, which Eliot phrases as "the peculiarity of expressing oneself through historical masks" (142). As a consequence, the order of literary chronology breaks into moments of "profound kinship" and of "imperative intimac[ies]" ("Reflections" 66).

Literary history becomes the question of a natality in language; it implies a bond with language that can be thought in terms of a possession based on self-dispossession. Each poet is *with* another, but, being in the neighborliness of another, he also writes with another, that is to say, through another. Far from consisting in a procession of authors, literary history is a corrosive and decontextualizing process. Eliot's "extinction of personality" sheds light on an oblique circuit of obligatory giving, of gift *and* debt. Monumental literary history breaks down, ceding to a more radical version of those moments of "profound kinship": an "imperative intimacy" that yokes gift and debt, in a similar way in which gift and obligation were linked in Esposito's analysis of community discussed in Chapter 3. What does it mean to talk about the artist? Eliot, as mentioned, talks about the "progress of the artist" to open to another problem: when it comes to the literary tradition, his theme is a writing of repetitions, a writing without a book and without *the* artist. The monumentality of literary history breaks down in favor of a coeval plane of repetitions, which can be conceived also as a common or public writing that writes itself, as an ongoing discourse started by others.

Like Saussure, T. S. Eliot was fascinated by the unruly aspect of language, by the shadowy realm of imprints and impressions that ask to be made less impermanent. An indeterminate realm of meaning acts on the self—"I am moved," writes Eliot in "Preludes"—and this affected state translates into the concrete image of the pierced self in the "The Death of Saint Narcissus." "Marina" begins with loss but climaxes with the gift or lease ("Given or lent?") of likenesses ("face") that dissolve in their kinetic passage: "What is this face, less clear and clearer / The pulse in the arm, less strong and stronger / Given or lent? More distant than stars and nearer than the eye" (Ricks and McCue 25).[3]

The referential armature of the poem protects signs that seem "more distant than the stars and nearer than the eye" (Ricks and McCue 25). The problem of the many, as we discussed in the previous chapter, played a role in Eliot's abandonment of philosophy for poetry. The experience of a vaster world and a human multiplicity that defies conceptuality required an empathetic observer and a public writing that would pierce the impersonal dimension of life.

Eliot's entire career can be grasped, to use Agamben's term, as an *experimentum* at a form of public life, in the sense of being born with another, that is to say, through a practice of co-writing that incorporates the practitioner in the continuum of repetitions. First manifested in "Tradition and the Individual Talent," the experimentum reaches its clearest formulation in "East Coker": "And what there is to conquer / By strength and submission, has already been discovered / Once or twice, or several times, by men whom one cannot hope / To emulate—but there is no competition— / There is only the fight to recover what has been lost / And found and lost again and again . . . (*Four Quartets* 19).[4]

Eliot seems to suggest a blank writing because what tradition really writes remains always residual and dependent on the next writer appearing on the literary horizon; on the other hand, the metaphor of recovering (and repairing) leans more toward a logic of circulation with recognition—or *méconnaissance*—as a key term.

Writing the "thing"

The last stanza of "Preludes" marks an important moment in what Eliot called the progress of "self-extinction," if with that term we understand the graduation from an individual to a public form of life:

> I am moved by fancies that are curled
> Around these images, and cling:
> The notion of some infinitely gentle
> Infinitely suffering thing. ("Preludes" IV, 16, lines 10–13)

In its entirety, the poem consists in a succession of scenes of city life; it is an attempt at representing different individual lives. In the last stanza, however, the singular lives merge in a more abstract configuration which commands attention because, despite its differing affective nuances (grace and pain), it is something raw, unnamable, and impersonal: the "thing." Eliot's speaker is affected by something that is utterly hostile to thought and language. The multiple individual lives that the modern artist ought to represent, in fact, merge into an impersonal fold that defies conceptualization.

"Preludes" informs us that Eliot is pulled in two different directions. The poem's cropped stanzas bespeak his attempt to synchronize with the seductive *tempo* of the modern city, staking his credibility as an artist on snapshots of singularities swallowed up by the city's alienating forward rhythm, as well as on his capacity to feel the aura of objects that ought to be attractive to the mind, things like "dingy shades," "[s]awdust-trampled streets," "thousand furnished rooms," signifiers of a post-Baudelaire lyrical realism. At the same time, the poem stages the waning of those objects that ought to be attractive to the mind. Following up on the late Victorians and members of Yeats's generation, Eliot had fashioned himself on Baudelaire's type of city poet, but he had also sought emancipation from that model. Texts like "The Love Song of J. Alfred Prufrock" attempt a departure from the late Victorian "dialectic of morbidity and joy" imposed by the influence of Baudelaire, registering the failure of that influence.[5] Eliot found that he lacked the master's conviction when it came to being "possessed" by the city, as he would write in a revealing introduction to Baudelaire's *Intimate Journals* in 1930: "Some poets, such as Baudelaire, similarly possessed by the town, turn directly to the littered streets, the squinting slums, the grime and smoke and the viscid human life within the streets, and find there the center of intensity" (Eliot qtd. in Schuchard 13).[6] His own "centre of intensity" was to differ. In "Preludes," that center appears through its absence from the frame of writing. We see body parts (the feet) of the people lined up at coffee stands, but not their faces: "The morning comes to consciousness / Of faint stale smells of beer / From the sawdust-trampled street / With all its muddy feet that press / To early coffee-stands" ("Preludes" II, 15, lines 1–5). Those missing faces suggest simultaneously Eliot's wonder at the many and his lack of appropriate means to address that wonder. The metonymic feet both assert and repress an unsayable that tarries before the concept, in the same manner that a film director would use close-ups of soldiers' feet to represent the horror of war.

Eliot would perhaps sympathize with the self-portrait of Jean-Bertrand Pontalis where the writer and psychoanalyst talks of himself as someone who has "never discovered anything other than the malady of being human—like everyone else" (*Finestre* 3).[7] The phrase "like everyone else" probably captures the position that is most desirable to Eliot. In "Preludes" he tried out that position without success. Stanza III reads like a set of stage directions, as if he were moving images unconvincingly, and in stanza IV the mind stalls before the "thing." At this early stage, Eliot fails at imagining others. His level of empathy remains fickle, a byproduct of the observer's absorption in his own capacity to feel, as in exercises like "In the Department Store" (probably 1915).[8] Here, the observer begins by portraying another, a woman at the counter of a department store: "She is business-like and keeps a pencil in her hair // But behind her sharpened eyes take flight / The summer evenings in the park // And heated nights in second story dance halls" ("In the Department Store" 268, lines 3–6). However, the closing epigram seals his failure, with the observer's impatient flight: "Man's life is powerless and brief and dark / It is not possible for me to make her happy" ("In the Department Store" 268, lines 7–8).

Only more allegorical poems like "The Death of Saint Narcissus" afford a glimpse of the center of Eliot's intensity. The poem can be read in light of what Jewel Spears Brooker identifies as the main reason for Eliot's turn from philosophy to poetry: the conflict of flesh and soul, body and mind.[9] Turning away from formalist dichotomies, he finds himself before a shared, vulnerable human condition. He harbors new ambitions, of the kind that surface in "The Death of Saint Narcissus." Here, elements of religious iconography—the "bloody cloth and limbs" ("The Death of Saint Narcissus" 270, line 6)—are recontextualized in abstract surroundings where the sacrificial images of saints become amalgamated with mythological echoes. The unnamed, anonymous "he," who "was stifled and soothed by his own rhythm," alludes to Orpheus's plaintive, solitary song (270, line 12). Part Narcissus, part saint, part Orpheus, Eliot's male figure is placed by a river, the setting for a momentous scene of individuation: "He could not live men's ways, but became a dancer before God" (270, line 17). Eliot profiles a poet whose distinctive trait is his capacity for an unusual exposition to others and to the elements: he is a fish, a tree, a disgusting old man. The trials of the flesh by the "burning arrows" "satisfied him" because they seem to prepare him for an enabling kind of speech named through the metaphor of the shadow: the "shadow in his mouth" (271, lines 34, 37, 39).

"The Death of Saint Narcissus" is a declaration of independence. Becoming a "dancer to God" (271, line 33) means something distinct and divergent from the swarming "phantasmagoria of shadows and specters" below the surface of city life and from the "dark angel" mythology that had forged generations of late Victorians (Schuchard 13, 11). Eliot's metaphor also suggests a writing without addressee, except for a loving You (God), a writing which in *Four Quartets* he would call "a raid on the inarticulate" (19). The metaphor calls attention to Eliot's pursuit of a relation to language in terms of gift (the progress of the poet is to be given speech), a fact pointed out by Rebecca Colesworthy when she helpfully recalls that Jacques Lacan concluded his 1953 paper "The Function and Field of Speech and Language in Psychoanalysis" with a reference to Eliot's quote from the Upanishads, at the end of *The Waste Land*, about the priority of "the gift of speech" (Colesworthy 15).

When, in the 1930 introduction to Baudelaire's *Intimate Journals*, translated by Christopher Isherwood, Eliot pays his dues to the master, he talks about himself. Baudelaire becomes a Christian poet: the grime, the slums, the poverty, the viscid human life in the streets, the proximity to abjection and evil are presented as the necessary, ecstatic path to redemption.[10] "The Death of Saint Narcissus" sketches in verse what Eliot would explain in criticism. When read together with early poems like "Preludes" and "The Love Song of Saint Sebastian" (Ricks and McCue, 265–6), it gives us a sense of Eliot's struggle with the model of the modern artist and of his turn toward a more abstract but attractively choreographic landscape of scenes, poses, and gestures. The anonymous voice in "The Death of Saint Narcissus" issues the call to come "under the shadow of this gray rock"; it points the way to a different *savoir* of shadows: "I will show you" ("The Death of Saint Narcissus" 270, lines 2–3).

Dance, it should be noted, becomes the primary metaphor for Eliot's symbolic natality, but it stands for a practice, not for an ideal. "He danced on the hot sand" indicates an action that is necessary until "the arrows came": "As he embraced them his white skin surrendered itself to the redness of blood, and satisfied him" ("The Death of Saint Narcissus" 271, lines 35–7). Dance names the practice aimed at fulfilling an experience in which speech ends up feeling like a kind of "touching," a way of being pierced. The progress is from motion (treading on "convulsive thighs and knees") to shelter ("under the rock"), indicating a less convulsive search as a result of "the burning arrows" (270–1, lines 19, 20, 34). Helen Vendler speaks of Eliot's writing as distinctly "theatrical" (81), thinking perhaps of those moments when verbal language sets in motion a series of poses and gestures. Susan Jones prefers to describe Eliot's writing as choreographic. Taking as an example the verbal directives of "La Figlia Che Piange," Jones argues that "the voice prompts a predominantly choreographed vision of the subject of poetry" ("Eliot" 230). Jones sees "La Figlia Che Piange" as inaugural of a writing entangled in "gesture" and "pose," and she goes on to propose that Eliot thinks of writing, and verbal expression more generally, in terms of choreography and dance. Connecting verbal expression to dance, Jones perceptively establishes that in "La Figlia Che Piange," an "equivocal indeterminacy in the speaker's voice generates an imagined movement between poses and hints at the poet's struggles to craft a scenario that eludes representation" "Eliot" 230). "The Death of Saint Narcissus" is an example of the appeal to dance in the attempt to convey a language of impermanent signs ("the shadow" in the dancer's mouth). The choreographic subject—both the writer and the reader of signs—at the center of Eliot's concerns sheds light on an exceptional, erotic intimacy with the medium. In "The Burnt Dancer," the dancer, a "broken guest," is twinned to the shadow of a presence, as if to an empty space that only deceptively is within the range of touch: "O broken guest that may return not" ("The Burnt Dancer" 263, line 40).[11] The moth's dance "with beat of wings that do not tire," neglects "more vital values" in favor of a single-minded devotion "To golden values of the flame," a fact that by poem's end is extended to the mind of the observer: "Within the circle of my brain / the dance continues" ("The Burnt Dancer" 262, lines 5–7; 263 lines 30–1). The burning arrows in "The Death of Saint Narcissus" signify incision, cut, and caesura; they are strong images of a simultaneous union and separation that seems necessary to ensure intimacy with the medium. They rise as an apt symbol of a writing that is virtuosically attuned to the stifling of life.

Work

In his book *Windows*, Jean-Bertrand Pontalis quotes a poem by Rainer Maria Rilke, where a window functions as a device that might contain "the great excess of the world."[12] Rilke's window can "balance out" a fluid external reality that exceeds conceptuality, framing an otherwise unmanageable world of "faces" that appears "as changeable as the sea." The Austrian poet governs the problem of the many with the poetic image: "reflecting and blending / our faces with what we see through you"; the window secures the observer's cognition ("see"). Eliot refuses. In our discussion of "Preludes" those faces become "the thing." He balks before something unthought, farther from Rilke's metaphor and closer to Pontalis's conceptuality: a conceptuality "that has vanished before awakening" (Pontalis, *Finestre* 21). This seems the center of Eliot's intensities and perhaps no one among his contemporaries can help us illuminate it better than Virginia Woolf.

More than anyone else in Eliot's London circle of acquaintances, Woolf was baffled by his inclination to tarry in a zone where intellectual productivity is articulated with constraint. Woolf was involved in the initiative by Richard Aldington to set up the Eliot Fellowship Fund (1922) to free the American writer from his bank job so that he could write full time, but in a letter to Bloomsbury fellow Roger Fry she called the whole thing "an appalling shindy" (*Letters*, 2, 572). She was irritated by Eliot's reticence about money and especially by his chronic indecision about the kind of life that would be most conducive to the productivity he wished. Writing to another Bloomsbury friend, Lady Ottoline Morell, Woolf reported the facts: "Anything less than £500, he says, would throw him into journalism, and he prefers the Bank" (*Letters*, 2, 561), only to wonder later about "Tom's psychology" which, as she put it, "fascinates and astounds" (*Letters*, 2, 572). The use of the term "psychology" suggests that she might have thought that Eliot had other reasons for rejecting his friends' plans to turn him into a full-time artist. What "fascinates and astounds" Woolf is Eliot's use of wage-earning work as a preservative defense of the life of the mind.

Eliot's form of life differed from the form of life that seemed desirable to more illustrious modernists. Marcel Duchamp, for example, rejected wage-earning work to rebel against the chronophagic pace of production and the assimilation of art to standardized industrial production. From 1923 on, Duchamp referred to himself as "defrocked" from art (Lazzarato 15). Ezra Pound shared Duchamp's views, as is manifest in his own portrait of the artist as a young man, the long poem "Hugh Selwyn Mauberley" (1920). Eliot departed from the dominant modernist view of work, not just because he worked in an institution associated with the evils of capitalism (something that he did only from 1917 to 1925), but because he insisted on holding a regular nine-to-five, wage-earning job throughout his life. When, in the autumn of 1925, he transitioned from Lloyds' Bank to his new office work, first as literary editor and member of the board of directors at the publisher Faber and Gwyer, later as director of the publisher Faber and Faber, his move from a bank to a publisher did not mean a graduation from capital to culture. Frank Morley (1899–1985), an executive at Faber and Faber, who shared a room and a telephone with Eliot, suggests that he was hired as "a man of business" with personal, rather than literary, qualities:

> He was a gentleman; he was literate; he was patient; he got on well with difficult people; he had charm, and he had been in the City. He had good qualifications for a man of business, and it was as a man of business, I suggest, that he was taken on.[13]

Morley conjectures that, for Faber and Gwyer, "there was possibly something solid and comforting, something magical, in having a banker in the crew."[14] The benefit for Eliot was that he could persevere in a form of life that implied a distinctive shape to his days, a shape that, as we shall see, bears directly on his theory of literature.

Eliot distinguished between "permanent" and "ephemeral" writing, writing that endures and writing that is forgotten ("Aim" 386). By the first type of writing, he meant eminently legible writing. In this kind of writing, which may be thought of as akin to argumentative writing, not only can the author "know exactly what he meant" but, having "a definite purpose, a thesis to demonstrate," he or she can choose to make him- or herself understood by the audience. However, "what he has written will cease to interest and excite, as soon as the circumstances, in which he formulated that thesis" cease to exist (386). In the case of the other writing, the "permanent" kind, "the author is making something which he does not understand himself. Only God understands the creature; in human creation humanity is only an instrument" (386). Eliot here is not encouraging automatic writing, a writing under dictation, nor is he defending willful hermeticism. He seems to return to what in "The Death of Saint Narcissus" he had rendered with the image of the dancer—becoming "a dancer to God"—to suggest a writing that is given by others. Eliot's problem is the exigency to write in a way that feels more than blank writing. Just as the dancer's body is an instrument in the hands of the choreographer, so Eliot's writer is the instrument of a writing that does not belong to him. The metaphor of the dancer conjoins writer and interpreter, poet and critic in one and the same act, in one and the same writing, poising Eliot midway between the notion of an "intensive process of interpretation" (Benjamin, "Letter" 388), and the dream of literature as a living-writing continuum, "an interminable ... polylogue" and infinite book which allows one to say "in every way" (Derrida qtd. in

Attridge, "Strange Institution" 35–6), even though Eliot argues that the sort of dispossession he describes is felt in poetry more than in prose, on the ground that "poetry releases more unconscious force, than prose can" ("Aim" 386). Work meant a form of life that might ensure "the potency" of this genre-defying writing, and Eliot's way of shifting closer to an unprecedented intimacy with the medium. He put it simply when he said that the work secured the ability "to think ... with a free mind": "The work is very interesting to me, and also, when 5 o'clock comes it is over, and I can think about my writing for Jourdain, or the New Statesman, or my class, with a free mind" (*Letters*, 1, 181).[15]

At Lloyds Bank Eliot had to file and tabulate balance sheets of all the foreign banks with which Lloyds did business, "in such a way as to show the progress or decline of every bank from year to year" (*Letters*, 1, 181). The "interesting" side of work does not lie in the tasks themselves, but in the "satisfaction" at the idea of having regular work: "It is a great satisfaction to me to have regular work, and I can do my own work much the better for it" (*Letters*, 1, 181). Money of course was a factor, as we know from his wife Vivien:

> He *writes* better, feels better and happier and has better health when he knows that money (however *little*) is *assured*, and coming in regularly—even tho' he has only a few hours a day to write in, than when he has *all* day—and nothing settled, nothing *sure*. (Eliot, *Letters*, 1, 192; original emphasis)

But Vivien could see the reason why Eliot stuck to a form of life that seemed to nullify his prospects as an artist. His "greatest ambition," she relayed to her mother-in-law, was "a congenial and *separate* money-making occupation—of *a sort* that will leave his mind and brain fresh enough to produce good literature" (*Letters*, 1, 197; original emphasis). Waged employment was not, as his modernist colleagues assumed, "the most horrible catastrophe" (*Letters*, 1, 197) but an apt preparation for the "permanent" writing he theorized ("Aim of Poetic Drama"). This does not mean that Eliot did not lament the "lack of continuous time" (*Letters*, 1, 557),[16] but he believed that the daily routine, with a weekly salary adding up to a yearly salary, set working hours 9.15 to 5.00, divided into blocks of time by lunch and tea, assigned tasks, and the accompanying sense of having his small "province" facilitated, he said, "my own work." What is meant by "work"?

Waged employment placed him in a network of others and set Eliot thinking about what in "Preludes" he called "the thing." His interdependence with others engaged his mind daily: "I share an office with Mr McKnight, who lives in a suburb, cultivates a kitchen garden out of hours, polishes his silk hat with great care when he goes out, and talks about his eldest boy" (*Letters*, 1, 185). Through work, he practiced the position that Pontalis calls "like anyone else," a position in which the self is part of a whole of unfamiliar others like Mr McKnight, who are both near, because of the daily proximity, and distant in form of life, habits, interests. The position is expressed simply in the letters when Eliot manifests his good fortune in "being liked," not for any special "acquirements" (*Letters*, 1, 427).[17] Work refined his capacity to be vigilant about the kind of human connection that remained hostile to thought, a fundamental yet tenuous connection which becomes confused with the spatial arrangement of the working environment ("I share an office with Mr McKnight" [*Letters*, 1, 185]). The degree to which Eliot welcomed this sort of vigilance also transpires from his letter of resignation from Lloyds' Bank, on 2 November 1925. In relating his transition from the Bank to the publishing firm Faber and Gwyer, he emphasizes his loyalty to the institution, setting himself amidst a body of co-workers united by reciprocal obligation.[18] In leaving, he will no longer "be encumbering the Bank" on account of his need to attend to "domestic anxieties," and will no longer be put in the position of "provid[ing] a bad example to others" (*Letters*, 2, 769). Eliot expresses concern about the injustice toward a colleague, James de Vine Aylward:

> For Mr Aylward has performed his work and that which was mine, alone since January; he has had one week of holiday and no more, and this only in October; he has had the responsibility without the authority of the Head of a Section, with scant respect and little aid, I sincerely believe (for this is my belief based on previous observation, not on complaints from him; he has not complained to me) from those who dislike to take orders or advice from a 'supplementary' man. (*Letters*, 2, 770)

The office may not be just an obvious microcosm of power relations, of affections and hostilities, but also a privileged point of view on the elusive aspects of community.

His need for this "window" punctuates his self-presentation in the letters to Virginia Woolf. Their correspondence thrusts into relief the endearing persona of a fatigued Tom who does not have time and writes late at night.[19] By the mid-1920s Eliot and Woolf had comfortably settled into a pattern in which she was Virginia, coy and in need of approval, and he was Tom, exhausted and in need of protection.[20] Eliot's self-presentation endured well into the 1930s, when the American writer was internationally recognized as a public intellectual.[21]

There was work and there was his "own" work, with a clear divide between the two, like day and night, and while he complained about "not getting more than a few hours together for myself, which breaks the concentration required for turning out a poem of any length" (*Letters*, 1, 557), the arrangement seemed preeminently desirable. In the relation of life to writing, it allowed him to understand the latter not in terms of self-creation but as "the relation to a practice" (Lucci 70; my translation). Joined to (and cut from) work, writing, to draw on Lucci's take on *forma-di-vita*, is a mode of action that shapes life without Eliot's being reduced to the object that he produces, consequently to the object that he becomes through the work (*un'opera*) that he produces (70). In this way, Eliot kept himself in relation to "the potency," that is to say, in a native relation to language that enabled him to think of himself as one who is given language.

The classical emblem of this intimacy is of course Orpheus. Eliot never explicitly wrote about Orpheus, but Orpheus, as the symbol of an attachment to language that has nothing conventional or artificial about it, runs through his writing and transpires in those moments when a shift toward the non-referential powers of language becomes more audible. In "Marina," for example, speech is anchored in nautical language until the speaker is in a position to describe "caulking," the technique consisting in the joining of planks so that the hull of a boat or ship might be protected and made impermeable. The technique is strikingly representative of Eliot's method. Signs can temporarily settle, as they do in "Marina" ("This form, this face, this place" [Ricks and McCue 157]), but they nevertheless address us as if transparently embalmed in the film of echoes and shadows that become the faces or appearances holding together the planks of the poem (as caulking does the planks of the hull). The poem is the armature of possible scenes of recognition. Even though the process of caulking involves transparency, its effect is to make the poem opaque and impermeable (just like the hull).

The epigraph of Marina, "Quis hic locus, quae regio, quae mundi plaga?" (What place is this? What kingdom, what quarter of the globe? [Ricks and McCue 156]), comes from Seneca's *Hercules Furens*, but the text is a retelling of Shakespeare's *Pericles*.[22] Two versions of truth overlap: the impoverished version of Hercules, who slays his children in a fit of madness, and the version of Pericles, the one who knows deeply because he experiences the healing power of recognition (Brooker 144). In his essay "The Development of Shakespeare's Verse" (1937), Eliot judged Act V, sc. I of Shakespeare's *Pericles* as "the finest of all the 'recognition scenes.'"[23] The retrieval of impermanent signs through recognition is the spring of his theory of literature, which makes his poetry and his criticism hard to keep apart. The non-blank, "permanent" writing celebrated by Eliot steeps the act of writing in the activity of interpretation; it is given to the author without him or her being able to understand what he or she writes. Writing seems always indebted to an act of reading that is not just hermeneutic decoding but, considering Susan Jones's brilliant reading of Eliot's choreographic subject, also a mode of hermeneutic animation.

Over time, Woolf remained baffled by Eliot's form of life. Their correspondence testifies to Eliot's respect for her literary taste and for her activity as a publisher, but reads like a series of ups and downs, with Eliot constantly trying not to let the connection die, while occasionally flaunting his own un-bohemian form of life. At the time of

Figure 6. T. S. Eliot, postcard to Virginia Woolf, 1926. T. S. Eliot Collection of Papers, The Henry W. and Albert A. Berg Collection of English and American Literature, The New York Public Library. Courtesy Eliot Estate.

his trip to Rome, in 1926, he sent her a postcard announcing that he was "on a secret errand to the Pope, of high philosophical and political importance," adding in closing: "We wish you were with us, but want to show you the little house if you will come to tea with us upon (?) return."[24] Woolf was an atheist; she would probably never think of joining Eliot on such a religious errand.[25] The Catholicism infusing Eliot's postcard endearingly points to their substantial divergences, while, in relation to the message, the illustration on the postcard takes on an enigmatic aura (Figure 6). It shows the symbol of a Parisian restaurant, "Le Boeuf à la Mode," which prided itself on having been founded in 1792: an overly accessorized cow, her trunk draped with a fringed shawl, a long pearl necklace with a big oval pendant hanging around her neck, sporting a bonnet with red and blue feathers. A provocatively grotesque self-portrait of the artist?

Who appears? The photographic portraits

A possible response to Woolf's bafflement about Eliot's choices seems to come from the twelve photographic portraits of Eliot by George Platt Lynes housed in the Berg Collection of the New York Public Library.[26] The portraits are undated, but they seem to have been taken—possibly in one sitting—in the New York studio of Eliot's friend Edward McKnight Kauffer. Kauffer's studio is identified through its characteristic bare surroundings and furniture and by one of the posters that the graphic artist created for American Airlines between 1946 and 1949, "Washington—Night and Day."[27] A portrait in the series is particularly meaningful for our discussion; I will refer to it as portrait N. 11, in the order in which I encountered the item in the archive (Figure 7). Eliot sits comfortably, facing the viewer; his hands rest on the armrests and his back is erect, adhering to the back of the chair. A cigarette pack and some matches are visible on the table. The orderly way in which these marginal props have been placed suggests the staged quality of the picture. The main source of light, from the right, is a window giving onto an outside that is kept out of the frame. If we look carefully, we see the window reflected on the wall. Eliot poses in a slightly rotated position so that, despite the erect back, the figure seems tilted toward the white wall and the barely visible shadow of the window. In N. 11, Eliot's nearness to the reflection beautifully captures his form of life, aimed at sustaining the relation of writing to a practice of separations and divides. All twelve photographic portraits in the Berg open to a fascinating web of connections that can further illuminate Eliot's practice, if only retrospectively given the portraits' dating in the late 1940s.

Lynes's twelve portraits have a way of pressing the question of "who": Who appears? (Figures 7–18). By the time he crossed paths with Lynes—whether the date is 1947 or 1950 or

Figure 7. George Platt Lynes, T. S. Eliot, twelve photographic portraits undated. T. S. Eliot Collection of Papers, The Henry W. and Albert A. Berg Collection of English and American Literature, The New York Public Library. Photographic Portrait N. 11. Courtesy Joshua R. Lynes.

anytime in-between—Eliot had achieved public fame and was especially sought as a public lecturer in his native country.[28] He was a desirable object of study for a photographer like Lynes who had collected an astonishing array of modernists. From the early 1930s to the early 1950s, George Platt Lynes (1907–55) had taken portraits of the likes of Gertrude Stein, Jean Cocteau, Edith Sitwell, E. M. Forster, Marsden Hartley, Aldous Huxley, Thomas Mann, Katharine Anne Porter, Marianne Moore, Dorothy Parker, of musicians like Igor Stravinsky, Aaron Copeland, Arnold Schoenberg, of painters like Salvador Dalí, Marc Chagall, Oskar Kokoschka, of photographers like Henri Cartier-Bresson and Cecil Beaton, to name just a few of his sitters (Leddick, *George Platt Lynes*). A flyer for the exhibition mounted five years after his death lists, among others, portraits of André Gide, Colette, Janet Flanner, Mina Loy, Somerset Maugham, Kay Boyle, E. E. Cummings, W. H. Auden, Christopher Isherwood, Marianne Moore, and Dorothy Parker.[29] As Lincoln Kirstein remarks in the text of the flyer, Lynes had photographed or, as Kirstein put it, "fixed the face," of "nearly every artist and writer and musician of importance in his epoch," proposing that the photographer's talent consisted in representing his subjects in ways that did not corroborate the public icon (Kirstein 1960, n.p.).

In his reading of Lynes, Kirstein attempts to redeem the photographer's version of modernism from the discourse on celebrity. He rejects the opposition of the truth of the individual versus the artificiality of the public persona, claiming that "Lynes' faces remained private faces."[30] Kirstein, however, must have been aware of Lynes's even greater talent for creating public icons, since he had hired him to invent the "successful, elegant, and glamorous" image of Ballet Society. The company that Kirstein had founded with George Balanchine on the ashes of Diaghilev's Ballets Russes was later to become the New York City Ballet, with Lynes's lavishly illustrated souvenir programs masking the company's financial difficulties (Weinberg 134). If Lynes knew well the difference between private individual and public mask, that is because he was versed in the making of modernist personae that display an unclear difference between truth and artifice. His "surprisingly direct" studies of Gertrude Stein (Prokopoff n.p.) are highly representative of a style that has been praised for its clarity and neat syntax:

> In much the same way as our verbal expression, written or spoken, wants to be in good order, reasonably and neatly tied together with

subject and predicate and relative clauses intelligibly related to the whole entity, there is a grammar of location, a syntax of pose and a cadence of the brightness and the blackness to guide the eye. (Scott n.p.)

But such directness is not diminished when the portrait suggests a melodramatic public mask, as in the instance of Edith Sitwell: "garbed in a costume of rich brocade, seated in majesty," she "seems to bless her admirers with a royal gesture" (Prokopoff n.p.).

The gap between the truth of the individual and the appearance of the public icon in Lynes's modernist portraiture is the effect of his "thoughtful control of the studio" (Prokopoff n.p.). The studied control came from his experience in fashion photography, which remained his primary occupation.[31] The main features of his studio work, especially "the strong contrast of shadows and lights" and the sculptural effect, inform his photography for Kirstein and Balanchine, combining with "a clear sense of line and gesture" (Weinberg 130). The same features are recognizable in his modernist portraiture, which stands out for Lynes's particular construction of space. He used light and "cramped and cropped composition" to highlight only what could be "brought clearly to the attention of the lens" (Scott n.p.). Such devices create the impression of a "natural space around his subject" (Scott n.p.), of "a close, containing environment around the figures that forces the spectator to share their space" (Prokopoff n.p.). His studies of male nudes provided opportunities to experiment with this type of construction of space, dislodging the spectator from his or her observer's position and asking him or her to occupy the place of a participant witness. Lynes does not fit the person to an essential trait (candor, or majesty, etc.), but uses the photographic session to redraw the boundary between photographer and photographed subject. Rather than aim the camera at the photographed subject, he seeks to bring into the field of vision what the sitter wants to let emerge.[32] When Kirstein speaks of Lynes's "private faces," therefore, the adjective "private" is highly suggestive of a collaboration that becomes an integral part of the final image.[33] Lynes's characteristic construction of space is key for reading his portraits of Eliot.[34] What does their collaboration tell us about Eliot?

Before answering, it would be helpful to consider what Balanchine said about Lynes's photography. As a choreographer, Balanchine appreciated the sculptural quality of Lynes's images, speaking of that quality as "Lynes' secret":

> For Lynes' secret was his sense of plasticity, his genius for lighting figures in space so that his bodies seemed to exist in actual aery ambience, akin to the three-dimensional vitality in sculpture. What it lacked in color or motion it more than made up in a quintessential permanence of characteristic silhouette and massive form. (105)

Balanchine was an expert in dancers' bodies and what attracted him to Lynes's photography was that, far from being driven by the desire to make something permanent, it wanted to show the fact of silhouette and form stolen from ephemerality and impermanence. His images were a perfect match for the ephemerality of Balanchine's own art, ballet, which he countered to the literary monumentality of Proust: "I have never considered my own repertory of more than passing interest; nor have I ever kept scrapbooks, letters, programs, posters or photographs. I have energy to make new works, not to recall old ones with original accuracy" (Balanchine 105). Balanchine favored Lynes's photography because it did not document dance steps, but gave what was essentially ephemeral some sort of "quintessential permanence" through lines, gestures and poses (105). We have seen that Eliot described his literary practice through dance; when considered from Balanchine's point of view, Lynes's portrait N. 11 captures Eliot's own idea of "permanent" writing: a certain execution of language, like the body's execution of a choreography, can cause writing to shift from "medium of flux" to "instrument of tradition" (Weinberg 135).

Like Balanchine, Eliot associated ballet with permanent forms. In "A Dialogue on Dramatic Poetry," one the participants (B) proposes that "The ballet is valuable because it has, unconsciously, concerned itself with a permanent form" ("A Dialogue" 400).[35] Ballet comes close to his idea of tradition: a continuum (a simultaneous order) in which voices are enfolded one in the other (and one writer speaks with the other in his bones). Like Eliot's tradition, ballet suggests "a training, an askesis ... which ascends for several centuries" ("A Dialogue" 400). Eliot had trained himself in the appearance of ordinarily invisible emotions of which all partake.[36] Lynes's photographic portrait N. 11 redeems the writer's daily askesis from the banality of meaning. We are made to inhabit his space. Lit from more than one angle, Eliot is more than a face; he appears fully embodied and concrete. As in other Lynes images, props direct the gaze to areas of vulnerability: the armrest, the pack of cigarettes and matches at close range cramp and crop the composition, and, although Eliot is perfectly attired, it is as if he were just a body next to the barely visible shadow.

Figure 8. George Platt Lynes, T. S. Eliot, twelve photographic portraits undated. T. S. Eliot Collection of Papers, The Henry W. and Albert A. Berg Collection of English and American Literature, The New York Public Library. Photographic Portrait N. 1. Courtesy Joshua R. Lynes.

Figure 9. George Platt Lynes, T. S. Eliot, twelve photographic portraits undated. T. S. Eliot Collection of Papers, The Henry W. and Albert A. Berg Collection of English and American Literature, The New York Public Library. Photographic Portrait N. 2. Courtesy Joshua R. Lynes.

Figure 10. George Platt Lynes, T. S. Eliot, twelve photographic portraits undated. T. S. Eliot Collection of Papers, The Henry W. and Albert A. Berg Collection of English and American Literature, The New York Public Library. Photographic Portrait N. 3. Courtesy Joshua R. Lynes.

Double portrait

Some of the twelve photographic portraits in the Berg Collection feature in the background the same American Airlines poster, "Washington—Night and Day," which can also be seen in the background of Lynes's beautiful and widely reproduced double portrait

Figure 11. George Platt Lynes, T. S. Eliot, twelve photographic portraits undated. T. S. Eliot Collection of Papers, The Henry W. and Albert A. Berg Collection of English and American Literature, The New York Public Library. Photographic Portrait N. 4. Courtesy Joshua R. Lynes.

of Eliot and his friend Edward McKnight Kauffer. The portrait is assumed to have been taken in 1950, but might as well have been taken during the same session as the twelve photographic portraits in the Berg, unless Eliot sat for Lynes more than once years apart.[37]

Figure 12. George Platt Lynes, T. S. Eliot, twelve photographic portraits undated. T. S. Eliot Collection of Papers, The Henry W. and Albert A. Berg Collection of English and American Literature, The New York Public Library. Photographic Portrait N. 5. Courtesy Joshua R. Lynes.

The portrait plays up the "dramatic resemblance" (Schulman 129) between Eliot and his artist friend, who were often mistaken for brothers.[38] Lynes, however, uses the physiognomic affinity—"both willowy and aquiline" (Schulman 129)—to suggest a deeper spiritual affinity.

American by birth, from Montana, Kauffer, who had taken the name McKnight from his benefactor, had become one of England's

Figure 13. George Platt Lynes, T. S. Eliot, twelve photographic portraits undated. T. S. Eliot Collection of Papers, The Henry W. and Albert A. Berg Collection of English and American Literature, The New York Public Library. Photographic portrait N. 6. Courtesy Joshua R. Lynes.

most popular advertising artists. His posters decorated the London Underground in the 1930s. Aldous Huxley argues that Kauffer used the main features of modernist aesthetics—"simplification, distortion and transposition" and "a simplified, formalized" representation of things through expressive symbols—in the service of a public

Figure 14. George Platt Lynes, T. S. Eliot, twelve photographic portraits undated. T. S. Eliot Collection of Papers, The Henry W. and Albert A. Berg Collection of English and American Literature, The New York Public Library. Photographic portrait N. 7. Courtesy Joshua R. Lynes.

art that would keep alive untapped areas of meaning ("Foreword" n.p.). Kauffer himself, commenting on "Derry and Toms, 1917," his advertisement for a London department store, described it as "an endeavor to dramatize shapes in space, to give an excitement to the

Figure 15. George Platt Lynes, T. S. Eliot, twelve photographic portraits undated. T. S. Eliot Collection of Papers, The Henry W. and Albert A. Berg Collection of English and American Literature, The New York Public Library. Photographic portrait N. 8. Courtesy Joshua R. Lynes.

mind with the use of non-naturalistic symbols and to suggest to the person who sees it a conflict of which he is a solitary witness" (Kauffer n.p.). Kauffer was the author of the first cubist poster, "Flight" (1919), the abstract representation of a soaring multiplicity.[39] He

Figure 16. George Platt Lynes, T. S. Eliot, twelve photographic portraits undated. T. S. Eliot Collection of Papers, The Henry W. and Albert A. Berg Collection of English and American Literature, The New York Public Library. Photographic portrait N. 9. Courtesy Joshua R. Lynes.

Figure 17. George Platt Lynes, T. S. Eliot, twelve photographic portraits undated. T. S. Eliot Collection of Papers, The Henry W. and Albert A. Berg Collection of English and American Literature, The New York Public Library. Photographic portrait N. 10. Courtesy Joshua R. Lynes.

celebrated the collectivity, but the emphasis on conflict and on the "solitary witness" in his technique suggests that, like Eliot, he was interested in releasing unconscious forces.

The Kauffer poster in the background of Lynes's double portrait functions as a linking device, connecting the two men in their artistic vision. The asymmetry in the composition contrasts with the

Figure 18. George Platt Lynes, T. S. Eliot, twelve photographic portraits undated. T. S. Eliot Collection of Papers, The Henry W. and Albert A. Berg Collection of English and American Literature, The New York Public Library. Photographic Portrait N. 12. Courtesy Joshua R. Lynes.

symmetry of the physiognomies. Kauffer has taken his jacket off and occupies a standing position, his willowy body in view, while Eliot is seated in his formal attire. As is often the case in Lynes's images, an asymmetrical distribution of agency between the two subjects photographed reveals a complicity and a shared silent knowledge.[40] Here, the uneven distribution of agency reveals a profound intellectual and spiritual correspondence. The source of light is the outside; they are both inside and are looking out as if their parallel gazes see the same thing in the same way. They seem solitary witnesses together. The sense of their shared lyrical view of the social bond (being alone together) is entirely a construction of Lynes's photography, and it may be a product of his own heroic version of modernist lives, but the double photographic portrait does remind us that it was Kauffer who appreciated what Susan Jones calls Eliot's "choreographic subject." Kauffer wrote to Eliot, "Your work awakens in me memories beyond myself and before myself . . ." (Kauffer qtd. in Haworth-Booth 55), sharing his own ambition to stir dormant cultural layers in the collective memory. The illustration that he provided for "Marina," a poem discussed above, shows two majestic, icastic male figures that recall in posture and pose Giorgio de Chirico's *Disquieting Muses* (1916–18).[41] More than illustrating the content of the poem, Kauffer's image foregrounds an affinity between the writer and the visual artist. The two statuary figures are not just linked; they appear as contained or incorporated one in the other.

At the time of Lynes's double portrait, Kauffer was an important bridge figure between Eliot and the New York cultural scene. The work of Terri Meister and Susan Jones has mapped those connections through dance.[42] Lynes's work adds to those connections and provides valuable material for Eliot's role in what Jones calls a "transatlantic poetics."[43] Lincoln Kirstein was an admirer of Eliot and had assimilated his influence, an influence that was not only palpable in the company's repertoire but also colored Kirstein's own assessment of Balanchine.[44] His portrait of the choreographer strikingly recalls the poet: "Balanchine has always attempted to find, refine and intensify those kinetic signs which even by short-circuit, dialectic, elision or antithesis provide at once a shock, a conviction and a deep, satisfactory recognition" (Kirstein, "American Ballet: II" 17). The notion of "kinetic signs" links the choreographer's lyrical corpus to Eliot's writing of shadows.

As the impresario of the New York City Ballet, Kirstein's mission was to transform the image of the American artist on the international scene, undoing familiar stereotypes that associated America with mechanization, commerce, and soulless capitalism. He appealed to literary models like Emily Dickinson to champion an American tradition that extolled not innovation but a certain asceticism:

> There is, in the best examples of classic American style, a leanness, a visual asceticism, a candour, even an awkwardness which is in itself elegant, shared also by some of our finest Colonial silver, the thin carving on New England grave slabs and in the quicksilver of Emily Dickinson's unrhymed quatrains. (Kirstein, "American Ballet: II" 18)

Kirstein included ballet in this tradition, arguing that the famed "technical efficiency" of American dancers, far from encouraging the "malignant narcissism" in dance ("American Ballet: II" 18), serves a higher aesthetic purpose.[45]

The London performances that Eliot attended in the summer of 1950 were part of this mission.[46] The Covent Garden repertoire included the celebrated *Orpheus*, in the original 1948 Balanchine production. *Orpheus* was commissioned by Stravinsky in 1946 and the production of 1948 resulted from an exceptional collaborative work, with the choreography by Balanchine, the music by Stravinsky and striking costumes and scenery by sculptor Isamu Noguchi. Noguchi renders compellingly the story of "the artist blinded by his vision" with the use of a mask (131). Drawing on the familiar myth, the production tells the story of Orpheus who, grief-stricken by the death of Eurydice, is led by the Dark Angel to the underworld, where he reclaims his wife only to lose her again when she insists on him tearing off the mask that he has sworn to wear. Back on earth, he is torn to pieces by the Thracian Bacchantes, and the ballet ends with the invocation of the spirit of Orpheus as the source of song by Apollo, who appears on the stage wearing a majestic mask. The mask is the gravitational force of the ballet; it decides the plot and underscores the association of the power of song with opaqueness and blindness, a fact also stressed by the Lynes photographs used for souvenir programs, like the beautiful souvenir program for 1951 showing the hands of the male dancers on a majestic mask.[47] But Orpheus's blindness means an exceptional union with the medium, and in Balanchine's production the mask becomes confused with the lyre as a positive symbol of creative power. One reviewer talked of the mask of Orpheus as "both a harp and a tree in the rich earth of the soul."[48] Both the mask and the lyre are on a continuum with Orpheus's body.[49]

The relation of the two objects created the opportunity for the male duet between Nicholas Magallanes, as Orpheus, and Francisco Monsion, as the Dark Angel who takes him to Hades. The duet became legendary and deemed unrepeatable for the sensuality of the execution.[50] When the Dark Angel comes to take Orpheus to the underworld, the two dancers join hands through the lyre.[51] The ballet was celebrated because it struck a balance of expressiveness and constraint (White 13–17).[52] The two dancers perform a score of "enchainments" and "entwinings" that bring forth the erotic dimension of the life of the mind, with the relation to song rendered as erotic relation, as shown by the confusion of lyre and mask.[53] Lynes continued to capture offstage this aspect of the production with separate photographs of Magallanes (as Orpheus) and Moncion (as the Dark Angel) in his studio in 1948.[54] In these more private portraits, the dancers have taken off their clothes and reenact some of the poses from Balanchine's ballet.[55] These images are marginal with respect to Balanchine's original production, but they prove valuable when reading Lynes's version of Eliot. In the Magallanes–Moncion photographic portraits, the mask and the lyre take center stage, as if they were a reflection of one another, just as the two bodies seem to echo each other, with lines that overshadow, follow, and protect each other.[56] The relation of two objects, the mask and the lyre, blends with the dialogue of the two figures. The portraits are a superb example of Lynes's gift for giving substance to a reality that belongs exclusively to the world of the studio.[57] The two objects stand out in their concreteness, with Naguchi's original design showcasing their uncanny autonomy, but they also enhance the nakedness of the sitters, calling the viewer's attention to their substitutive function: like clothes, they are necessary to the self; they prepare the self for those who see. They are part of the body, as suggested in one of the opening sequences where the lyre rests against the back of the right leg of a masked Orpheus.[58] In Lynes's magnetic portraits of Magallanes and Moncion, the lyre and the mask are the visual transcript of the problem of the artist understood in terms of an intimacy with the medium. Lynes's double portrait of Eliot and Kauffer echoes the same motif, but the motif, as we have seen, can be traced in Eliot's solo portraits in the Berg batch.

When, in the summer of 1950, during the intermission of a performance of *Orpheus* at Covent Garden, Kirstein asked Eliot to write a sequel to the ballet, Eliot refused (Kirstein, *New York City Ballet* 102).[59] It was as if someone were asking him to become an artist.

Notes

1. She writes to her brother-in-law: "Come to lunch, Eliot will be there in a four piece suit" (Virginia Woolf qtd. in Gordon 83–4).
2. "The Method of Mr. Pound" was first published in *The Atheneum*, 4669, 24 October 1919; "Reflections on Contemporary Poetry [IV]" in *The Egoist*, 6 (1919): 39–40; "Tradition and the Individual Talent" was published in two installments, the first in *The Egoist*, 6 (1919): 54–5, the second in *The Egoist*, 6 (1919): 72–3. See the editor's notes to volume two of *The Complete Prose of T. S. Eliot* (*The Perfect Critic, 1919–1926*).
3. Unless otherwise specified, quotations from Eliot's poems in this chapter are from *The Poems of T. S. Eliot. Volume I: Collected and Uncollected Poems*, edited by Christopher Ricks and Jim McCue (Baltimore, MD: Johns Hopkins University Press, 2015). The poems will be referenced either as "Ricks and McCue" followed by the relevant page number, or by the poem's title, the page number in Ricks and McCue, and the line numbers.
4. Eliot's artist is like Wallace Stevens's scholar: a reader who, in the confined space of a room, becomes the book he reads, a fact that Stevens calls "a perfection of thought" (358).
5. The emblems of such a dialectic were Hamlet and Faust. "I am not Prince Hamlet," Eliot's Prufrock famously declares. Ronald Schuchard discusses the "sensual-spiritual malaise" that infuses the work of the French master, and the influence of "the dark angel" on the late Victorian poet Lionel Johnson and on all the members of Yeats's generation, who considered Baudelaire as an essential part of their formation: "Dowson, Johnson, Beardsley, and Wilde all knew the dark angel" (5).
6. For Eliot's Baudelaire, see also Rainey.
7. I am working with the Italian edition, *Finestre*, and all translations from it are mine; for the English edition, see Pontalis, *Windows*.
8. See Christopher Ricks's commentary to the poem in Eliot, *Inventions* 211.
9. See especially the first three chapters of Brooker.
10. Eliot's Baudelaire authors a "poetry of flight" which is itself the search "for a form of life" (Eliot, "Introduction" 15) guided by "a dim recognition of the direction of beatitude" (22).
11. See also Schuchard 9, 12.
12. In the English translation, the poem is entitled "Measure of Longing" and can be found in Rilke, *When I Go: Selected French Poems of Rainer Maria Rilke*. Eliot's "Preludes" (composed between 1910 and 1911) is earlier than Rilke's poem which, like all the other poems in this collection, dates between 1923 and 1926.

13. "T. S. Eliot as Publisher," Frank Vigor Morley Collection of Papers, The Henry W. and Albert A. Berg Collection of English and American Literature, The New York Public Library, p. 3. Morley's text, "T. S. Eliot as Publisher," originally a lecture delivered in 1949, appeared in *T. S. Eliot: A Symposium*, eds. Tambimuttu and Richard March.
14. "T. S. Eliot as Publisher," Frank Vigor Morley Collection of Papers, The Henry W. and Albert A. Berg Collection of English and American Literature, The New York Public Library, p. 4. See also Morley, "A Few Recollections"; and, on Eliot as publisher, Gupta.
15. A letter to his mother in March 1917.
16. For a description of the constraint that Eliot's nine-to-five job put on his writing both as a poet and as a critic, see Crawford 339–40.
17. "Yet I am very fortunate in having got into the bank and being so highly thought of there—not only for the acquirements which they overestimate (I am supposed to be a profound economist, and a special scholar in French, German, Spanish and Norwegian) but in being liked" (Eliot, *Letters*, 1, 427).
18. Eliot had created the "Intelligence Section" as separate and autonomous from the Colonial and Foreign Department.
19. T. S. Eliot to Virginia Woolf, 12 November 1918, "Correspondence: Outgoing Correspondence," Correspondence to V. Woolf, Folder 1, T. S. Eliot Collection of Papers, The Henry W. and Albert A. Berg Collection of English and American Literature, The New York Public Library. See also, in the same folder, Eliot's letter to Woolf, 12 April 1919.
20. T. S. Eliot to Virginia Woolf, 7 April 1924, "Correspondence: Outgoing Correspondence," Correspondence to V. Woolf, Folder 3, item 1, T. S. Eliot Collection of Papers, The Henry W. and Albert A. Berg Collection of English and American Literature, The New York Public Library.
21. See, for example, Eliot's letter of 9 January 1935, "Correspondence: Outgoing Correspondence," Correspondence to V. Woolf, Folder 7, item 2, T. S. Eliot Collection of Papers, The Henry W. and Albert A. Berg Collection of English and American Literature, The New York Public Library. For a heady description of his own academic success, see the letter of 25 April 1933 (Eliot, *Letters*, 6, 574–7).
22. For a reading of "Marina" that explicates this incongruity, see Brooker 142–6.
23. Eliot qtd. in Ricks and McCue's commentary to "Marina," 773.
24. Correspondence to V. Woolf, Folder 4, item 1, T. S. Eliot Collection of Papers, The Henry W. and Albert A. Berg Collection of English and American Literature, The New York Public Library. The postcard is dated 23 April 1926. Eliot traveled to Rome with Vivien, his brother Henry and his wife.

25. "I have had the most shameful and distressing interview with poor dear Tom Eliot, who may be called dead to us all from this day forward. He has become an Anglo-Catholic, believes in God and immortality, and goes to church. I was really shocked. A corpse would seem to me more credible than he is. I mean, there's something obscene in a living person sitting by the fire and believing in God" (Virginia Woolf's letter to Vanessa Bell, 11 February 1928, *Letters* 3, 457–8).
26. George Platt Lynes, twelve portrait photographs of Thomas Stearns Eliot, unsigned and undated, 18 x 19.5 cm, T. S. Eliot Collection of Papers, The Henry W. and Albert A. Berg Collection of English and American Literature, The New York Public Library.
27. In the checklist of posters by Kauffer included in Mark Haworth-Booth's biography, *E. McKnight Kauffer: A Designer and His Public*, the American Airline poster depicted here in George Platt Lynes's photographic portrait, "American Airlines to Washington—Night and Day," is listed as n. 309 and included among the posters dated c. 1946–9 (Haworth-Booth 124).
28. I have not been able to find any evidence for an exact date. The twelve photographic portraits comprise an image of Eliot that is very similar to the portrait acquired by the National Portrait Gallery, which is dated 1947: <https://www.npg.org.uk/collections/search/portrait/mw213832/TS-Eliot?LinkID=mp01450&role=sit&rNo=1>. Accessed 21 April 2022.
29. The exhibition was held at the Art Institute of Chicago Gallery of Photography, 15 July–28 August 1960, and it included Lynes's portraiture from 1931 to 1952. Lincoln Kirstein Papers (1907–91), Box 16, Jerome Robbins Dance Division, The New York Public Library for the Performing Arts.
30. Lincoln Kirstein Papers (1907–91), Box 16, Folder 97–255, Jerome Robbins Dance Division, The New York Public Library for the Performing Arts.
31. Lynes had originally set up a studio in New York in 1932. His life-long collaboration with choreographer George Balanchine started the following year, in 1933. In 1945 his fashion work, which had appeared in *Town and Country*, *Harper's Bazaar*, and *Vogue*, earned him the directorship of the Vogue Studio in Los Angeles, where he moved only to return to New York two years later, in 1947, to collaborate with Kirstein and Balanchine. I am drawing on the biographical note and the chronology included in Lynes, *Photographic Visions*.
32. Kirstein speaks of his portraiture as a practice of friendship: "George Lynes was the friend of painters and writers all his life; he saw through the eyes of their observings and this schooling was a permanent academy" ("Untitled" 79).
33. From this perspective, Lynes's portraiture may be considered as an example of that art of collaboration that is distinctive of the New York

School. Balanchine too notices a capacity for empathy with the sitter: "George loved dancers around his studio and his home. They were not alone his subjects but his intimates—like his beautiful pictures: his early Picasso, the Klees, the magnificent Tchelitchew 'Golden Leaf,' and his fine modern American drawings. His true family consisted of painters and poets" (105).

34. See the first section, "Nudes," in Woody.
35. Susan Jones discusses Eliot's view of ballet, especially this concern for an impermanent form that a choreographic effort must bring forth into visibility ("Eliot" 235).
36. For this askesis, Eliot had turned from philosophy to poetry. See Brooker's work, in particular chapter 2, "Eliot's First Conversion: 'Rhapsody on a Windy Night' and the 1913 Critique of Bergson," and chapter 3, "Eliot's Debt to F. H. Bradley," of her book.
37. I do not have any knowledge of the dates. The verso of most of the photographs in the Berg Collection says "George Platt Lynes" and "Vogue Studios," which does not necessarily prove that they were printed in Los Angeles, where Lynes was director of the Vogue Studios from 1945 to 1947. I am particularly grateful to Grace Schulman for the conversation we had in the summer of 2019 in her New York apartment. She confirmed that the portrait of Eliot and her mentor, Kauffer, was taken in 1950; she also confirmed that the setting of the portraits in the Berg Collections is Kauffer's studio. What is strange is that, in the Berg pictures, Eliot seems to be wearing the same suit as he does in the twin portrait with Kauffer. For a memoir discussing the double portrait, and including a reproduction, see Schulman.
38. In a tribute to his friend, Eliot begins to describe Kauffer's appearance but stops short to avoid being self-referential: they looked, in fact, alike: "He was in appearance very much the same figure that he is to-day: tall, slender and elegantly-dressed, and wearing whatever he wore with a grace that would make the best of the best efforts of the best tailor. (I cannot venture to say much about his appearance, because there is said to be a facial resemblance between Kauffer and myself—at any rate, when I have asked for him at the building in which he lives, several successive porters have taken for granted that I was his brother)" (Eliot qtd. in Ricks and McCue 775).
39. The poster was printed by the London newspaper *Daily Herald* with the title "The Early Bird: Soaring to Success."
40. This is the case, for example, in Lynes's portrait of W. Somerset Maugham, 1941, where the writer is standing up, fully dressed in his striped suit, kerchief poking from his pocket and right arm akimbo in a pose that evokes the dandy, looking down at a younger man with nude torso whose portrait is taken from the back so that the viewer can see only his naked torso (Woody 93).

41. Eliot wrote to Kauffer that his art reminded him of de Chirico (Haworth-Booth 56).
42. Meister, "Dance"; Jones, "Eliot," "'At the still point,'" and *Literature*.
43. See Jones, "'At the still point.'"
44. He acknowledges this influence, for example, in the company's production of "Transcendence" (1935), one of Balanchine's earlier American works: "Ingredients were from a mixture of sources, including ... Sir James Frazer's *The Golden Bough*, Jessie L. Weston's *From Ritual to Romance*, T. S. Eliot" (Kirstein qtd. in Jones, "Eliot" 238).
45. "The technical efficiency of American dancers is comparable to the general high level of our mechanization, but even automobiles possess personalities. Look at a jeep. Balanchine has taught those dancers for whom he is responsible and who are responsible to him for the maintenance of his repertory, that hot mime is bad manners. (Kirstein, "American Ballet: II" 18).
46. Lincoln Kirstein's New York City Ballet opened at the Royal Opera House on 10 July 1950 with a program including: *The Age of Anxiety* (Bernstein–Oliver Smith–Robbins), *Orpheus* (Stravinsky–Noguchi–Balanchine), and *Symphony in C* (Bizet–Karinska–Balanchine). Eliot had been sent an anonymous gift of tickets and attended the premiere of *The Age of Anxiety*. In a letter to Lincoln Kirstein on 19 July 1950, he writes to thank him because he suspected that the director of the New York City Ballet had a role in the gift. He writes: "I have been meaning to write to you ever since the first night of the New York Ballet," and lets Kirstein know that he "was much impressed" by *The Age of Anxiety*, even though during the intermission, having spotted Kirstein, he was unable to talk to him. With the letter, Eliot responds to Kirstein's invitation to attend "the Stravinsky ballet." In the summer of 1950 both *Fire Bird* and *Orpheus* were brought to Covent Garden, but we know from Kirstein that Eliot attended *Orpheus*. In the 1973 edition of his book, *The New York City Ballet*, under the section "Covent Garden," Kirstein recalls: "During an intermission after a performance of *Orpheus* to which I'd asked Eliot, we spoke of a possible sequel for which his words might conceivably be set by Stravinsky, as he had handled André Gide's Perséphone" (102). White 13–17; T. S. Eliot, letter of Eliot to Lincoln Kirstein, 19 July 1950, Manuscript Box, T. S. Eliot Collection of Papers, The Henry W. and Albert A. Berg Collection of English and American Literature, The New York Public Library. For the conversation between Eliot and Kirstein in Covent Garden in the summer of 1950, as reported by Kirstein, see also Jones, "Eliot" 238.
47. New York City Ballet, Seventh New York Season, June 1951, souvenir program. Jerome Robbins Dance Division, New York Public Library for the Performing Arts, Special Collections.

48. Seymour Raven, "New 'Orpheus' Ballet Shows Genius' Touch," unknown source, Jerome Robbins Dance Division, New York Public Library for the Performing Arts.
49. In one of his portraits of Magallanes and Moncion, Lynes shows Orpheus, shot from the back, wearing the mask, with the lyre resting against his right leg (see Woody).
50. Commenting on a 1979 revival of *Orpheus* by Baryshnikov, Clive Barnes recalls Magallanes's performance as "largely one of unstressed presence." "Slow-eyed and slow-paced," Magallanes "offered Orpheus as if it were an autobiographical lyric poem." Barnes had no doubts: "No one has done it like him since. No one will." Clive Barnes, "Baryshnikov Revives 'Orpheus' for the City," *New York Post*, 5 February 1979, Jerome Robbins Dance Division, New York Public Library for the Performing Arts.
51. See the reproduction in Woody 108.
52. Eric Walter White helpfully points out the cross-historical valence, referring to Monteverdi's, Gluck's, and Offenbach's conceptions of the myth, while defining Stravinsky's version as "a score of grave beauty and restraint, which provides in musical terms a moving understatement to the deep and sometimes terrifying emotions roused by that myth" (15).
53. Rene Dumesnil, "Une semaine dans le monde," 9 August 1947, quoted in a compilation by Maitland McDonagh for the New York City Ballet Program, January 1989; Anna Kisselgoff, "Why Do Some Ballets Seem Dated?," *New York Times*, Late Edition, 15 June 1980, A.22, Jerome Robbins Dance Division, New York Public Library for the Performing Arts.
54. For photographs of the original 1948 production of the ballet, see George Platt Lynes, "Photographic Scrapbooks," Vol. 13, "Orpheus (Balanchine)," Jerome Robbins Dance Division, New York Public Library for the Performing Arts, Special Collections.
55. For a reproduction of some of these images, see Woody 107–13. The photographs of Monsion and Magallanes are also reproduced in Lynes, *Ballet*.
56. See the reproduction in Woody 107.
57. As Weinberg observes: "We are not asked to imagine these two figures inhabiting any world but that of the studio" (130).
58. See the reproduction in Woody 113.
59. Kirstein's account of the time he approached Eliot to ask him to collaborate on a sequel to *Orpheus*, with Stravinsky setting the poet's words to music, continues: "But Eliot knew of the composer's notorious difficulties with French prosody and Gide's poetics, and was not enthusiastic. A sung prayer for dancers could be imagined, but would take consideration. Eliot, remote, courteous, attentive, thought dancing was

sufficient unto itself, requiring nothing by way of words, at least from him. I reminded him of his excellent notices of dancing and music halls when he edited the Criterion; he replied that those were 'evocation not invocation'" (*New York City Ballet* 102).

Chapter 6

Text and Method: Cixous–Joyce–Lispector

> Stephen watched the three glasses being raised from the counter as his father and his two cronies drank to the memory of their past. An abyss of fortune and of temperament sundered him from them.
> James Joyce, *A Portrait of the Artist as a Young Man*

Overview

In the previous chapter we followed T. S. Eliot's erosion of the linear concept of tradition from the vantage point of the conflict of Life and Form. Eliot's theory of literature hands down to us a circuit of gift and debt, tying one writer to the other, that resonates with Esposito's plane of coevalness. Eliot's plane of repetition and recognition exceeds the figure of the artist as it was understood by his contemporaries; it takes away the stress from self-fashioning and tips the scales toward the search for an enabling intimacy with the medium of language. It is in his relation to language as pure potentiality that Eliot can be enlisted in living thought, as someone who felt the exigency of a writing that aspires to pierce the impersonal dimension of human experience. This chapter follows up and discusses contemporary feminist theorist Hélène Cixous back to back with Eliot because her recuperation of Brazilian writer Clarice Lispector activates the conflict of Life and Form, latent in modernism and now overtly redirected in the theorization of an alternative line of reflection which the French feminist thinker, similarly to Esposito, qualifies as "living." For Cixous, "writing is something living."[1]

Cixous interests us here because, even though she has been assimilated to French poststructuralism, her idea of literature strays from what has become customary to associate with the poststructuralist attitude. She neither assumes a competitive relation with the text nor does she feed the hostility of text and critic which has been lamented, in postcritical times, as an effect of poststructuralism (Marcus and Best 18). Her gaze is neither impassive nor distancing; it does not nullify the text in the attempt to go against "received wisdom" or secrete "an exemplary self-consciousness and a heightened aesthetic sensibility" (Felski, *Limits* 74).[2] Cixous places center stage the activity of reading, with the sense of wonder and discovery that we associate with it. Reading, like philosophy, Toril Moi reminds us, begins in wonder (26). Cixous's discovery of Lispector provides an example.

Cixous inaugurated the transnationalization of the great Brazilian writer before the geo-cultural reorientation and expansion of the New Modernist Studies (Mao and Walkowitz). Now that Lispector has entered the Olympus of world literature, we can look back at Cixous's audacious discovery of the Brazilian writer. The critic reads the writer from the vantage point of Eliot's tradition, finding in the writer something that she wants to repeat. However, scholars have found her way of reading troubling, taking it as the example of a critic who incorporates the writer, dispossessing the latter of his or her authority. Lispector is thought to have provided Cixous "with a frame, a name and a voice, an external authority, within which to speak of her own ideas, obsessions and dreams" (Carrera 86). The writer, it has been argued, has acted as a "mirror device" for Cixous's own feminist brand of literary criticism (*écriture feminine*), and the critic is found "guilty of not leaving much space for Lispector to be other than that" (Carrera 93). This chapter takes another look at Cixous's treatment of Lispector. Cixous's comparative reading of Joyce's *A Portrait of the Artist* and Lispector's first novel, *Near to the Wild Heart*, will lead to a dialogue with Esposito's living thought. In fact Cixous's recuperation of Lispector calls attention to the enfolding of modernism and living thought one in the other more overtly than we could perceive in Eliot. Echoed and amplified by Esposito's living thought, which we discussed in the previous chapters, Cixous's living writing concerns our critical practice, compelling us to re-examine the ways we conceptualize the text and think about method in literary studies.

Living writing

Cixous's comparative reading of Clarice Lispector's *Near to the Wild Heart* (1943) and James Joyce's *A Portrait of the Artist as a Young Man* (1916) was widely circulated in English in the early 1990s. It was less a study of influence (an influence that Lispector always denied) and more a milestone in the identification of a cluster of texts that are representative of a type of text, comprising, as Cixous proposes, "texts that are 'near to the wild heart'" (WL 1). We will discuss Cixous's work on this type of text shortly. Before doing so it is helpful to recall that her formulation of such a text coincided with the transnationalization of the concept of modernism in the anglophone world. This meant the translation of the concept from a term of literary periodization to the name for a cross-temporal, cross-cultural aesthetics. Her reading of Lispector had no small role in this transnationalization. No longer understood as a chronologically and geographically localized phenomenon, modernism was reinvented. It was reconceived as a field of motifs that come and go, appear and disappear, are intensified and retranslated. The attention was directed to the *fort/da* movement of certain themes, to the persistence and resilience of a weave of concerns.

Combining Joyce and Lispector, Cixous inaugurated what Susan Stanford Friedman was to call "the scholar's act of paratactical cutting and pasting," a practice of literary criticism inspired by the modernist mode of collage, fueled by the notion of literature as an "archive of radical juxtapositions" (*Planetary Modernisms* 77). Undoubtedly, the attractiveness of paratactical collage lies in its productiveness for the critic. The juxtapositions can reveal new clusters and thematic concerns; they can also modify and extend key concepts, making them more capacious and inclusive. Friedman offers the example of Aimé Césaire and Theresa Kyung Cha, two writers from different geographies and from different temporalities. Thus, the juxtaposition of Césaire's *Notebook for a Return of the Native Land* and Cha's *Dicteé* reveals "a diasporic modernism based in the instabilities of colonial exile and the imaginative recreation of lost homes" (77).[3] Césaire's negritude and Cha's maternal body emerge as modernist themes across time and cultural climates, with the paratactical collage making room, within the preeminently chronological concept of modernism, for a movement forward and backward: "for Césaire, Negritude reuniting the diaspora of slavery with black Africa; for Cha, the maternal body as route to a syncretic phenomenology of home and homeland. Both invoking the rhythm of aller/retour" (77). In the case of Cixous, this rhythm regards the idea of the artist.

We have discussed with Eliot a form of life that resists reduction to the idea of the artist. Cixous makes the modernist motif of the artist resonate with the psychoanalytic motif of the father; in doing so, she amplifies the question that Eliot had skirted around: What kind of relation to language does the term "artist" name? Eliot's answer was that the relation is like an empty space separating potency and existence. In Cixous's reading, Joyce and Lispector, together, "produce" the artist understood less as a cultural phenomenon and more as a type of relation to language. When approached through Lispector, Joyce's foundational text, *A Portrait of the Artist as a Young Man*, thrusts into relief the notion of a paternal adoption in language which Cixous understands as inseparable from the "unformulated hypothesis that writing is something living" (WL 1). If we start from the assumption that language and thought are connected, Cixous's hypothesis of a living writing is comparable to Esposito's proposal of a latent line of reflection called living thought, which exceeds poststructuralism and coexists with it. But what does Cixous mean by "living"?

Joyce and Lispector both raise the question of a living writing, a question that addresses criticism in relevant ways, with consequences for our notion of the text. The text changes. It is no longer an object: "not the book as a sacred object" (WL 1); but neither is it just a semiotic texture, a tapestry of interwoven signs (Henry James's figure in the carpet) commanding the critic's chase and her labor to exit the labyrinth; nor is it a field of decentered signifiers intoxicating (and overwhelming) the critic with its sublime multiplicity. Cixous takes us back to a primary scene: there is a writer in search of a reader. The text "comes from within" (WL 1), she says, but this does not mean that the text is the actualization of the individual life of the author, its documentary evidence, so to speak. Cixous's idea of the text is closer to the hermeneutic tradition than we might think. It is an externalization of life, but with a difference: what is externalized is not an individual life necessarily, but the fact that there is nothing between the body and the world. No wedge there. What she calls "the artist" is produced there, in that nothing between the body and the world. This implies that the relation to language is forged through a weak, vulnerable, trembling body (like the enfeebled body of Joyce's myopic Stephen), a body that *resonates* with words.

Cixous's literary criticism rests on the notion of the subject; it is a discourse that cannot do without that notion. The scene of subject formation provides an ordering element within textual variety; it affords a palimpsest shared by widely different texts. From this perspective, perhaps her criticism is theory, not in the sense of Jameson, as an excess at the edge of philosophy, a not-philosophy that founds a new discourse, but in the more traditional sense of a model that can predict future cases. She formulates a poetics that yokes together different authors, through a paratactic collage that instates what Friedman would call the "diasporic" order of modernism: Blanchot, Joyce, Kafka, Kleist, Lispector, and Tsvetayeva, with each reading as a different version of the same fundamental scene of subject formation. Cixous's theory interests us because she weaves feminism and psychoanalysis to move beyond the Oedipal grid which assumes the relation to language as a gender-determined access to a symbolic order governed by the father figure. To do so, she places a resonating body at the center of her scene of subject formation. This allows Cixous to raise the question of language otherwise: she shifts from the question of the sovereignty of language, with its imperious, radical mediation of experience (there is nothing but the text), to the question of a paternal adoption *in* language. The "unformulated hypothesis that writing is something living" (WL 1) signals the nearness to this adoption, where paternal is not to be understood in the Oedipal sense but in the sense of a beneficial resourcefulness of language associated to the possibility of natality and well-being. This scenario does not dispose of interpretation. Cixous does not seek to cut the bond with hermeneutic depth;[4] on the contrary, she advocates an "intense deciphering" (WL 3) that assumes a writer more familiarly addressed ("Clarice") by the critic. What, on the wings of the presumed poststructuralist competitiveness between critic and text, has been taken as an act of dispossession and appropriation by Cixous of the writer's authority can, in fact, be grasped as a shift closer to a hermeneutic approach, an approach that considers writing and discourse (the text) within a set of social actions.

The hermeneutic approach (the cut)

To clarify what we mean when we talk about hermeneutic approach in this chapter, we will draw on Paul Ricoeur. For Ricoeur, we produce signs to appropriate our effort to exist. These signs call others; the signs of others call us, initiating the spiraling movement of reflection and interpretation. Ricoeur defines thinking (reflection) as "a reappropriation of our effort to exist" (*Della interpretazione* 61).[5] He therefore does not distinguish between the firstness of thinking and the secondariness of interpretation, and offers the example of Descartes. The "cogito" is an example of what Ricoeur means by "reappropriation." I have the certainty that I think, therefore I am, but this certainty, argues Ricoeur, is a "feeling," an affective state we could say, not a certifiable or verifiable idea (60). The roots of the hermeneutic problem for Ricoeur are to be found "in this primitive connection between the act of existing and the signs that we exhibit in our works" (63). For Ricoeur thinking and interpretation are mutually incorporated: "Reflection must become interpretation because it is never possible to grasp the act of existence in any place other than the signs disseminated in the world" (63). The ego, the subject of language and thought, is at the center of Ricoeur's hermeneutic problem as it is in Cixous's feminist criticism.

For Ricoeur, the aim of reflection "is to capture the ego in the effort to exist, in our desire to be" (*Della interpretazione* 26). Through such desire—akin to Plato's eros or Spinoza's conatus—reflection passes into interpretation, which is close to the "affirmative position" of a singular being, not a lack of being (62). Reflection needs interpretation. It is this mutual incorporation of thinking and of the art of reading signs that confronts us when we think of something like the desire to exist, the desire to recover someone else's effort to exist. Reflection seeks precisely to transform itself into a hermeneutic (63), yet the paradox of this hermeneutic is that the effort to reappropriate being is attested only by works whose meaning remains doubtful and expendable. Approaching Lispector from this angle, Cixous finds that the Brazilian writer is the kind of writer who addresses her critic with the responsibility of a "reappropriation" of those efforts (61).

This does not mean that the text that Lispector produces dissolves the figure of the critic; it rather invites an analysis of this figure. First and foremost, we have a reader, with reading as always blended with reflective activity. Cixous's notion of "intense deciphering" endorses Ricoeur's view of the unavoidable confusion of tongues between reflection and interpretation. Deciphering still entails an understanding based on the erosion of a distance; it pursues the breakdown of a foreignness through the mode that Gadamer calls "dialogue" (390), except that, for Cixous, the foreignness to be negotiated is not the gap between producer and receiver, writer and reader, but a shared foreignness common to both parties involved in the activity of deciphering. The main reason for the mutual incorporation of Cixous–Clarice is this common foreignness—the foreignness of language itself.

Cixous's critic is moved by the problem of "an inscription" (WL 1), by the question of a nearness to the foreignness of language. She seeks to describe the problem through the notion of the text: "I want to work on texts that are as close as possible to an inscription—conscious or unconscious—of the origin of the gesture of writing and not of writing itself" (WL 1). Nearness does not mean an intimacy, a mirroring, a familiarity, but it suggests that, when reading, one is near to an incision, a cut (another meaning of "inscription"). What Cixous calls "gesture" is a cut; but the cut does not manifest in the same way as in Eliot, through distancing devices. Texts like Joyce's *Portrait* leave us no choice but an unmediated knowledge of the cut. Working on texts that are close to the cut is like retracing "the origin of the gesture of writing" (WL 1). Judging from her vocabulary— "I want"; "the origin of"—Cixous would seem to advocate depth, a willful excavation, a meaning that must be dragged into the light, except that "the gesture of writing," which is not the content of the writing (somewhat recalling Benjamin's distinction between criticism and critique),[6] is rendered as a wound, like the wound of palpitating flesh.

Beyond the performance of power: unwritten writing

Clarice Lispector is supposed to have been given the name of her first book by her friend Lúcio Cardoso. After reading her manuscript, Cardoso suggested a title borrowed from a passage in James Joyce's *A Portrait of the Artist as a Young Man*: "He was alone. He was unheeded, happy, and near to the wild heart of life" (Joyce qtd. in Moser, "Hurricane Clarice" viii). Lispector is supposed to have been annoyed by the baptism and claimed that she read Joyce only after writing the book (Moser, "Hurricane Clarice" viii), but in the end she must have been quite happy with the chancy connection since she kept the title. She knew the importance of names. Against the transnational modernist horizon, she would probably have remained "hidden" longer,[7] if she had not appeared under someone else's name. This is the problem that Eliot called "tradition," the plane of recognition and repetition. We said that the notion dovetails with

Esposito's plane of coevalness, discussed in Chapter 3, by which the philosopher referred to the circulation of ideas that, having started elsewhere, reach thematic relevance on other horizons. From the perspective of Cixous, this thematic relevance manifests under a name. Lispector's living writing reaches thematic relevance under the name of Joyce, the modernist writer.

It is not just a question of the paratactic nearness of Lispector and Joyce that we are dealing with here but, simultaneously, the question of the nearness of fields and critical approaches. Cixous's focus on the body and on gender brings modernism near to feminism and both near to psychoanalysis. Her formula, *écriture feminine*, woman-writing does not mean an antipatriarchal criticism by women but the idea of a concern which, regardless of genders, unites different fields and approaches, making for their productive convergence on a particular idea of writing: writing as the question of speaking. Cixous's "coming to writing" presupposes the other question: What does it mean to speak?

In pairing Joyce and Lispector, Cixous has in mind Lacan's Seminar XXIII (1975–6), *The Sinthome*, on Joyce. In Lacan's reading, Joyce is one of those men in whose writing "there appears to be the trace" of a knowledge about language that most men seem to ignore. Joyce does not ignore that knowledge, concludes Lacan, and that is why he becomes a "saint homme" (the pun in the seminar's title), one of those holy men who know that "the word is a parasite" (*Seminario* 91).[8] Lacan alludes to the fact that language is "a strange relation," a non-relation whereby one can speak of something only insofar as it has a name, as an *as if* (Agamben, *Che cos'è la filosofia?* 16). In the words of Cixous, "the signifier always represses" ("Foreword" xv).

It is from the point of view of this non-relation that Cixous illuminates Lispector. I will focus on a page of her foreword to Lispector's *The Stream of Life*, where she contrasts Lispector's "technique" with Gertrude Stein's. She points to the American modernist's famous motto "A rose is a rose is a rose," from "Sacred Emily," to argue that "the hidden message behind Gertrude Stein's sentence would be something about the impossibility of language to be adequate to the object" ("Foreword" xv). Stein "subverts" through repetition: "She subverts something of what might be repressive in the use of language, in the fact that the signifier represses" (xv). Lispector, Cixous argues, walks the opposite path of her anglophone modernist colleague: she proceeds by designation and facsimiles. Her purpose is "to refuse the phantasm of the book," the book "posited as an object containing something on the side of knowledge" (xv). When Cixous talks about knowledge here, she means formalized knowledge, something akin to what Moi would call traditional theory, Benjamin an "externality full of yearning," and Latour "objective statements," in other words, repressive concepts.[9] For Lispector, "every book is a facsimile of expression, of representation, of reality, etc." (xv), in the sense that every book restitutes to her reader the question that the critic decides to pursue: "the inscription" before "the gesture of writing." A text does not assume a subject (a critic) grasping something and, although the incision and cut alluded to by the inscription call to mind the metaphor of touch, there would be nothing to grasp when one traces and retraces the rim of the cut. Cixous operates with the notion of the subject (a subject of speech and thought) but she does not support the subject/object divide because it is the emblem of a cruel dynamics of humanization: we become human when we make another desire us (*Terza persona* 136). Her critic avoids this dynamic.

Lispector enables Cixous to introduce an idea of criticism beyond the performance of power and invulnerability that reading becomes when one approaches the object-book from all the other books one has read, in a kind of siege or spectacle of consumption (quite different from Benjamin's "method of [the work's] consummation" ["Goethe's Elective Affinities" 153]).[10] The critical act loses its spectator, if it ever needed one. With her first book, Lispector feared that she had written fragments that could not cohere in a novel, but the fragments, Cixous suggests, are in line with the writer's technique: not the subversion of the book but an affirmative "inscription" of a nearness to language.

The fragments do not subvert the book as a symbol of human knowledge but inform us that the relation to language is not inconspicuous. Writing *is* this relation to language, and that is why Cixous speaks of "the drive to write" that precedes every book as a closed and finished object. If writing "is already something finished, something that follows the drive to write," the latter, instead, is an unfinished writing that accompanies what we read, giving the writer's book the quality of the "firstborn" (WL 1). Some texts are more audacious than others: whenever they come to be, in whatever sequel of texts, they are not afraid to be the writer's firstborn. Lispector's *Near to the Wild Heart* "is just such a text" (WL 1): its parts signal its unwritten quality,[11] and it is one of these parts—its title—to give the earlier modernist classic the audacity of unwritten writing.

Life vs. Form according to Cixous–Lispector–Joyce

What does it mean to work on texts that are "near to the wild heart"? The audacious firstborn takes from the predecessor; in taking, it inscribes the problem of the gesture of writing back in the classic; it brings the critic near the scene of a subject formed through the cut of his or her relation to language:

> Reading Clarice's text, I was struck by its extraordinary power. It is a text that has the audacity to let itself be written close to the very drive to write. At the same time, it gives the impression of being poorly written. It does not display a mastery of form or language and does not raise the question of art. It is the contrary of Flaubert. (WL 1)

Cixous's Lispector powerfully illustrates the polarity of Life vs. Form.

As we saw in Chapter 3, Esposito turns to the modernist critic Adriano Tilgher (1890–1941) to reconsider the predecessor's defense of a "radical conflict" between Life and Form which sees life as "a force that exceeds the limits of any economy" (*Da Fuori* 165).[12] Cixous embeds the Life vs. Form conflict in the formation of the subject:

> Clarice's first movement as a child was to put herself at the *écoute* of, in tune with, writing, of something that happens between the body and the world. One has to have a touch of something savage, uncultured, in order to let it happen. It is the contrary of having been so much of a student, of a scholar, that one thinks that a book is a book, and that, if one vaguely has the desire to write, one says: I have to write a book. (WL 1)

The child becomes attuned to writing in the sense of a relation to language which acts as a wedge between the body and the world, as it must, from Cixous's point of view, for there to be the "drive to write." Literature is not just a question of genres and taxonomies. One writes even as one lives. The shift toward the listening metaphor in the quotation above ("in tune") remedies a condition; it repairs another beginning: the fact that one is a body, not in any abstract sense or mitigated condition but rather as palpitating flesh. Lispector's writing bears the memory of this fleshy condition, of this not-language, this "onomatopoeia" or "convulsion of language" in lieu of speech acts: "I'm transmitting to you not a story but only words which live off of sound," she writes in *The Stream of Life* (59). Lispector writes from this weakness, from this thorn in the flesh.

This condition is not exactly the same as the story of the artist in the traditional sense, as Cixous makes clear with the example of Flaubert. Flaubert "called it art, not writing" (WL 2). In this example, art means a care of the self, the implementation of practices aimed at transforming the self into "the lover of writing": "He organized the totality of his material, psychological, and affective life in such a way that he became forever the lover of writing" (WL 2). The set of practices included dividing the self—not only his material life but also his innermost, spiritual life—into parts and fitting the parts in a totality. Flaubert features in Cixous as the example of an askesis in the sense of a technique of life, a series of procedures that train the body and the soul to a lasting transformation.[13] Flaubert's artist subjects himself to the calculated and repeated practice of welding parts into forms. Cixous emphasizes the calculated procedure, the steps in Flaubert's self-fashioning: "He made love with his art throughout his entire life" (WL 2). A decisive step in the transformation is flexing the self to a bond that she calls the "production of art" (WL 2), with an exercise in economizing himself, preserving himself, fixing "a rendezvous with [Louise Colet] only after completion of such and such a chapter" (WL 2). In this sense, "art" and "the artist" are the names for a dispositif, a government of the self which is a government of life that is worth more than life. The askesis that Cixous describes under the name of Flaubert might also apply to the phenomenon of the avant-garde as defined by its early theorizer, Renato Poggioli. Poggioli quotes from a letter in which Paul Valéry reminds Mallarmé of the value of his writing, reminding the master that "there is, in every city of France, a youth who would let himself be cut into pieces" for the master's work, "difficult to find, difficult to understand, difficult to defend" (Valéry qtd. in Poggioli 91). What Poggioli called "the avant-garde in general"—a cross-historical and cross-cultural notion which survives its death and rises from its ashes like the phoenix—is what Cixous (pointing to Flaubert) calls writing that is worth more than life.

At first, Cixous places Joyce in a line of reflection that associates the artist to a calculated procedure for the control of "living and liveable" relations with other human beings (WL 2). Joyce seems Flaubert's "successor," implicated in a "tyrannic" circuit of gift and debt: "First one pays the price oneself, then one makes others pay" (WL 2). But this version of Joyce evaporates when he is brought near to Lispector. From a mechanism of immunization from others, we shift to the "gesture of writing." Near Joyce's *A Portrait of the Artist*, Lispector's *Near to the Wild Heart* becomes a "portrait of the primitive portrait" (WL 3), and next to Joyce's modernism, Lispector's "foreign" text displaces our relationship to the concepts and categories that we use. It is the kind of displacement that does not weaken interpretation but heightens its intensity: "One has to be audacious in one's reading, so that it becomes an intense deciphering" (WL 3). Audacity is not just an affect or a passion of the self; it is a critical category congruent with literary inquiry. Cixous champions reading as a discovery and a sense of purpose: "We need not be afraid of wandering, though one should read in terms of a quest" (WL 3). The audacious inquiry has to do with the deeper layers of culture: she finds that the artist is a relation to language that emerges in a cluster of texts, in a collective discourse which poses the question of a relation to language produced by the father—by the fact of there being a father.

What is a father?

But what is a father? Cixous connects Lispector and Joyce by reading the "embryonic scene" of Joyce's *Portrait of the Artist* through the image of the egg or an opaque shell of calcium in Lispector's "Sunday, before falling asleep," a text in which the question of the father produces the artist (WL 3). When Cixous reads Lispector's treatment of the father back into Joyce, the motif of the father accounts for modernist hermeticism: "One understands everything and nothing" (WL 4). Cixous, an expert on Joyce, repeats the "apparent naiveté" of Joyce's text in her critical practice while reading Lispector and systematically calling the author by her first name, "Clarice" (WL 4). The modernist difficulty of Lispector's text is proportional to the content: in "Sunday, before falling asleep" there are many referents "but nothing is more condensed, or more allusive" (WL 4). Both Joyce and Lispector offer primal scenes of the birth of the "I" into the intellectual dimension. The first begins "with the enormous O that recurs in the first pages" (WL 4). She focuses on the graphic and phonic o's, on marks that have a sound: "Once upon a time ... baby tuckoo." Joyce begins with "a failed bird linked through its double *o* to the moocow," an evocation of the Minotaur (via Stephen's last name, Dedalus), "the child of a (false) cow" (WL 5). The failed phonic signifier ("tuckoo" should be cuckoo) leads Cixous to "the formation of the subject through the intervention of a third," the Oedipal setting suggested also via references to Kafka's parable "Before the Law": Stephen's father's "hairy face" recalls the keeper of the law in Kafka's parable, "who was also said to have a hairy face" (WL 5). The crisscrossing brings to light questions of authority, which Joyce's text manifests through Stephen's oscillation between rebellion (*non serviam*) and obedience. The bifurcation is simple and brutal, and it is there, the very backbone of a text that returns to decisions, cuts, and separations with a plot propelled as much by Stephen's achievement of severance from the biological father as by the persistence of a symbolic father alluded to by the old father, old artificer of the ending. The artist is produced by prohibitions—"he who will become the artist is in open opposition to the law and to authority" (WL 3)—without its being about a romancing of rebellion. The text is also about the shift from the father motif (theme) to the paternal function, and about the transfer of the paternal function to language. The event of this transfer is signaled, after the text grieves the great distance that separates Stephen from his biological father, by the quote from the literary precursor, Shelley, in Chapter 2: "Art thou pale for weariness / Of climbing heaven and gazing on the earth, / Wandering companionless . . . ?" Cixous assists us in seeing the transfer when she talks of the young artist's "system of thought":

> The system of thought of the young artist is put in place. From thinking about things, the artist ends up understanding them. Joyce says this along these lines: If one reflects on words, if one warms them like a hen, one ends up understanding them. (WL 9)[14]

Cixous talks about Stephen's "fixation on language" (WL 9). If we study how this fixation unfolds, we find that Stephen places himself under the tutelage of words. The two writers' words, their naming—"Clarice is into chickens and worms, Joyce into roses and eagles"—puts into place "the system of thought" of the young artist, of the artist in the process of making himself one: the system is about a particular relation of language to thought. Language resonates in the weak and trembling body, which provides hospitality and friendship for words; it is because of his retreat into words that Stephen gains access to knowledge: "from thinking about things the artist ends up understanding them" (WL 9), in a circuitous route that echoes Augustine's achievement of praise along his path to logos in *Confessions*. The "system" begins with a nearness to words. But it is not a question of reciprocity; *reciprocus* means returning the same way, suggesting an interchange and thus, somehow, an obligation to give that has the aim of annulling differences. Reciprocity is a kind of erasure. Stephen, instead, moves over near words, in a relation of mutuality with them, and this nearness modulates his idea of action as a clear-cut decision: "Joyce's motto reads *non serviam*, 'I will not.' He is obliged to begin from a refusal, from a retreat" (WL 8). The retreat marks the beginning of recognition: Stephen makes himself be recognized by words. He subverts our idea of language as a system of signs or as an instrument of communication, in favor of a relation to words that resembles a dynamic of recognition, steeped in mutuality rather than in struggle (Ricoeur, *Course*; Helenius 53). Shifting near words, he becomes passively recognized by them. Joyce's *Portrait* shows that Stephen's problem is to become reconciled with the otherness of language. This is the reason for Cixous's paratactical juxtaposition with Lispector: "It's the portrait of someone . . . who is outside norms" (WL 8). *Portrait* opens with this otherness, with the knowledge that language is a phonic maze before it becomes a spoken chain. The sound of "moocow"—a translinguistic mark (one can hear it as the Italian word *mucca*, meaning "cow")—proves the inauthenticity of the biological father's speech, though it immediately modulates in the euphony of the father's song. The "embryonic scene" in *Portrait* is, as Cixous also notices, a sequence of parts, but the sequence highlights something that is missing: (1) the moo-cow; (2) the father sings; (3) the child wets his bed; (4) the father's smell is queer. We move from the father's song to the son's weak body and to the father's smell. We do not know the whys in between the song and the bed, place of birth and love and death all at once, a symbol of circular time, which is a form of arrested time. We know that something is wrong; we are informed that there is a connection between the father and Stephen's weak body, and that the father's smell signals an inoperative entrance in the intellectual dimension since smell is the farthest from intellect. The parts inform us that Stephen's association with his father amounts to a weakness, a fact that surfaces when the talk among the other fellows at school touches on the question of fathers, of who their fathers are and what they do: "he felt his body small and weak amid the throng of players and his eyes were weak and watery" (*Portrait* 6). Joyce places Stephen's weak and vulnerable body in the midst of others who command him to be: "What is your name?"; "What kind of name is that?"; "What is your father?" (6). The latter question refers to the métier ("Is he a magistrate?"), but it also asks "what": What fathers you? Rather than tell a story, Joyce's fragments talk to each other; they are like the pieces of a rebus: "that was not a nice expression" (7) seems to respond to the incontinence of the text when it asks the troubling question: "What is your father?" By now, this is not a question for Stephen; rather, it is the question we need to take on if we wish to understand *this* artist.

Stephen wants to know. He has the same audacity that Cixous counsels in reading ("One has to be audacious in one's reading"); it causes him to feel "small and weak" (*Portrait* 14): "It was better to go to bed to sleep" (14). Joyce begins to describe the loveliness of falling asleep, with the cold all about and "the cold shivering sheets" (14), his weak body resonating in stark relief, "shaking and trembling" (16): "he shivered and wanted to yawn. It would be lovely in a few minutes. He felt a warm glow coming up from the cold shivering sheets, warmer and warmer till he felt warm all over, ever so warm" (14). In that bed/tomb the artist is born. Stephen is wounded in his desire to know, but his weak, shivering flesh becomes the house of words. When he gets into bed after praying, the night, the sleep, the tomb of his bed, first cold then warm, the dark, cold and strange (15)—all become the elements of Joyce's own primary scene, which corrects the Oedipal struggle with a structure of recognition: as his shaking body clings to the restricted space of his bed—dark, cold, warm, strange—he becomes "the artist," a subject recognized by words. In Cixous's terms, he comes to writing.

Later in the text, his "savage desire" for birth resembles a terrible cry, a "furious cry at having been abandoned" (*Portrait* 84). Abandoned by whom? By what? Both questions lead us back to the "embryonic" question of *Portrait*: What is a father? We can now see how "the inscription of the origin of the gesture of writing" translates the question of language from one of seizing—seizing speech, seizing the word—to the other of being given words, of a "wherefrom" of speech, around which Cixous joins Lispector's Clarice and Joyce's Stephen in the knowledge that "the father always has to be dead" (WL 9). The father must be overtaken by a paternal adoption that takes place in the mutuality with language. That is what Joyce gives an account of in *A Portrait of the Artist*. That is why, in his reading of Joyce, Lacan talks of a "paternal deficiency" (*Seminario* 90), a paternal that is "not enough."

The search for method

Cixous and Esposito collaborate at the hypothesis of a living writing-thought which ought to be distinguished from vitalism. In Modernist

Studies, the notion of vitalism refers to an interest in primitivism, the unconscious and myth (Tonning 8), all of which have joined in the effort to posit what Eirik Vassenden defines as "a special Life Force, a creative impulse that is not explicable in terms of mechanical laws" (Vassenden qtd. in Tonning 8). The line of living writing-thought at the center of our discussion here is not to be confused with the vitalist immanence which is often implied in celebrations of modernity, with factories, collectivities, urban life, and machines seen as the pathway to a life force previously lying dormant. In living writing-thought the conflict between Life and Form calls attention to life in tension with history and its context (Esposito, *Da Fuori* 165). The Joyce–Lispector pairing highlights the *fort/da* movement of the Life vs. Form conflict within the extended field of "diasporic modernism" posited by Friedman. Cixous's critic is called by texts that speak to this conflict. In her reading of modernism, life is no longer a vitalist rupture of the effects of industrial life, neither does it stand for the rupture and innovation of an avant-garde. In asking "What are the stakes in the text?" (WL 2), she pays close attention to a "formation of the subject" (WL 4) that does not get rid of the question of speaking—What does it mean to speak? That is to say, where from do you take the word?—keeping us wondering why such questions are important, rather than disposable, for literary studies and the Humanities more broadly.

The text that calls and the critic who is called: that is the primary scene of the critical act for Cixous. It does not follow that the critic should impersonate a reader lost in the labyrinth of signifiers, absorbed in resisting hermeneutic depth because it would repress multiplicity. Neither is Cixous's critic worried about the dynamics of power and how a text illustrates them, though of course her "woman-questions" react to the politics of criticism in a male-dominated academia (as hers was in France). Her critic wants to make sense of the text; she asks questions of critical method, and these are, as Edward Said would put it, "enmeshed in circumstance" ("Text" 4). When she places Joyce's *Portrait* side by side with Lispector's *Wild Heart*, questions of method arise: "What is a writer looking for? What are the stakes in the text? How does one search for something?" (WL 2). These questions concern how one knows through reading literature.

From the vantage point of Cixous, reading does not stop being a purposive inquiry about the writer. It might even be possible to see her "woman-questions" as a reaction to the theory of the "death of the author" (Barthes, "Death"). What is certain is that her feminism asks for the audacity of interpretation. It builds on formalist and hermeneutic notions of interpretation as the main ingredients of critical experience, only heightened.

The audacity she advocates, in fact, closely recalls Russian Formalism's notion of *ostranenie* or estrangement. Her reading attends to the strange details of a text, like "the enormous O" in Joyce's *Portrait*. The paratactic juxtaposition of texts from different cultural latitudes such as Joyce's Europe and Lispector's South America only heightens the illuminating power of defamiliarization. Cixous herself comments on the benefits of defamiliarization when she observes, referring to Lispector's text in translation, that, being "transgrammatical," foreign texts "displace our relationship to grammar" (WL 3), suggesting that the displacement affords new meanings beyond the frame of "automatization" (Shklovsky 162). Formalist defamiliarization was concerned with objects that "follow a formula of sorts without ever reaching consciousness" and life that is "as if [it] had never been," says Shklovsky quoting Tolstoi (Shklovsky 162). Cixous echoes Shklovsky with the idea that "writing is something living," and the implication is that criticism follows as a reparative activity that, as the Russian formalist put it, aims "to restore the sensation of life" (Shklovsky 162).

At the same time, Cixous also builds bridges with a hermeneutic tradition predicated on the dialogue of reader and work. We already discussed her "intense deciphering" as an inflection of the hermeneutic approach earlier on. Here we might note that the deciphering she advocates, especially when combined with the notion of a text that calls, is not entirely foreign to the notion of "hermeneutical conversation" proposed by Hans-Georg Gadamer in response to the vexed question of method in the Humanities (Gadamer 390). As developed by Gadamer, the concept refers to a way of understanding that revolves around a difference—a distance and a foreignness—to be negotiated in the mode of a dialogue between reader and text. Understanding a text amounts to a kind of historical knowledge, but it does not equal the historical reconstruction of the text. Instead, it calls for a "re-awakening" of the meaning of the text (Gadamer 390). As with Ricoeur, reflection and interpretation become conjoined for the reader whose stake is the vital dimension of the text. In the pursuit, of course, the interpreter's subjectivity—"the interpreter's horizon," in Gadamer's terminology—constitutes a risk in the process of cognition; cognition is not a *savoir* (knowledge) from which the interpreter's self comes away unscathed; rather, it is closer to a spiritual *savoir*, with the incorporation of "what the text says" in the self of the reader. Gadamer writes:

> In this sense understanding is certainly not concerned with "understanding historically"—i.e., reconstructing the way the text came into being. Rather, one intends to understand the text itself. But this means that the interpreter's own thoughts too have gone into re-awakening the text's meaning. In this the interpreter's own horizon is decisive, yet not as a personal standpoint that he maintains or enforces, but more as an opinion and a possibility that one brings into play and puts at risk, and that helps one truly *to make one's own* what the text says. (390; my emphasis)

Gadamer's "horizon of the interpreter"—Said's "circumstance"—does not determine or govern the interpretation of the text but helps in truly possessing what the text says. Possessing what the text says marks the shift from cognition to knowing that is at the basis of the notion of hermeneutic dialogue. It is in this shift that the question of method in the Humanities appears. If in the natural sciences, method is a matter of identifying "the uniformities, the regularities and the conformities to laws/rules that make possible to foresee (or predict) certain phenomena and processes," the concept of hermeneutical conversation, Gadamer affirms, does not aim "to grasp the concrete phenomenon as a specific case for the general rule" (26) but rather to "understand how this man, this people, or this state is what it has become or, more generally, how it happened that it is so" (4).

As we saw with Eliot in Chapter 5, part of the knowledge that arises in the hermeneutical conversation is the recovery of "what has been lost / And found and lost again" (*Four Quartets* 19); from Eliot's vantage point, what Gadamer calls "re-awakening" equals the repetition of a text that others may have written before us. Tellingly, Eliot does not specify whether he is talking about the reader or the critic; the two are linked in the process of restoration. One of the leading practitioners of the approach known as "close reading," Helen Vendler, follows Eliot in encouraging the confusion. In her introduction to her marvelous *The Ocean, the Bird and the Scholar* (2015), she insists on being perceived as "a critic rather than a scholar," as someone "taken by texts" (3). Vendler's critic illustrates Gadamer's reader, a subject of knowledge who gives birth to herself in the hermeneutical conversation, a fact corroborated by her anecdote of the discovery of the poetry of Wallace Stevens. Vendler's discovery of Stevens expounds on Gadamer's notion of truly possessing what the text says:

> It was as if my own naked spirit spoke to me from the page. I'd read dozens of poets by the time I came across Stevens, and I'd memorized scores of poems ... Before I could make out, in any paraphrasable way, Stevens's poems, I knew, as by telepathy, what they meant emotionally. (Vendler 1–2)

For Vendler, as for Cixous, being a critic means being a reader. Vendler does not deny that she is a sort of "learned" reader, nevertheless she is a reader, and that means someone that

> has a memory for stories, styles, and structures she has seen before, and she understands the expressive possibilities latent in writing ... She remembers the combinations and permutations of words and syntax that she has come across and is curious about the power of new assemblages. (3)

Thinking of herself as a scholar would diminish that fusion of horizons that Gadamer assumes as part of the hermeneutical conversation. In talking about criticism in terms of reading, Vendler takes a distance from anything that would interfere with what she calls "telepathy," rendering in a more ordinary way what Eliot, speaking of the method of Pound, had called "imperative intimacy."[15] In Vendler's and Eliot's case, Gadamer's notion of hermeneutical conversation yields the instability of the figure of the critic, with the process of deciphering—Gadamer's "re-awakening"—becoming confused with Vendler's "telepathy." Along similar lines, Cixous's text—the text that calls—manifests the paradox at the heart of literary studies whenever we talk of method.

As discussed in the Introduction, Toril Moi, surveying the current state of literary criticism, finds that one of the outcomes of the past theoretical climate is that literary critics "mistake political and existential investments for methods, specific practices of reading" (179). Today, the search for method in the Humanities has taken the form of a new objectivity in criticism (Fleissner 102). The term "postcritique" sums up, even though inadequately of course, a debate that testifies to the deeply felt need for "an accurate knowledge of texts" (Marcus and Best 17). Moi reminds us that the search for method distracts us from the more radical problem of our field, that is reading, and reading is not a method but a practice: "to read is to pay attention to a particular text, to look and think in response to particular questions. Is reading a 'method'?" (178). Cixous's blend of feminism and psychoanalysis illustrates the paradox. She reads exactly in Moi's terms: she pays attention, looks, and thinks in response to certain questions ("What is the writer looking for? What are the stakes in the text?"), and, like Moi, she wonders whether reading is a method, since the questions she asks of, in Moi's phrase, a "particular text" imply the examination of our own reading procedures ("How does one search for something?"). But the fact that Cixous turns to psychoanalysis to decipher in the text the structures of culture matters: different texts, distant in time and space, begin to resonate with each other showing an affinity with those structures on the basis of a common concern. This common concern owes to her feminist sensibility and targets the issue of a natality in language. Cixous starts with a subject *before* the threshold of language; she must therefore deal with the strange ban or exclusion that, from the vantage of point of feminist thought, is the experience of the speaking subject. The predicament of this subject resembles the condition of the woman in W. B. Yeats's controversial sonnet "Leda and the Swan," who is given a knowledge that she cannot certify: "Did she put on his knowledge with his power / Before the indifferent beak could let her drop" (Yeats 221).[16] In the feminist analysis of the ban, the speaking subject remains, like Kafka's man in his celebrated parable "Vor dem Gesetz," one of the most inspiring texts for poststructuralist thought, before the law.[17] Although Cixous retraces the ban in both Lispector and Joyce, her paratactic collage enables her to see a relation to language beyond rupture and beyond the rebellion against the father.

Her deciphering can be considered as a hermeneutical conversation because it is not limited to the isolated dialogue with a text; she reads for cultural structures that, incorporated in the text, appear and are reoriented under the attentive and loving gaze of the reader. The text by which Cixous's critic is called is the text that appears on condition that, as Claude Lefort would say, we "give it our thoughts" (Lefort qtd. in Esposito, *Pensiero istituente* 198). Giving "our thoughts" to the work is a condition for the text, but the latter means the existence of an "open exchange" (what Gadamer calls "conversation") of such nature that, each time, a response to a question does not nullify the question but calls for new ones, instituting a collective discourse that determines the text's advent, that is to say, the fact of its institution. It is by interrogating this institution, says Lefort, that we are already interrogating the work (Lefort qtd. in Esposito, *Pensiero istituente* 198). Gadamer's conversation becomes here a "hermeneutic vortex" from which reader and text "resurface transformed" (Esposito, *Pensiero istituente* 199). This instituting giving is possible because text and reader are highly representative of a distance (separation) that unites them; the question of the hermeneutical conversation subsists when the text calls me, when "it meets me in a lack that regards me" (Esposito, *Pensiero istituente* 199).

Thus, Cixous's poetics recalls Gadamer's conversation. In Cixous's words:

> When choosing a text I am called: I obey the call of certain texts or I am rejected by others. The texts that call me have different voices. But they all have one voice in common, they all have with their differences a certain music I am attuned to and that's the secret. (*Three Steps* 5)

Cixous begins by detecting a common cultural structure around which the readers' questions are articulated, and indeed it is by interrogating this discourse that we also interrogate the text. Her paratactical collage may prove that literary texts incorporate cultural structures across different latitudes, and one could certainly go on reading with the aim of proving that those structures are not fixed and transcendent but are produced; consequently one could get to the point of arguing that literature reveals the production and enforcement of norms. However, in our reading we have found that the norm put in place by Joyce's modernist text (via Kafka's subject before the law) does not suffice, and we have seen how Cixous interrogates Joyce–Lispector beyond Oedipus, toward the question of a paternal adoption in language. The question will be discussed in detail in the next chapter. Here, we will conclude this chapter by suggesting that Cixous's feminist hermeneutics is a form of reparative reading.

From the hermeneutical conversation to attachment

The interpretation advocated by Cixous may be said to aim at undoing cultural structures and beliefs, and one could certainly conclude that it is a form of symptomatic reading, a way of reading invested in repressed meaning. We explained in the Introduction that symptomatic reading has been questioned. We have seen that, drawing on psychoanalytic theory, Eve Kosofsky Sedgwick introduces the twin notion of reparative reading ("Paranoid Reading" 2003). Symptomatic reading and reparative reading, Sedgwick stresses, are not two mutually exclusive positions but the two poles between which the reader oscillates. In her remarkable *A Dialogue on Love* (1999), Sedgwick continues to have recourse to psychoanalysis, to flesh out an idea of reparative criticism steeped in the notion of dialogue. The word "dialogue" in Sedgwick's title refers primarily to the psychoanalytic setting, but the fact that Sedgwick's analyst, Shannon, is a Ferenczian therapist is no negligible detail. Sándor Ferenczi was a Hungarian psychoanalyst and a dissident disciple of Freud. His attempt to solve the problem of the analyst's lack of sincere understanding led Ferenczi to experiment with the radical technique of mutual analysis, a fact that resulted in his fall from grace within the psychoanalytic community (see Ferenczi).[18] The point of mutual analysis was to diminish the analyst's power over the analysand so that the analyst, too, could experience the position of a subject in need, and thus be better able to help.

The Ferenczian analyst embodies a weak subjectivity, different from the face-to-face combat, which shifts the focus toward empathy. Sedgwick reorients Gadamer's hermeneutical conversation through the Ferenczian inflection of dialogue to provide an appropriate setting for a re-examination of the turn to Theory in ways that might reconcile critical practice with the weakened body of the critic undermined by illness. *A Dialogue on Love* is an important document for literary criticism, one in which the latter is interrogated precisely in its nature as a dynamic discipline innervated in the love of language. Sedgwick retraces the rise of Theory in the uncertain boundary between poetry and criticism, reading and writing. She questions the divide between criticism and literature. The structure that Cixous calls "the artist" emerges in Sedgwick's discourse, too, as a particular relation to language. Sedgwick presents herself as a poet who turned to theory in postwar America. National culture and intellectual autobiography merge and, in the narrative of the literary critic divided between two loves, criticism emerges as the loss of poetry. In the analytic setting, Sedgwick recounts the loss of her muse:

> It was my first vocation, first identity—from early childhood on into my thirties. (When my grandmother lost her memory and didn't know our names or relationships. She still mouthed, pointing at me, "The poet?") Poetry both my first love, I guess, and first self—always with the most excruciating blockages—gone now for years. Really gone for a decade. I can't think about it; I don't; when I used to, it would make me crazy. I don't know if it was depression that drove this muse away or if it was the long rocky strand of her loss that made depression. (*Dialogue* 65)

Far from a station in a solitary path, an incident in the making of a public intellectual, being abandoned by the muse of poetry is an event of national dimensions and the cost paid by the postwar generation for its protest against the invasive power of institutions.[19] The loss of poetry for a criticism capable of such an adversarial energy remains a generational rite of passage. In Sedgwick's case the passage from poetry to theory parallels the confusion of public and private realms and the discovery of power within the Jewish family hearth. The analytic dialogue stresses the mutuality of individual life and national collectivity, with the latter putting the muse out of work as if it were an invention of childhood. In her account of the transformation of the poet in post-World War II America, Sedgwick, like Cixous, poses the question of "the artist." Giving an account of the transition from poet to theorist, she too understands the artist to be the name of a relation to language. Like Cixous's writing, Sedgwick's theory is "something living saved from books, from narratives" (Cixous, "*Coming to Writing*" 59). In Sedgwick, the Ferenczian setting gestures toward a reconciliation beyond the Oedipal struggle and aggression, and the turn from poetry to theory points to a concern similar to that of Cixous, that is to say, the formulation of a relation of tutelage in language.

Peter Szondi was the first to understand *écriture*, a name he used for poststructuralism more broadly, as a contemporary turn within the tradition of hermeneutics. Before he could see the developments of poststructuralism because of his premature death, Szondi illuminated *écriture* through the "vital moment" theorized by Schleiermacher, who conceived writing and discourse as acts among other acts of another kind, thus "not only as documentary evidence but as the active and relevant externalization of a life" (Szondi 158). Szondi argued that

> the decision of Schleiermacher who, moved by his lack of satisfaction for the "solitary contemplation of an isolated text," returned from writing to discourse represents today, especially in France, the focal point of the discussion, even though Schleiermacher's name is not mentioned. (159)

When considered from Szondi's vantage point, Cixous's quest for the inscription beyond writing itself recalls Schleiermacher's "active and relevant externalization of a life," by which we can understand an ampler meaning of Life that is not reduced to the conflict with Form but considered at the meaningful intersection of context, history, politics, and language. Language is shown to be the wedge between the body and the world. Joyce's Stephen and Lispector's Joana are united by a weak body which makes them into a lost cause.[20] But, in receiving the paternal adoption *in* language, they challenge the view that life is technique. As Rebecca Colesworthy writes, the gift was "central to [modernist] aesthetic projects" and many modernist writers "cast their writing as gift" (2). As receivers of the paternal adoption in language, Joyce's Stephen and Lispector's Joana are an example of the modernist centrality of the gift and they are both guides, as Cixous brilliantly points out, to a question that, borne through modernism, slides into psychoanalytic as well as feminist interests, as we have seen with Cixous, and that is the question of the gift of speech. Our discussion of Eliot in the previous chapter has revolved around this question, which will be examined in greater detail in the next chapter via Lacan. In the case of Joana and Stephen, the gift of/in language received in their weak bodies specifically counters a representation of life "that is structurally linked to its own transformability" (Bazzicalupo, *Biopolitica* 76).

Cixous may be said to champion a feminist hermeneutics that involves a consideration of the whole and its parts (Dersken and Halsema 205). The recourse to psychoanalysis helps identify the structures that make the whole cohere. If, as Moi reminds us, the main activity of literary studies is reading, reading calls attention once again to the paradox of the field practitioner. For Moi the paradox lies in the term "method." Perhaps, however, the doubt about method is amplified by a marked dependence of readers like Cixous and Sedgwick on other disciplines. For such readers, the text does not seem enough. Cixous and Sedgwick are emblematic of the critic who seeks theoretical grounding in neighboring disciplines, in their case psychoanalysis. As mentioned in the Introduction to this book, some scholars are suspicious of this dependence on the neighbor, perhaps because it is thought to betray a lack of method (Lesjak 18). But the problem of a field's strong relation to its outside is a good problem. As we have seen, for Cixous questions of method coincide with questions of reading: "What is a writer looking for? What are the stakes in the text? How does one search for something?" (WL 2). In her case, the transition from Oedipal combat to paternal adoption in language may be taken as an example of reparative criticism; it brings about and gives its due to the symbolic birth of Joana and Stephen at the same time that it enables Cixous to redraw the inclusiveness of the concept of modernism. But it is interesting that the reparative moment is made possible by the critic's nearness to the "wild heart" of the literary text through the relation of the literary to its outside (in this case psychoanalysis).

Can we entirely separate the practice of reading from this reparative recourse to the outside?

It would probably be wrong to say that postcritique is a return to the hermeneutic method, and my discussion of Cixous in this chapter does not aim at closing the circle. But, to the extent that the question of how we can be more receptive to literary texts and to works of art more generally is one of the main concerns of postcritique, then the notion of dialogue becomes productive, especially when dialogue is understood as a type of relation in which one puts oneself in a position to be affected (Felski, *Hooked*). Cixous of course does not talk of hermeneutics but of "poetics" to convey that, while interpretation matters, reading for interpretation is not the "pursuit of the meaning (singular) of a work," but of a type of relation, a relation that, as Rita Felski proposes in her most recent study, can be called "attachment" (*Hooked* 131).

Notes

1. Cixous, "Writing and the Law" 1. Hereafter referred to as WL.
2. See the Introduction to this book.
3. For the problematic aspect of the "non-hierarchical" aspirations of paratactical collage, I refer the reader to the conversation on comparison between Friedman and R. Radhakrishnan in Friedman, "Why Not Compare?" See also Radhakrishnan.
4. See Derrida, "Signature Event Context" 1988.
5. I am working with the Italian edition of *De l'interprétation, Della interpretazione*, and all translations from it are mine.
6. See discussion in Chapter 1.
7. In a blurb for Benjamin Moser's celebrated biography of Lispector, *Why This World*, Colm Tóibín speaks of Lispector as "one of the hidden geniuses of twentieth-century literature."
8. I am working with the Italian edition of *Le Sinthome, Seminario*, and all translations from it are mine; for the English edition, see Lacan, *Sinthome*.
9. See discussion in Chapter 1.
10. See also discussion in Chapter 1.
11. I am using the English title of Lispector's book as it appears in Verena Andermatt Conley's English translation of Cixous.
12. See Chapter 2.
13. Foucault, *Hermeneutics*, lecture of 24 February 1982.
14. Stephen studies words like a monk studies the Scriptures in his cell; through hermeneutic devotion, words warm up; words alone suffice. Words already constitute thought.

15. See discussion in Chapter 5.
16. The language of Yeats's sonnet—the "sudden blow," the "staggering girl", "her nape caught in his bill," "those terrified vague fingers," the girl "so caught up," and "mastered"—gives critics reason to think that it is about rape (Holstad; Cullingford).
17. Giorgio Agamben, in *Homo Sacer* 2005, reads Kafka's parable "Von dem Gesetz" as an exemplary illustration of the structure of sovereignty (*la struttura del bando*) transferred to language (57). The man from the country in the parable illustrates the Law in its pure form, when it does not prescribe anything. In this form, and following the model of sovereign exception, the law applies at the moment of its suspension: it keeps the man in its grip (*bando*) by abandoning him outside itself. The open door becomes the symbol of what Agamben means by "state of exception": "The open door which is destined only for him includes him by excluding him and it excludes him by including him" (58). Jacques Derrida, in "Before the Law," proposes that the parable is about the withholding of a pass: "The door is physically open, the doorkeeper does not bar the way by force. It is his discourse, rather, that operates at the limit, not to prohibit directly, but to interrupt and defer the passage, to withhold the pass. The man has the natural, physical freedom to penetrate spaces, if not the law. We are therefore compelled to admit that he must forbid himself from entering" (203). Massimo Cacciari agrees with Derrida that it is the man's decision not to enter, and elaborates on the power that the pass exerts on him. As Cacciari writes, the man from the country could challenge the prohibition of the guardian and enter, but he decides to wait for permission to enter to be given to him (75). For Cacciari, the door is open "to testify to our unreasonable insistence on begging to enter" (76; my translation). Judith Butler, in *The Psychic Life of Power*, shows that the imaginary threshold continues to wield its power when she reminds us that there are "linguistic requirements for entering sociality at all" (29).
18. Ferenczi experimented with his American patient, Elizabeth Severn, in 1932 (Fortune).
19. In her book of verse *Fat Art, Thin Art*, Sedgwick explains the loss of poetry as a historical event defining her generation ("Who Fed This Muse" 6).
20. See Recalcati's commentary on the character of Maggie in Clint Eastwood's movie *Million Dollar Baby* (131).

Chapter 7

Poststructuralism: Faith and Lacan

Overview

In the last chapter, in the hands of feminist poststructuralist thinker Hélène Cixous the modernist motif of the conflict of Life vs. Form took on centrality. The question of a living writing, which issues directly from Cixous's own belaboring of the conflict, caused our interest to shift from language seen as an all englobing, even imprisoning, horizon to a principle of natality within language in spite of the symbolic order and the symbolic structure that fix the subject in the social order. The notion emerged of a paternal donation. This chapter expands on that notion, presenting it as a neglected aspect of poststructuralism. Within the context of poststructuralism, we shall see that the notion of paternal donation consigns us a subject that is constituted through the idea of the gift and of giving. Discussion will open this chapter's keyword, poststructuralism, to wider, far-reaching effects.

The term "poststructuralism" embraces critical and philosophical trends that mark a crisis in the capacity of human consciousness to scrutinize itself, in the capacity of the "subject" to be the object of analysis and investigation. If structuralism had assumed that knowledge of the world and of the self *is* language, then language can no longer be viewed as an external vantage point. Poststructuralism rejects the idea of "a knowable reality independent of language" (Berman 173). The correspondence between language and reality seems lost, and language points to itself: "what exists are 'texts'" (Berman 173). However, in the previous chapter we have seen that Cixous, even though she has been classified as poststructuralist, diverts attention from this problem. Her turn to Lispector's living writing recuperates, via Joyce's modernism, not so much the adherence of language to reality but the question of a beneficial principle in language. Following on from the previous chapter, this chapter pursues the sense of a beneficial principle concentrating on a donation supplemented by language.

The spatial component of poststructuralism

When we think of the reader and the text, we often think of a subject before an object. It is from this perspective that the problem of mastery appears, with the risk of reducing understanding to a question of power. The spotlight is turned on the mastery that the interpreter comes to exert over the text or, conversely, the power of the text to silence the interpreter. Reading for interpretation, with the aim, that is, of producing literary criticism, may rigidify into a battle of prestige and insight, with the reader attempting to surpass the text and keep it under control, in order to experience the crossing of that undefined ever so spectral threshold beyond which the reader becomes the critic. Poststructuralism has been an important moment for literary studies, but it has displaced the elusive problem of this threshold.

The trends clustered under the label "poststructuralism" mark the shift to a new literary model. This is still under the influence of the notion of system, central to structuralism, but while structuralism's aim is to "demonstrate that the system is built up of elements," poststructuralism is identified with a methodology that "begins with a presumed systemic unity and proceeds to a disentangling of elements rather than vice versa" (Berman 175–6). Poststructuralism helps to neutralize the rigidification of the boundary between reader and text in the name of the production of literary criticism; thus it also neutralizes the specter of an unfounded difference between reader and critic. It does so by positing a radical otherness that meets us in unpredictable ways, an otherness that we cannot "plan for, progress towards, imagine, expect or anticipate" (Russell 405). In philosophy, the turn to otherness is motivated by the attempt to breach the difference between the metaphysical notion of Being and singular beings; in literary studies, the opening to radical otherness primarily affects the way we think about meaning, with an increasing reliance on the notion of space (Berman 177). Jacques Derrida, who is included in a larger constellation of male thinkers, such as Foucault and Lacan, usually called "poststructuralism" in English, provides an example with his notion of *différance* which, meaning both "differing" and "deferring," adds an important spatial component to thought about language.

Derrida posits a radical otherness by deriving from his reading of Saussure and his idea of language a neglected, inaudible difference that insists before the phonic signifier but is not yet, as Hélène Cixous would say, a failed phonic signifier. As an example, he offers the French equivalent for the word "difference." When the word is (mis)spelled with an "a"—"différance"—rather than with an "e" as it normally should be, it illustrates a lapse in writing which shows the "law" that "keep[s] it seemly" ("Différance" 3). The letter "a" is an "infraction" that one can pass over as if it did not matter, since it is a difference that cannot be heard (3): "The difference which establishes phonemes and lets them be heard remains in and of itself inaudible, in every sense of the word" (5). Derrida pushes Saussure's concept of the sign beyond the presumed unity of signifier and signified, and proposes the concept of trace, which he variously defines as a "noneconomical" sign, "an expenditure without reserve," or "the irreparable loss of presence, the irreversible usage of energy" (19). Erasure, rather than dichotomy, constitutes the structure of the trace: "the trace is never as it is in the presentation of itself. It erases itself in presenting itself, muffles itself in resonating, like the *a* writing itself, inscribing its pyramid in *différance*" (23).

As a philosopher, Derrida's main interest is to take stock of the history of thought as a great text ("the text of Western metaphysics" ["Différance" 25]) and to work with its critics (Levinas and Heidegger) and with Saussure, since at the time, in the 1960s and 1970s, linguistics was a dominant discipline with a consolidated influence over many other disciplines, so that the margins of the history of thought might be preserved and recuperated as traces. His intent is essentially reparative, targeting what, with Cixous, we might call a "living writing" that is buried under a dead writing. Derrida himself echoes the terminology we have examined with Cixous in the previous chapter: traces, he proposes, are signs that are "simultaneously living and dead" ("Différance" 24).

By his own admission, Derrida argues nothing new: we can signify only through signs, but he goes on to draw out the consequences of "the banality of the characteristic of the structure of the sign" ("Différance" 9), and that is that the sign is not a thing but substitutes for what is present: it defers. The sign is deferred presence: "The sign represents the present in its absence" (9). The trace reveals the rift with the present: "When we cannot grasp or show the thing, state the present ... we signify. We go through the detour of the sign. We take or give signs" (9). Paul Ricoeur had this basic structure of deferral in mind when he posited a "primitive connection between the act of existing and the signs that we exhibit in our works" (*Della interpretazione* 63). Our existence too can only be grasped or shown in signs. As discussed in Chapter 6, this entails a particular view of interpretation: interpretation is reflection that inevitably becomes interpretation because "it is never possible to grasp the act of existence in any place other than the signs disseminated in the world" (Ricoeur, *Della interpretazione* 63). Not only are existing and understanding the signs of existing one and the same thing, but thinking (reflection) and understanding signs are one and the same thing, too. The sign's basic structure of deferral results, for Ricoeur, in the mutual enfolding of reflection and interpretation. Yet, interpretation can only be a failed reappropriation of existence; the sign's structure of deferral causes meaning to remain doubtful and expendable. When Arendt affirms that everything that exists must appear, like Ricoeur, she is thinking about this "primitive connection" between existence and signs. For Ricoeur, and for Arendt, thinking seeks precisely to transform itself into a hermeneutic, into a reappropriation of the signs disseminated in the world (Ricoeur, *Della interpretazione* 63). Such a mutual enfolding of reflection and interpretation does not wane with the rise of the Derridean trace, the sign that signifies as it erases itself. Deconstruction does not collapse the hermeneutical dialogue as discussed in Chapter 6, but it no longer thinks of it as an exchange. In the act of reappropriating the signs of existing, an otherness interferes, an otherness that had not been foreseen and that surprises us.[1]

As we said earlier, poststructuralism has an important literary dimension. The metaphorical space that opens between Saussure's signifier and signified not only weakens the difference between the two (Berman 177) but also simultaneously pushes back into a faraway world of shadows and forgetfulness the problem of the unsteady identitarian boundaries between reader and critic with the latter condemned as if to a perpetual weakness. Promising to generate meaning, the metaphorical space neutralizes the specter of the secondariness of the critical act. The term "poststructuralism" seems to have arisen out of the need to give a name to a newfound, unprecedented autonomy of literary criticism, beyond the confines of the discipline of literature, as an inclusive line of reflection, as a thought. When not confused with the traditional task of the philologist, who is called to be a keeper of the text's authenticity and place in history—"to record and explain" (von Jagemann)—the critical act has traditionally aimed at reducing textual heterogeneity to a harmony of elements. Even after Wolfgang Iser's reception theory, understanding a text still largely amounted to the construction of coherence. The interpreter is a reader who has the means of appreciating the interaction of the parts within the text, can admire how the heterogeneous parts are harmonized, and conceives of meaning in terms of the detection of this harmonizing capacity.[2] Opening a metaphorical space for generating meaning, poststructuralism intercepts the problematic enfolding of the pursuit of meaning in criticism, which is inevitably contiguous with the preoccupation with the new (whether producing new readings, discovering new texts, etc.), and the unsteady identitarian boundary between reader and critic with the latter condemned to a sort of endlessly delayed legitimation.

Poststructuralism builds a privileged bridge with literary studies.[3] But the emphasis on radical otherness (of which Derrida's trace is the symbol) changes the attitude and the role of the interpreter. It might be helpful to consider here that Derrida's trace does not necessarily exclude Arendt's luminosity (when she says that everything that exists must appear) and Ricoeur's "affirmative position" (*Della interpretazione* 62), which we introduced in the previous chapter, since the trace is still caught in the lexicon of appearance/disappearance: the trace is a sign that appears in disappearing; it appears in the space of reading.[4] But it does change our idea of the text. This can no longer be an object, and we move from the allure of harmonized heterogeneous structures to the puzzling question of what, with Barbara Johnson, we might call the structure of address, that is to say, the reader's insertion in "a dialogic situation," in "a play of specific desires and expectations" (288). The reader's insertion may restitute the metaphorical space of the "suspension of reference" (288), but it is also true that this suspension only delays further the real problem, which is the uncertain grounding of the critic. Yet, the shift from the text as object to the text as a structure of address is important because the insertion of the reader and that play of desires and expectations make possible the hypothesis of the gift as a relevant critical category. The next section will clarify this hypothesis, expounding on what we mean by the gift in the triangulation of reader, critic, text.

The problem of the gift

The notion of gift punctuates poststructuralism even though its consequences for the ways we conceive of reading and meaning remain to be explored. Brian Russell thinks of the metaphorical space open to a radical otherness as gift. Russell writes: "The coming of otherness is gift, not *demanding* our response, but challenging us with force in positive and negative ways" (405–6; original emphasis). The problem of meaning—the meaning of a literary text—rises under the aegis of reconciliation: reading becomes the trial and test to which the erased subjects the human:

> While we should react responsibly, our action does not *bring* the Other. Nonetheless, we must live a "performed" faith, as if the Other will come in ways which bring about friendship, justice, hospitality, forgiveness, which are all needed if humanity is to become real Humanity. (Russell 406; original emphasis)

Literary critical practice is the recipient of a gift in being made accountable for its contribution to an evolving humanity.[5] But what is meant by "gift"?

The term "gift" is inevitably associated with the work of anthropologist Marcel Mauss. Because of his findings, Mauss remains one of the most original thinkers of the gift. Studying it within a symbolic economy of exchange, Mauss found that the gift issues from a "principle of separation" and reveals, contrary to what we might assume, an antithetical relation to the other (Esposito, *Pensiero istituente* 181).[6] In order to understand the link between poststructuralism's radical opening to otherness and the gift, however, it is necessary to look at poststructuralism's transformation of Mauss's idea. We will do so with the help of Jean-Luc Marion.

Marion builds on Mauss's idea, revising it. He begins by considering that in the economy of efficiency (exchange), the gift "must acquire the consistency of objectness, its visibility, its permanence, its availability" (*Being Given* 82). This view posits the gift as accessible "to all the potential partners of economic exchange," but Marion directs his attention to the givenness of the gift (82). The givenness of the gift—the phenomenon of donation—demands that the giver remain unknown and the bracketing of the givee. It is this bracketing that characterizes the givenness of the gift since, if the givee expected it, the gift would be disqualified (85). Marion suspends the economic meaning of gift as barter, endowment, or transfer. If the gift presupposes, on the one hand, an unknown giver and, on the other hand, a givee who does not know that she or he has received, then it interrupts the possibility of a return. He reconceives of the gift in terms of subtraction and suffuses it with poverty and loss, proposing to think of it "outside of presence and outside of self-subsistence" (81). Thus transformed, Marion's gift has a similar structure to Derrida's uneconomical sign (the trace), which "erases itself in presenting itself" ("Différance" 23).

The gift as donation, what Marion calls "the givenness of the gift," may be inscribed among the effects of the poststructuralist opening to a radical otherness. Both Marion's donation and poststructuralist otherness assume a speech context or structure of address outside the face-to-face. If poststructuralism assumes language as the field of an otherness that does not demand a response, Marion's givenness similarly dispenses with meaning ("truth") as an appearance into presence. Donation is something that moves in language, and beyond the subject/object divide. The similarity accounts for Marion's crowning of Augustine as a poststructuralist thinker. His reading of Augustine's *Confessions*, a text that eludes genre classification, sheds light on its central position in poststructuralist thought for its capacity to illustrate Marion's own redescription of the gift. The following section builds on Marion's reading of Augustine to understand the gift as a speech situation in which the stake is a paternal adoption. Through this route, Cixous's feminist and modernist inflected question of language will re-emerge within poststructuralism, which will be able to pose the problem of the event/experience of a receiving (a being given) beyond the Oedipal model and symbolic structures.

A different relation to language

Marion declares that he reads Augustine from a non-metaphysical point of view, as "a contemporary utopian": "He would guide, in advance and without intending it, our hesitant steps by having thought *before* this *after* which we are trying to pass—metaphysics and possibly the very horizon of Being" (*In the Self's Place* 9; original emphasis). Turning to Augustine, Marion, much like Derrida, makes inroads into a pre-theoretical zone beyond the questioning mode of philosophy, a zone where truth is "something which cannot be denied" and "happens beyond any performativity and beyond any theory" (Kearney, "Confessions" 33). In that zone, Derrida affirms "a sort of yes, a sort of 'anterior' acquiescence" to the relation to the other ("On Being"). The inquiry implies a special focus on what we are calling here the "structure of address" which can be compared to a kind of interpellation that eludes the face-to-face setting and the economy of power. From Derrida's perspective, everyone and everything leaves a trace, and, while the trace may address me because it is in my own language, it also addresses others who are therefore unknown addressees: "The indeterminacy of the addressee is part of the structure of the trace" (Derrida qtd. in Kearney, "Confessions" 35).[7] Marion's reading illustrates Augustine's movement toward a similar structure, that is to say, beyond the notion of subject and the "struggle for recognition" (Honneth). In Augustine's text, God is the ultimate otherness.

As Marion points out, *Confessions* is only apparently a text of theology and Augustine only apparently speaks as a philosopher would about the world, about something (*In the Self's Place* 19). The unique trait of *Confessions* lies in the fact that "Saint Augustine does not so much speak *of* God as he speaks *to* God" (Marion, *In the Self's Place* 9; original emphasis). Privileging the vocative case, Augustine addresses himself to a radical otherness—neither person, object, or animal—whose place is left empty. Marion calls the text a "praising text" or "a performance of praise" (*In the Self's Place* 19). Readers of *Confessions*, however, may come to realize that, as Augustine cares to stress, praise is a different form of cognition to which the protagonist accedes on his intellectual quest. At the start of *Confessions*, we read: "Grant me, Lord, to know and understand whether a man is first *to pray to you* for help or to praise you" (I, 1, 21; my emphasis). The text begins to raise questions: Does prayer come before praise? Or does praise come first? "If he does not know you, how can he pray to you? For he may call for some other help, mistaking it for yours" (I, 1, 21). Is it possible to praise something without knowing it? The otherness of God in *Confessions* is an intellectual quest. Turning away from the philosophical tradition, Augustine leans toward a more dialogic mode. As Marion observes, "the word of praise is the dialogical space in which God and myself are in relation" (*In the Self's Place* 19).

Praise is a form of cogitation that differs from reasoning on the basis of doubt, argument, confutation, and so on. It is a new beginning for the thinker who, released from the experience of ideas that seem to vanish into thin air every time that he tries to grab them, can look at the world as an expanding organism, as the affirmative rhythmic correspondence between the created and its Creator.[8] Praise names an epistemology of abundance: "You create them, nourish them, and bring them to perfection . . . You support, you fill and you protect all things . . . You love your creatures, but with a gentle love. You treasure them, but without apprehension" (*Confessions* I, 4, 23). But why confess praise?[9]

What compels Augustine to confess praise is not, he specifies, some kind of reward. Though this is often the case—"We give abundantly to you so that we may deserve a reward"—he adds "yet, which of us has anything that does not come from you?" (*Confessions* I, 4, 23). In the space where God and myself are in relation, the economy of exchange is suspended, replaced by the structure of what Marion calls "the gift." God as creator is also the ultimate giver, but we do not realize what we receive because it is natural for him to give. God, whose wisdom is inscrutable, is also the giver who remains inscrutable, unseen, invisible, and unknown. Confessing praise, therefore, argues Marion, is essential to bringing the giving into visibility. By confessing praise the givee brings to visibility the giving he has received and builds a community of readers who, all together, will amplify the praise:

> why do I lay this lengthy record before you? Certainly it is not through me that you first hear of these things. But by setting them down I fire my own heart and the hearts of my readers with love of you, so that we all may ask: Can any praise be worthy of the Lord's majesty? (*Confessions* XI, 1, 253)

The praising text positions its readers as witnesses of the gift in Marion's sense, but Augustine's text also makes the point that language *is* the gift. I will now build on Marion to expand on this view of language.

If, as Marion points out, what the readers witness in *Confessions* is "the return of my word through the Word" (*In the Self's Place* 27), readers witness the restoration of language (and thought), a fact that is illustrated by the make-up of the text. Augustine borrows the words from the Scriptures, for example when he quotes from Psalm 144: "Those who look for the Lord will cry out in praise of him" (*Confessions* I, 1, 21); he completes the repetition with his own words—"because all who look for him shall find him"—which, in turn, repeat the message of the psalm. The text enacts the recovery of its author's linguistic power, the repetition testifying to the living meaning of those words: the silent Word of the Scriptures "renders possible my own living word" (*In the Self's Place* 23). The praising text confesses the event of being given language. Augustine writes: "I say nothing correct to men that you did not hear me say to you *first*, and you hear nothing correct said by me which *you did not first say to me*) (Augustine qtd. in *In the Self's Place* 24; original emphasis).

While not neglecting the importance of language, Marion is more interested in the issue of proprietorship and of control brought out by the words of praise: "In short, do the words that I say in praise come from me or from him whom I praise?" (*In the Self's Place* 21). The question of the proprietorship of the word allows the philosopher to highlight the weakening of the subject/object boundary and the interchangeability of the two actors in the dialogue: speaker and listener (21). And this is because my speech is made possible by the one who has interpellated me. Yet, it is significant that Marion himself adds: "Of myself, reduced to my dumb solitude, I could not yet say anything *to* anyone, if no one had not already interpellated me" (21; original emphasis). The "dumb" solitude suggests that, in being interpellated, it is language that is restored. In fact, the fascination of *Confessions* is that the narrative shifts from a master scene in which language is learned through the effort of imitation, by observing what Wittgenstein would call language games, to another primal scenario that is compellingly reminiscent of Jean Laplanche's scene of subject formation.

In Laplanche's primal scene the child is addressed by the adult in a verbal and extra-verbal manner with messages that are eminently "enigmatic" because they exceed the child's interpretive system and remain beyond the child's grasp ("Unfinished Copernican Revolution"). Laplanche's child, however, seems no passive actor in the scene as he or she tries to make meaning out of a signifier which exceeds his or her means, and that is why we can read the primal scene as one of receiving. For Laplanche, the enigmatic signifier that exceeds the addressee constitutes subjectivity and the unconscious (Stack). The important point for our argument is not what exceeds and eludes (for that emphasis is responsible for awakening the ghost of an overwhelming sovereignty of language), but the fact that what Laplanche calls "enigmatic" signifier is a frayed, damaged signifier at the origin. In reaching its addressee, the enigmatic signifier involves him or her in an activity of recovery, mending, and restoring which, as Augustine's chain of well-being and praise demonstrates, hatches the relation to language as a "gift of speech," in the terms of Lacan, or as paternal donation in our terms.[10] The part of Laplanche's paradigm that is important for our argument is the damaged message at the origin, the enigmatic signifier which, from the beginning, confuses the gift of language (the enigmatic signifier given) with the gift of speech (the attempted interpretation by the child). This is the gift that Augustine's text enacts in that mutuality that, as Marion emphasizes, bespeaks recovery.

Those who read—*Tolle lege* (take it, read it)—"thereby receiving it [the text] as a call" (Marion, *In the Self's Place* 26), are first and foremost called to this gift: a signifier that addresses them in enigmatic ways that exceed their means of translation. Marion admits that Augustine reached God by way of inquiry into the self and we have argued that a different relation to language is crucial to his conversion. What bears emphasizing is that this different relation to language implies a shift from the biological father to quite another paternal function. If the aim of the praising text is to build an ever-expanding community of readers, it would be important to ask why everyone can read the text. What does it mean to speak of readers in *Confessions*? What is it that readers witness in Augustine's text?

From the father to paternal donation

Confessions is an intellectual quest which features someone seduced by the aesthetic and rhetorical power of language. When describing Faustus, the Manichee leader, Augustine recalls: "The ease with which he found the right words to clothe his thoughts delighted me, and I was not the only one to applaud" (*Confessions* V, 6, 97). The seduction takes hold under the sign of the father, who wanted his son to have a "gifted tongue" (V, 6, 97). The central questions of the narrative—the pleasure that language affords and what it means to have a relation to language—are intertwined with Augustine's progress toward *caritas*, the love of God. The protagonist finds himself in a labyrinth of competing doctrines struggling to find the right belief to embrace and attain an independence of mind: his love of learning, science, philosophy, his need to belong to a school or to a discipline, as well as the seductiveness of language all form one big knot. As a seeker, Augustine is like Joyce's Stephen, Arendt's Rahel, Cixous's Clarice; like them, he burns with intellectual ambition: How does one know? When it comes to language and knowledge, Augustine, in dandy-like fashion, is always in admiration of form, of the clothes and vesture in which thoughts present themselves. Language, is, therefore, on one side; the world, on the other. He has been schooled in this aural seduction by his father, who went out of his way to make him study public speaking (II, 3, 45). When he meets Ambrose, he realizes for the first time that the aesthetic appeal of language can combine with its hermeneutic power: "nevertheless his meaning, which I tried to ignore, found its way into my mind together with his words, which I admired so much" (V, 14, 108), a fact that initiates his self-examination: "I only made use of [language] to try and please others, and I only tried to please them, not to teach them" (VI, 6, 119). In the course of the narrative, just as language breaks from instrument of power into instrument of praise, so understanding breaks from philosophical inquiry into access to a principle of thriving to which he clings ("manebo in illo") and in which he wants to dwell (VII, 11, 147). Augustine reaches God before his conversion, not as a man of faith, but as a man of intellect who discovers a principle of abundance.[11] His conversion comes, quite anticlimactically, in Book IX, when he resigns from his position as a professor of rhetoric because he feels he is cured of the split between the aesthetic and the hermeneutic dimensions of language: "The day came when my release from the profession of rhetoric was to become a reality, just as, in my mind, I was free from it already. The deed was done, and you rescued my tongue as once you had rescued my heart" (IX, 4, 185). They must find, he writes, "another vendor of words" (IX, 5, 189). Caritas, or love of God, is the point of arrival of an inquiry that culminates in the destitution of language and the rise of a donation *in* language. His attempt to put into words this transition for his readers constitutes the praising text: "My love for you, Lord, is not some vague feeling: it is positive and certain. Your word struck into my heart and from that moment I loved you" (X, 6, 211). The entire narrative of *Confessions*, which is a narrative of resistance, illustrates that Augustine has decided not because he has willed but because he has received without knowing it. From this perspective, the narrative follows the structure of the gift in Marion's sense, but because the gift is inseparable from the experience of receiving language otherwise, it highlights unambiguously the necessity of the destitution of the father. Augustine must undo the traditional symbolic knot that ties the capacity to speak to the symbolic order of the father, the Oedipal dimension, and reach a state of *désêtre* which announces the destitution of the tie between speaking subject and biological father. The allure of Augustine's text is that, in its treatment of the question of speaking, it pushes beyond the symbolic Oedipal dimension.

If, as Marion argues, by confessing praise the givee brings to visibility the giving he has received, Augustine's text institutes a community of readers who witness what Cixous would call his coming to language; it is for them that receiving is enacted. As Marion observes, "the *confessio* will have no other function than to teach my speech little by little the call from which it comes" (*In the Self's Place* 23). What Marion calls "hermeneutic recovery" (27) concerns a return to (and of) language under different uneconomical auspices. Such a return resonates with the poststructuralist opening beyond the subject/object divide. Marion prefers the term "encounter" to the notion of subjectivity. Praise permits an encounter, but how?

Poststructuralist dialogic views of subjectivity lodge difference in the self; they emphasize an opening that puts the "I" in relation with a "you," an otherness that could be anyone (Kristeva, *Strangers*). But the "you" or otherness that is coterminous with the "I" also diminishes the "I"; in this case the "you" is a reminder of our non-difference, thus of the fact that we are a subjectivity. In Marion's definition, faith is a different kind of "face-to-face" vis-à-vis this scenario (*In the Self's Place* 42).[12] The "you" is not there to elicit our address; it does not, to use Marion's vocabulary, impose itself to incite the interlocution (*In the Self's Place* 153). Faith, in Marion's definition, is a face-to-face without intermediaries and closely entwined with the question of welcoming the word of another. Augustine's vocative—"Saint Augustine does not so much speak *of* God as he speaks *to* God" (9)—builds up an intimate address that is one with the turn toward an unknown addressee outside the boundaries of what the speaker could predicate of the addressee. As Marion shows, the confession of praise affirms an I–you encounter beyond subjectivity. I would add that we should not forget that praise is hinged on the particular face-to-face of faith. Augustine, in fact, ties the view of language as paternal donation with faith, inviting an examination of faith as a structure of address.

The experience of speaking

Key poststructuralist thinkers have drawn on Saint Augustine's *Confessions*, but it was Jacques Lacan perhaps who more than anyone else carried on Augustine's reflection on language in terms of paternal adoption. In the seminar *On the Names-of-the Father* (1963) the psychoanalyst reminds his audience: "I have been reading St. Augustine since I was an adolescent" (63), and, more pertinently, in the same seminar he suggests that his move beyond Freud's mythological treatment of the father supplements Augustine (64–5).

In this seminar, Lacan specifies his own restructuring of the functions of subject and object beyond Hegel's dialectic. "Hegel's dialectic is false," says Lacan; it is "a twofold gap between the subject and the object that has fallen away from him" (*Names-of-the Father* 62).[13] But his difference from the philosophers is articulated most compellingly in a text about religion, "Discourse to Catholics" (1960), delivered before an audience that would be familiar with Augustine and, through Augustine, would be interested in the conjunction of psychoanalysis and religion on the question of the word. Lacan asks, with Augustine: "What does it mean to speak?"[14]

To outline the difference, Lacan argues that, in instituting desire as an object of inquiry, Freud went further than the philosophers because he considered a truth that is such even though it remains undeciphered:

> What are we to think of a desire with which consciousness no longer has anything to do except to know it to be as unknowable as the "thing in itself" but which is nevertheless recognized to be the structure of the for "itself *par excellence* that a chain of discourse is?" ("Discourse" 16)[15]

Before an audience that would comprise a number of theologians, he asks: "Doesn't Freud seem to you to be more applicable than our philosophical tradition as regards conducting oneself correctly in relation to this extremity of intimacy that is at the same time excluded internality?" (Lacan, "Discourse" 16).

His terms—"extremity of intimacy" and "excluded internality"—resonate with Augustine's intellectual journey toward faith. For Lacan, as for the author of *Confessions*, the self is unknown, a void without a core: "The self crushes me because I do not have access to it" (Marion, *In the Self's Place* 157). As someone who spent his life "listening to lives that are told, that are confessed (*s'avouent*)," Lacan speaks of the "scandal" of his discovery "that will remain palpitating after me" ("Discourse" 7). The scandal concerns the imaginary direction of the self:

> *How does it happen that these good and accommodating men or neighbors*, every one of whom props up a certain knowledge and is propped up by a certain knowledge, who are thrown into this business of existence, *let themselves go to the point of falling prey to captivation by mirages by which their lives, wasting opportunity, allow their essence to escape*, by which their passion is toyed with, and by which their being, in the best of cases, only attains the scant reality that is affirmed only insofar as it has never been anything but disappointed? (Lacan, "Discourse" 8; my emphasis)

As an auditor, the psychoanalyst is presented with an affected subject engendered by the power of symbols. His patients, like the author of *Confessions*, are ravaged by language. Yet, the affinity of views with Augustine only helps Lacan to reinstate the divide between psychoanalysis and religion. In the face-to-face with the other, of which the analytical relation is one of the noblest expressions, "one of the goals of the silence that constitutes the rule of my listening is precisely to silence love" ("Discourse" 7).

Psychoanalysis and religion must keep silent one about the other, divided yet linked by a space between.[16] Lacan tirelessly delimits the boundaries to prevent a confusion of tongues between the two. In *The Triumph of Religion* (originally a press conference held in Rome in 1974), he insists on the rigor of the analyst: "When one is an analyst, one is constantly tempted to skid, to slip, to let oneself slide down the stairs on one's backside, which is, all the same, not very dignified as regards the analyst's function. One must know how to remain rigorous ..." ("Triumph" 84).[17] Still in *The Triumph of Religion*, he is careful to outline the diverging interests of psychoanalysis and religion. He offers a narrative of modernity in which psychoanalysis emerges as a historical phenomenon, a product of the age of science and technological reproducibility. It is with regard to *this* time that psychoanalysis finds itself almost inevitably in relation and in tension with religion. While religion produces meaning (it tries to cure all sorts of distressing things)— "And they know quite a bit about meaning. They can give meaning to absolutely anything ... They are trained to do that" (64–5)— psychoanalysis is a symptom; "psychoanalysis is concerned with what does not work" (61). But across the divide that separates them, psychoanalysis and religion amplify the centrality of speech to human experience. The question of psychoanalysis is speech— "What does the experience of speaking involve? What is the essence and exchange of speech" ("Symbolic" 8–9)—but the same question becomes an issue for religion when one considers, from Augustine's vantage point, that faith is inseparable from the experience of speaking, from the experience, that is, of being given language otherwise, of being addressed.

The structure of the act of faith

Christian theology defines faith as Revelation; it is inseparable from Christ, incarnation, and the Cross. In the encyclical *Fides et Ratio*

(1998) John Paul II argued that faith "produces thought" (*produce pensiero*) (27), setting for contemporary theologians the task of deconstructing the divide between faith and science, with science understood not only as method (based on observation and experiment) but also as philosophical rationality and, more broadly, the speculative knowledge that includes critical thought. Contemporary theologians reject the traditional opposition of faith and method (observation, verifiability, credibility). Marco Vanzini, for example, appeals to John Henry Newman's notion of "illative sense" (the faculty of judging and conceptualizing on the basis of experience, which allows one to reach a certainty based on the accumulation of signs), and Jean-Pierre Rousselot's "synthetic capacity" (the capacity of the human subject to build on signs, or clues) to take up faith in a semiotic and hermeneutic network that allows the definition of the "structure of the act of faith": (1) God approaches me in the signs of the visible world; (2) it is true that I have no evidence; yet I see truths that are meaningful to me because I recognize that God is talking to me with love; (3) following from the assent, my intellect desires to know more and better the subject of faith (belief) ("La fede").[18] Although Vanzini acknowledges no poststructuralist influences, dismissing poststructuralism as the "culture of disenchantment" ("La fede"), his analysis of faith closely recalls Marion's description of the dialogical relation to God. He adds an important element, however, when he takes into account the role of affect: "faith is an organ of affect" ("La fede").

In Marion's reading of Augustine, faith (the face-to-face without intermediaries) is entwined with the question of welcoming the word of another; it is inseparable from the question of an address to an unknown addressee outside the boundaries of what "I could say, predict, or predicate of him starting from myself alone" (*In the Self's Place* 19). From this point of view, faith is enmeshed in what Lacan calls the "primordial question" ("Symbolic" 8), which he spells out in "The Function and Field of Speech and Language in Psychoanalysis" (delivered in Rome, 1953): "there is no speech without a reply, even if it is met only with silence, provided that it has an auditor" (*Écrits* 40). The function of speech in psychoanalysis echoes the function of speech in faith, while of course remaining other from it: speech is always the presupposition of a reply, even when there is only silence. Vanzini emphasizes the mutuality in welcoming the word of another—the act is twofold, double—and thus supplements Marion's description. In Vanzini's account not only does God turn his face to me but I also turn *my* face, because

I find God to be infinitely worthy of trust.[19] Only the emphasis on this mutual face-to-face, which highlights the lack of intermediaries, makes the discourse on faith resonate with Lacan's (and poststructuralism's) interest in the subject beyond philosophy at the center of Lacan's "Discourse to Catholics."

To belabor this resonance, we can consider Marion's uses of Derrida. Derrida's notion of the trace implies an unmastered and therefore unknown destination. Marion builds on Derrida's trace in order to shift *from* the unknown addressee *to* the "encounter": "*the word that brings about an encounter*" (*In the Self's Place* 20; original emphasis). According to the poststructuralist view of the trace, any unknown addressee can be called "God" (Derrida qtd. in Kearney, "Confessions" 35).[20] As if mindful of this problem, Augustine, this post-metaphysical utopian, enacts exactly the problem of names: "If he does not know you, how can he pray to you? For he may call for some other help, mistaking it for yours" (*Confessions* I, 1, 21).[21] The progress of the narrative toward the love of God represents the kind of truth that Lacan called "extremity of intimacy": this is a truth that does not wait to be deciphered.[22] Marion retranslates Lacan's "extremity of intimacy" in terms of the givenness of the gift, which affords "hermeneutic recovery" (*In the Self's Place* 27). But what interests us here is that faith is presupposed in Marion's notion of "hermeneutic recovery" and thus confuses itself with this notion.

The linguistic utterance in Augustine has a reparative function; as we have argued, Marion's "encounter" is simultaneous with "the return of the Word" (*In the Self's Place* 27), that is to say, with the experience of receiving language.[23] As we have also argued, the remarkable thing about Augustine's text is that faith is cast in terms of the destitution of the symbolic law of the father as the law of language. Augustine is a public intellectual, a lover of language and a professor of literature and rhetoric, and as such the product of his father's wish (II, 3, 45). Conversion means the abandonment of all this; it amounts to a reorientation of his *affectus* for language, with the suspension of the command to be that is borne in language and inseparable from the ravaging power of the gaze of the other. He realizes that he sins and speaks because he wants to please and be pleased. Lacan refers to this fact in *On the Names-of-the-Father*, where, in lieu of Marion's "hermeneutic recovery," he introduces the enigma of speaking: "what is there whose voice the subject assumes each time he speaks?" (72).

"A slice of the Word"

In the press conference held in Rome in 1974, which became the text of *The Triumph of Religion*, the interviewer provoked Lacan: "According to what I have understood, in Lacanian theory, at the basis of man there is not biology or physiology but rather language. St. John had already said: 'In the beginning was the Word.' You have added nothing to that" ("Triumph" 73). Lacan replied: "I am in favor of John and his 'In the beginning was the Word,' but it is an enigmatic beginning" (74), adding:

> It is when the Word is incarnated that things really start going badly. Man is no longer at all happy, he no longer resembles at all a little dog who wags his tail or a nice monkey who masturbates. He no longer resembles anything. He is ravaged by the Word. (74)

Why "ravaged"? We can begin to reply if we consider the neighborliness of Lacan's view with the representation of human language in the Biblical text.

Take for instance the extraordinary passage from Sirach that reads: "Do not praise anyone before he speaks, for this is the way people are tested" (27, line 7).[24] Humans give proof of themselves; they appear in language, just as the refuse appears when the sieve is shaken (27, line 4). Speaking is the test of the human, which means that it is both the proof of the human and the human temptation, in the sense of trial or ordeal. The word used for "test" in the Greek text—*peirasmós* (from *peirázō*)—means both temptation and test (πειρασμὸς ἀνθρώπων), and both senses can apply simultaneously, depending on the context: the positive sense of "test" and the negative sense of "temptation" (*peirázō*, from *peíra*, "test, trial"). God tests the faith of Abraham precisely in this double sense.

When Lacan says "ravaged by the Word," he suggests this double sense of speaking, as proof and temptation. The enigma unfolds through the description of his own psychoanalytic practice. We have already quoted from a "Discourse to Catholics": the analyst is the auditor; he must listen, not love. In *The Triumph of Religion* he speaks of his "sordid profession" ("Triumph" 75). He sees that his clients go back again and again, and the thing "gives them pleasure, they rejoice in it" (75). At this point, he introduces the notion of "a slice of the Word": "why would they come back if it weren't to treat themselves to a slice of the Word each time?" (75). Speaking is being toyed with by symbols, and it is temptation: it is taking . . . that slice. The analytic scene confesses this taking: "what is there whose voice the subject assumes each time he speaks?" (Lacan, *Names-of-the-Father* 72).

In *On the Names-of-the-Father*, an interrupted seminar, the enigma of this slice of speech is presented through the question of the father, the father understood not in the mythical or Oedipal sense but dispersed in a plurality of names. Lacan discusses two Biblical passages from Exodus, the passage about Moses in the burning bush (chapter 3) and another from chapter 6, when Moses hears that the God of Abraham, Isaac, and Jacob has announced himself under another name, El Shaddai (Exodus 6: 2–3; Lacan, *Names-of-the-Father* 79).[25] With reference to the passage about Moses in the burning bush (Exodus 3:14), "When you go to them you will tell them that my name is Ehyeh asher ehyeh. *I am what I am*," it is important to Lacan that what Moses hears in the burning bush (probably his body) be translated "I am what I am" (*Names-of-the-Father* 79), not "I am the one who is," because the sense of this "I am" is that it is only a name, a name that defers the name and follows another name (79). When Lacan says that the pen of Freud stops before the God of Moses, he indicates that he (Lacan) does not want any myth to fix the identity of the father. The plurality of names suggests that to have a name does not grant you that you are the one who speaks.

The enigma is illustrated with two icons of the father, two paintings by Caravaggio of the sacrifice of Isaac (*Names-of-the-Father* 82), one in which Abraham, the father, seems a blind executor, the other in which he appears to debate with an angel, while Isaac waits.[26] Commenting on the first, which is the later of the two, a version probably painted in 1603, now at the Uffizi in Florence, Lacan writes: "There is a boy whose head is pushed up against a small stone altar. The child is suffering and grimacing. Abraham's knife is raised above him. The angel is there—the presence of the one whose Name is not pronounced" (82). Lacan's description halts on the question: "What is an angel?" (82). The question actually gains more urgency when one looks at the second image, an earlier version from 1598, now in Princeton. At the center of this painting we find what we might call a dialectical rendition of Abraham, the father of Isaac. Abraham debates with the angel, and the son appears as a witness at the margin of the debate. Isaac is naked, his shoulders are lit, he is almost an accessory; the face of the angel is lit, too, and his gaze holds Abraham's gaze. Isaac does not seem afraid; he is waiting for them to make a decision. In this human–animal–father configuration, the animal's gaze is fixed on Isaac waiting. Alluding to the Florence painting, where the angel arrests Abraham's hand, Lacan observes that

> after all, prior to the gesture that restrains him, Abraham went to this specific spot for a reason. God gave him a son and then gave him the order to bring that son to a mysterious meeting place. There the father bound him hand and foot, as one would bind a lamb, to sacrifice him. (83)

By contrast, we might add, in the Princeton version the son is in a position, a formalist subject position; anyone could be in that position, but that would not make him a son. Isaac here is a witness to the debate. In its winning theatricality it is a perfect painting. The suspended action suggests that the father is always listening to others, to angels and others; he is suspended on a speech act. Unlike *this* Abraham, the father in the later canvas is a man under trial, following through: he is blindly executing, and the angel points to the animal as if to divert the father's violence. In the earlier canvas there is no such wilderness, where your father is the enemy. "What is an angel?" is an appropriate question there because we have an interlocution suspended in the darkness, with the angel—perhaps an inner phantasm?—as the other term, one sent in the name of another, a Giver (Isaac is a miraculous gift). What is an angel? What is another? These questions in the two Caravaggios seem strictly linked to another question: When is faith faith? And all three questions are hinged on the question of the "father" grasped as a spacing of names, as the various names of a withdrawn addressee.

Once the recognition of another has been woven into the imaginary trajectory, and the image is found to be deceitful, "God's power resides in the capacity to advance into emptiness," as Lacan writes, echoing Saint Augustine's ordeal (*Ethics* 242). The recognition of another, "reveals itself as an adventure" (242); it means groping in darkness. By way of this darkness, faith enters the poststructuralist redescription of subjectivity, in which Lacan the auditor becomes a major actor.

The spacing created by the multiplicity of names informs us that not only is Lacan's speaking being (*parlêtre*) determined by a network of symbols, and thus speaking always implies a reply, but also that this reply is tied up with the question of a donation in language. The question of psychoanalysis—What is speaking?—concerns the production of a "symbolic adoption" (Recalcati 132;

my translation). This, Massimo Recalcati suggests, is an anterior affirmation, "the 'Yes!' of the father" (a formulation that recalls Derrida's "anterior acquiescence") which has the power to "love the other precisely because she is a lost cause" (132; my translation). In *On the Names-of-the-Father*, the plurality of names is an interlocution in the darkness and the spacing of an anterior affirmation.

The seminar is strange, in part because it was interrupted by the ban on Lacan and his teaching and bears the mark of those circumstances. It could be said, in fact, that Isaac is Lacan himself, the son that the institution of psychoanalysis is about to sacrifice; this father wants to see at least a bit of blood. We perceive the metaphorical dimension when Lacan quotes Rashi (Rabbi Solomon ben Isaac, an Ashkenazi from Troyes, France), who, in a commentary to Abraham's sacrifice of his son, writes: "Then what? If that's the way it is, have I come for nothing? I am going to give him at least a flesh wound, to draw a little blood" (*Names-of-the-Father* 85–6). Lacan stops but he will continue in *The Ethics of Psychoanalysis*, which might be considered his response to the (philosophical) notion of the subject based on the struggle for recognition. Lacan intercepts the negative path of recognition and redirects it through the imaginary. The response to recognition is the identification with the other "that arises at the extreme moment of our temptation. We refrain from assaulting the image of the other because it was the image in which we were formed as an ego" (*Ethics* 241).

Notes

1. For a discussion of the common points between Ricoeur and his poststructuralist contemporaries, including the shared concern about the autonomy of the Cartesian subject, see Johann.
2. Iser proclaims the death of the traditional interpreter: "an interpreter can no longer claim to teach the reader the meaning of the text" (19). What he or she can do is analyze what actually happens when one reads a text (19). That is why his theory of interpretation is a theory of reception. As overdue as it was, Iser's reorientation left problems unsolved. It might be said that his updated theory of interpretation, in fact, made even more glaring some of the problems that had always inhered in criticism, especially in light of the effort to be a discipline. First of all there is the question of the interpreter's and the reader's identities: In what sort of relation do they stand? Is there a point at which a reader becomes an interpreter? If so, which one? What enables him or her to transit from one identity to another?

3. For more on the legacy of poststructuralism, see Braidotti.
4. The sign redefined as trace is an erasure "which constitutes itself from the outset as a trace, which situates it as the change of site, and makes it disappear in its appearance, makes it emerge from itself in its production" (Derrida, "Différance" 24).
5. For another discussion of the gift as a poststructuralist concern, see Moore.
6. Esposito calls what is exchanged "the negative"; in Claude Lefort's terms, it is "the distance" that each must take from the other, the separation and demarcation that ensures and preserves the bond that unites the members of a society (Esposito, *Pensiero istituente* 181). As Esposito observes, that separation is the precondition of the face-to-face, where the stake is not the gift in the sense of Mauss—a thing exchanged, given, restituted—but the subjectivity of the giver, which is augmented or decreased by the disproportion between gift and countergift (182).
7. "The addressee—precisely because of the structure of the trace, when a trace is addressed and left without any firm and assured destination—[is indeterminate]; we don't know whom we are addressing. Even if I know that I'm addressing you, I know that because my language is intelligible, to some extent it can be addressed to others. The indeterminacy of the addressee is part of the structure of the trace." (Derrida qtd. in Kearney, "Confessions" 35).
8. The text may be said to begin at the end, at the point of the quest's arrival: with Augustine's discovery that the world is the created and God is the creator. God has majesty, magnificence, strength, inscrutable wisdom because he is the creator of creatures, and it is man's instinct, that is, natural inclination, as "one of [his] creatures," to praise him. The world is no longer something to be described and understood, but something that can be understood insofar as man exerts his natural ability to praise. Insofar as language and thought are proper to man, as one of the created creatures, these properties in man are realized in the capacity to praise. The first words are: "Can any praise be worthy of the Lord's majesty?" (*Confessions* I, 1, 21).
9. We associate confession with guilt and sin or crime; one usually confesses one's sins. But Augustine specifies: "Confessio enim, non peccatorum tantum *dicitur*, sed et laudis," confession is not said only of sins, but also of praise (Augustine qtd. in Marion, *In the Self's Place* 13). To confess praise modifies the meaning of confession, and by expanding the meaning of confession he gives birth to this text which is just as much an intellectual autobiography as it is a spiritual autobiography.
10. For an article exploring the implications of Laplanche's paradigm for creativity, see Wyatt.
11. He reaches God as the principle of all beings: "in an instant of awe, my mind attained to the sight of the God who IS" (*Confessions* VII, 17,

151). Augustine says this even before he is converted; he names God belatedly, retrospectively.
12. Marion also quotes the expression "face to face" from 1 Corinthians 13:12 (*In the Self's Place* 248).
13. Freud and psychoanalysis, Lacan suggests here, move beyond philosophy: Freud "does not allow us to handle desire in the logician's immanence of violence as the only dimension that can force open logic's deadlocks." In this enterprise, Freud, says Lacan, brings us back to the question of religion, which he thought of as an illusion (*Names-of-the-Father* 62–3).
14. The text of two conferences held in Brussels at the University of Saint-Louis, to which Lacan also refers in *Ethics of Psychoanalysis*. See Miller.
15. As Lacan weighs Freud's contribution, his truth, similar to Derrida's truth, "happens beyond any performativity and beyond any theory" (Kearney, "Confessions" 33).
16. The split between psychoanalysis and religion reflects the larger divide between science and religion in which the two parties enact "a sort of mimesis of powers" (Lacan, "Discourse" 17), in which their division actually works to neutralize questions, not to bring them to light. Lacan argues for the breakdown of the separation between the two branches of knowledge, religious inquiry and critical inquiry, against "[a] sort of strange division in the field of truth," adding that "to me . . . an epistle by St. Paul is as important to comment on in ethics as one by Seneca" (17).
17. He recalls something that he had said a decade earlier in a "Discourse to Catholics": the analyst must listen before the threshold of love.
18. All translations from Vanzini, "La fede è conoscenza" are mine; for a print article that elaborates on the ideas of this talk, see Vanzini, "L'esperienza."
19. We are away from the God of theology here, or the God of philosophy, but closer to what Marion calls "Gxd" with the cross (*God Without Being*), and Vanzini simply calls "il Dio di ogni uomo," everyone's God (*Il Dio*).
20. In the roundtable moderated by Richard Kearney, Derrida says: "When someone leaves a trace—an animal leaves a trace—not mastering the destination of the trace, then these unknown addressees might be called God" (Derrida qtd. in Kearney, "Confessions" 35). However, as Richard Kearney observers elsewhere, *différance* and God "are not the same thing" ("Deconstruction" 303).
21. And: "Grant me, Lord, to know and understand whether a man is first to pray to you for help or to praise you" (*Confessions* I, 1, 21). Praying for help is something; knowing is something else.
22. As Gerald Bruns observes, Lyotard, too, in his reading of *Confessions* emphasizes in Augustine's intimate address to God a relation "outside

cognition, outside the alternatives of propositions and negations, and thus highlights the importance of *Confessions* for the kind of alternative view of the subject to which Lacan was committed through psychoanalysis" ("Senses" 4). See Lyotard, *Confession*.

23. In Marion's reading there is an emphasis on reparation (the relation to the Scriptures is key): "the silent word that, in advance (in the immemorial advance of a creation), renders possible my own living word" (*In the Self's Place* 23).

24. When a sieve is shaken, the refuse appears;
so do a person's faults when he speaks.
The kiln tests the potter's vessels;
so the test of a person is in his conversation.
Its fruit discloses the cultivation of a tree;
so a person's speech discloses the cultivation of his mind.
Do not praise anyone before he speaks,
for this is the way people are tested.

Ἐν σείσματι κοσκίνου διαμένει κοπρία, οὕτως σκύβαλα ἀνθρώπου ἐν λογισμῷ αὐτοῦ.
σκεύη κεραμέως δοκιμάζει κάμινος, καὶ πειρασμὸς ἀνθρώπου ἐν διαλογισμῷ αὐτοῦ.
γεώργιον ξύλου ἐκφαίνει ὁ καρπὸς αὐτοῦ, οὕτως λόγος ἐνθυμήματος καρδίας ἀνθρώπου.
πρὸ λογισμοῦ μὴ ἐπαινέσῃς ἄνδρα· οὗτος γὰρ πειρασμὸς ἀνθρώπων.

25. "*Elohim* spoke to Moses, 'I am *Yahweh*. I appeared to Abraham, Isaac, and Jacob as *El Shaddai*, but I didn't make myself known to them by my name, *Yahweh*.'"

26. Both images have helpfully been included in the Italian translation of *On the Names-of-the-Father* by translator and editor Antonio Di Ciaccia. The images are missing in the English edition.

Conclusion: Depending on Your Neighbor

We began with ordinary encounters with others who call on us to understand them. The call seems unavoidably connected with a common need for recognition. Yet, if acts of understanding are one with the activity of interpretation, this suggests the entanglement of interpretation with the problem of recognition. The problem is at once political, philosophical, and ethical, and it has concerned, even shaped, literary criticism, steering it in more experimental, theoretical directions. It accounts, for example, for the centrality of the notion of subjectivity—of scenes of subject formation—in the attempt to understand the ways in which the texts we read reflect or react to the symbolic structures that underpin the social order. It accounts for the insight that we exist through the gaze of another, and the exclusions of this symbolic texture of the human. The distance between reader and text, which we try to bridge in the attempt to understand, does not remain confined to the activity of interpretation but, as Elaine Scarry reminded us (see the Introduction to this book), it is connected to the labor of imagining others (45). This labor has been central to literary criticism in the past decades without this entailing a dispersal or, worse, the death of the discipline. Quite the contrary, what we call critique is ambitious criticism committed to reflection on the uses of literature, not only to expand the latter's meaning but especially to probe its uses.

As the need arises for a "new breed of thinker" who asks "questions about the nature of reality independently from human thought and from humanity more generally (Bryant et al. 3), this speculative desire prompts us to open our eyes to the network of radical relationality of which the world is made. As scholars appeal to a newfound importance of wonder, hermeneutics, the practice of understanding and interpreting, ceases to be "a privilege of humans" to become "a property of the world itself" (Latour, *Reassembling* 245). The current critical climate, defined by many as postcritical, far from being a turn away from interpretation, frees this activity from its human confinement and extends it to the world. The challenge is for us to place literature and cultural objects in a larger network of other things but also to argue and write differently. All this invites a re-examination of the central tools of literary studies. How might the new thinker look from the vantage point of the literary critic for whom words like "text" or "discourse" name indispensable concepts? Each chapter you have read has taken its cue from a basic keyword in literary studies (critique, theory, critic, language, tradition, text and method, poststructuralism) but there is an overarching narrative, and this is held together by the enigmatic figure of the critic—the field practitioner—who appears in all its simultaneous attractiveness and instability. One of the defining traits of critique as presented here lies in the critic's vocation for the outside, as someone who seeks his or her grounding in literature's neighboring disciplines.

The current debate on postcritique has turned the spotlight on reading as the central activity in literary studies, asking us to reflect on how we read (and how we talk about what we read) and examine the consequences of that centrality. As mentioned in the Introduction, the fact that reading is a practice (not a method) by definition privileges the unforeseen; it implies a degree of experimentalism and an openness to transformation, both of which, in the past, have fostered the critic's reliance on other disciplines—linguistics, psychology, philosophy, and so on—for theoretical grounding. One of the messages of this book is that such a reliance on the neighbor is a defining aspect of critique: it determines the sliding of literary criticism into something more desirable called "critique." Such a reliance has been condemned in the past, and it is at risk today, often overshadowed by the louder rejection of the hermeneutics of suspicion.

Why should the critic's dependence on the neighbor be a source of anxiety? If, "[u]nderstood as the work of reading, literary criticism has no method" (Moi 178), and if method is not to be confused with the practitioner's political leanings, at best we can talk about approaches. If so, close proximity with other disciplines may itself be constitutive of the field. Perhaps, it is precisely in that proximity that criticism is enabled to perceive itself, as Jameson hoped, as "genuine thinking" (*Marxism and Form* xiii).

While the rise of a new cross-disciplinary thinker who wants to ask about reality may result in a craving for objectivity in literary studies, here I have foregrounded the vulnerability and instability of the figure of the field practitioner, with his or her dependence on the neighbor as the living trait of criticism as critique. Research has highlighted a continuity between Jameson's desire to be near thought and the desire of scholars in the present for a criticism that feels like "the ongoing labor of thought" (Sarah Chihaya, Merve Emre, Katherine Hill, and Jill Richards qtd. in Dabashi 950), as well as for styles of argumentation that might reflect that neighborliness and thus for a critical practice that shares in the ardor and audacity of thought. This continuity encourages us to assume that while the generalized imperative to think of reality independently of human thought may imply a serious questioning of the centrality of language, indeed of its sovereignty in past versions of critique, it does not necessarily mean that we should turn our back on language.

We began with the face-to-face with which the activity of interpretation is entangled—the face-to-face with another that parallels in ineludible ways the negotiation of textual meaning, opening to a multiplicity of meanings—and we ended with the dispersal of the face-to-face, and ultimately of the subject/object combat model, in the other question of a donation in language. Even before feminist theory, language was thought in the same breath as the event of a receiving. This was a central concern for German-American philosopher Hannah Arendt, for example. In fact, Arendt may be considered as a pioneer of those relational ontologies which today are prompting us to revise our priorities in literary studies. At the center of her thought is a bustling world of happening and becoming, much like the world in the sense of William James and Alfred North Whitehead, but with a difference. For Arendt, in this ineluctably relational world one does not cease to be at risk of being reduced to "the mute spell of mere happening" (*Rahel* 248). The risk is true for humans as well as for things, both of which are interconnected in a world-wide web that is as immaterial as it is real. In Arendt, being is a movement of externalization shared by all agents and all elements: "Everything that is, must appear" (*Human Condition* 173). Language is important in that movement of externalization because it reveals (rather than conceals) the network of relations. In *Rahel Varnhagen: The Life of a Jewess* language is considered neither as an acquired definition of the human nor in its duplicitous nature as a system of signs but as an "opportunity": the central problem in this study is "the great opportunity to confide in history, in language" (248). For Rahel, it is another that creates the conditions for language to "become her friend"; it is another whose words "free . . .

her from the mute spell of mere happening" (248). At times, Rahel seems a fold for the twentieth-century philosopher, with the narrative emphasizing an immaterial gift that makes a difference:

> It was the great fortune of Rahel's that she found the one person she had trusted. It was her great opportunity to confide in history, in language ... Only in the wholly liberated purity of the poetic, in which all words are, as it were, spoken for the first time, can language become her friend, one to whom she is willing to entrust herself and the unprecedented life. Goethe provided her with the language to speak ... Again and again his words freed her from the mute spell of mere happening. And her ability to speak provided her with an asylum in the world, taught her how to trust what she had heard. She had Goethe to thank for being able to speak. (248)

The question of language amounts to the question of speaking: there is something called "being able to speak," and it clearly does not have to do with the ability to pronounce words correctly but with the sense of a friendship with language. One must know how to cultivate this friendship.

As already mentioned, for Arendt, the world is not divided between human and non-human. Like the world of contemporary realists and materialists who return to the modernists James and Whitehead, it is a buzzing and blooming world of happening. But Arendt's Rahel seeks the "ability to speak," which will give her an "asylum" in it.[1] Rahel's gender and her Jewishness of course play an important role in her search for the certainty of the knowledge that she has entered the world.[2] "No tradition had transmitted anything to her" (*Rahel* 109). Experiencing herself in the position of the givee, of the one who receives, language, as for Joyce's Stephen, is Rahel's obsession. Arendt's Rahel imagines language in the terms of Stanley Cavell, as "a birthright." Cavell considers the act of speaking ("giving voice") in conjunction with freedom: "freedom of language, having the run of it, as if successfully claimed from it, as of a birthright" (Stanley Cavell qtd. in Eldridge 1; Cavell 55).

Arendt's focus on the exodus from "the mute spell of mere happening" implies a speaking subject who turns toward the world (*Rahel* 248). For Arendt it makes sense to speak of the "world" if by the term one means a hospitable world, with language as part of that hospitable world.[3] Affirming the irrefutable event of a turn toward "the world," she presents the question of language as the question of an ease in the world. In this, Arendt shares the position of one of her predecessors in the land of adoption, Henry David Thoreau.[4]

Like Thoreau, Arendt assumes that to "live in" the world does not imply its reduction to a human place of dwelling. Like Thoreau, she suggests a basic meaning of living, which entails a recalibration of relations among all the other agents and elements that have equally come to live in the world.

In *The Human Condition*, things are elements in the world. Not only do they relate to us, but they put us in relation, with their intermediary function providing the sense of a "shared" world. The burden of biological life, "weighing down and consuming the specifically human life-span between birth and death" (Arendt, *Human Condition* 119), prompts the recalibration of the world as an environment. In some really striking passages, it is possible to hear the readjustment of our relation to things. It is by being related to the same chair and to the same table that I know myself, that the self is not void, that I am not mere happening. The ability to speak (in Rahel's sense of a confidence in language) depends on this web of relations. What we find in the empty chair (which is empty when *we* look at it) is the idea of a puzzling bond with another that—if not recollected—would be in danger. This is the danger dramatized by Rahel, who needs to receive friendship in language, even if she already speaks and thus may be said to already belong in a world of others. Thoreau deals with the same danger and, at the start of *Walden*, he staves it off with reading:

> I have no doubt that some of you who read this book are unable to pay for all the dinners which you have actually eaten, or for the coats and shoes which are fast wearing or are already worn out, and have come to this page to spend borrowed or stolen time. (9)

Thoreau is to his readers as Goethe is to Rahel, or Heidegger to Rahel's biographer: his readers are indebted to necessity (they must work for a living), but they "come to [his page]," which Thoreau presents as a potential space of symbolic birth: a birth in language and thought. While it is only a parenthetical space, it nevertheless provides a break from the archaic temporality that Arendt calls *animal laborans*. The point, however, is that Thoreau's page functions like Arendt's chair and table: it reminds its reader of his or her sameness, of his or her self or, as Thoreau puts it, of "my being with and by myself" (Thoreau qtd. in Arendt, "Civil Disobedience" 63). In Arendt's sense, language, that is to say the ability to speak, is synonymous with being seen and heard by others in the space of appearance, but it also means the balancing function of things, which allows us to stand in a world rather than be exiled in a not-world.

We began our Introduction with the example of artist Airan Kang, who uses books to transform space and incorporate them in ordinary life. We introduced her art because it furthers Arendt's question about the role of language and thought in the intangible reality of the space of appearance while also resonating with postcritique's interest in different ways of reading. Like postcritique the art of Airan Kang treats books as vulnerable artifacts to be conserved and curated. But she is especially concerned with how we package knowledge, imagining books as bundles, thus raising the question not only of how books may be accessed but also of how incomplete they are. Her gendered perspective, especially her concern with the incompletely recorded negative experiences of women in patriarchal cultures, implies that encountering bound books "bear[s] social and cultural implications," and that the encounter promises as if "to alleviate" loss, what is missing from culture and history. We said that her installations align reading with "creative changes" planting the encounter with the book in its dream-like dimension in ordinary life, as if to comment on Rahel's need for a hospitable world (Kang 121).

The meaning of "world" has changed since Arendt, and perhaps, as Dipesh Chakrabarty observes, her account of a human condition centered on the idea of dwelling has been inflected by the threat of homelessness posed by technology, a line of inquiry compromised by the ascendency of the term "global" (146). Chakrabarty dates the change to "Earthrise," the view of the earth photographed on Christmas Eve 1968 by the crew of Apollo 8, which "places humans firmly within a larger view of life and planetary dynamics" (155).[5] Yet, it is possible that the question of language in Arendt's terms may have increased in fascination since the inception of planetary consciousness. The awakening to the smallness of the world has meant a greater visibility on a larger scale of the contrasting desires for displacement and (multiple) belonging. If angst and restlessness were once the psychological and spiritual luxury of a few, with all the rest abandoned to a local cultural unevenness that seemed the inevitable consequence of the march of modernity, with planetary consciousness the clash of contrary feelings, especially an anatopism or sense of displacement mixed with anachronism vs. a longing for rootedness, becomes everyone's planetary legacy. With the transition from the notion of the human subject to a more impersonal notion of the living,[6] the need for a space of appearance where we are seen and heard by others might have become only more acute (as proponent of weak thought Pier Aldo Rovatti has suggested in Chapter 3). Arendt preferred to look at the lexical-conceptual transition from earth to globe not so much as a hollowing out of the social and political dimension of the human but as an opportunity for change in our philosophical and critical vocabularies, a change that, however, cannot easily dispose of Rahel's exodus from "the mute spell of mere happening." Arendt's Rahel invites us to see the promise, which is held in the term "global," of a dual citizenship for everyone, with each "as much an inhabitant of the earth as [he or she] is an inhabitant of [his or her] country" (*Human Condition* 250). Moreover, as a woman and a Jew, she helps us think of the turn toward the "zoecentric" in terms of bios, that is to say, of life as we understood it with Italian Theory, always with and through the categories of language, history, politics, both in relation and in tension with them.[7] The question of a receiving in/through language risks remaining unthought today. Yet, as it manifests in Arendt's notion of a place of mutual recognition where "I appear to others as others appear to me" (*Human Condition* 198), in the notion, that is, of an intangible but constitutive reality of relations (*Human Condition* 183), it resonates with our postcritical concerns with the "wounded and vulnerable artifacts of history" (Felski, "Introduction" 217). Perhaps this receiving is itself one of those wounded artifacts which we have come to as a matter of concern in our postcritical climate.

Notes

1. Her sense of lack is strange since language and thought are already "her" world. The dramatic structure that Karl Jaspers admired in Arendt's manuscript would not be there without this "redundant" knowledge that friendship with language means friendship with the world; it means finding a refuge in the world. In his letter dated 23 August 1952, Jaspers writes to his former pupil: "I've read your *Rahel* straight through and with great interest. There is no doubt in my mind: this book is powerful and significant ... The whole book could be tightened up, all to the benefit of the already existing dramatic structure" (Arendt, *Hannah Arendt/Karl Jaspers Correspondence* 192).
2. "To enter society all alone, marked with the blemish and condemned to be one of the last, was far worse than waiting outside and hoping for better conditions. Always having to represent oneself as something special, and having to do it all alone, in order to justify her bare existence, was so strenuous that it nearly consumed all her strength. 'How loathsome it is always having to establish one's identity first. That alone is enough to make it so repulsive to be a Jew'" (Arendt, *Rahel* 252).

3. "Everything that is, must appear" (Arendt, *Human Condition* 173). *Human Condition* is an unrestrained exodus toward the well-being of existing. The term "world" enters importantly into play, but it means something profoundly intangible: it is put in place by the confidence in language and history, received (given), the experience of an exit into light that is given, the great overhaul of the self from shadow to light. It makes sense to speak of "world" because of this experience of transformation. Getting back to Rahel, being able to speak is the experience of finding an "asylum" in the world, the world as hospitable.
4. In her essay on "Civil Disobedience," Arendt applies pressure to the term "world" in the sense of Thoreau, quoting the American predecessor saying that our aim is not to make the world "a good place to live in" but "to live in it, be it good or bad," without undoing the delicate balance of justice among agents (60).
5. As historian Dipesh Chakrabarty reminds us, Arendt has been commonly viewed as part of a group of Western modernist thinkers of epochal change (the group includes Jaspers and Heidegger), for whom dwelling, fear of homelessness due to technology, and the standardization of life constitute the tenets in the analysis of modernity and require a new understanding of the human condition (146). According to Chakrabarty, these thinkers raised the question of the meaning of "world," and their line of inquiry was indeed carried over into the early 1990s, but at that point the word "global" obscured the term "world," making it sound insufficient.
6. Chakrabarty refers to the transition by the name "Anthropocene."
7. This understanding of life is at the center of the line of reflection that Esposito calls *pensiero vivente* (*Pensiero vivente* 32). Arendt might be included in this line of reflection.

Bibliography

Adorno, Theodor W. *Minima Moralia: Reflections from the Damaged Life.* Trans. E. F. N. Jephcott. London: New Left Books, 1974. First German ed. 1951.

Adorno, Theodor W. *Negative Dialectics.* Trans. E. B. Ashton. London: Seabury Press, 1973. First German ed. 1966.

Adorno, Theodor W. "Resignation." *The Culture Industry: Selected Essays on Mass Culture.* Ed. and intro. J. M. Bernstein. London: Routledge, 1991. 198–203.

Adorno, Theodor W., and Walter Benjamin. *The Complete Correspondence 1932–1940.* Ed. Henry Lonitz. Trans. Nicholas Walker. Cambridge: Polity Press, 1999.

Adorno, Theodor W., and Max Horkheimer. "The Culture Industry: Enlightenment as Mass Deception." *The Dialectic of Enlightenment.* Trans. Edmund Jephcott. Stanford, CA: Stanford University Press, 2002. 94–136.

Adorno, Theodor W., and Max Horkheimer. "L'industria culturale: Quando l'illuminismo diventa mistificazione di massa." *Dialettica dell'illuminismo.* Trans. Renato Solmi. Turin: Einaudi, 2010. 126–81.

Agamben, Giorgio. "Bartleby o della contingenza." *Bartleby: La formula della creazione.* Eds. Gilles Deleuze and Giorgio Agamben. Macerata: Quodlibet, 1993. 45–89.

Agamben, Giorgio. *Che cos'è la filosofia?* Macerata: Quodlibet, 2016.

Agamben, Giorgio. *The Coming Community.* Trans. Michael Hardt. Minneapolis: University of Minnesota Press, 1993.

Agamben, Giorgio. *Homo Sacer: Sovereign Power and Bare Life.* Trans. Daniel Heller-Roazen. Stanford, CA: Stanford University Press, 1998.

Agamben, Giorgio. *Homo sacer: Il potere sovrano e la nuda vita.* Turin: Einaudi, 2005.

Agamben, Giorgio. *Means Without End: Notes on Politics.* Trans. Vincenzo Binetti and Cesare Casarino. Minneapolis: University of Minnesota Press, 2000.

Agamben, Giorgio. "What is the Contemporary?" *"What is an Apparatus?" and Other Essays.* Trans. David Kishik and Stefan Pedatella. Stanford, CA: Stanford University Press, 2009. 39–54.

Agamben, Giorgio. *What is Philosophy?* Trans. Lorenzo Chiesa. Stanford, CA: Stanford University Press, 2017.

Alaimo, Stacy, and Susan Hekman, eds. *Material Feminisms*. Bloomington: Indiana University Press, 2008.

Anker, Elizabeth S., and Rita Felski. "Introduction." *Critique and Postcritique*. Eds. Elizabeth S. Anker and Rita Felski. Durham, NC and London: Duke University Press, 2017. 1–28.

Anzaldúa, Gloria. "How to Tame a Wild Tongue." *Borderlands/La Frontera: The New Mestiza*. San Francisco: Aunt Lute Books, 1987. 53–64.

Arendt, Hannah "Civil Disobedience." *Crises of the Republic*. New York: Harcourt Brace Jovanovich, 1972. 49–102.

Arendt, Hannah. *Hannah Arendt/Karl Jaspers Correspondence, 1926–1969*. Eds. Lotte Kohler and Hans Saner. Trans. Robert and Rita Kimber. New York: Harcourt Brace Jovanovich, 1992.

Arendt, Hannah. *The Human Condition*. Intro. Margaret Canovan. Chicago and London: University of Chicago Press, 1998. First ed. 1958.

Arendt, Hannah. *Rahel Varnhagen: The Life of a Jewess*. Ed. Liliane Weissberg. Trans. Richard and Clara Winston. Baltimore, MD and London: Johns Hopkins University Press, 1997. First ed. 1957.

Aristotle. *Politics*. Trans. Carnes Lord. Chicago and London: University of Chicago Press, 1984.

Attridge, Derek. "In Praise of Amateurism." *The Critic as Amateur*. Eds. Saikat Majumdar and Aarthi Vadde. New York: Bloomsbury Academic, 2020. 31–48. *Bloomsbury Collections*. 30 July 2021. <http://dx.doi.org/10.5040/9781501341441.ch-002>. Accessed 19 April 2022.

Attridge, Derek. "'This Strange Institution Called Literature': An Interview with Jacques Derrida." *Jacques Derrida: Acts of Literature*. Ed. Derek Attridge. New York and London: Routledge, 1992. 33–75.

Badiou, Alain. "Definition of Philosophy." *Conditions*. Trans. Steven Corcoran. London and New York: Continuum 2008. 23–5.

Baert, Barbara. *Nymph: Motif, Phantom, Affect: A Contribution to the Study of Aby Warburg (1866–1929)*. Leuven: Peeters, 2014.

Balanchine, George. "Untitled" (1956). In "Dance." *George Platt Lynes: Photographs, 1931–1955*. Ed. Jack Woody. Pasadena, CA: Twelvetrees Press, 1981. 103–13.

Barad, Karen. "Posthumanist Performativity: Toward an Understanding of How Matter Comes to Matter." *Material Feminisms*. Eds. Stacy Alaimo and Susan Hekman. Bloomington: Indiana University Press, 2008. 120–54.

Barthes, Roland. "The Death of the Author." *Image, Music, Text*. Trans. Stephen Heath. New York: Hill & Wang, 1977. 142–8.

Barthes, Roland. *A Lover's Discourse*. New York: Hill & Wang, 2010.

Basile, Esther. *Anna Maria Ortese*. Perugia: Ali&no Editrice, 2014.

Bazzicalupo, Laura. *Biopolitica: Una mappa concettuale*. Rome: Carocci, 2012. First ed. 2010.

Bazzicalupo, Laura. "L'economia come logica di governo." *Spazio Filosofico*, vol. 7 (2013): 21–9.

Bazzicalupo, Laura, ed. *Impersonale: In dialogo con Roberto Esposito*. Milan-Udine: Mimesis, 2008.

Bazzicalupo, Laura. "La politica e le parole dell'impersonale." *Impersonale: In dialogo con Roberto Esposito*. Ed. Laura Bazzicalupo. Milan-Udine: Mimesis, 2008. 57–76.

Benjamin, Walter. "The Concept of Criticism in German Romanticism." Trans. David Lachternman, Howard Eiland, and Ian Balfour. *Selected Writings: Volume 1, 1913–1926*. Eds. Marcus Bullock and Michael W. Jennings. Cambridge, MA and London: Belknap Press of Harvard University Press, 1999. 116–200.

Benjamin, Walter. "On the Concept of History." Trans. Harry Zohn. *Selected Writings: Volume 4, 1938–1940*. Eds. Howard Eiland and Michael W. Jennings. Cambridge, MA and London: Belknap Press of Harvard University Press, 2003. 389–400.

Benjamin, Walter. "Goethe's Elective Affinities." Trans. Stanley Corngold. *Selected Writings: Volume 1, 1913–1926*. Eds. Marcus Bullock and Michael W. Jennings. Cambridge, MA and London: Belknap Press of Harvard University Press, 1999. 297–360.

Benjamin, Walter. "Letter to Florens Christian Rang." Trans. Rodney Livingstone. *Selected Writings: Volume 1: 1913–1926*. Eds. Marcus Bullock and Michael W. Jennings. Cambridge, MA and London: Belknap Press of Harvard University Press, 1996. 387–90.

Benjamin, Walter. "On the Middle Ages (1916)." *Early Writings*. Trans. Howard Eiland and Others. Cambridge, MA and London: Belknap Press of Harvard University Press, 2011. 238–40.

Benjamin, Walter. *Origin of the German Trauerspiel*. Trans. Howard Eiland. Cambridge, MA: Harvard University Press, 2019.

Benjamin, Walter. "The Task of the Translator." Trans. Harry Zohn. *Selected Writings: Volume 1, 1913–1926*. Eds. Marcus Bullock and Michael W. Jennings. Cambridge, MA and London: Belknap Press of Harvard University Press, 1996. 253–63.

Bennington, Geoffrey. "Saussure and Derrida." *The Cambridge Companion to Saussure*. Ed. Carol Sanders. Cambridge: Cambridge University Press, 2004. 186–202.

Benveniste, Émile "Subjectivity in Language." *Problems in General Linguistics*. Trans. Mary Elizabeth Meek. Miami, FL: University of Miami Press, 1971. 223–30.

Berlant, Lauren. *Cruel Optimism*. Durham, NC and London: Duke University Press, 2011.

Berman, Art. *From the New Criticism to Deconstruction: The Reception of Structuralism and Post-structuralism*. Urbana: University of Illinois Press, 1988.

Bertens, Hans. *Literary Theory: The Basics*. London: Routledge, 2007.

Bérubé, Michael. "An Audacious Argument for Modesty." *PMLA*, vol. 135, no. 5 (2020): 970–5.

Binswanger, Ludwig, and Aby Warburg. *La guarigione infinita: Storia clinica di Aby Warburg*. Ed. Davide Stimilli. Trans. Chantal Marazia and Davide Stimilli. Vicenza: Neri Pozza, 2005.

Booth, Wayne. "My Life with Rhetoric." *A Companion to Rhetoric and Rhetorical Criticism*. Eds. Walter Jost and Wendy Olmsted. Malden, MA: Blackwell, 2004. 494–504. ProQuest Ebook Central. <https://ebookcentral-proquest-com.flagship.luc.edu/lib/luc/detail.action?docID=214214>. Accessed 30 September 2021.

Booth, Wayne. *The Rhetoric of Fiction*. Chicago: University of Chicago Press, 1983. First ed. 1961.

Braidotti, Rosi, ed. *After Poststructuralism: Transitions and Transformations*. New York: Routledge, 2010.

Brooker, Jewel Spears. *T. S. Eliot's Dialectical Imagination*. Baltimore, MD: Johns Hopkins University Press, 2018.

Brooks, Cleanth, and Robert Penn Warren. *Understanding Poetry*. Belmont, CA: Wadworth Publishing, 1976. First ed. 1938.

Brouillette, Sarah. "Work as Art and Art as Life." *Literary Materialisms*. Eds. Mathias Nilges and Emilio Sauri. New York: Palgrave Macmillan, 2013. 95–111.

Bruns, Gerald L. *Hermeneutics: Ancient and Modern*. New Haven, CT and London: Yale University Press, 1992.

Bruns, Gerald L. "The Senses of Augustine (On Some of Lyotard's Remains)." *Religion & Literature*, vol. 33, no. 3 (Autumn 2001): 1–23.

Bryant, Levi, Nick Srnicek, and Graham Harman. "Towards a Speculative Philosophy." *The Speculative Turn: Continental Materialism and Realism*. Eds. Levi Bryant, Nick Srnicek, and Graham Harman. Melbourne: re.press, 2011. 1–18.

Buchanan, Ian. *Fredric Jameson: Live Theory*. London: Continuum, 2006.

Butler, Judith. *The Psychic Life of Power: Theories of Subjection*. Stanford, CA: Stanford University Press, 1997.

Butler, Judith. *Undoing Gender*. New York: Routledge, 2004.

Butler, Judith. "What is Critique? An Essay on Foucault's Virtue." *The Judith Butler Reader*. Ed. Sara Salih. Malden, MA: Blackwell, 2004. 302–22.

Cacciari, Massimo, *Icone della legge*. Milan: Adelphi, 2002.

Carrera, Elena. "The Reception of Clarice Lispector via Hélène Cixous: Reading from the Whale's Belly." *Brazilian Feminisms*. Ed. Solange Ribeiro and Judith Still. Nottingham: University of Nottingham, 1999. 85–100.

Cavarero, Adriana. "Per una teoria della differenza sessuale." *Diotima: Il pensiero della differenza sessuale*, by Adriana Cavarero et al. Milan: La Tartaruga, 1987. 42–79.

Cavell, Stanley. *This New Yet Unapproachable America: Lectures After Emerson After Wittgenstein*. Albuquerque, NM: Living Batch Press, 1989.
Chakrabarty, Dipesh. "The Human Condition in the Anthropocene." *The Tanner Lectures in Human Values*. Delivered at Yale University, 18–19 February 2015. <http://tannerlectures.utah.edu/Chakrabarty>. Accessed 17 August 2017.
Cheng, Mel Y. *Animacies: Biopolitics, Racial Mattering, and Queer Affect*. Durham, NC: Duke University Press, 2012.
Chiesa, Lorenzo, and Alberto Toscano, eds. *The Italian Difference*. Melbourne: re.press, 2009.
Cimatti, Felice. "Introduzione: più di uno, meno di due. Linguaggio e riconoscimento dell'altro." *Come bipede implume: Corpi e menti del segno*, by Daniele Gambarara. Acireale-Rome: Bonanno Editore, 2005. 9–17.
Cimatti, Felice. "Vita e linguaggio nel pensiero italiano." *Effetto Italian Thought*. Eds. Enrica Lisciani-Petrini and Giusi Strummiello. Macerata: Quodlibet, 2017. 87–107.
Cixous, Hélène. *"Coming to Writing" and Other Essays*. Ed. Deborah Jenson. Intro. Susan Rubin Suleiman. Trans. Sarah Cornell, Deborah Jenson, Ann Liddle, and Susan Sellers. Cambridge, MA and London: Harvard University Press, 1992.
Cixous, Hélène. "Foreword." Trans. Verena Conley. *The Stream of Life*, by Clarice Lispector. Trans. Elizabeth Lowe and Earl Fitz. Minneapolis: University of Minnesota Press, 1989. ix–xxxv.
Cixous, Hélène. *Reading with Clarice Lispector*. Ed., trans., and intro. Verena Andernatt Conley. Minneapolis: University of Minnesota Press, 1990.
Cixous, Hélène. *Three Steps on the Ladder of Writing*. Trans. Sarah Cornell and Susan Seller. The Wellek Library Lectures at the University of California Irvine. New York: Columbia University Press, 1993.
Cixous, Hélène. *Volleys of Humanity: Essays 1927–2009*. Ed. Eric Prenowitz. Edinburgh: Edinburgh University Press, 2011.
Cixous, Hélène. "Writing and the Law." *Readings: The Poetics of Blanchot, Joyce, Kafka, Kleist, Lispector, and Tsvetayeva*. Ed., trans., and intro. Verena Andermatt Conley. Minneapolis: Minnesota University Press, 1991. 1–27.
Claverini, Corrado. *La tradizione filosofica italiana: Quattro paradigmi interpretativi*. Macerata: Quodlibet, 2021.
Claverini, Corrado. "Localizzare il pensiero. Filosofia italiana e migrazione delle idee." *La passione del pensiero. Studi in onore di Enrica Lisciani-Petrini*. Ed. Daniela Calabrò. Macerata: Quodlbet: 2021. 383–93.
Colesworthy, Rebecca. *Returning the Gift: Modernism and the Thought of Exchange*. Oxford Scholarship Online, 2018. DOI:10.1093/oso/9780198778585.001.0001.
Collini, Stefan. "The Identity of Intellectual History." *A Companion to Intellectual History*. Eds. Richard Whatmore and Brian Young.

Chichester: Wiley-Blackwell, 2015. *ProQuest Ebook Central.* <http://doi.org/10.1002/9781118508091.ch1>. Accessed 30 April 2020.

Contemporary Italian Thought. Intro. Timothy Campbell, double special issue of *Diacritics*, vol. 39, nos. 3 and 4 (2009).

Cook, Deborah. *The Culture Industry Revisited: Theodor W. Adorno on Mass Culture.* Lanham, MD: Rowman & Littlefield, 1996.

Crane, Mary Thomas. "Surface, Depth, and the Spatial Imaginary: A Cognitive Reading of *The Political Unconscious.*" *Representations*, vol. 108, no. 1 (2009): 76–97.

Crawford, Robert. *Young Eliot: From St Louis to The Waste Land.* London: Jonathan Cape, 2015.

Cullingford, Elizabeth Butler. "Pornography and Canonicity: The Case of Yeats' 'Leda and the Swan.'" *Representing Women: Law, Literature, and Feminism.* Ed. Susan Sage Heinzelman and Zipporah Batshaw Wiseman. Durham, NC: Duke University Press, 1994. 165–87.

Cunningham, Valentine. *Reading After Theory.* Oxford: Blackwell, 2002.

Dabashi, Pardis. "Introduction to 'Cultures of Argument': The Loose Garments of Argument." *PMLA*, vol. 135, no. 5 (2020): 946–55.

Davies, Anna. "New Romance: Art and the Posthuman—Curatorial Essay." Museum of Contemporary Art Australia (MAC), 30 June–4 September 2016. <https://www.mca.com.au/stories-and-ideas/new-romance-art-and-the-posthuman-curatorial-essay/>. Accessed 21 April 2022.

Day, Gail. *Dialectical Passions: Negation in Postwar Art Theory.* New York: Columbia University Press, 2010.

de Man, Paul. "Rhetoric of Persuasion (Nietzsche)." *Allegories of Reading: Figural Language in Rousseau, Nietzsche, Rilke, and Proust.* New Haven, CT and London: Yale University Press, 1979. 119–31.

Deleuze, Gilles. *Pure Immanence: Essays on a Life.* New York: Zone Books, 2005.

Derrida, Jacques. "Before the Law." *Acts of Literature.* Ed. Derek Attridge. London and New York: Routledge, 1992. 181–220.

Derrida, Jacques. "Circumfession." *Jacques Derrida*, by Geoffrey Bennington. Chicago: University of Chicago Press, 1993.

Derrida, Jacques. "Différance" (1968). *Margins of Philosophy.* Trans. Alan Bass. Chicago: University of Chicago Press, 1982. 1–27.

Derrida, Jacques. "On Being." Interview; bonus material from the documentary *Derrida*. Dir. Amy Ziering Kofman. Zietgeist Films; Jane Doe Films, 2002. <https://www.youtube.com/watch?v=gjmp0ZAz5yk>. Accessed 19 April 2022.

Derrida, Jacques. "Signature Event Context." *Limited INC.* Trans. Samuel Weber and Jeffrey Mehlman. Evanston, IL: Northwestern University Press, 1988. 1–23.

Derrida, Jacques. "Signature Event Context." *Margins of Philosophy.* Trans. Alan Bass. Chicago: University of Chicago Press, 1982. 307–30.

Derrida, Jacques. *Specters of Marx.* London: Routledge, 1994.

Dersken, Louise D., and Annemie Halsema. "Understanding the Body: The Relevance of Gadamer's and Ricoeur's View of the Body for Feminist Theory." *Gadamer and Ricoeur: Critical Horizons for Contemporary Hermeneutics*. Eds. Francis J. Mootz III, George H. Taylor. London: Bloomsbury, 2013. 203–25. *ProQuest Ebook Central*. <https://ebook-central.proquest.com/lib/unive2-ebooks/detail.action?docID=686918>. Accessed 21 April 2022.

Di Leo, Jeffrey R. "Introduction: Theory in the New Millennium." *The Bloomsbury Handbook of Literary and Cultural Theory*. Ed. Jeffrey R. Di Leo. London: Bloomsbury Academic, 2018. 1–14. *Bloomsbury Collections*. 25 September 2021. <http://dx.doi.org/10.5040/97813500 12837.0005>. Accessed 19 April 2022.

Didi-Huberman, Georges. *The Surviving Image: Phantoms of Time and Time of Phantoms: Aby Warburg's History of Art*. Trans. Harvey L. Mendelsohn. Philadelphia: Pennsylvania State University Press, 2016. First French ed. 2002.

Dillet, Benoît. "What is Poststructuralism?" *Political Studies Review*, vol. 15, no. 4 (2017): 516–27.

Dimock, Wai Chee. "A Theory of Resonance." *PMLA*, vol. 112, no. 5 (1997): 1060–71.

Dimock, Wai Chee. "Weak Theory: Henry James, Colm Tóibín, and W. B. Yeats." *Critical Inquiry*, vol. 39, no. 4 (2013): 732–53.

Dinshaw, Carolyn, et al. "Theorizing Queer Temporalities: A Roundtable Discussion." *GLQ: A Journal of Lesbian and Gay Studies*, vol. 13, no. 2–3 (2007): 177–95.

Duncan, Pansy. "Once More, With Fredric Jameson." *Cultural Critique*, vol. 97 (2017): 1–23.

During, Simon. "The Eighteenth-Century Origins of Critique." *Critique and Postcritique*. Eds. Elizabeth S. Anker and Rita Felski. Durham, NC and London: Duke University Press, 2017. 73–96.

During, Simon. *Foucault and Literature: Towards a Genealogy of Writing*. London: Routledge, 1992.

Eldridge, Richard. "Introduction: Between Acknowledgement and Avoidance." *Stanley Cavell*. Ed. Richard Eldridge. Cambridge: Cambridge University Press, 2006.

Elias, Amy J., and Christian Moraru. "Introduction: The Planetary Condition." *The Planetary Turn: Relationality and Geoaesthetics in the Twenty-First Century*. Eds. Amy J. Elias and Christian Moraru. Evanston, IL: Northwestern University Press, 2015. xi–xxxvii.

Eliot, T. S. "The Aim of Poetic Drama" (1949). *The Complete Prose of T. S. Eliot: The Critical Edition: A European Society, 1947–1953*. Eds. Iman Javadi and Ronald Schuchard. Baltimore, MD: Johns Hopkins University Press, 2018. 376–88.

Eliot, T. S. *The Complete Poems and Plays*. London: Faber and Faber, 2004.

Eliot, T. S. *Four Quartets*. London: Faber and Faber, 2001.

Eliot, T. S. "Introduction." Charles Baudelaire, *Intimate Journals*. Trans. Christopher Isherwood. London: Blackamore Press, 1930.

Eliot, T. S. *Inventions of the March Hare, Poems 1909–1917*. Ed. Christopher Ricks. New York, San Diego, and London: Harcourt Brace, 1996.

Eliot, T. S. *The Letters of T. S. Eliot. Volume 1: 1898–1922*. Eds. V. Eliot and H. Haughton New Haven, CT: Yale University Press, 2011.

Eliot, T. S. *The Letters of T. S. Eliot. Volume 2: 1923–1925*. Eds. V. Eliot and H. Haughton. New Haven, CT: Yale University Press, 2011.

Eliot, T. S. *The Letters of T. S. Eliot. Volume 6: 1932–1933*. Eds. V. Eliot and J. Haffenden. New Haven, CT: Yale University Press, 2016.

Eliot, T. S: "The Method of Mr. Pound." *The Complete Prose of T. S. Eliot: The Critical Edition: The Perfect Critic, 1919–1926*. Eds. Anthony Cuda and Ron Schuchard. Baltimore, MD: Johns Hopkins University Press and Faber and Faber, 2014. 141–6.

Eliot, T. S. *The Poems of T. S. Eliot. Volume I: Collected and Uncollected Poems*. Eds. Christopher Ricks and Jim McCue. Baltimore, MD: Johns Hopkins University Press, 2015.

Eliot, T. S. "Reflections on Contemporary Poetry [IV]." *The Complete Prose of T. S. Eliot: The Critical Edition: The Perfect Critic, 1919–1926*. Eds. Anthony Cuda and Ron Schuchard. Baltimore, MD: Johns Hopkins University Press and Faber and Faber, 2014. 66–71.

Eliot, T. S. "Tradition and the Individual Talent." *The Complete Prose of T. S. Eliot: The Critical Edition: The Perfect Critic, 1919–1926*. Eds. Anthony Cuda and Ron Schuchard. Baltimore, MD: Johns Hopkins University Press and Faber and Faber, 2014. 105–14.

Eliot, T. S. "A Dialogue on Dramatic Poetry." *The Complete Prose of T. S. Eliot: The Critical Edition: Literature, Politics, Belief, 1927–1929*. Eds. Frances Dickey, Jennifer Formichelli, and Ronald Schuchard. Baltimore, MD: Johns Hopkins University Press, 2015. 396–412.

Esposito, Roberto. *Bíos: Biopolitica e filosofia*. Turin: Einaudi, 2004.

Esposito, Roberto. *Bíos: Biopolitics and Philosophy*. Trans. Timothy Campbell. Minneapolis: University of Minnesota Press, 2008.

Esposito, Roberto. *Communitas: The Origin and Destiny of Community*. Trans. Timothy Campbell. Stanford, CA: Stanford University Press, 2009. Italian ed. 1998.

Esposito, Roberto. *Da Fuori: Una filosofia per l'Europa*. Turin: Einaudi, 2016.

Esposito, Roberto. *From the Outside: A Philosophy for Europe*. Trans. Zakiya Hanafi. Cambridge: Polity Press, 2018. Italian ed. 2016.

Esposito, Roberto. "German Philosophy, French Theory, Italian Thought." Trans. Mena Mitrano. *Forum: American Studies and Italian Theory*. Ed. Mena Mitrano. *RSA Journal*, 26 (2015): 104–14.

Esposito, Roberto. *Living Thought: The Origins and Actuality of Italian Philosophy*. Trans. Zakiya Hanafi. Stanford, CA: Stanford University Press, 2012. Italian ed. 2010.

Esposito, Roberto. "Melanconia e comunità." *Termini della politica: Comunità, immunità, biopolitica*. Milan: Mimesis, 2008.
Esposito, Roberto. *Pensiero istituente: Tre paradigmi di ontologia politica*. Turin: Einaudi, 2020.
Esposito, Roberto. *Pensiero vivente: Origine e attualità della filosofia italiana*. Turin: Einaudi, 2010.
Esposito, Roberto. *Persons and Things: From the Body's Point of View*. Trans. Zakya Hanafi. Cambridge: Polity Press, 2015.
Esposito, Roberto. *Politica e negazione: Per una filosofia affermativa*. Turin: Einaudi, 2018.
Esposito, Roberto. "Il sintomo immaginario nel 'difetto di politica.'" *Il Manifesto*, 28 May 2016.
Esposito, Roberto. *Terza persona: Politica della vita e filosofia dell'impersonale*. Turin: Einaudi, 2007.
Esposito, Roberto. *Third Person: Politics of Life and Philosophy of the Impersonal*. Trans. Zakiya Hanafi. Cambridge: Polity Press, 2012.
Eyers, Tom. *Speculative Formalism: Literature, Theory, and the Cultural Present*. Evanston, IL: Northwestern University Press, 2017.
Faraone, Rosella. *Adriano Tilgher: Tra idealismo e filosofie della vita*. Soveria Mannelli: Rubettino, 2005.
Felski, Rita. "Critique and the Hermeneutics of Suspicion." *M/C Journal: A Journal of Media and Culture*, vol. 15, no. 1 (2012). <http://journal.media-culture.org.au/index.php/mcjournal/article/viewArticle/431>. Accessed 20 April 2022.
Felski, Rita. *Hooked: Art and Attachment*. Chicago and London: University of Chicago Press, 2020.
Felski, Rita. "Introduction." *Re-composing the Humanities—with Bruno Latour, New Literary History*, vol. 47, no. 2–3 (2016): 215–29.
Felski, Rita. *The Limits of Critique*. Chicago and London: University of Chicago Press, 2015.
Fenves, Peter D. "Of Philosophical Style—From Leibnitz to Benjamin." *boundary 2*, vol. 30, no. 1 (2003): 67–87.
Ferenczi, Sándor. *The Clinical Diary of Sándor Ferenczi*. Ed. Judith Dupont. Cambridge, MA: Harvard University Press, 1988.
Fish, Stanley. *Is There a Text in This Class? The Authority of Interpretive Communities*. Cambridge, MA: Harvard University Press, 1980.
Fleissner, Jennifer. "Romancing the Real: Bruno Latour, Ian McEwan, and Postcritical Monism." *Critique and Postcritique*. Eds. Elizabeth S. Anker and Rita Felski. Durham, NC and London: Duke University Press, 2017. 99–126.
Fortune, Christopher. "The Case of 'RN': Sándor Ferenczi's Radical Experiment in Psychoanalysis." *The Legacy of Sándor Ferenczi*. Eds. L. Aron and A. Harris. Hillside, NJ: The Analytic Press, 1993. 101–20.

Foucault, Michel. *The Birth of Biopolitics*. Ed. Michel Senellart. New York: Picador, 2010.

Foucault, Michel. *The Hermeneutics of the Subject: Lectures at the Collège de France, 1981–82*. Ed. Frédéric Gros. Trans. Graham Burchell. New York: Palgrave Macmillan, 2005.

Foucault, Michel. *On the Government of the Living: Lectures at the Collège de France 1979–1980*. Ed. Michel Senellart. New York: Picador, 2012.

Foucault, Michel. *Soggettività e verità: Corso al Collège de France (1980–1981)*. Trans. Deborah Borca and Carla Troilo. Ed. Pier Aldo Rovatti. Milan: Feltrinelli, 2017.

Foucault, Michel. "What is an Author?" *Language, Counter-memory, Practice: Selected Essays and Interviews*. Trans. Donald F. Bouchard and Sherry Simon. Ithaca, NY: Cornell University Press, 1980. 113–38.

Foucault, Michel. "What is Critique?" Trans. Lysa Hochroth. *The Politics of Truth*. Eds. Sylvère Lotringer and Lysa Hochroth. New York: Semiotext(e), 1997. 23–82.

Freeman, Elizabeth. "Introduction." *GLQ: A Journal of Lesbian and Gay Studies*, vol. 13, no. 2–3 (2007): 159–79.

Freeman, Elizabeth. *Time Binds: Queer Temporalities, Queer Histories*. Durham, NC: Duke University Press, 2010.

Freundlieb, Dieter. "Foucault and the Study of Literature." *Poetics Today*, vol. 16, no. 2 (1995): 301–44.

Friedman, Susan Stanford. "Musing Modernist Studies." *Modernism/Modernity*, vol. 17, no. 3 (2010): 471–99.

Friedman, Susan Stanford. *Planetary Modernisms: Provocations on Modernity Across Time*. New York: Columbia University Press, 2015.

Friedman, Susan Stanford. "Why Not Compare?" *Comparison: Theories, Approaches, Uses*. Eds. Rita Felski and Susan Stanford Friedman. Baltimore, MD: Johns Hopkins University Press, 2013. 34–45.

Fromm, Erich. *The Erich Fromm Reader*. Ed. Rainer Funk. New York: Open Road Distribution, 2014. *ProQuest Ebook Central*. <https://ebookcentral-proquest-com.flagship.luc.edu/lib/luc/detail.action?docID=4457721>. Accessed 4 August 2020.

Gadamer, Hans-Georg. *Truth and Method*. Trans. Joel Weinsheimer and Donald G. Marshall. London and New York: Continuum, 2004.

Gambarara, Daniele. "Il Linguista e il Filosofo." *Istituzione e Differenza: Attualità di Ferdinand de Saussure*. Ed. Francesco Raparelli. Milan-Udine: Mimesis, 2014. 49–57.

Gardner, Helen. *The Art of T. S. Eliot*. London: Cresset Press, 1949.

Gentili, Dario. *Italian Theory: Dall'operaismo alla biopolitica*. Bologna: Il Mulino, 2012.

Gentili, Dario, and Elettra Stimilli, eds. *Differenze italiane*. Rome: DeriveApprodi, 2015.

Gilloch, Graeme. *Walter Benjamin: Critical Constellations*. Cambridge: Polity Press, 2002.

Gordon, Lyndall. *Eliot's Early Years*. Oxford: Oxford University Press, 1977.
Grattan, Sean. "Affect Studies." *The Bloomsbury Handbook of Literary and Cultural Theory*. Ed. Jeffrey R. Di Leo. London: Bloomsbury Academic, 2018. 333–42. Bloomsbury Collections. 25 September 2021. <http://dx.doi.org/10.5040/9781350012837.0032>. Accessed 19 April 2022.
Gregg, Melissa, and Gregory J. Seigworth. "An Inventory of Shimmers." *The Affect Theory Reader*. Eds. Melissa Gregg and Gregory J. Seigworth. Durham, NC: Duke University Press, 2010. ProQuest Ebook Central. <https://doi.org/10.1515/9780822393047-002>. Accessed 25 September 2021.
Groys, Boris. *Introduction to Antiphilosophy*. Trans. David Fernbach. London: Verso, 2012.
Guglielmi, Marina. "Ripensare lo studio della traduzione: Politiche, effetti, migrazioni." Presented at "Migrazioni: Incontri tra lingue, letterature, arti e musica." Ca' Foscari University of Venice, Venice, 11–13 November 2019.
Gupta, Suman. "In Search of Genius: T. S. Eliot as Publisher." *Journal of Modern Literature*, vol. 27, no. 1/2 (2003): 26–35.
Hagen, Margareth. "Mapping, Bridging, Quilting: Tracing the Relations Between Literature and Science." Margareth Hagen et al., *The Art of Discovery: Encounters in Literature and Science*. Aarhus: Aarhus University Press, 2010. 9–28.
Harman, Graham. *Dante's Broken Hammer: The Ethics, Aesthetics, and Metaphysics of Love*. London: Repeater, 2016.
Harman, Graham. *Guerrilla Metaphysics: Phenomenology and the Carpentry of Things*. Chicago and LaSalle, IL: Open Court, 2005.
Harman, Graham. *Prince of Networks: Bruno Latour and Metaphysics*. Melbourne: re.press, 2009.
Haworth-Booth, Mark. *E. McKnight Kauffer: A Designer and His Public*. London: V&A Publications, 2005.
Hayot, Eric. "Then and Now." *Critique and Postcritique*. Eds. Elizabeth S. Anker and Rita Felski. Durham, NC and London: Duke University Press, 2017. 279–95.
Heidegger, Martin. "The Thing." *Poetry, Language, Thought*. Trans. and intro. Albert Hofstadter. New York: Harper & Row, 1975. 163–86.
Helenius, Timo. *Ricoeur, Culture, and Recognition: A Hermeneutic of Cultural Subjectivity*. Lanham, MD: Lexington Books, 2016.
Holstad, Scott C. "Yeats's 'Leda and the Swan': Psycho-sexual Therapy in Action." *Notes on Modern Irish Literature*, vol. 7, no. 2 (1995): 45–52.
Honneth, Axel. *The Struggle for Recognition: The Moral Grammar for Social Conflicts*. Trans. Joel Anderson. Cambridge, MA: MIT Press; London: Polity Press, 1995.
Huxley, Aldous. "Foreword." *Posters by E. McKnight Kauffer*. New York: The Museum of New York: Museum of Modern Art, 1937.

Huxley, Aldous. *Literature and Science*. New York: Harper & Row, 1963.
Iamurri, Laura. *Un margine che sfugge: Carla Lonzi e l'arte in Italia 1955–1970*. Macerata: Quodlibet, 2016.
Iamurri, Laura. "Prefazione." *Autoritratto*. Milan: et al./Edizioni, 2010. vii–xv.
Iovino, Serenella. *Ecocriticism and Italy: Ecology, Resistance, and Liberation*. London: Bloomsbury, 2016.
Irr, Caren, and Ian Buchanan, eds. *On Jameson: From Postmodernism to Globalization*. New York: SUNY Press, 2005.
Iser, Wolfgang. *The Act of Reading: A Theory of Aesthetic Response*. Baltimore, MD: Johns Hopkins University Press, 1978.
Italian Thought Network. "About." <https://italianthoughtnetwork.com/about-us/>. Accessed 26 April 2022.
Jaffe, Aaron. *Modernism and the Culture of Celebrity*. Cambridge University Press, 2005.
Jameson, Fredric. *Allegory and Ideology*. London and New York: Verso, 2019.
Jameson, Fredric. *Late Marxism: Adorno, or, The Persistence of the Dialectic*. London and New York: Verso, 1990.
Jameson, Fredric. *Marxism and Form: Twentieth-Century Dialectical Theories of Literature*. Princeton, NJ: Princeton University Press, 1971.
Jameson, Fredric. *The Political Unconscious: Narrative as a Socially Symbolic Act*. Ithaca, NY: Cornell University Press, 1981.
Jameson, Fredric. *Postmodernism, or, The Cultural Logic of Late Capitalism*. Durham, NC: Duke University Press, 1991.
Jameson, Fredric. *Valencies of the Dialectic*. London: Routledge, 2009.
Jankélévitch, Vladimir. *Music and the Ineffable*. Trans. Carolyn Abbate. Princeton, NJ and Oxford: Princeton University Press, 2003.
Jankélévitch, Vladimir. *Il non-so-che e il quasi-niente*. Trans. Carlo Bonadies. Intro. Enrica Lisciani-Petrini. Turin: Einaudi, 2011. First French ed. 1980.
Jeong, Young-Do. "The Space of Sensuous Experience and the Simulation of the Sublime." *Airan Kang: 2006–2010*. Ed. Hong-Hee Kim et al. Seoul: Gallery Simon, 2010. 116–22.
Johann, Michel. *Ricoeur and the Post-Structuralists: Bourdieu, Derrida, Deleuze, Foucault, Castoriadis*. Trans. Scott Davidson. London: Rowman & Littlefield, 2015.
John Paul II. *Fides et Ratio: Lettera enciclica circa i rapporti tra fede e ragione*. Milan: Edizioni Paoline, 2018. First ed. 1998.
Jones, Susan. "Eliot and Dance." *The Edinburgh Companion to T. S. Eliot and the Arts*. Eds. Frances Dickey and John D. Morgenstern. Edinburgh: Edinburgh University Press, 2016. 225–45.
Jones, Susan. *Literature, Modernism, and Dance*. Oxford: Oxford University Press, 2013.

Jones, Susan. "'At the still point': T. S. Eliot, Dance, and Modernism." *Dance Research Journal*, vol. 41, no. 2 (2009): 31–49.
Johnson, Barbara. "Thresholds of Difference: Structures of Address in Zora Neale Hurston." *Critical Inquiry*, vol. 12 (1985): 278–89.
Johnson, Christopher D. *Memory, Metaphor, and Aby Warburg's Atlas of Images*. Ithaca, NY: Cornell University Press, 2012.
Jonsson, Stefan. *Crowds and Democracy: The Idea and Image of the Masses from Revolution to Fascism*. New York: Columbia University Press, 2013.
Joyce, James. *A Portrait of the Artist as a Young Man*. London: Penguin Classics, 2003. First ed. 1916.
Kang, Airan. "Airan Kang." *Asia Time: The 1st Asia Biennial and the 5th Guangzhou Triennial*. Eds. Yiping Luo et al. Guangdong Museum of Art, 2015. 120–3. <https://universes.art/fileadmin/user_upload/Biennials/Guangzhou/2015/5GZTcat.pdf.120-123.https://universes.art/fileadmin/user_upload/Biennials/Guangzhou/2015/5GZTcat.pdf>. Accessed 26 April 2022.
Kauffer, Edward McKnight. "A Note on Technique." *Posters by E. McKnight Kauffer*. Foreword by Aldous Huxley. New York: Museum of Modern Art, 1937.
Kearney, Richard. "Confessions and 'Circumfession': A Roundtable Discussion with Jacques Derrida." Moderated by Richard Kearney. *Augustine and Postmodernism: Confessions and Circumfession*. Eds. J. D. Caputo and M. J. Scanlon. Bloomington: Indiana University Press, 2005. 28–49. *ProQuest Ebook Central*. <http://ebookcentral.proquest.com>. Accessed 3 March 2019.
Kearney, Richard. "Deconstruction, God, and the Possible." *Derrida and Religion: Other Testaments*. Eds. Yvonne Sherwood and Kevin Hart. London: Routledge, 2004. 297–307. *ProQuest Ebook Central*. <http://ebookcentral.proquest.com/lib/unive2-ebooks/detail.action?docID=182995>. Accessed 2 September 2020.
Kim, Hong-Hee. "Airan Kang's Digital Book Project." *Airan Kang: 2006–2010*. Ed. Hong-Hee Kim et al. Seoul: Gallery Simon, 2010. 6–20.
Kim, Hong-Hee, et al. *Airan Kang: 2006–2010*. Seoul: Gallery Simon, 2010.
Kirstein, Lincoln. "American Ballet: I." *Ballet*, vol. 9, no. 5 (1950): 24–33.
Kirstein, Lincoln. "American Ballet: II." *Ballet*, vol. 9, no. 6 (1950): 15–22.
Kirstein, Lincoln. *The New York City Ballet*. Photographs by Martha Swope and George Platt Lynes. New York: Alfred A. Knopf, 1973.
Kirstein, Lincoln. "Untitled" (1960). In "Portraits." *George Platt Lynes: Photographs, 1931–1955*. Ed. Jack Woody. Pasadena, CA: Twelvetrees Press, 1981. 77–101.
Kristeva, Julia. "A New Type of Intellectual: The Dissident." Trans. Seán Hand. *The Kristeva Reader*. Ed. Toril Moi. New York: Columbia University Press, 1986. 292–300.

Kristeva, Julia. *Strangers to Ourselves*. Trans. Leon S. Roudiez. New York: Columbia University Press, 1994.
Lacan, Jacques. *Dei Nomi-del-Padre e Il trionfo della religione*. Ed. Antonio Di Ciaccia. Turin: Einaudi, 2006.
Lacan, Jacques. "Discorso di Roma." *Altri scritti*. Ed. Antonio Di Ciaccia. Turin: Einaudi, 2013. 133–64.
Lacan, Jacques. "Discourse to Catholics" (1960). *The Triumph of Religion: Preceded by Discourse to Catholics*. Trans. Bruce Fink. Cambridge: Polity Press, 2013. 5–52.
Lacan, Jacques. *Ethics of Psychoanalysis. The Seminar of Jacques Lacan: Book VII*. Trans. Dennis Potter. London and New York: Routledge, 2008.
Lacan, Jacques. "The Function and Field of Speech and Language in Psychoanalysis." *Écrits: A Selection*. Ed. Alan Sheridan. New York and London: W. W. Norton, 1977. 30–113.
Lacan, Jacques. *On the Names-of-the-Father*. Trans. Bruce Fink. Cambridge: Polity Press, 2013.
Lacan, Jacques. *Il Seminario, Libro XXIII: Il Sinthomo*. Ed. Antonio Di Ciaccia. Rome: 2006.
Lacan, Jacques. *The Sinthome: The Seminar of Jacques Lacan. Book XXIII*. Ed. Jacques-Alain Miller. Cambridge: Polity Press, 2018.
Lacan, Jacques. "The Symbolic, the Imaginary, and the Real." *On the Names-of-the-Father*. Trans. Bruce Fink. Cambridge: Polity Press, 2013. 1–52.
Lacan, Jacques. "The Triumph of Religion." *The Triumph of Religion: Preceded by Discourse to Catholics*. Trans. Bruce Fink. Cambridge: Polity Press, 2013. 53–85.
Lacoue-Labarthe, Philippe, and Jean-Luc Nancy. "La Panique Politique." *Retreating the Political*. Ed. Simon Sparks. London and New York: Routledge, 1997. 1–31.
Laplanche, Jean. "The Unfinished Copernican Revolution." Trans. Luke Thurston. *Essays on Otherness*. Ed. John Fletcher. London: Routledge, 1999. 52–83.
Laplanche, Jean, and Jean-Bertrand Pontalis. *The Language of Psychoanalysis*. Trans. Donald Nicholson-Smith. New York: W.W. Norton, 1973.
Latour, Bruno. *Reassembling the Social: An Introduction to Actor-Network Theory*. Oxford: Oxford University Press, 2005.
Latour, Bruno. *We Have Never Been Modern*. Trans. Catharine Porter. Cambridge, MA: Harvard University Press, 1993.
Latour, Bruno. "Why Has Critique Run Out of Steam? From Matters of Fact to Matters of Concern." *Critical Inquiry*, vol. 30, no. 2 (2004): 225–48.
Lazzarato, Maurizio. *Marcel Duchamp and the Refusal of Work*. Los Angeles: Semiotext(e), 2014.

Leddick, David. *George Platt Lynes, 1907–1955*. Foreword by Anatole Pohorilenko. Cologne, London, Madrid, New York, Paris, and Tokyo: Taschen, 2000.

Leddick, David. *Intimate Companions: A Triography of George Platt Lynes, Paul Cadmus, Lincoln Kirstein, and Their Circle*. New York: St. Martin's Press, 2000.

Lehman, Robert S. *Impossible Modernism: T. S. Eliot, Walter Benjamin, and the Critique of Historical Reason*. Stanford, CA: Stanford University Press, 2016.

Lesjak, Carolyn. "Reading Dialectically." *Literary Materialisms*. Eds. Mathias Nilges and Emilio Sauri. New York: Palgrave Macmillan, 2013. 17–47.

Liming, Sheila. "Fighting Words." Review of *Hooked: Art and Attachment*, by Rita Felski. *Los Angeles Book Review*, 14 December 2020. <https://lareviewofbooks.org/article/fighting-words/>. Accessed 5 August 2021.

Lisciani-Petrini, Enrica. "Per una 'Filosofia dell'Impersonale': In dialogo con Roberto Esposito." In *Impersonale: In dialogo con Roberto Esposito*. Ed. Laura Bazzicalupo. Milan-Udine: Mimesis, 2008. 39–55.

Liska, Vivian. "Kafka, Modernism, and Literary Theory." *A Handbook of Modernism Studies*. Ed. Jean-Michel Rabaté. Chichester: Wiley-Blackwell, 2013. 75–86.

Lispector, Clarice. *Near to the Wild Heart*. Trans. Alison Entrekin. Intro. Benjamin Moser. New York: New Directions, 2012.

Lispector, Clarice. *The Stream of Life*. Trans. Elizabeth Lowe and Earl Fitz. Foreword by Hélène Cixous. Trans. Verena Conley. Minneapolis: University of Minnesota Press, 1989.

Lonzi, Carla. *Autoritratto*. Milan: et al./Edizioni, 2010. First ed. 1969.

Lonzi, Carla. "La solitudine del critico." *Scritti Sull'Arte*. Eds. Lara Conte, Laura Iamurri, Vanessa Martini. Milan: et al./Edizioni, 2012. 353–6.

Love, Heather. "Close but Not Deep: Literary Ethics and the Descriptive Turn." *New Sociologies of Literature*, special issue of *New Literary History*, vol. 41, no. 2 (2010): 371–91.

Love, Heather. "Close Reading and Thin Description." *Public Culture*, vol. 25, no. 3 (2013): 401–34.

Lucci, Antonio. "L'opera, la vita, la forma: La filosofia delle forme-di-vita di Giorgio Agamben." *Giorgio Agamben: La vita delle forme*. Eds. Antonio Lucci and Luca Viglialoro. Genoa: Il Melangolo, 2016. 69–94

Luglio, Davide. "Biopolitica e letteratura: Note per una letteratura alter-moderna." *Differenze italiane*. Eds. Dario Gentili and Elettra Stimilli. Rome: DeriveApprodi, 2015. 273–85.

Luisetti, Federico. "Dopo il Leviatano: Gaia, Cthulhu e i mostri dell'Antropocene." *Effetto Italian Thought*. Eds. Enrica Lisciani-Petrini and Giusi Strummiello. Macerata: Quodlibet, 2017. 149–60.

Lynes, George Platt. *Ballet*. Pasadena, CA: Twelvetrees Press, 1985.

Lynes, George Platt. *Photographic Visions*. Institute of Contemporary Art. Boston, MA. 5 March–27 April 1980. Boston, MA: Institute of Contemporary Art, 1980.

Lynes, George Platt. *Portrait: The Photographs of George Platt Lynes, 1927–1955*. Intro. Lincoln Kirstein. Santa Fe: Twin Palms, 1994.

Lyotard, Jean-François. *The Confession of Augustine*. Stanford, CA: Stanford University Press, 2000. First French ed. 1998.

Lyotard, Jean-François. *Libidinal Economy*. Trans. Iain Hamilton Grant. Bloomington and Indianapolis: Indiana University Press, 1993.

Mahaffey, Vicki. "'The Death of Saint Narcissus' and 'Ode': Two Suppressed Poems by T. S. Eliot." *American Literature*, vol. 50, no. 4 (1979): 604–12.

Mao, Douglas, and Rebecca L. Walkowitz. "The New Modernist Studies." *PMLA*, vol. 123, no. 3 (2008): 737–48.

Marcus, Sharon. *Between Women: Friendship, Desire, and Marriage in Victorian England*. Princeton, NJ: Princeton University Press, 2007.

Marcus, Sharon, and Stephen Best. "Surface Reading: An Introduction." *The Way We Read Now*, special issue of *Representations*, vol. 108 (2009): 1–21.

Marcus, Sharon, Heather Love, and Stephen Best, eds. *Description Across Disciplines*, special issue of *Representations*, vol. 135, no. 1 (2016).

Marion, Jean-Luc. *Being Given: A Phenomenology of Givenness*. Trans. Jeffrey L. Kosky. Stanford, CA: Stanford University Press, 2002.

Marion, Jean-Luc. *God Without Being: Hors-Texte*. Trans. Thomas A. Carlson. 2nd ed. Chicago: University of Chicago Press, 2012. First French ed. 1982. *ProQuest Ebook Central*. <https://ebookcentral-proquest-com.flagship.luc.edu/lib/luc/detail.action?docID=951112>. Accessed 13 January 2019.

Marion, Jean-Luc. *In the Self's Place: The Approach of Saint Augustine*. Trans. Jefferey L. Kosky. Stanford, CA: Stanford University Press, 2012. *ProQuest Ebook Central*. <http://ebookcentral.proquest.com/lib/luc/detail.action?docID=1031944>. Accessed 7 January 2019.

Meister, Terri. "Dance." *T. S. Eliot in Context*. Ed. Jason Harding. Cambridge: Cambridge University Press, 2011. 114–24.

Miller, Jacques-Alain. "Nota." *Dei Nomi-del-Padre e Il Trionfo della Religione*, by Jacques Lacan. Ed. Antonio Di Ciaccia. Turin: Einaudi, 2006. 3–4.

Mitrano, Mena. "Che cos'è la teoria." *Englishness and Its Discontents*. Eds. Iain Chambers, Sara Marinelli, and Mena Mitrano, special issue of *Anglistica AION An Interdisciplinary Journal*, vol. 4, no. 2 (2000): 51–78.

Mitrano, Mena. *In the Archive of Longing: Susan Sontag's Critical Modernism*. Edinburgh. Edinburgh University Press, 2016.

Mitrano, Mena. "Voglia di realtà (aura, storia, pensiero critico)." *Un legame obbligato: Letteratura e storia oltre l'Europa*. Eds. Mario Martino and Antonella Gargano. Rome: Lithos Editrice, 2021. 29–83.
Moi, Toril. *Revolution of the Ordinary: Literary Studies After Wittgenstein, Austin, and Cavell*. New York: Columbia University Press, 1986.
Moore, Gerald. *The Politics of the Gift: Exchanges in Poststructuralism*. Edinburgh: Edinburgh University Press, 2011.
Morley, Frank Vigor. "A Few Recollections of Eliot." *T. S. Eliot: The Man and His Work*. Ed. Allen Tate. London: Chatto & Windus, 1967. 90–113.
Morley, Frank Vigor. "T. S. Eliot as Publisher." *T. S. Eliot: A Symposium*. Eds. Tambimuttu and Richard March. London: Frank Cass, 1965. 60–70.
Moser, Benjamin. "Hurricane Clarice." *Near to the Wild Heart*. Trans. Alison Entrekin. Intro. Benjamin Moser. New York: New Directions, 2012. vii–xii.
Moser, Benjamin. *Why This World: A Biography of Clarice Lispector*. London: Penguin 2009.
Motoe, Kunio. "On Airan Kang's Art World: Digital Book Project and Heterotopian Space." *Airan Kang: 2006–10*. Seoul: Gallery Simon, 2010. 134–41.
Muñoz, José Esteban, et al. "Theorizing Queer Inhumanisms." *GLQ*, vol. 21, no. 2–3 (2015): 209–48.
Nancy, Jean-Luc. *Corpus*. Trans. Richard Rand. New York: Fordham University Press, 2008. First French ed. 1992.
Nancy, Jean Luc. *The Inoperative Community*. Ed. Peter Connor. Foreword by Christopher Fynsk. Minneapolis: University of Minnesota Press, 1996. First English ed. 1991.
Negri, Antonio. "Un pensiero vitale messo fuorigioco." *Il Manifesto*, 17 May 2016. <https://ilmanifesto.it/un-pensiero-vitale-messo-fuorigioco>. Accessed 21 April 2022.
Noguchi, Isamu. *A Sculptor's World*. Foreword by R. Buckminster Fuller. New York and Evanston, IL: Harper & Row, 1968.
Okabe, Aomi. "Airan Kang: Towards the Sublime." *Airan Kang: 2006–2010*. Ed. Hong-Hee Kim et al. Seoul: Gallery Simon, 2010. 41–58.
Olmsted, Wendy. *Rhetoric: An Historical Introduction*. New York: John Wiley & Sons, 2008.
Ortese, Anna Maria. "Da Moby Dick all'Orsa Bianca." *Da Moby Dick all'Orsa Bianca*. Milan: Adelphi, 2011. 97–102.
Parmenides. *On the Order of Nature*. Edited by Raphael. New York: Aurea Vidya, 2009.
Pease, Donald E. "Gramsci/Agamben: Re-configurations of American Literary Studies." *Forum: American Studies and Italian Theory*. Ed. Mena Mitrano. *RSA Journal*, 26 (2015): 115–20.

Pease, Donald E., and Robyn Wiegman. "Futures." *The Futures of American Studies*. Eds. Donald E. Pease and Robyn Wiegman. Durham, NC: Duke University Press, 2002. 1–42.

Peirce, Charles S. "Some Consequences of Four Incapacities." *Peirce on Signs*. Ed. James Hoopes. Chapel Hill: University of North Carolina Press, 1991. 54–84.

Poggioli, Renato. *Theory of the Avant-Garde*. Trans. Gerald Fitzgerald. Cambridge, MA: Belknap Press of Harvard University Press, 1968.

Pontalis, Jean-Bertrand. *Finestre*. Trans. Linda Ferri. Rome: E/O, 2001.

Pontalis, Jean-Bertrand. *Windows*. Trans. Anne Quinney. Lincoln: University of Nebraska Press, 2003.

Ponzi, Mauro. *Nietzsche's Nihilism in Walter Benjamin*. New York and London: Palgrave Macmillan, 2017.

Prigogine, Ilya, and Isabelle Stengers. *Tra il tempo e l'eternità*. Turin: Bollati Boringhieri, 2014.

Prokopoff, Stephen. "George Platt Lynes." *George Platt Lynes: Photographic Visions*. Institute of Contemporary Art. Boston, MA. 5 March–27 April 1980. Boston, MA: Institute of Contemporary Art, 1980. N.p.

Radhakrishnan, R. *Theory in an Uneven World*. Oxford: Blackwell, 2003.

Rainey, Lawrence. "The Lesson of Baudelaire." *The Annotated Waste Land with Eliot's Contemporary Prose*. New Haven, CT and London: Yale University Press, 2005. 144–5.

Rainey, Lawrence, and Robert von Hallberg. "Introduction," *Modernism/Modernity*, vol. 1, no. 1 (1994): 1–3.

Recalcati, Massimo. *Cosa resta del padre? La paternità nell'epoca ipermoderna*. Milan: Raffaello Cortina Editore, 2017. First ed. 2011.

Ricoeur, Paul. *Della interpretazione: Saggio su Freud*. Trans. E. Renzi. Milan: Il Saggiatore, 1967. First French ed. 1965.

Ricoeur, Paul. *The Course of Recognition*. Cambridge, MA: Harvard University Press, 2007.

Ricoeur, Paul. *Freud and Philosophy: An Essay on Interpretation*. Trans. Denis Savage. New Haven, CT and London: Yale University Press, 1970.

Rilke, Rainer Maria. *When I Go: Selected French Poems of Rainer Maria Rilke*. Trans. Susanne Petermann. Eugene, OR: Cascade Books, 2017.

Ross, Stephen, ed. *Modernism and Theory: A Critical Debate*. London: Routledge, 2009.

Rovatti, Pier Aldo. *Etica minima*. Milan: Raffaello Cortina Editore, 2010.

Rovatti, Pier Aldo. "Foucault Docet." Trans. Lorenzo Chiesa. *The Italian Difference*. Eds. Lorenzo Chiesa and Alberto Toscano. Melbourne: re.press, 2009. 25–9.

Rovatti, Pier Aldo. *Inattualità del pensiero debole*. Udine: Forum Edizioni, 2011.

Rovatti, Pier Aldo. "Trasformazioni nel corso dell'esperienza." *Il pensiero debole*. Eds. Gianni Vattimo e Pier Aldo Rovatti. Milan: Feltrinelli, 1983. 29–51.

Russell, Brian. "Developing Derrida: Pointers to Faith, Hope and Prayer." *Theology*, vol. 104, no. 822 (2001): 403–11.

Said, Edward. *Representations of the Intellectual*. The 1993 Reith Lectures. New York: Vintage Books, 1996.

Said, Edward. "The Text, the World, the Critic." *The Bulletin of the Midwest Modern Language Association*, vol. 8, no. 2 (1975): 1–23; 4.

Saint-Amour, Paul K. "Weak Theory, Weak Modernism." *Modernism/Modernity*, vol. 25, no. 3 (2018): 437–59.

Saint Augustine. *Confessions*. Trans. R. S. Pine-Coffin. London: Penguin, 1961.

Sanders, Carol. "The Paris Years." *The Cambridge Companion to Saussure*. Ed. Carol Sanders. Cambridge: Cambridge University Press, 2004. 30–44.

Saussure, Ferdinand de. *Course in General Linguistics*. Eds. Charles Bally and Albert Sechehaye. Trans. Wade Baskin. New York, Toronto, and London: McGraw-Hill, 1966.

Scarry, Elaine. "The Difficulty of Imagining Other Persons." *The Handbook of Interethnic Coexistence*. Ed. E. Weiner. New York: Continuum, 1998. 40–62.

Schuchard, Ronald. *Eliot's Dark Angel: Intersections of Life and Art*. Oxford: Oxford University Press, 1999.

Schulman, Grace. "Gift from a Lost World." *Yale Review*, vol. 85, no. 4 (1997): 121–34.

Schwebel, Claudia L. "Intensive Infinity: Walter Benjamin's Reception of Leibniz and its Sources." *Modern Language Notes, German Issue: Walter Benjamin, Gershom Scholem, and the Marburg School*, vol. 127, no. 3 (2012): 589–610.

Scott, Glenway. "George Platt Lynes and the Ballet." *George Platt Lynes: Photographic Visions*. Institute of Contemporary Art. Boston, MA. 5 March–27 April 1980. Boston, MA: Institute of Contemporary Art, 1980. N.p.

Sebeok, Thomas A. *Encyclopedic Dictionary of Semiotics*. Vol. 1. Berlin, New York, and Amsterdam: Mouton de Gruyter, 1986.

Sedgwick, Eve Kosofsky. *A Dialogue on Love*. Boston, MA: Beacon Press, 1999.

Sedgwick, Eve Kosofsky. "Paranoid Reading and Reparative Reading; or, You're So Paranoid, You Probably Think This Introduction is About You." *Novel Gazing: Queer Readings in Fiction*. Ed. Eve Kosofsky Sedgwick. Durham, NC and London: Duke University Press, 1997. 1–37.

Sedgwick, Eve Kosofsky. "Paranoid Reading and Reparative Reading, or, You're So Paranoid, You Probably Think This Essay is About You."

Touching Feeling: Affect, Pedagogy, Performativity. Durham, NC: Duke University Press, 2003. 123–52.

Sedgwick, Eve Kosofsky. "Who Fed This Muse?" *Fat Art, Thin Art*. Durham, NC and London: Duke University Press, 1994. 3–8.

Shaviro, Steven. "The Actual Volcano: Whitehead, Harman, and the Problem of Relations." *The Speculative Turn: Continental Materialism and Realism*. Eds. Levi Bryant, Nick Srnicek, and Graham Harman. Melbourne: re.press, 2011. 279–90.

Shklovsky, Viktor. "Art, as Device." Trans. and intro. Alexandra Berlina. *Poetics Today*, vol. 36, no. 3 (2015): 151–74.

Singh, Julietta. *Unthinking Mastery: Dehumanism and Decolonial Entanglements*. Durham, NC: Duke University Press, 2017. *Project Muse*. <https://muse.jhu.edu/book/64085>. Accessed 20 April 2022.

Sloterdijk, Peter. *Globes: Spheres II*. Trans. Wieland Hoban. South Pasadena, CA: Semiotext(e), 2014.

Smith, Bernard. *The Formalesque: A Guide to Modern Art and Its History*. Melbourne: Macmillan, 2007.

Smith, Bernard. *Modernism's History*. New Haven, CT and London: Yale University Press, 1998.

Snow, C. P. *The Two Cultures*. Cambridge: Cambridge University Press, 2012.

Sontag, Susan. *As Consciousness is Harnessed to Flesh: Journals & Notebooks 1964–1980*. Ed. David Rieff. New York: Farrar, Straus, and Giroux, 2012.

Sontag, Susan. "The Idea of Europe (One More Elegy)." *Where the Stress Falls*. New York: Vintage, 2003. 285–9.

Sontag, Susan. *On Photography*. London: Penguin, 2002. First ed. 1977.

Sontag, Susan. *Regarding the Pain of Others*. New York: Picador, 2003.

Stack, Allyson. "Culture, Cognition, and Jean Laplanche's Enigmatic Signifier." *Seductions and Enigmas: Laplanche, Theory, Culture*. Eds. John Fletcher and Nicholas Ray. London: Lawrence and Wishart, 2014. 63–80.

Stein, Gertrude. "Sacred Emily" (1913). *Writings: 1903–1932*. Eds. Catharine R. Stimpson and Harriet Chessman. New York: Library of America, 1998. 387–96.

Stengers, Isabelle. "Wondering About Materialism." *The Speculative Turn: Continental Materialism and Realism*. Eds. Levi Bryant, Nick Srnicek and Graham Harman. Melbourne: re.press, 2011. 368–80.

Stevens, Wallace. "The House Was Quiet and the World Was Calm." *Collected Poems*. New York: Vintage Books, 1982. 358–9.

Strandberg, Ake. *T. S. Eliot and the Mallarmean Quest for Meaning*. Uppsala: Uppsala University Library, 2002.

Stimilli, Elettra. *Debito e colpa*. Rome: Ediesse, 2015.

Šumič, Jelica. "Giorgio's Agamben's Godless Saints: Saving What Was Not." *Angelaki: Journal of the Theoretical Humanities*, vol. 16, no. 3 (2011): 137–47.

Szondi, Peter. *Introduction to Literary Hermeneutics*. Trans. Martha Woodmansee. Cambridge: Cambridge University Press, 2009.

Tagliapietra, Andrea. *Il dono del filosofo. Sul gesto originario della filosofia*. Turin: Einaudi, 2009.

Tambimuttu and Richard March, eds. *T. S. Eliot: A Symposium*. London: Frank Cass, 1965. 60–70.

Tanning, Dorothea. "Graduation." *A Table of Content: Poems*. New York: Graywolf Press, 2004. 20.

Thoreau, Henry David. *Walden*. New York, The New American Library, 1960.

Tilgher, Adriano. "Le estetiche di Luigi Pirandello." *Il problema centrale: Cronache teatrali 1914–26*, by Adriano Tilgher. Ed. Alessandro d'Amico. Genoa: Edizioni del Teatro Stabile di Genova, 1973. 385–94.

Tilgher, Adriano. "Immagine e sentimento nell'opera d'arte." *Rivista di Filosofia*, vol. 5, no. 2 (1913): 206–25. Reprinted in *Teoria del Pragmatismo Trascendentale*. Milan, Turin, and Rome: Fratelli Bocca Editori, 1915. 83–115.

Tilgher, Adriano. "Il teatro di Luigi Pirandello." *Studi sul Teatro Contemporaneo*. Rome: Libreria di Scienze e Lettere, 1923. 135–93.

Tilgher, Adriano. *Studi di poetica*. Rome: Bardi, 1934.

Tilgher, Adriano. *Teoria del pragmatismo trascendentale*. Naples: Fratelli Bocca Editori, 1915.

Tonning, Erik. *Modernism and Christianity*. Basingstoke and New York: Palgrave Macmillan, 2014.

Tuana, Nancy, and Charles Scott. "An Infused Dialogue, Part 1: Borders, Fusions, Influence." *The Journal of Speculative Philosophy*, vol. 30, no. 1 (2016): 1–14.

Vanzini, Marco. *Il Dio di ogni uomo: Una introduzine al mistero cristiano*. Rome: Edizioni Santa Croce, 2018.

Vanzini, Marco. "L'esperienza dell'amore di Dio nell'atto di fede." *Forum: Supplement to Acta Philosophica*, vol. 4 (2018): 59–80.

Vanzini, Marco. "La fede è conoscenza: Ma di che cosa?" Fede Cristiana e Pensiero Filosofico: Di fronte alle sfide della scienza. Pontifical University of the Holy Cross, Rome. 2 March 2019.

Vattimo, Gianni, and Pier Aldo Rovatti, eds. *Weak Thought*. Trans. and intro. Peter Carravetta. Albany: State University of New York Press, 2012. First Italian ed. 1983.

Vendler, Helen. "The Waste Land: Fragments and Montage." *The Ocean, the Bird, and the Scholar: Essays on Poets and Poetry*. Cambridge, MA and London: Harvard University Press, 2015. 79–91.

Virno, Paolo. *A Grammar of the Multitude: For an Analysis of Contemporary Forms of Life*. Los Angeles: Semiotext(e), distributed by MIT, 2004.

Virno, Paolo. *Grammatica della Moltitudine*. Rome: DeriveApprodi, 2014. First ed. 2002.

Virno, Paolo. "Pensare il presente con Saussure." *Istituzione e Differenza: Attualità di Ferdinand De Saussure*. Ed. Francesco Raparelli. Milan-Udine: Mimesis, 2014. 41–8.

Virno, Paolo. *Quando il verbo si fa carne: Linguaggio e natura umana*. Turin: Bollati Boringhieri, 2003.

Virno, Paolo. *Saggio sulla negazione: Per un'antropologia linguistica*. Turin: Bollati Boringhieri, 2013.

Virno, Paolo. "Virtuosity and Revolution: The Political Theory of Exodus." *Radical Thought in Italy: A Potential Politics*. Eds. Michael Hardt and Paolo Virno. Trans. Maurizia Boscagli, Cesare Casarino, Paul Colilli, Ed Emory, and Michael Turits. Minneapolis: University of Minnesota Press, 2006. 189–212.

von Hallberg, Robert. "Intellectual Eloquence: East Coker." Forty-first Annual T. S. Eliot Memorial Lecture. The International T. S. Eliot Society. Forty-first Annual Meeting. 1–3 October 2020, via Zoom. <https://www.youtube.com/watch?v=L5F8VRG7U68>. Accessed 21 April 2022.

von Jagemann, H. C. G. "Philology and Purism." *PMLA*, vol. 15, no. 1 (1900): 74–96. <https://doi.org/10.2307/456494>. Accessed 21 October 2021.

Warburg, Aby. *Images from the Region of the Pueblo Indians of North America*. Trans. Michael P. Steinberg. Ithaca, NY: Cornell University Press, 1995.

Weinberg, Jonathan. "Substitute and Consolation: The Ballet Photographs of George Platt Lynes." *Dance for a City: Fifty Years of the New York City Ballet*. Eds. Lynn Garofala with Eric Foner. New York: Columbia University Press, 1999. 129–51.

White, Eric Walter. "'Fire Bird' and 'Orpheus.'" *Ballet*, vol. 10, no. 2 (1950): 13–17.

Williams, James. *Understanding Poststructuralism*. Hoboken, NJ: Taylor and Francis, 2014. ProQuest Ebook Central. <https://ebookcentral-proquest-com.flagship.luc.edu/lib/luc/detail.action?pq-origsite=primo&docID=1900170>. Accessed 1 May 2020.

Woody, Jack, ed. *George Platt Lynes: Photographs, 1931–1945*. Pasadena, CA: Twelvetrees Press, 1981.

Woolf, Virginia. *The Letters of Virginia Woolf: The Question of Things Happening, 1912–1922*. Vol. 2. Ed. Nigel Nicholson. London: Hogarth Press, 1976.

Woolf, Virginia. *The Letters of Virginia Woolf: A Change of Perspectives, 1923–1928*. Vol. 3. Ed. Nigel Nicholson. London: Chatto & Windus, 1977.

Wyatt, Jean. "Laplanche, Freud, Leonardo: Sustaining Enigma." *American Imago*, vol. 76, no. 2 (2019). Project Muse. <https://muse.jhu.edu/article/728527/pdf>. Accessed 20 April 2022.

Yeats, W. B. "Leda and the Swan." *Collected Poems*. Ed. and intro. Augustine Martin. New York: Hill & Wang, 1977. 142–8.

Archives

Archivio Tilgher. National Central Library of Rome.
Frank Vigor Morley Collection of Papers. The Henry W. and Albert A. Berg Collection of English and American Literature. The New York Public Library.
George Platt Lynes Papers. Jerome Robbins Dance Division. The New York Public Library for the Performing Arts.
Lincoln Kirstein Papers (1907–91). Jerome Robbins Dance Division. The New York Public Library for the Performing Arts.
Susan Sontag Papers. Charles E. Young Research Library. Special Collections. UCLA.
T. S. Eliot Collection of Papers. The Henry W. and Albert A. Berg Collection of English and American Literature. The New York Public Library.

Index

Abraham, 232–4, 238n25
acknowledgment, 93
  and Toril Moi, 83
act of reading, 8, 162
Adorno, Theodor W., 37, 46, 50–9, 65n4, 68–9, 74, 76, 117
"adventure of interpretation," the (Stengers), 13, 24, 43n2
affect theory, 98, 131
"after man" (Esposito), 21, 38, 45n46
Agamben, Giorgio, 45n47, 66n8, 101–2, 118n9, 119n15, 144n3
Age of Anxiety, The (ballet), 186n46
Aldington, Richard, 157
amor vitae (Tilgher, A.), 116–17
Angelou, Maya, 7
Arendt, Hannah, 6–7, 9, 22, 29, 41n8, 126, 218, 241, 242–5, 245n1, 245n2, 246n3, 246 n4, 246n5, 246n7
argumentation, 91, 241; *see also* "Cultures of Argument" (*PMLA* cluster)
art, 4–5, 7, 15, 52, 58, 62, 74, 115–16, 157, 198–9, 244
  and literature, 33
  and philosophy, 69, 76
  art criticism, 36
  art practice, 15
  avant-garde, 82
  media, 6
  public, 173
artifact(s) 4–5, 25, 32, 36, 75, 244–5
artist, 1, 6–8, 12–13,16, 22, 147n26, 165, 179–81,189, 199–201, 203, 210–11, 244
  and Joyce, 192

and Lispector, 192
and T. S. Eliot, 150–1, 153, 155, 157, 159, 163, 182n4
as a technology of the self, 21
as "exemplary sufferer" (Sontag), 149
askesis, 167, 185n36, 199
attachment, 13, 18, 20–1, 33, 40, 124–6, 131, 138–40, 144n2, 161
Auden, W. H., 165
Aufklärung, 50
Augustine, 41n8, 201, 221–31, 234, 236n8, 236n9, 237n11, 237n22
  and Lacan 227–29
  and paternal donation, 224, 227
  as poststructuralist thinker, 221

Bacon, Francis, 102
Balanchine, George, 165–7, 179–80, 184n31, 185n33,186n45, 186n46, 187n54
Ballets Russes, 165
Barthes, Roland, 73, 99
Baryshnikov, Mikhail, 187n50
Baudelaire, Charles, 113, 153, 155, 182n5, 182n6, 182n10
Bazzicalupo, Laura, 113–15, 120n29, 121n35, 212
Beaton, Cecil, 165
Benjamin, Walter, 28, 44n39, 46, 60, 64, 66n15, 69, 73, 82, 89, 92, 110, 113, 120n25, 158
  criticism and critique, 61–3
  "Goethe's Elective Affinities", 61–2, 67n16, 150, 197
  "Letter to Florens Christian Rang", 61–2

"On the Concept of History", 88n6, 121n33
"The Concept of Criticism", 62, 67n18
Benveniste, Émile, 122n45, 123–4
biopolitics, 103,
Blanchot, Maurice, 101, 193
bodies, 5, 30, 128–30, 143, 167, 181
books, 1, 5–9, 12, 22, 40–1, 197, 211, 244
   art, 41n4
   bojagi, 5
   digital, 5, 9
   luminous 7, 8, 22, 40
   real, 1, 7
   virtual, 1, 7
Borch-Jacobsen, Mikkel, 102
Brooker, Jewel Spears, 149, 154, 162, 182n9, 183n22, 185n36
Boyle, Kay, 165
Bruns, Gerald, 75, 237n22
Butler, Judith, 50–1, 58–9, 68, 121n32, 127, 214

Cacciari, Massimo, 214n17
Caravaggio, 233
Cardoso, Lúcio, 195
Cartier-Bresson, Henri, 165
Cavell, Stanley, 83, 94, 242
Chagall, Marc, 165
Chakrabarty, Dipesh, 244, 246n5, 246n6
charm, 8–9, 12, 41n5, 50, 158
Cixous, Hélène, 73, 189–205, 207–13, 215, 217, 226
Cocteau, Jean, 165
Colette, 165
Consagra, Pietro, 15
Copeland, Aaron, 165
critical attitude, 46, 48, 50, 58, 60–2, 64, 66n12
critique, 5–6, 13–20, 23, 26–28, 32–6, 38, 40, 44–51, 56–66, 68–71, 78–80, 91–2, 98, 101–2, 104, 106–8, 110, 112, 115, 117–119, 121 n33, 124, 148, 195, 198, 239–41
"Cultures of Argument" (*PMLA* cluster), 14

culture industry, 52–6, 65n5, 76, 117, 130
Cummings, E. E., 165

Dalí, Salvador, 165
Dante, 37
de Chirico, Giorgio, 186n41
   Disquieting Muses, 179
de Man, Paul, 50
"death of the author" (Barthes), 204
debt, 30, 52, 87, 103, 126, 141, 151, 189, 199
   guilt and, 53, 55–6, 65n6, 68
deconstruction, 12, 14, 17, 32, 64, 79, 88n9, 91, 98, 102, 109, 131, 218
Denkraum (Warburg), 83, 86, 88
Derrida, Jacques, 34, 44n42, 73, 88n8, 1012, 109, 120n25, 137, 146n22, 158, 214n17, 216–17, 221–2, 231, 236n4, 236n7, 237n20
"diasporic modernism" (Friedman), 191, 204
différance, 217, 221, 236n4, 237n20
Dickinson, Emily, 179
Didi-Huberman, Georges, 87
Dimock, Wai Chee, 33, 91–7, 99, 109–10
Duchamp, Marcel, 157
Dürer, Albrecht, 5
During, Simon, 57–9, 65n7, 66n10

écriture, 73, 87, 211
   feminine, 190, 196
Eliot, T. S. 17, 20–1, 67n19, 100, 129, 148–50, 156, 159, 180, 182n1, 182n10, 190, 192, 195, 207, 212
   and Baudelaire, 153, 155, 182n5
   and dance, 155–6, 167, 179
   and Lincoln Kirstein, 186n46, 187–8n59
   and Orpheus, 154, 161
   and the many, 127–8, 142
   and theory of literature, 54, 161, 149, 158, 162, 189
   and Woolf, 149, 157, 160, 162–3,182n1, 184n25
   photographed by George Platt Lynes, 163–78
   sustainability of the writing life, 149

Eliot, T. S. (cont.)
  Four Quartets, 152, 155, 206
  "La Figlia Che Piange", 156
  "Marina", 152, 161, 179
  "Preludes", 151–4
  "Reflections on Contemporary Poetry [IV]", 150, 182n2
  "The Death of Saint Narcissus", 152, 154–6, 158
  "The Development of Shakespeare's Verse", 162
  "The Love Song of J. Alfred Prufrock", 153
  "The Love Song of Saint Sebastian", 155
  "The Method of Mr. Pound", 150, 182n2
  The Waste Land, 127, 129, 155
  "Tradition and the Individual Talent", 150, 152, 182n2
environment of thought, 86, 110
Esposito, Roberto, 19, 21, 36, 42n19, 44n42, n45, n46, 57, 79, 91, 93, 102, 107, 113, 117, 119n16, 120n27, 121n31, 122n44, 123, 127, 129, 132, 140–1, 143, 148–9, 190, 192, 196, 198, 203–4, 208–9, 220, 236n6, 246n7
  analysis of community, 101–4, 119n21, 120n23, 126, 151
  and Theory, 38, 106, 116
  concept of reality, 23
  "living thought" 18, 20, 37–9, 106, 108–12, 116, 148, 246n7
  impersonal, 102, 122n45, 130
  negative, the, 236n6
  other modernity, 104, 112, 115, 121n33, 145n8
  plane of coevalness, 88, 90, 101
euēmeria, 125, 144n3
European philosophies, 37, 105, 108–9
Eyers, Tom, 32

Fanon, Franz, 98
father, the, 201–3, 208, 225–8, 231, 233–5
Felski, Rita, 13, 19, 27, 32–4, 36, 39, 43n35, 44n42, 59, 91, 110, 131n8, 190, 213, 245
  and Rovatti, 96
  and wonder, 25
  on Foucault's style, 25, 49
feminism, 39, 102, 106, 140, 146n24, 196
  and psychoanalysis, 20, 193, 207
feminist theory, 43n33, 82, 146n21, 241
Ferenczi, Sándor, 210, 214n18
Fides et Ratio (John Paul II), 229
"formalesque" (Smith, B.), 121n38
forms, 1, 5, 9, 27, 30, 36, 39, 41, 57, 63–4, 66 n11, 66n12, 73–4, 86, 94, 112, 115–16, 121n29, 167, 199
Flanner, Janet, 165
Forster, E. M., 165
Foucault, Michel, 6, 39, 44n42, 46, 51, 61, 63, 65n1, 66n10, 66n12, 68–9, 82, 103, 107, 129n25, 129n28, 216
  and American academy, 34
  and critique, 47–50, 57–60, 64, 66n11
  and indocility, 46, 50, 60
  and living thought, 37
  in Felski, 25, 49
Frankfurt School, 37, 146n18
French Theory, 34, 37–8, 73, 105–6
Freud, Sigmund, 36, 55, 147n17, 210, 228, 233, 237n13
Friedman, Susan Stanford, 27, 33, 113, 191, 193, 204, 213n3

Gadamer, Hans-Georg, 95, 111–12, 118n5, 194, 205
German Critical Theory, 34, 37–8, 106
Gide, André, 165, 186n46, 187n59
Goethe, Johann Wolfgang von, 61, 76, 242–3
gift, 25, 85, 87, 141, 181, 186n46, 189, 199, 215, 219, 224, 234, 236n5, n6, 242
  Arendt, 242
  Eliot, 151–2, 155
  Esposito, 103, 123
  Joyce, 212
  Lacan, 155, 224

Lefort, 92–3, 110
Lispector 212,
Marion, 220–21, 223, 225–6, 231
Mauss, 220
governamentality, 70
guilt, 53–6, 65n6, 68, 236n9

Haraway, Donna, 43n28
Harman, Graham, 9, 23, 28, 29, 44n36, 70
Hartley, Marsden, 165
Hayot, Eric, 34, 36, 38, 44n42
Heidegger, Martin, 23–4, 104, 120n23, 146–7 n25, 217, 243, 246n5
Heraclitus, 144n2
"hermeneutic recovery" (Marion), 227, 231
hermeneutical conversation (Gadamer), 205–10
hermeneutics of suspicion, 14, 92, 98, 109, 240
history, 5–6, 18, 20, 25, 31, 35, 37, 39–40, 48–9, 51–2, 56, 63, 66n12, 74, 76, 80–1, 89n10, 92, 94, 101, 106, 108, 110–11, 113, 116, 121n33, 150–1, 204, 211, 217, 219, 241–2, 244–5, 246n3
Hobbes, Thomas, 108, 121n34
"human separation" (Moi, T.), 30
humanitarian scene, 30
human condition, 9, 29, 104, 131, 143, 154, 244, 246n5
Huxley, Aldous, 25, 42n26, 165, 173

institution, 20, 83, 157, 159–60
  language, 138, 141, 143
  literary work, 92–3, 208
  philosophy, 81
  psychoanalysis, 235
introspective thinker (Adorno), 54, 76
Isaac, 233–5, 238n25
Iser, Wolfgang, 40, 72, 235n2
Isherwood, Christopher, 155, 165
Italian Theory, 17, 19–21, 34–7, 39, 45n46, 102, 104–7, 110, 112, 114, 119n11, 120n27, 120n28, 124, 245
  and the linguistic turn, 18, 38, 90, 98, 104, 106–7, 116–18

see also Italian Thought; living thought; *pensiero vivente*
Italian Thought, 37, 105–6, 120n27

James, Henry, 94
James, William, 27–8, 129, 144n4, 241–2
Jameson, Fredric, 70–83, 88n9, 98n12, 91–2, 95, 118n4, 120n25, 193, 240
  Late Marxism, 74–5
  Marxism and Form, 27, 71–5, 77, 81, 92, 240
  Political Unconscious, The, 73–5, 77, 79, 81, 83
  Postmodernism, or, The Cultural Logic of Late Capitalism, 77
  Valencies of the Dialectic, 80, 88n9, 89n12
Jankélévitch, Vladimir, 8, 41n5, 129–30, 142
Jaspers, Karl, 245n, 246n5
Johnson, Barbara, 219
Joyce, James, 20–1, 74, 189, 191–3, 195–6, 199–204, 208–9

Kafka, Franz, 193
Kang, Airan, 1–11, 16, 22, 40–1, 244
  Digital Book Project, 1, 7, 12
  Light of the World, Light of the Intelligence, 9, 11, 41n9
  Otheca Luminosa—Cella Penthesilea 6;
  Lord Byron (Hyper Open Book), 41n6
Kant, Immanuel, 47, 50
Kauffer, Edward McKnight, 171–3, 177–79, 181, 184n27, 185n37, 185n38, 186n41
  "Derry and Toms" (poster), 174
  "Flight" (poster), 175
  "Washington—Night and Day" (poster), 163, 170
Kirstein, Lincoln, 165–6, 179–81, 184n31, 184n32
  and T. S. Eliot, 186n46, 187n59
  and the New York City Ballet, 179, 186n46,
  on American dancers, 186n45

Kleist, Heinrich von, 193
Klimt, Gustav, 7
Kokoschka, Oskar, 165
Kounellis, Jannis, 15
Kristeva, Julia, 60, 227

Lacan, Jacques, 23, 84, 120n25, 126, 203, 212, 216, 224, 237n13, 237n15, 238n22
  "Discourse to Catholics", 228–9, 237n16
  Le Sinthome, 196
  On the Names-of-the-Father, 227, 231, 233, 235
  The Ethics of Psychoanalysis, 234–5
  "The Function and Field of Speech and Language in Psychoanalysis", 83, 127, 155, 230
  The Triumph of Religion, 232
language, 6, 8–9, 16, 19–20, 22–4, 30, 36, 41, 42n26, 48, 69, 74, 80, 86, 98, 105, 107, 114, 117–18, 127, 129, 131, 133–7, 140, 142, 145n5, 146n24, 147n26, 148–9, 151, 155, 161, 167, 189, 192, 195, 197–8, 210–11, 214n17, 215–16, 240, 245
  alienation of, 118n9
  and community, 104, 120n23, 123
  and *différance,* 217, 221
  and Lacan, 230, 232–4
  and thought, 31, 38, 65, 128, 130, 143, 192, 194, 236n8, 243–4, 245n1
  as an institution, 138, 141
  as non-relation, 196
  as pure potentiality, 150, 189
  faculty of, 125, 133, 140
  limits of, 128
  in Arendt, 126, 241–4, 246n3
  in Augustine, 223–7, 229, 231
  in Joyce and Lispector, 200–3, 208
  paternal adoption in, 21, 192–3, 209, 212
  sovereignty of, 18, 38, 90, 119n11, 193, 224
  well-being in, 124, 146n21
Laplanche, Jean, 65n2, 224

Latour, Bruno, 24–5, 27, 31, 43n26, 43n29, 46
  and critique, 63–5
Lefort, Claude, 92–3, 208
Lesjak, Carolyn, 70, 75, 79–80, 83, 212
life, 6, 13–14, 18, 22–3, 36–7, 40, 42n24, 46, 50–1, 55–8, 61–2, 66n12, 77, 79–80, 82, 103–7, 112–14, 116–17, 120n22, 121n29, n34, 122n47, 124, 130, 134, 137, 138, 143, 144n6, 145n12, 148, 150, 161, 181, 189, 195, 199, 204–5, 211–12, 245, 246n5, 246 n7
  academic, 65, 142
  American, 55
  biological, 243
  form of, 16–17, 44n38, 125, 158–60, 162–3, 185n10, 192
  hidden, 28
  impersonal dimension of, 102, 152
  in Eliot, 153–7
  naked, 21
  of women, 5–7
  ordinary, 1, 5, 30, 149, 151, 52–3, 151, 244
  precarious, 14
  repression of, 19–20, 53, 126, 145n8
  social, 74, 118n9, 125
  spectacularization of, 97
  techniques of, 16
  "unheard" (Adorno), 53, 117
  U.S. intellectual, 91
Life vs. Form, 19, 39, 90, 115, 198, 204, 215
Lispector, Clarice, 20–1, 189–205, 208–9, 211–12, 213n7, 216
  and Joyce, 191–3, 195–6, 200, 204, 208, 209
  beyond Oedipus, 209
  Near to the Wild Heart, 190–1, 197, 200
  Stream of Life, 196, 199
  "Sunday, before falling asleep", 200
literary critic, 5, 13, 17, 19, 25, 29, 42n26, 50, 57, 59, 65, 71–2, 80, 91, 93, 109, 115, 148, 210, 240
literary history, 63, 92, 94, 150–1

literary studies, 4, 12–13, 18–19, 23–7, 29, 32–3, 40, 42n22, 43n28, 45n45, 46, 50, 60, 99, 111,113, 119n13, 190, 204, 207, 212, 216, 219, 240–1
literature,14–15, 32, 41, 48, 59, 61, 66n10, 69–70, 72, 74–5, 78–9, 92, 94, 99, 143, 159, 190–1, 198, 204, 209–10, 219, 231, 240
   and philosophy, 23, 45n45, 50, 67n18, 68–70, 109, 112
   theory of, 119n13, 149, 158, 162, 189
   uses of, 239
   value of, 33
living thought, 18, 20, 36–40, 106–12, 115–16, 121n31, 148
   and Cixous, 189, 192
   and T. S. Eliot, 189
Lonzi, Carla, 12, 15–16, 29, 82, 89n11
Loy, Mina, 165
Lynes, George Platt 64, 163–78, 180–1, 184n31, n32, 185n37, 187n49, n54
   and Balanchine, 166–7
   and construction of space, 166
   and modernist portraiture, 165–6
   photographic portrait of T. S. Eliot (N. 11), 167
Lyotard, Jean-François, 88n7, 114, 237–8n22

Machiavelli, 37, 42n19
Magallanes, Nicholas, 180–1, 187n49, n50
Mallarmé, Stéphane, 143, 199
Mann, Thomas, 165
many, the, 20, 124, 127–9, 133
   and Anna Maria Ortese, 130
   and Eliot, 152–3
   and Jankélévitch, 130
   and Rilke, 156
   and Saussure, 135, 140, 142–3
Marion, Jean-Luc, 220–8, 231, 237n12, n19
Marx, Karl, 23, 77, 121n35, 134, 144n4, 145n11, 147n26
materialism, 23, 39, 101, 146n23
Maugham, Somerset, 165, 185n40

Mauss, Marcel, 220, 236n6
Meillassoux, Quentin, 88n1
Merleau-Ponty, Maurice, 9
method, 16–9, 26, 46, 49, 58, 76, 81, 86–7, 95, 109–11, 113, 118n5, n6, 161, 190, 203–8, 212–13, 230, 240
method of consummation (Benjamin), 61–2, 110, 150, 197
Miller, Perry, 78
Million Dollar Baby (movie), 214n20
modernism, 18, 21, 27–8, 33, 39, 74–5, 100–1, 104, 113–15, 119n12, 146n24, 148, 165, 189–91, 193, 198, 200, 212, 216
   and Anglophone Theory, 20
   aesthetic, 27
   and feminism, 196
   and Italian Theory, 19–20, 39, 90–1, 112, 117
   and photography, 165;
   and Saussure, 124, 134, 140, 143;
   and the public intellectual, 44n35
   literary, 19, 24
   see also modernism and theory
modernism and theory, 91, 101, 124; *see also* Theory
modernism/postmodernism, 78
modernity, 18, 20, 23–4, 27, 40, 42n26, 50–1, 56–8, 82, 103–4, 108, 112–15, 121n33, 121 n35, 127, 132, 145n8, 204, 229, 244, 246n5
modesty, 14, 47, 50, 60, 64, 71, 97–100, 119
Moi, Toril, 13, 30, 43n33, 95–6, 98, 109–10, 190, 197
   on Cavell, 83, 93–4
   on reading, 17, 26, 29, 111, 207–8, 212, 240
   Revolution of the Ordinary, 17, 80
Moore, Marianne, 165
Morrell, Lady Ottoline, 157
multitude, 130–3, 137, 141; *see also* many, the
Murray, Les, 131–3
muse, 35, 46, 68, 210–11
"mute spell of mere happening," the (Arendt), 21, 241–2, 245

Nancy, Jean-Luc, 36, 101, 103, 119n13, 124, 128–31, 133, 144n6
New Criticism, 32, 72
New Modernist Studies, The, 100, 190
New Romance—Art and the Posthuman (exhibition), 1–3
New York City Ballet, 165, 179, 186n46
Nietzsche, Friedrich, 9, 37, 58, 62, 66n8, 96, 116, 120n28
Noguchi, Isamu, 180, 186n46
non-human, 23, 25, 242
non-person, 102, 130,
"not philosophy" (Jameson, F.), 75

onomatopoeia, 198
Orpheus (ballet), 180–1, 186n46, 186n50, 186n59
Ortese, Anna Maria, 130, 142
ostranenie, 205
"outer limits of philosophy," the (Foucault), 50, 69

Parker, Dorothy, 165
Parmenides, 22, 24, 129, 144n7
paternal donation, 215, 224–5, 227
Pease, Donald E., 77–8, 89n16
Peirce, Charles Sanders, 41n7
pensiero debole, 96
pensiero vivente (Esposito), 110, 246n7
philosophy, 7, 16, 23, 26, 45n45, 48, 50, 54, 56, 63, 74, 76, 80–1, 88n9, 96, 99, 109, 127, 190, 193, 216, 221, 225, 231, 237n13, 240
  and literary criticism, 71–2, 74, 81, 95
  and T. S. Eliot, 127, 149, 152, 154, 185n36
  and the critical attitude, 50
  European, 37, 73
  French, 12
  German, 71, 105
  Italian, 37, 120n27
  margins of, 47, 68
  modern, 37
  see also European philosophies
Picasso, Pablo, 7, 185n33
plane of coevalness (Esposito), 39, 79, 88, 90, 101, 109–10, 143, 149, 189, 196
  and *méconnaissance*, 20, 40
  and the temporality of Theory, 112
plurality, 20, 102, 113, 126–7, 130, 233, 235
PMLA, 14
Poe, Edgar Allan, 7
poetry, 7, 35, 128, 149, 152, 154, 156, 159, 162, 182n10, 185n36, 206, 210–11, 214n19
Poggioli, Renato, 44n38, 118n6, 199
Pontalis, Jean-Bertrand, 65n2, 154, 156–7, 160
Porter, Katherine Anne, 165
Postcolonial Theory, 45n46
postcritique, 5, 12–18, 20, 22–3, 25–7, 34–6, 46, 49, 56, 70, 79–80, 90, 96, 110, 129, 132, 207, 213, 240, 244
posthuman, 21
postmodernism, 75–6, 78–80, 82, 84, 87, 88n3
poststructuralism, 12–14, 17–19, 21, 23, 27, 38–9, 43n33, 73, 98, 104, 106, 123, 148, 190, 192, 211, 215–21, 230, 236n3, 240
Pound, Ezra, 149, 151, 157, 207
Proust, Marcel, 167
psychoanalysis, 13, 20–1, 22–3, 27, 40, 42n20, 83, 102, 126, 140, 144n5, 145n16, 155, 193, 196, 207, 208–9, 212, 228–30, 234–5, 237n13, n16, 238n22

Queer Theory, 35, 45n46, 110

Race Theory, 45n46
realism (philosophical current), 18, 23, 32, 39, 63, 90, 101, 143
Recalcati, Massimo, 234–5
reception theory, 72, 219
reparative reading, 79, 83, 209
repetition, 20, 46, 47, 50–1, 57, 60, 149, 189, 195–6, 206, 223
Ricoeur, Paul, 73, 193–4, 202, 205, 218–19, 235n1
Rilke, Rainer Maria, 156
Rotella, Mimmo, 15

Rovatti, Pier Aldo, 95–100, 118n9, 244
Russian Formalism, 205

Said, Edward, 60, 204
Saint-Amour, Paul, 27, 100, 102, 104, 119n12
Sanders, Carol, 141–3, 146n20, n23, n24
Saussure, Ferdinand de, 20, 118, 125, 131, 133–42, 145n15, n16, 146n18, 146n22, 148, 217
  and the many, 135, 140, 142–3
  and T. S. Eliot, 151
  as modernist thinker, 124, 143, 146n22
"scalar leap" (During, S.), 58
Scarry, Elaine, 31, 130, 239
Schleiermacher, Friedrich, 211
Schoenberg, Arnold, 165
Schulman, Grace, 172, 185n37
Scriptures, 31, 213n14, 223, 238n23
Sedgwick, Eve Kosofsky, 35–7, 51, 79, 87, 98, 209–12, 214n19
self, 6, 9, 22, 59, 139, 149, 151–2, 160, 181, 200, 205, 210, 215, 225, 227, 228, 243, 246n3
  and other, 123, 129, 206
  as a void, 41n8
  care of, 199
  hermeneutics of the, 64, 66n12
  technologies of the, 149–150, 161
Shaviro, Steven, 27–9, 44n36, 90
sign (Saussure), 134, 138–9, 141–2
Simondon, Gilbert, 119n16, 145n16
Singh, Julietta, 21, 35, 45n46
Sitwell, Edith, 165–6
Snow, C. P., 25, 42n26
Sontag, Susan, 17, 31, 33, 44n35, n39, 56, 86, 115, 120n25, 149
space of appearance (Arendt), 6, 243–4
Spinoza, Baruch, 37, 116, 120n28
Stein, Gertrude, 149, 151, 165, 196
Stengers, Isabelle, 13, 24–5, 31, 42n25, 43n28
Stevens, Wallace, 149, 182n4, 206–7
Stimilli, Elettra, 55–6
Stravinsky, Igor, 165, 180, 186n46, 187n59

"surface reading" (Marcus and Best), 12
Szondi, Peter, 211
symbolic recognition, 19, 21, 30–1, 45n46
  Cimatti, F., 19, 38
Symphony in C (ballet), 186n46
symptom, 229
  history as, 76, 82, 89n10
symptomatic reading, 14, 22, 26, 29, 209; *see also* hermeneutics of suspicion

Tagliapietra, Andrea, 25, 43n27
Tanning, Dorothea, 12–13
text, 8–9, 13, 15–17, 19, 32, 42n22, 46–7, 50, 54, 56, 58–9, 61, 69–70, 81, 84, 92, 102, 211, 216, 220, 239–40
  and Cixous, 191–95, 197–8, 200–1, 203–5, 208–9, 212
  and poststructuralism, 12, 216
  and the critic, 40, 204
  and the reader, 8, 31–2, 205, 208, 216, 239
  as action and expression, 73, 93
  Biblical, 232
  in Augustine, 221–3, 225–6, 231, 236n9
  in Benjamin, 61–3, 67n16
  in Dimock, 93, 109
  in Gadamer, 205–6
  in Iser, 73, 219, 235n2
Theory, 13–14, 19–20, 22–3, 27, 33, 37–8, 69, 72, 91–2, 100, 106–9, 112, 116–17, 120n25, 131, 210
Thoreau, Henry David, 242–3, 246n4
Tilgher, Adriano, 115–17, 121n39, 122n40, 122n44, 122n45, 148, 198
Tóibín, Colm, 94, 213n7
transatlantic transmission, 70, 72, 108
Tsvetayeva, Marina, 193
Turcato, Giulio, 15
Twombly, Cy, 15

Valery, Paul, 143, 146n24, 199
Vendler, Helen, 155, 206–7
Vermeer, Jan, 5

Virno, Paolo, 119n11, 124–6, 129–35, 137, 139, 143, 145n11, n16, 146n18, 147n26

Warburg, Aby, 84–8
Weak Theory, 15, 33–4, 43n29, 91–2, 94–6, 110, 119n12, 133,
well-being, 122, 124–5, 127, 138, 140, 142, 146n21, 193, 224, 246n3
Whitehead, Alfred North, 27–9, 44n36, 129, 241–2

Wiegman, Robyn, 78, 89n16
Williams, Raymond, 46, 50–1, 57–9, 61, 70, 111
Wittgenstein, Ludwig, 224
wonder, 13, 19, 25, 40, 43n27, 72, 91, 128, 130, 133, 142, 153, 190, 239
Woolf, Virginia, 149, 157, 160–3
work(s) of art, 15–16, 61–2, 136, 213
"wounded and vulnerable artifacts" (Felski), 4, 25, 245

EU representative:
Easy Access System Europe
Mustamäe tee 50, 10621 Tallinn, Estonia
Gpsr.requests@easproject.com